OPEN SPACES

Machine Knit
Eyelets, Ladders and Slits

Susan Guagliumi

Photography by Jim Mullen

GUAGLIUMIDOTCOM
NORTHFORD, CT

Open Spaces: Machine Knit Eyelets, Ladders, and Slits

Susan Guagliumi

ISBN — 13: 978—1986317733

ISBN — 10: 1986317730

Publisher: Guagliumi Dot Com

Produced with Create Space Independent Publishing Platform, North Charleston, So. Carolina

Photography by Jim Mullen

Cover Design by Jeanne Criscola, Criscola Design

Charts and Illustrations by the author

www.guagliumi.com

www.susanguagliumi.com

Other books by Susan Guagliumi

Hand Knits by Machine

More Hand—Manipulated Stitches for Machine Knitters

Hand—Manipulated Stitches for Machine Knitters

Twelve Sweaters One Way: Knitting Cuff—to—Cuff

Twelve Sweaters One Way: Knitting Saddle Style

Handmade for the Garden

For Benjamin and Brayden

Your dad was the sun, the moon and *most* of the stars in my sky,
but the two of you are my universe.

Acknowledgments

Thank you, thank you,
thank you, one and all.
You make me as good
as I'll ever be and
better than I am alone.

THIS BOOK WAS A HUGE UNDERTAKING and over the last four years there have been so many people who helped me. The words "thank you" sound so inadequate because I know that, without their help, I would not have succeeded in producing such a beautiful, comprehensive book.

The folks at Cascade Yarns have been supporting my efforts for years, supplying me with unlimited skeins of their Cascade 220 Worsted. It is a high quality wool yarn that knits perfectly on the middle of the stitch dial of my midgauge machines so that yarn difficulties are eliminated from the process of experimenting and developing fabrics.The colors are gorgeous and it remains one of my favorite yarns.

I produced all of the charts for my last two books with Adobe Illustrator software, but it meant drawing my grids and symbols from scratch. It was time consuming and cumbersome — to say the least! Mathew Bragg at Soft Byte supplied me with Design—A—Knit software and cut my chart production time exponentially. The pre—designed symbols and grids made it as easy as a coloring book and almost as much fun.

Early in the process I had access to the Stoll America fabric archives in New York City. I spent hours poring over rack after rack of incredible samples, photographing what was relevant and making (never enough) notes. The archives are no longer there so I feel very fortunate to have explored them when I did. Both Beth Hofer and then Carol Edwards were welcoming and helpful in getting additional information for me from the German offices of Stoll. Chui King Lai, one of the knit lab technicians (i.e. wizards!), worked out instructions for a couple of the more baffling fabrics and shared the information with me. There are not enough chocolate chip cookies to thank her for that!

An entire book of swatches would be so boring which is why I am grateful to Cari Morton, Jo Bee, Rita Nylander and Anne Grut Sørum (the dynamic duo at DuoDu in Norway) and Cornelia Tuttle Hamilton for providing me with photos of their beautiful garments. Britt—Marie Christoffersson's fabric added just the "pop!" that her book promises. Over the years, I have been fortunate to know and connect with so many wonderfully talented people and fortunately, many of them just happen to be knitters!

Anyone who has ever received an email from me knows that I am a terrible typist, creating errors previously unknown to man! I have relied on the generosity of friends — some of whom are great knitters or have a keen eye for the incorrect coma — to help proof the chapters in progress and the completed document. Sincere thanks to Nancy Roberts, Mijung Jay, Carol Edwards, Carol Scott and Olivia Creser, who did some of the original color corrections to compensate for my lack of photo skills.

Jeanne Criscola of Criscola Design, who is a superb graphic designer, has been a dear friend for 35 years. She adapted the "grid" from the first Taunton Press book (*Hand—Manipulated Stitches for Machine Knitters*) for *More Hand—Manipulated Stitches* and *Hand Knits by Machine* so that they were all fairly similar in layout. She redesigned the grid for this book with a slightly larger format to help me save pages (i.e. reduced cost for you and for me). She has answered endless dumb questions at all hours of the night and day as I laid out the pages and photos. My part in the layout was like color by numbers, but Jeanne supplied all the numbers to begin with.

Jim Mullen, who has worked in television for years and had the good sense to marry my cousin, offered to photograph the swatches. He saw me struggling with lighting and depth of field issues and refused to take no for an answer. How lucky am I?! I think the photos are just gorgeous and clear as can be. If pages didn't cost what they do to print, I would have sized every single photo to fill half a page. As an added bonus, having Jim in Connecticut for photo sessions meant that his wife, Daralynn, and her daughter, Sasha, were also here and willing to model.

Last, but never least, is my husband, Arthur, who cooked so many dinners and spent endless days supervising a criminally inclined Labrador puppy so that I could finish this book. Without Arthur's support we might have starved — except for Arlo, who seems to do just fine eating cushions and parts of the coffee maker.

Contents

INTRODUCTION

Manipulating Stitches and Creating Patterns

BACK IN THE LATE 80'S when I wrote *Hand–Manipulated Stitches for Machine Knitters* for Taunton Press, I was fortunate to work with a talented editor named Chris Timmons. She polished me as an author and was largely responsible for the way that first book (and the others that followed) was organized. Chris taught me that when I say something like "this is my favorite method to do thus and so", I also need to give examples of other methods and explain *why* that particular method is a favorite. I still hear her voice in my head when I write.

At our initial meeting, Chris asked me exactly what hand—manipulated stitches were and suggested I list the ways that one could manipulate stitches on a knitting machine. I started compiling lists, which ultimately became the six major chapters in *HMS.* More than 30 years later they are still my guidelines when I sit down to "play" at a machine to challenge old ideas or explore new ones.

In one of the first chapters of *HMS*, I talked about casting–on and binding–off, as well as other motions I called "basic moves" because they were required in order to have stitches to manipulate in the first place or because they provided a base for further expansion. That chapter also included information on holding position, reforming stitches and a brief summation of garter stitch — all basic moves and not necessarily ends unto themselves.

Each of the remaining chapters explored one of the six ways I had originally defined stitch manipulation on a knitting machine: twisting, wrapping and weaving, lifting, rehanging, transferring and crossing stitches. I can honestly say that since that time, I haven't discovered any other ways of working my magic on the needles and stitches of my machines that don't fall into these categories or the basic moves.

Employing any of the six methods listed might alter an existing pattern and give you a springboard for new ideas, but there are lots of other factors to consider when developing patterns and textures. They are what I call my "what ifs".

If any of you have taken classes with me or read my previous books, you've probably heard me say that "if there is a repetition or rhythm to what you do with your hands and transfer tools, there must be a repetition, rhythm or pattern in the resulting fabric." This book is a search for those patterns.

What if.........

What will happen if I do *this* six times instead of five? What will happen if I work in two or more colors? Knit an even or odd number of rows between repeats? Use more or fewer stitches per repeat? What if, what if, what if. Those are the two words that keep me exploring and experimenting and *excited* about machine knitting.

In addition to twisting, wrapping, weaving, lifting, rehanging, transferring and crossing stitches, you might want to consider some of the following possibilities. Just make sure that you do as I do and keep a notepad close by to record *every* detail. What seemed crystal clear while you sat at the machine can become a frustrating mystery when you revisit your swatches a day later. I keep detailed notes on both the good *and* the bad outcomes for later development or exploration because you never know where your next great idea is going to come from.

Sometimes, the simplest variation can create a totally different pattern; other times there is hardly any difference. I find, however, that the more I play with a pattern, the more variations I discover as each new effect builds upon the last.

One of the most obvious variations is the number of stitches or rows used for a particular effect or the number of stitches/rows between repeats. Sometimes just changing the scale of things is enough to create a totally different look.

Consider whether or not it matters if you use an odd or an even number of stitches. While a 3x3 cable may be difficult to cross, a 3x2 cable will give you the same effect with less strain when you cross 3 stitches to the front and 2 behind. An odd number of rows between repeats will give you the option of alternately starting each repeat at the opposite end of the bed, which might also make it easier to keep track of the direction you perform a specific motion like crossing cables or reversing the entire direction of each alternate repeat.

You can repeat a particular maneuver every row, every other row or every ten rows and probably see very different results. Also, keep in mind that the number of rows between repeats doesn't always have to be the same.

I like to think in terms of "stitch recovery" after manipulations that create a lot of tension on the stitches. Allowing more or less space (i.e. plain stitches and/or rows) for the stitches to recover their alignment after each repeat will affect the way the stitches look and how the background stitches react—or not — to the manipulation. For example, if you knit just four rows after crossing a 2 x 2 cable, the column of cabled stitches will look narrower and tighter than if you had knitted six or eight rows between crossings because the stitches have not worked enough plain rows to recover their initial width. See swatch (A1).

A1 The cables at the left of this swatch were crossed every four rows. The softer looking cables on the right were crossed every eight rows, giving the stitches space to recover their original alignment. Both cables cross 2 x 2.

Don't be timid! How many times you repeat a particular motion in a given repeat or the entire fabric can change the way the stitches look or position themselves in the final result. For example, twisting a group of stitches twice will yield a very different effect than twisting them just once.

The knit side is not always the right side of the fabric. Sometimes the purl side can be even more interesting. You can turn the fabric over every so—many—rows to alternate the knit and purl faces of the fabric. And you can, of course, knit the base fabric in tuck or slip, rather than stockinette.

The location of the manipulation in the fabric — all over, isolated or along the edge — often affects the way that neighboring stitches respond. Just as you can knit an isolated motif in Fair Isle, you can also place isolated textures throughout your fabric. Not every technique has to be worked over the entire fabric. Remember, if the entire fabric is the same, sometimes there is no textural contrast to help the featured stitches stand out from the background. I once heard someone say that an effect should be visible on a galloping horse, 50 yards away, and while that might be a *bit* of an exaggeration, texture is meant to be seen and to stand out.

You can choose the direction of the motion you perform so that it is always to the left or right or you can alternate the direction with each partial or full repeat. Many of us have learned that the most interesting Fair Isle designs are created by varying the order of the colors we use so that simple motifs take on some visual complexity. You can also vary the order when working with textures. For example, there is likely to be a difference between ABC, ABC and ABC, CBA, whatever methods the variables ABC represent in your pattern.

With many techniques, it won't matter whether you manipulate stitches to the left or to the right. With others, like traveling twisted stitches, you need to twist in the direction the stitches are traveling when you want to emulate traditional twisted stitch effects. On the other hand, doing it "wrong" just might lead to something new and, if you know what you did and can do it again, it is perfectly correct.

When removing stitches from their needles and replacing them on the same/other needles, where and when you replace the stitches will affect the outcome. Stitches that are placed on the needles first always show on the knit side, which is why some of the patterns' directions specify using the two—step transfers, explained on page 20 along with their symbols.

The alignment of the repeats — vertical, staggered, alternate or random — is often what defines a pattern so shake it up! Try combining or reversing placement. Just as stitches can travel across the fabric, so can a motif or texture if you consistently work one needle further to the left (or right) with each repeat.

I've included some samples that were consistently worked in one direction so that you could see the biasing that sometimes results. While you might be able to work with a biased fabric for *some* projects, in most traditional garments it would be a problem, which begs two questions: (1) Does it need to be a traditional garment and (2) is it really a problem? What about using a biased strip as a feature to build off with join—as—you—knit or re—hung methods? Maybe you can straighten the fabric visually by filling in with short rows. If not, perhaps the biased fabric is useful as a scarf, shawl or other item where it does not need to conform to a body shape.

The size, texture or color is often what leads us to choosing one yarn over another to begin with so think about using color and texture in combination. Sometimes, even simple stripes can have a profound effect on pattern, as evidenced by many two—color tuck patterns. Some effects are lost on very fine yarn, but explode with interest when knitted with heavier or textured yarn. That said, the majority of the swatches in this book were worked in a single color *only* so that the stitch structures would stand out more clearly for photography. You could use many of those one—color fabrics as springboards for multi—color variations.

Remember that the stitch size doesn't have to be the same throughout a project. Think about changing the stitch size between repeats so that the background fabric is more, or less, pronounced, allowing the texture to recede or pop. Also remember to include any stitch size or other variations when swatching for gauge. In some instances I find that the actual stitch and row count is less helpful for garment planning than simply counting repeats, which is how I work with something like the winged ladder fabric on page 113,

Some effects can be worked on either single or double bed machines. I often find that it is more convenient for me to latch up a few stitches on a single bed fabric than to have the ribber in the way, blocking my view the entire time. It all depends on how many purl stitches are involved. For more than a few stitches or when the surfaces are dealt with separately, the double bed option might require a lot less manipulation on your part and justify the fact that you will need to work "blind" between the beds. It becomes a matter of practicality as much as preference when the ratio of purls to knits increases.

While we're considering equipment, let me also say that some of the patterns may be suitable for use with a lace carriage. I have not included the charts for those partly because my focus is on hand—manipulations, but also due to the differences between machines and the additional pages it would require for charts and explanations. Hand—manipulated stitches allow me to address the greatest number of machines and knitting skills, but if you are well versed in using your lace carriage, do experiment with some of the transfer techniques for punch card or electronic patterning.

I am a huge fan of *profusion* because sometimes seeing lots of repetitions creates more interest than a single motif or a scattering of motifs across a fabric. When in doubt, more is often more!

And, when all else fails, if you have knitted with an animal fiber like wool or alpaca, you can always try felting the finished fabric in hope of salvaging or enhancing what your efforts have failed to produce thus far.

Hopefully these suggestions will provide you with a road map to discovering new patterns and methods. Whenever I sit at the machine I am conscious of these variations as well as the manipulations and basic moves I referred to earlier. I usually find myself playing the "what if" game as I work through the possibilities. Even when it feels like I am beating a dead horse, I seldom just give up on an idea without thoroughly exploring as many possibilities as I can.

While I may not like the first fabric I create, the "what ifs" usually send me in other directions and introduce new variables so that, sometimes, the experimentation pays off. Other times, I end up right back where I started. In any case, I divide each attempt with a few rows of waste knitting and I write down everything I did so that I can evaluate my swatches when I remove the work from the machine.

Every once in a while, the most exciting results are what one of my weaving teachers used to call "happy accidents": the unexpected pattern or effect. As always, if you know what you did and can do it again, its right. If, however, you have no idea how the pattern developed, you are just looking at a delightful mistake. You can never take too many notes!

Open Spaces

Sometimes, what we *don't* say has as much impact as the words we choose. The same thing is true from a design perspective where negative spaces are important design elements — sometimes even the focus — of a fabric.

There are lots of ways to create negative spaces in a machine knitted fabric: transferring stitches, binding off and casting on and picking up and rehanging edges. Depending on the way the yarns are joined—or not — you can also create deliberate openings when working intarsia or short rows. Needles out of work create ladders and sometimes the ladders turn into something else entirely. In short, open spaces offer all kinds of opportunities for creating beautiful, original and interesting fabrics. These methods, combined with and modified by the What Ifs are the focus of this, my fourth machine knitting book.

If you have been machine knitting for a while, some of the material may be familiar to you, but I hope that you will appreciate the progression from one idea to the next and that some of my happy accidents will delight you as much as they did me. I am the first to admit that some of the samples are far more interesting than others and have greater value for practical use, but I have included them all so that you can see the progression of my ideas and learn as much from my lesser attempts as those that succeeded beautifully.

The pages that follow are the result of hours of experimentation and development of new techniques as well as some variations on established methods. There are some ideas that date back to Silver Reed in the 1960's and others that were inspired by contemporary photos on the internet. When ideas show up in half a dozen different places, it is impossible to know who to credit, but where I was able, I have cited my sources or inspiration.

I was extremely fortunate to have access to the archives of Stoll America in NYC. Stoll is a major manufacturer of industrial knitting machines that can do things we can only dream of doing on our home knitters. Many of my swatches were inspired by their industrial fabrics.

I'm sure you'll think of other ways of manipulating and changing patterns once you start playing with the possibilities. Stitch development can be an exciting and challenging process as long as you are willing to experiment and don't expect every effort to yield something wearable and wonderful. Once you begin welcoming your mistakes and learning from them, you never know what you will discover next.

Some of the fabrics I've included in this book are labor intensive, while others are deceptively simple and quick to do. I am a firm believer that none of us spends substantial sums of money or effort buying and learning to use a machine because we *need* a sweater. It is supposed to be a fun, creative craft and I hope you will join me in a quest for fewer sweaters, but better, more interesting and imaginative sweaters. Think of the money you will save on yarn!

I have to say that this was a complicated book to write that took almost twice as long to complete as any of my earlier books. Although I tried to group related swatches, there were times when it really wasn't clear whether a swatch belonged with eyelets or ladders. Also, there are some swatches that may appear quite similar, but they are usually just different approaches to the same end.

Laying out this book was a major undertaking. I have labeled the photos and charts with the same (red) numbers I refer to in the text. It isn't always possible to position the photos and charts right next to the text descriptions so you may have to flip to the next page to see the visuals. The red numbering should help you keep things straight. Also, there are a few references that do not have charts or photos.

There are literally hundreds of swatches and charts in the chapters that follow and although there have been several rounds of edits and knit—downs to proof the directions, there are apt to be some errors (to err *is* human). If (or *when*) I find any errors, I will post an errata sheet on my web site so do check there if you are having a problem with a particular technique. It may not be you.

Lastly, let me say that a number of these fabrics sport some *really* extreme textures. You can always change them or tone them down to suit your own taste. I just didn't think that any of us needed a book filled with the same old fabrics so this book became a journey of experimentation and discovery. I hope you enjoy the trip as much as I did!

Susan

Northford, CT
March 2018

web site: www.guagliumi.com
blog: www.susanguagliumi.com

All of the samples were knitted on a mid—gauge (6.5 mm) machine with Cascade 220, worsted weight wool. Some techniques will translate better than others to standard or chunky gauge machines and different yarns.

The stitch charts were first created with Design—A—Knit and then exported to Adobe Illustrator for final changes and additions, including original symbols and directional arrows.

THE BASICS

I WAS A SEWING ENTHUSIAST, weaver, hand knitter and a beader long before I discovered machine knitting and I have always been captivated by hand work and finishing details. For me, craft in general is always about the process, rather than the product so it didn't take long for me to be seduced by the hand—manipulated possibilities on the machine and to begin tackling the limitations the machine imposed on my efforts. Early on I began to develop and exploit some of the following tricks and techniques to bend the machine to my will. Please take the time to familiarize yourself with the methods that follow because I refer to them throughout this book.

Bridging

First and foremost, more than any other method, I rely on bridging to help me achieve a variety of unusual effects on the machine. Bridging has unlocked all kinds of possibilities for me and I used it extensively in all three of my previous machine knitting books; I specifically dedicated the entire second book, *More Hand—Manipulated Stitches,* to the subject. You can see examples of bridging in action in the video that accompanied the first book and there is also a short (free) video on my blog and on You Tube that illustrates the method.

At one time or another, you have probably used some form of bridging without even realizing that it was part of a much broader concept, but if bridging is a new subject for you, the following explanations (and the video) should get you started. Chances are you will realize that this is information you already knew on some level.

Simply stated, bridging is a method of using holding position to isolate and manipulate needles in one of several ways. Most machines are capable of holding some needles and knitting others, though there are differences in how this is done from one brand of machines to the next.

Although the Passap doesn't have a holding position as such, it does allow you to hold needles by manipulating the pushers. I first developed my bridged method for knitting popcorns on the Passap so I know it is possible, if a little clumsier than working on single bed Japanese machines. That said, there are times when it is very convenient to have that second bed of needles to work with.

You will find that I often rely on several (sometimes many) passes of the carriage to complete a single row of knitting, so at the very start of any bridged rows, make sure you turn off your row counter. At the end of the bridged row, turn the row counter back on and advance it by one row. Also, make sure that your claw weights are always underneath the *working* needles, not those in hold.

Many of my charts include a serpentine arrow to indicate the path the carriage follows for bridging a row. Each red arrow, no matter how many times it turns back on itself, indicates a single knitted row of fabric.

Sometimes the serpentine arrows represent actual, extra knitted rows. Those arrows are blue. When the arrows represent "dead" passes to simply return the carriage to the correct side they are shown in red. The text directions that accompany each sample will also indicate which is the case for that particular example.

Bridging for Stitch Size

Many times you will find that although the background fabric looks perfect, the stitches you want to cross or twist are just not large enough for easy manipulation. There are two ways to increase the size of those stitches while retaining the appropriate stitch size for the background fabric.

First of all, you can change the size of those stitches by adjusting the stitch dial on the carriage. Even larger stitches can be produced by manually knitting the needles. Please note that in the following explanations I have instructed you to begin with the carriage on the right only to make my directions as specific and helpful as possible. Bridging can begin at either side.

USING THE STITCH DIAL TO CHANGE STITCH SIZES

Assume that you want to increase the stitch size of some cable stitches and that the cables cross every six rows. After the fifth row, turn off the row counter and, beginning with the carriage on the right, proceed as follows and as shown in row 2 of the chart B1 for three cables crossing in one row:

Begin COR and set the carriage to hold NDLS placed in HP. The ST size should be set for the normal background (i.e. stockinette) fabric. Bring all NDLS to HP *except* the first bridge on the carriage side (NDLS 1-5). The first bridge in this case is the group of NDLS between the edge of the fabric and the first group of cable NDLS. There are 4 bridges in this example.

Knit 1 row across the bridge NDLS. COL. Move those NDLS to HP so that all NDLS are now in HP and return the carriage to the right end of the bed.

Nudge the first group of 8 cable NDLS (NDLS 6-13) to UWP and increase the ST size by one number. Knit those NDLS, hold them (once again, all NDLS are in HP) and return the carriage to the right end of the bed.

Bring the next group of bridge NDLS (14-18) to UWP and return the ST dial to normal size. Knit, hold the NDLS just knitted and return COR.

Nudge the next group of cable NDLS (19-26) to UWP. Increase the ST size. Knit, hold and return COR.

Knit the next bridge (27-31), then the third cable (32-39) and then nudge the last group of bridge NDLS to UWP, return to normal ST size and knit, ending COL. Cross all cables.

Turn the row counter back on and advance it by one number. Set the carriage to knit all NDLS back from HP. Knit five rows and then repeat the bridging sequence for the next row of cable crossings.

The *extra* carriage passes shown by the red serpentine arrow over each group of bridge and cable NDLS are non—knitting passes because the NDLS are in HP. They only serve to keep the carriage moving and knitting continuously in the same direction to the end of the row. The *first* pass over each group of NDLS is a knitted pass, so although the carriage makes 7 passes, only one row of STS is actually knitted by the time the carriage finishes at left.

The second and third examples on the chart illustrate the path the carriage would follow to increase the ST size for half of each cable group. Normally, this is all that is necessary to help cables cross more easily. The enlarged STS will not show on the knit side because they are always the second group of STS returned to their NDLS which ensures that they are on the back of the fabric.

Although its tempting to really crank up the ST size for the cable STS, you should only increase their size enough to facilitate the crossing because it is important to retain some cross tension on the STS to help define the cables. Overly—large STS cross easily, but the resulting cables look flat and limp.

MANUALLY INCREASING STITCH SIZE

If your background fabric is already knitting near the top of the stitch dial or for techniques that require *really* huge stitches, you can manually increase the size of specific stitches. To manually knit a stitch, just use your finger to push the needle butt forward, lay yarn into the hook and then push the needle back so that the old stitch slides over the closed latch and forms a new stitch. The further back you push the needle butt, the larger the resulting stitch.

B1

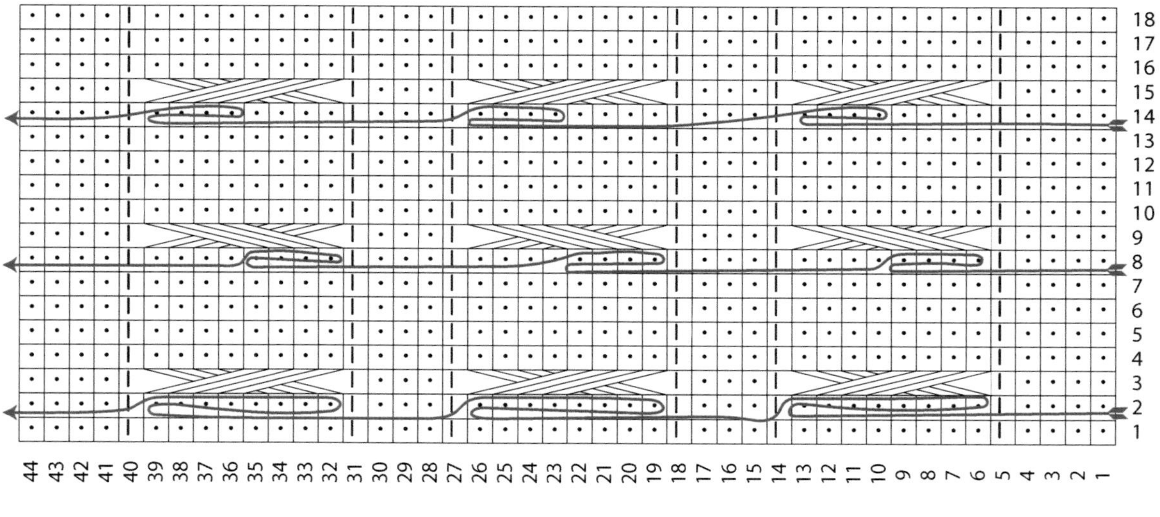

Begin COR and set the carriage to hold NDLS placed in HP. The ST size should be set for the normal background (i.e. stockinette) fabric and will not be changed. Bring all NDLS to HP *except* the first bridge on the carriage side then follow these steps:

Knit 1 row across the bridge NDLS. COL. Move the bridge NDLS to HP. Before returning the carriage to the right, manually knit the next group of NDLS to the left all the way back to the rail to NWP and leave them there. Return the carriage to the right end of the bed.

Nudge the next group of bridge NDLS to UWP and knit 1 row to the left. Hold the NDLS just knitted and then manually knit the next group of NDLS back to NWP. Return COR.

Continue knitting bridge STS with the carriage and pattern NDLS manually until you knit the last bridge, ending COL.

Complete any manipulations (i.e. crossing, twisting, etc.). As you push NDLS from NWP to WP, make sure you tug down lightly on the enlarged STS to prevent them from slipping off the NDLS. Advance the row counter by one number and set the carriage to knit all NDLS back from HP to WP. Continue knitting to the next prep row.

With this method, there is no need to change the stitch dial on the carriage. The NDLS back in NWP will stay there as long as you make sure they are knitted all the way back against the rail. When I do this, I keep a finger on the butt of the last NDL I knitted as I work the next one. Otherwise, the NDLS in NWP can slip forward as you knit the following row and you are likely to jam the carriage.

Its also possible to knit the NDLS part way back to the rail so that they are halfway between WP and NWP (I think of it as Half—WP) to form stitches that are larger than those on the stitch dial but not quite as huge as the ones described above. To do this, you must immediately push the NDLS out to HP after manually knitting them because the carriage will not pass over NDLS in this position. Try to knit all the STS the same size when you do this and, although you could lay a dowel or other gauge across the bed to help you, it needs to be removed and replaced every time you move the carriage. So, better to just do it by eye.

Remember that the carriage only knits in one direction in a single row, in these two examples from right to left. When the carriage backs up from left to right, it is a dead pass because all of the NDLS are in HP. It needs to return to the right so that the yarn knits continuously from the last ST on the left of one group to the first ST on the right of the next without interruption. Apart from the enlarged STS, the completed row bears no other evidence of the bridging itself.

B2 There is a free pattern for this Loopity Lou hat available on my web site that features an even faster, 2-transfer tool method for lifting the popcorns as you knit them than I have described in this book. Because you can download the pattern for free, there isn't much point in repeating the specifics here, but I have to tell you that I didn't stumble onto this newer, improved method until I had been knitting popcorns for many years using the "old method". Its a good method, but the fine tuning described in the hat pattern makes it so much faster and easier to find and lift the stitches that complete each popcorn. There's always room for improvement!

When bridging is used to increase stitch size by either of these methods, it is usually represented by a red serpentine arrow on my charts. If there are a lot of other things happening in the fabric, these arrows tend to make the charts more confusing to follow and may be omitted. In that case I specifically refer to bridging in the directions.

However, when bridging is used to add extra rows, as it is in the examples that follow, the carriage motion is represented by a blue serpentine arrow that indicates every pass of the carriage as it knits in both directions. In those examples there are no dead passes.

Bridging to Add Extra Rows

More than anything else, I use bridging to add extra rows to specific needles when knitting popcorns, dimensional cables and raised textures.(b2)The stitch size never changes. Instead, the bridges just connect one group of "special" needles to the next and, as always, the bridges only knit once.

This is how I would add extra rows to a series of 3 x 3 cables:

Turn off the row counter and begin COR, set the carriage to hold NDLS in HP and set the ST size for the background/main fabric.

Hold all NDLS except the first bridge on the carriage side and the first three of the six NDLS for the first cable. Knit one row to the left and then hold the bridge NDLS.

Three cable NDLS remain in WP. Knit one row over these three NDLS, ending COR.

*Push the other three cable NDLS, the next bridge and the next three cable NDLS to UWP. Knit one row to the left. Hold the first three cable NDLS and the bridge. Only the first three NDLS for the second cable remain in WP. Knit one row over these NDLS, ending COR.**

Repeat from * to ** until you reach the left end of the bed with the final bridge. Cross all cables, returning the three right hand stitches from each cable to the machine first so that the two extra rows on those STS stand up from the knit surface where they can be seen.

The above directions are for adding two extra rows on just the first three needles of a six stitch cable and could have been illustrated by the second example on the chart on page 8 if it had been drawn with a blue serpentine arrow instead of red.

The method is a little different (and so is the path of the serpentine arrow) when adding extra rows to all six cable stitches or the stitches for the left half of a cable. This is an important distinction because as cables become more complex (braided, "Hugs and Kisses", etc.) their direction is always determined by which stitches return to the needles first. There is no point in adding extra rows to the stitches that will lie on the back of the fabric where they won't show. The extra rows on select needles do make cables easier to cross, but, more importantly, they really increase the depth of the cables themselves because those extra rows pop right up off the knit surface of the fabric.

POPCORN

I use the same method to add extra rows to specific needles to knit popcorns and to create really bold effects like my stegosaurus and horizontal cables. (photo b2) In fact, it was the popcorn method that follows that initially inspired further uses for bridging. To knit an entire row of 2-stitch popcorns separated by 3-stitch bridges, try this:

Begin with COR set to hold needles in HP and background ST size. Hold all needles except the first 3 bridge NDLS and the first 2 popcorn NDLS. Knit one row. Place the bridge NDLS in hold *Knit 3 more rows on the remaining popcorn NDLS, ending COR.

Nudge the next 3-ST bridge and the next 2-ST popcorn NDLS to UWP and knit one row to the left. Lift the STS in the bottom row of the first popcorn onto the NDLS above, forcing the extra rows to the knit side of the fabric. Hold the completed popcorn and the bridge.**

Repeat from * to **, ending with a bridge at the left edge. Make sure you use some finger tensioning as you add the extra rows to the popcorn NDLS or the STS will not knit cleanly and may drop.

Bridges are the needles leading up to and between the needles that will receive special treatment. Bridges only knit once, regardless of whatever else is happening in the row, and they always knit with the background (main) stitch size.

NOPS

You'll notice that the directions for the popcorns include lifting the stitches from the first row of the popcorn onto the needles above. This is what forces the extra rows to pop out on the knit side of the fabric, while the purl side of the fabric remains smooth and flat.

If you do not lift the first row of stitches, the texture becomes what is called "nops", raised areas of texture that are forced off the surface of the fabric simply because of the extra rows. Some of the examples in the following chapters make use of nops, which are knitted like popcorns that are not lifted at all; others, however do employ lifting specific stitches.

Bridging to Access the "Free Yarn" Mid—Row

I refer to the yarn between the last needle knitted and the carriage feeder as the "free yarn". You can pull as much yarn as you need through the feeder and use it for a variety of purposes as you bridge across a row.

After bridging to the desired NDL, use the FY to wrap NDLS or STS, hang beads and feathers or create loops that you hang on the NDLS for all kinds of effects.

More often, however, I use the free yarn to B/O and/or C/O STS in the middle of a row. For example, beginning with the COR, hold all the NDLS except the first bridge on the carriage side. Knit those NDLS and then place them in HP. Then use whichever method you prefer to B/O the next group of NDLS. Transfer the last ST to be B/O to the next NDL in HP, place the emptied NDLS in NWP and then return the COR. Push the next bridge (the NDLS on the left of the ones you just B/O) into UWP and knit 1 row to the left. You can bind off another group of STS or perhaps this finishes the row.

At the start of the next row, just knit the first bridge on the left, hold those NDLS and then either e—wrap or chain onto the empty NDLS (the ones you B/O in the previous row) and bridge your way to the end of that row (or to the next group of NDLS that need to be C/O).

I usually find that I am happiest with the edges of the latch tool/chained B/O if I also bridge the row prior to increase the size of the STS I plan to bind off. In addition, to avoid a large gap between the B/O and the working STS, I usually start B/O by inserting my latch tool through the purl bump of the first ST in hold adj to those I am B/O Its a small detail, but one that can really affect the finished look of the fabric.

Initially, Bridging sounds like a lot of extra steps to worry about, but keep in mind that bridging is usually only necessary the row before you perform a specific action, not row after row in a fabric. Once you understand the method, it won't slow you down at all and it definitely facilitates all kinds of manipulations that would otherwise be impossible.

Drop Stitch

Drop stitch is an excellent method for creating open, all—over patterns or for enlarging specific stitches in order to manipulate them more easily.

Both of my first machines were double bed machines, the Superba and the Passap, and removing the front bed was never an option. I learned to do all kinds of hand manipulations on those machines and I also learned to make the front/ribber bed work to my advantage by using drop stitch to facilitate single—bed manipulations.

Double Bed Drop Stitch

Drop stitch is usually worked double bed with most of the stitches knitting on the main/back bed. As you probably know from catching your sleeve on a needle hook, any needles brought into work on the ribber/front bed will immediately start knitting if the ribber carriage is engaged and set to knit. And, as you also probably know from experience, if you release that stitch from its needle once you discover that it has knitted, the stitch will run and create a loose stitch (in the main bed fabric) that always shows, no matter how much you tug at the fabric later. A stitch, however, can only run to the point where it was cast on, which is the main idea behind Drop Stitch. Rather than allowing these accidental stitches to form, you can take control and purposely drop stitches to your advantage.

CONDO STITCH

Back in the 80's, hand knitters were excited about knitting "condo stitch" where they worked garter stitch with two different sized needles. The difference in needle sizes was huge — maybe a size 4 and an 11 — so the resulting fabric had very open rows of stitches alternating with rows of small, tighter stitches.

You can knit stockinette "condo stitch" on any double bed knitting machine by starting with all of the stitches on the main bed. Either cast on single bed to begin with or transfer the ribber stitches to the main bed after the band or ribbing is complete. Set the stitch size on the main carriage for a normal or slightly tighter stitch size for stockinette. B3

Initially, set the ST size on the ribber carriage fairly low — around ST size 1 or 2 to start. Once you see how the fabric knits and looks, you can always fine tune the ST sizes. Set the ribber carriage to knit in one direction and to slip in the other — it doesn't matter which way as long as the rows alternate between knitting and slipping. The main carriage knits every row.

With the beds in half pitch so that the NDLS do not collide, bring a corresponding number of NDLS to WP on the RB. Thread and couple the carriages and knit two rows. The NDLS on the MB will knit both rows, but the RB will only knit in one direction or the other, depending on how you have set the levers for knitting and slipping. In fact, after two passes of the carriage, all you will see in the hooks of the ribber NDLS is zigzag loops of yarn that look more like tuck STS or a cast on.

Uncouple the carriages and make two passes with ribber carriage alone. The ribber STS will drop the one row they knitted when the two carriages were connected. You can repeat these directions for the length of the fabric, but the truth is that you only need to drop the ribber STS after many rows have been knitted. Also, if you own a Silver Reed machine, instead of uncoupling the carriages to drop the STS, you can use the little "P carriage" that comes with the ribber for working drive lace.

I'll admit that the first few times you try this you are apt to hold your breath and hope for the best. As machine knitters, we generally try to avoid dropping a whole row of stitches at once. If you decide to drop the ribber stitches every 20 rows, for example, the stitches on the ribber needles will look like regular stitches (not the tuck loops you saw initially), but they can still only drop to the point where they began. The dropped ribber stitches will be absorbed into every other row of the main bed stitches.

Remember, you can adjust the stitch size on the ribber to create even larger dropped stitches, but be aware that the carriages will be that much harder to push across the beds if you do. It would be like trying to knit full needle rib (close rib) with the stitch size on both carriages set for stockinette instead of the smaller stitch sizes you normally use for knitting ribs. Even though stitches may appear quite small on the ribber needles, remember that once the ribber stitches are dropped, the yarn forming the zigzags across the beds is absorbed into the main bed stitches.

Instead of working Condo Stitch, if you allow the ribber to continually knit in both directions, you can produce a softer, more open stockinette fabric than might normally be possible on your machine. This is especially true for yarns like mohair, brushed wool and many novelty yarns. It also increases the range of yarns you can use on any machine.

Most knitters are aware that they can work on every—other—needle to accommodate heavier yarns than their machine was designed to handle. On single bed machines, this always produces a much narrower fabric, sometimes limiting you to smaller garments. However, with a 1 x 1 (rib) needle arrangement for drop stitch, the fabric is usually wider than it would have been if knitted on every—other—needle. In this particular case, drop stitch gives you one more option to try and, perhaps, one more use for your ribber.

To get a feel for drop ST, C/O and begin with all the STS on the MB the main carriage set to ST size 5. Increase the ribber ST size progressively by one ST size every row, starting with size 1 in the first row and working up to ST size 5. The carriage will be progressively harder to move as the ribber ST size increases.

B3

The purl side is more interesting than the knit side when Condo Stitch is worked in stockinette on a knitting machine.

Drop stitch works because a stitch can only ravel to the point where it was initially cast on.

Rather than increasing the size on the ribber alone, it might be easier to start with a smaller stitch size on the main bed and progressively increase both carriage stitch sizes. Unlike Condo Stitch, which only knits in one direction, the ribber carriage will knit in both directions and then, after every ten rows (for example), the carriages should be uncoupled and the ribber carriage moved across the bed alone to drop the stitches from the ribber bed.

As long as you precede any dropping of stitches by transferring the actual ribber stitches to the main bed where they are safe, you can knit as many or as few rows as you want before dropping ribber stitches from their needles. Remember, a stitch can only drop to the point where it was cast on to an empty needle. Stitches that have been transferred to the opposite bed are safe and secure. You can work a pattern of enlarged stitches/ladders by choosing different stitches to transfer and then drop or you can reform the dropped columns of stitches with some twists or other manipulations that needed more length.

If you only work one row of drop stitch at the very end of a piece of knitting, you can create a row of really huge stitches for binding off by hand or with a linking accessory. The bound off edge will be far less likely to pull in when the stitches have been enlarged. To do this, begin with all the stitches on the main bed. Bring the ribber needles to working position, knit one row and then run the ribber carriage across the bed alone to drop the newly formed loops.

ENLARGING SPECIFIC STITCHES

When working double bed, if you only need to enlarge a few specific stitches to ease a cable crossing (B4) or to weave some stitches through another set of stitches, you can selectively (i.e. manually) drop individual stitches. If the dropping needles are the only ribber needles in use, you can drop them as described earlier. However, when knitting a double bed fabric where some of the ribber stitches continue to knit and are not meant to drop, you cannot use the ribber carriage or the "P" carriage to release stitches from their needles. You will need to individually, manually drop those stitches.

For most cables, knit to the row just before crossing the cables and then bring one empty ribber needle to working position opposite the center of each of the groups of main bed cable needles. Knit 1 row and then manually drop the loops just formed and push the empty needles to non—working position. The remaining needles on the ribber will continue knitting normally, but you will be able to cross the cables more easily.

If you want to enlarge a group of 5 stitches for a fancy woven or twisted stitch design, chances are you won't

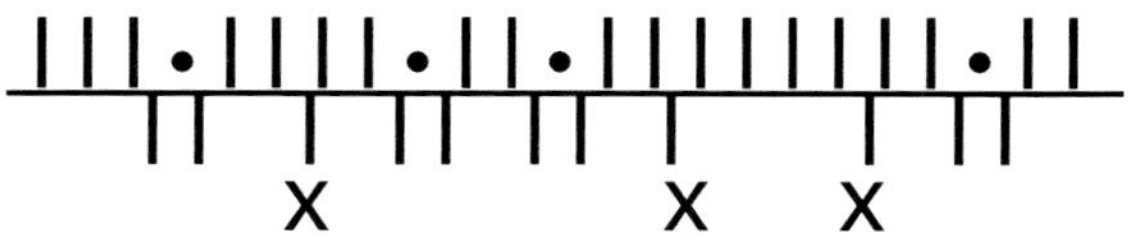

B4 This Half Pitch double bed NDL set up shows the placement of dropping NDLS for both a 4-stitch cable and an 8-stitch cable. The "X" indicates NDLS that are only brought into WP for the row *before* the cable crossings, dropped and then returned to NWP. Because there are also regular RB STS between the groups of main bed NDLS, the ones marked "X" must be dropped manually, not with the ribber carriage or the P—carriage. The chart does not show the RB NDLS in NWP.

have any other needles working on the ribber bed (though you could). In that case, the row before the manipulation in question, with the beds in half pitch, bring four needles into working position opposite the main bed stitches you plan to manipulate. Knit 1 row, drop the loops and put the empty ribber needles back in non—working position. If these are the only stitches being formed on the ribber bed, move the ribber carriage across the bed alone to drop the stitches. It is only necessary to perform the drop stitch maneuver the row before crossing, twisting or otherwise imposing your will on the stitches. All other rows are knitted normally.

OPEN STITCH PATTERNS

If you vary the needles you use on the ribber bed to knit the dropped stitches, you can create open stitch patterns in the fabric. Probably the easiest patterns to keep track of are those where the stitches travel in a single direction or reverse direction every ten rows or so. You can also select needles to form a diamond motif or other simple shapes.

B5 Sometimes, rather than selecting different needles every two rows, you can just rack the bed one position, reversing direction when the bed reaches the limit at either end. When the stitches drop, they will do so in a zigzag fashion.

When I do this I usually work with the fabric on the main bed and accomplish the dropping on the ribber bed. However, on machines with automatic needle selection, you can work very elaborate patterns by knitting the main fabric on the ribber bed and allowing the punch card or electronics to select the needles on the main bed that will be knitted and then dropped. This is what Silver Reed calls "drive lace" and why they provide a P—carriage with their ribbers.

Always work a couple of samples before you decide what stitch size to use on the ribber carriage. If you want to enlarge a specific group of main bed stitches, use as few ribber needles as possible for dropping so that the enlarged stitches retain some tension and don't appear sloppy or too different from the other stitches. Also, make sure the beds are in half pitch and remember that groups of main bed stitches will require one less (or one more)needle on the ribber bed to enlarge them.

You need to make sure that the fabric is well weighted when you work drop stitch so that as the stitches are released from the ribber bed, they are more easily absorbed by the adjacent stitches. You may still have to give the knitting a tug every so often to facilitate the dropping. Also, try to develop a rhythm so that you always knit the same number of rows before dropping the ribber stitches. It may affect the overall appearance of the fabric and minimizes any difficulty in dropping the stitches. Yarns that have any hair or texture to them tend to stick and drop unevenly. Dropping stitches more often ensures that they drop properly, evenly, and are easily absorbed into the main fabric. Unless you are knitting with slippery rayon, you certainly don't want to wait until the very last row of a project to drop all the stitches at once.

While I have used drop stitch for patterned effects, I find it most useful for lengthening stitches for the hand manipulations I love exploring. I have included the information on drop stitch primarily for that reason.

B5 With every fifth needle on the ribber in WP, the bed was racked every two rows, reversing direction when it reached its limit at either side. The main carriage was set for stitch 5 and the ribber for size 2. Move the ribber carriage across the bed alone to drop the stitches after each complete repeat of the pattern.

Although drop stitch is most often associated with double bed machines, it is also possible to work some drop stitch methods on single beds by capitalizing on adjacent needles and accessory gauges, rather than a second bed of needles.

Single Bed Drop Stitch

First of all, remember that a stitch can only drop to the point where it was cast on. If, at some point in your knitting, you transfer a stitch to its adjacent needle and put the empty needle out of work, a ladder will form. B6 However, if instead of forming a ladder, you bring the emptied needle back to working position and allow it to knit some rows and then drop the stitch from that needle, it will run back to the row where you initially transferred the stitch to create the ladder in the first place. The dropped stitch will form an even wider ladder than would have been formed by leaving the needle in non—working position to begin with.

This method can be useful on a single bed machine to add extra ease for wide cables or working other bold textures. The ease provided by the dropped stitch(es) make many manipulations easier and put less strain on the yarn. And, after a number of repeats, you can also reform the stitches of the ladder to create purl stitches alongside the cable. In that case, rather than transferring the stitch to an adjacent needle at the start, simply place it on a stitch holder so you can retrieve it later to begin latching up. If you do transfer the stitch to an adjacent needle and then decide to latch up the resulting ladder, there is usually a hole at the bottom of the ladder, much like an eyelet. You can minimize that effect by first catching the purl bump of an adjacent stitch in the hook of your latch tool.

In *Hand—Manipulated Stitches for Machine Knitters,* I showed a method of catching the yarn around the sinker posts of the ribber bed after manually knitting each main bed needle in order to produce really huge sinker loops that could be manipulated for specific stitches. The sinker posts on the ribber bed serve as a gauge to ensure that all of the loops are the same size. I also showed how to use a hand knitting needle as a gauge to form loops and textures with the free yarn, but if you are willing to do the hand—work, there are so many more possibilities!

On a single bed machine, there are no ribber sinker posts opposite the main bed to catch the yarn around, but you can extend that approach to using something else for a gauge to form a row of loops. The loops, in turn, can be used for decorative purposes or dropped to form really huge stitches.

B7 For occasional rows of incredibly huge stitches, you can manually knit an entire row, passing the yarn around a ruler, dowel or other gauge after knitting each stitch to enlarge the size of the loops between the stitches.

When the gauge is removed at the end of the row, the stitches on the machine will absorb all the extra length from the loops that were formed around the gauge.

B6 Both the left and right ladders were formed by bringing an empty needle to working position and then dropping the stitches that formed. The ladder at left was secured by transferring the stitch to a safety pin for easy retrival later on. The ladder at right was formed by transferring the stitch to an adjacent needle. The barely visible ladder at center was formed by leaving a needle out of work, without drop stitch.

B7

This opens up a whole new range of stitches because when you manually knit each of the needles, you can knit them to any position between Working and Nonworking. However, unless you have the patience of a saint, this is not a practical way to work an entire garment, though it will allow you to create accent rows of really open stitches for crochet or other special effects.

B8 I like using a regular, flat ruler as my gauge because, after the first 4-5 wraps, it is easier to hold onto. Whatever gauge you choose, hold it close to the bed and always wrap the yarn around it before manually knitting each needle back to working or non—working position. Make sure you wrap the same direction each time just to ensure that all the stitches look the same. At the end of the row, slide the gauge out and give the fabric a good tug so that the stitches absorb all the length of the loops. With some yarns, you will find that this is more easily done after first knitting one regular row. B9

B8

B9 The first row of enlarged stitches was formed by wrapping the yarn around a wooden size 10 hand knitting needle. The middle row was worked by winding the yarn around a ruler and manually knitting the needles back to WP to form 1" stitches. The top of the swatch was worked by knitting the needles back to NWP after wrapping the same ruler and produced 1.5" stitches.

Symbols, Terms & Abbreviations

In addition to descriptive text, I have also relied on stitch charts to explain how the various examples throughout this book were knitted. You may not be familiar with symbol—type charts, but let me assure you that these charts save pages of wordy explanation and are easy to read once you get used to them. You'll find that they help you visualize what you need to do and what has already happened in the fabric.

Each row on a gridded chart represents one row of knitting and each vertical column represents a single stitch. Hand knit charts generally show the knit side of the fabric. However, as the purl side of the fabric faces us on a machine, these charts represent the purl side.

Most of the decrease and traveling stitch symbols are the same as they would be if shown for the knit side of the fabric because it is nearly impossible to represent them with the purl symbol.

In addition to symbols for knit and purl stitches, there are specialized symbols to represent various manipulations. Some of these symbols are fairly standard, but others are my originals, developed to represent very specific manipulations. I have also utilized shading and color in various charts to indicate specific motions.

With only a couple of exceptions, all of the charts are numbered from right to left even though I usually work centered on either side of zero on the bed. I thought the directions would be confusing if I needed to continually specify needle 7 *left or right*. I suggest working your initial attempts on the needles left of center zero so that the needle numbers on the bed agree with the charts and then, when you understand the stitch and the directions, you can work your final project centered on the bed.

In order to keep directions (and the whole book!) from becoming too lengthy , I have opted to use some standard abbreviations, but I have tried to keep their use to a minimum because I know they can be confusing for some knitters. For many of the short rowed fabrics, the charts have been adapted to specific motions so please follow the written directions as well as the charts.

Abbreviations

A/R	every alternate row
#/R	substitute "#" with a number. 3/R indicates every 3rd row, 5/R every 5th row, etc.
adj	adjacent needle or stitches
alt	alternate needles or stitches
BB	bridge bar(s)s
B/O	bind off
C/O	cast on
CC	contrast color
COL	carriage on left
COR	carriage on right
Dec	decrease(s) (ing)
E/R	every row
EON	every other needle
EOR	every other row
FY	free yarn
GB	garter bar
HK	hand knit
HP	holding position
Inc	increase(s) (ing)
K/M	knitting machine
MB	main bed/back bed of double Japanese machines; front bed of Passap
KWK	knit, wrap, knit back
MC	main color
Ndl(s)	needle(s)
NWP	non—working position
P/U	pick up
RB	Ribber bed/front bed of double bed Japanese machines
RC	row count(er)
S/O	scrap off
S/R	short row(s) (ing)
St(s)	stitch(es)
Tog	together
UWP	upper working position
WP	working position
[.....]	brackets are used in patterns to indicate a group of stitches or directions to be treated as a single unit
*....**	Repeat stitches or directions between the asterisks

BRIDGING

A method for using HP and short rows to change the stitch size, access the free yarn or add extra rows on specific needles. It may take several passes of the carriage to complete a single row. Bridges are the groups of needles that divide "special effect" needles. Bridges only knit once and always with the main stitch size.

BRIDGE BARS

The lengths of yarn that extend, unknitted, from one short rowed section to the next.

DROP STITCH

Allowing empty needles to cast on for the sole purpose of later dropping those stitches to enlarge adjacent stitches. Although usually a double bed method, it is possible to work single bed drop stitch.

FREE YARN

The yarn between the carriage feeder and the first working needle that can be pulled through the feeder and utilized for special effects anywhere in a row, usually when bridging.

LADDER

Ladders are formed by leaving an empty needle in NWP between working needles *or* by dropping stitches and allowing them to run. They are defined by the unknitted bars of yarn that lie across the space where stitches should be.

NOPS

Raised areas formed by workling extrea rows on specific needles, without lifting stitches to secure the texture.

ONE—STEP DECREASE

Standard decreasing where the transferred stitches are placed on top of existing stitches and remain on the purl side of the fabric.

PREP ROW

Prep rows are used to arrange stitches and needles according to the pattern chart and are never knitted. Very often, the next row on the chart will include some manipulation or moving needles into position before it is knitted. Prep rows are not numbered and are shaded to distinguish them from the knitted rows of the chart.

SERPENTINE ARROW

The red or blue arrows used to indicate the path the carriage follows to knit a bridged row. Red arrows indicate sequences where the carriage only knits each needle once, but backs up regularly to keep the work flowing from right to left (or left to right). Blue arrows indicate sequences where extra rows are knitted on specific needles.

SKIPPED DECREASES

Stitches are transferred left or right, bypassing the first (or first few) adjacent needles before replacing them on the next needle(s). The skipped stitches remain on the knit face of the fabric with the decreases behind.

SINKER POSTS

Also called gate pegs, the metal dividers between needles on Japanese manufactured machines. European machines have flow combs, as do most of the plastic hobby machines.

SPLIT PAIRS

Combining half the stitches from one group with half the stitches from the next to form a new group. Groups AB and CD would split to form BC.

STACKED DECREASES

Each transferred stitch is placed on needles already holding stitches, unlike full fashioned decreasing where only the leading stitch is doubled.

STITCH RECOVERY

The number of rows required for stitches to return to their normal placement, size or tension after performing a specific manipulation that causes distortion.

STITCHES THROUGH STITCHES

One set of stitches is pulled through another stitch or group of stitches with a latch tool and replaced on the needles individualy or as a group. The stitches they were pulled through are dropped from their needle(s) and will encircle them.

TRAVELING STITCHES

Stitches appear to travel across the knitting when a manipulation like twisting, cabling or transferring progresses towards the left (or right) with each repeat. This is usually done by including one less stitch from the previous repeat and one new one on the advancing side.

TWISTED STITCHES

Twisted stitches include single, e—wrap type twists as well as classic twisted stitches that require a pair of transfer tools. Remove the stitches on the first tool then insert the second tool through the same stitches from the opposite direction. Remove the first tool and rotate the remaining tool 180° to the left or right. For vertical columns of stitches, either direction is correct but it is important to be consistent. For designs with traveling stitches, the tool is always twisted in the same direction the stitches are traveling.

TWO—STEP DECREASE

The transferred stitches show on the knit face of the fabric and usually contribute to the pattern/design. First remove the stitch(es) from the needle(s) that will receive the transferred stitch(es). Transfer the appropriate stitches to the now—empty needles and then replace the original stitch(es) on top of them.

TWISTED LIFTED STITCHES

Insert the tip of a transfer tool under the first (lowest) bar of a 2-bar ladder, then over the second bar, tipping the tool twards you. Place on the needle above either by pushing the needle through the back of the stitch or using a second tool, inserted through the front of the stitch.

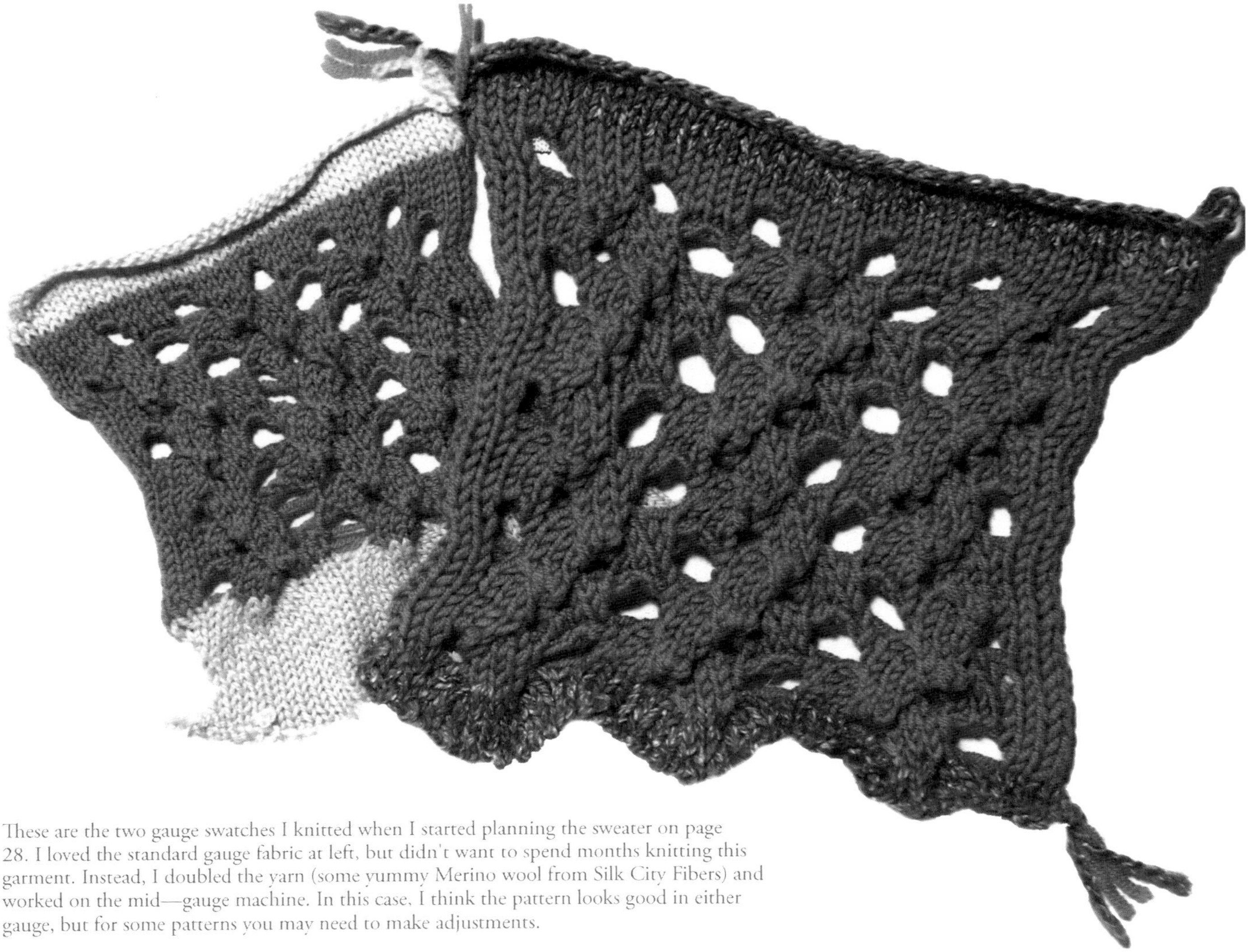

These are the two gauge swatches I knitted when I started planning the sweater on page 28. I loved the standard gauge fabric at left, but didn't want to spend months knitting this garment. Instead, I doubled the yarn (some yummy Merino wool from Silk City Fibers) and worked on the mid—gauge machine. In this case, I think the pattern looks good in either gauge, but for some patterns you may need to make adjustments.

Symbols

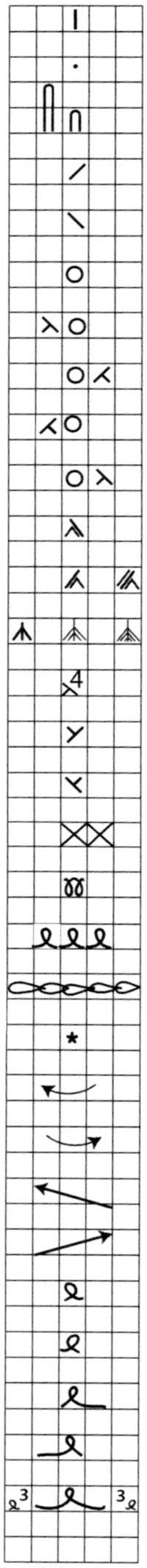

knit stitch: This ST must be latched up/reformed or worked on the ribber.

purl stitch as formed by the carriage.

tuck stitch needle in HP for one (or two) rows before knitting or as formed by punch card or electronics.

stitch traveling to the right.

stitch traveling to the left.

eyelet formed by NDL in NWP, usually paired with a decrease symbol.

1-step transfer to the lef:tCenter ST is transferred to adjacent NDL at left.

1-step transfer to the right: Center ST is transferred to adjacent NDL at right.

2-step transfer to the left: Left ST is transferred to center NDL then both STS are moved to left NDL.

2-step transfer to the right: Right ST is transferred to center NDL then both STS are moved to right NDL.

Two STS transferred to the same NDL at left.

two (three) STS transferred to same NDL at right.

two (four, six) STS transferred to the center NDL.

four STS transferred to same NDL at left (alternate symbol).

lifted increase to left: Pick up purl bar of center ST and hang on adjacent empty NDL at left.

lifted increase to right: Pick up purl bar of center ST and hang on adjacent empty NDL at right.

stacked decrease : Two STS from right and two STS from left transferred to same two center NDLS.

e—wrap

e—wrap

chaining/latch tool C/O or B/O

designated needle indicates which NDL to wrap when short rowing, etc

left motion Transfer or lift a ST or purl bump to NDL at left

right motion Transfer or lift a ST or purl bump to NDL at right.

left motion

right motion

stitch twisted left

stitch twisted right

2 stitches twisted left

2 stitches twisted right

3 stitches twisted left, center and right

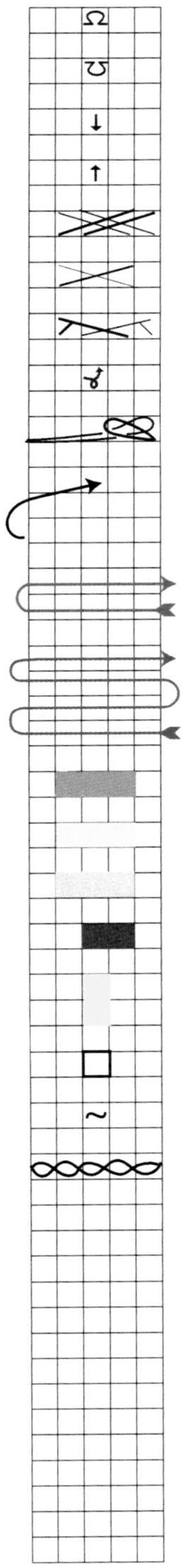

main bed stitch

ribber bed stitch

drop stitch or transfer ST from main bed to ribber.

lifted stitch/bar or transfer ST from ribber bed to main bed.

cable: darker lines indicate which STS are returned to the needles *LAST*

skipped cable 1 x 1 cable crossed behind a center ST.

cabled decrease: remove 2 STS on 2 single prong tools. Cross STS and return them 1 NDL to right or left so that there are 2 empty NDLS at center — not the original NDLS — to form an eyelet

twisted lifted stitch

stitches through stitches: 4 STS at left are pulled through single ST at right and returned to right NDL.

lifted edge stitch/loop hung on center NDL.

bridging: carriage knits first pass over NDLS, but following passes are "dead" passes with NDLS in HP.

bridging: carriage knits all 4 rows indicated by the arrow

latched up stitches or ribber bed stitches

prep row: arrange STS as indicated on chart but do not knit this row.

dropped stitches

popcorn/bobble

ladder formed by NDL(s) in NWP

needles in HP when short rowing/bridging (empty squares).

repeat needle arrangement across the bed

twisted C/O

EYELETS

AT THE SUGGESTION of an open fabric, most of us think first and foremost of lace knitting where single stitches are transferred to an adjacent or nearby needle to create delicate, simple or elaborate open—work designs.

Eyelets can generally be defined as open spaces made by transferring a stitch(es) to an adjacent or nearby needle(s) and then filling or casting on the empty needle(s) in a way that creates clean and unobstructed holes (for lack of a better word) in the fabric. This is usually done by leaving an empty needle in working position to cast on with the next pass of the carriage, then knitting one more rows to complete the stitch. Unlike other open spaces, eyelets are generally rounder and cleaner and do not contain un—knitted bars or ladders of yarn across their openings.

Sometimes an eyelet is adjacent to the doubled stitch that formed it, but often (in more elaborate lace patterns) there are several plain stitches between the eyelet and the doubled stitches. The arrangement of the emptied needles in relation to the doubled stitches is a basic variable that creates or accents these patterns. They can be changed by varying the number of stitches between each eyelet and the doubled stitch that formed it, the number of stitches between eyelets, the direction the stitches are transferred or by using a 1–step versus a 2–step transfer (see page 20).

E2 is from a 1960's knitting machine pattern book and is unusual only because there are double decreases made every row in alternating positions, stacking up in a way that looks more like ladders than eyelets. On close examination, these eyelets are actually pretty standard. After each set of transfers is made, the empty needles return to working position before knitting the next row and then those needles knit a second time when the next set of alternate transfers is made.

Even on a midgauge or bulky machine, this pattern requires a lot of transfers and would be a good candidate for conversion to automatic knitting with a lace carriage. I've included it here as an example of an unusual, but "standard", 1-stitch eyelet pattern to contrast with the variations that follow (and because I think it is a great fabric!).

There are lots of patterns and information about lace knitting for both hand and machine knitters, but I wanted to explore eyelets that emphasize scale and texture. My first modifications to simple eyelets were to the number of stitches removed from their needles, how they were transferred to nearby needles and the ways that the emptied needles were allowed to cast back on and resume knitting. After that, I simply allowed myself to play and explore various "what ifs".

Rather than common single stitch eyelets, I decided to pump up the scale of these fabrics by working 2, 3 and even 5 stitch eyelets. The doubled stitches gener-

E2

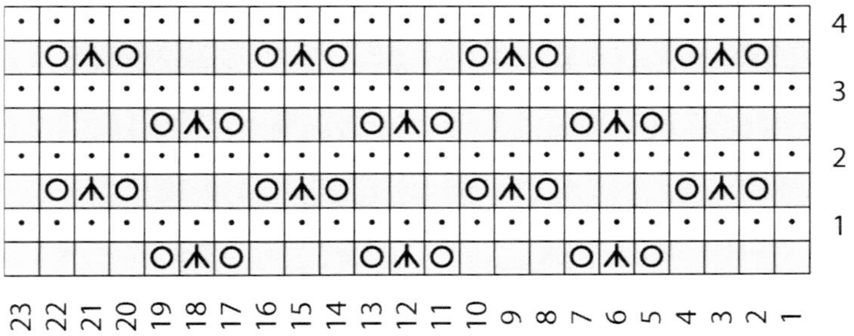

E2

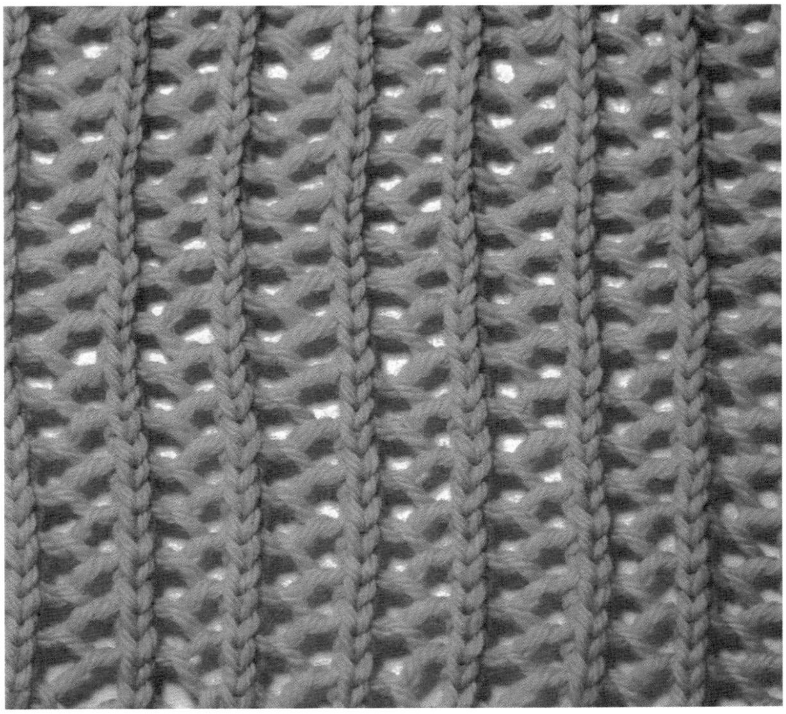

ally, though not always, take a back seat to these much more obvious "holes" and the resulting fabric is far more contemporary than typical lace fabrics.

The majority of the variations that follow are based on 3 and 5 stitch eyelets. I found that eyelets much larger than 5 stitches were more closely related to slits that required mid—row binding off and casting on or to open spaces created with intarsia methods and I will deal with those possibilities in other chapters. I did include some 2 and 4 stitch eyelets, but as you begin to explore these methods for yourself you will see that eyelets formed by transferring an even number of stitches require extra steps that odd—numbered eyelets do not. Because I like to make things as easy for myself as I can, I usually opt for the odd—numbered eyelets, but you can adapt any of the following methods to whatever size eyelets best serve your purposes and taste.

All of the variations on these outsized eyelets began with my usual "what if...." questions. Some of the results are more interesting than others and, as with many hand–manipulated methods, may be most practical on mid–gauge or bulky machines. The double bed method on page 62, where a second color peeks through the eyelets, is easiest with a color changer, but can also be worked in a single color or by manually changing yarns. And, because there is a second layer of fabric involved, this method is probably most practical on fine or standard gauge machines which use much lighter weight yarns to begin with so the thickness of a double—layered fabric is not an issue.

The most obvious variations are defined by how and where the stitches are decreased to make the eyelet; whether they are all deposited on the first adjacent working needle, or on the second or third working needle at one side or the other; some of the stitches can be deposited at each side, which is especially useful with 5 stitch eyelets. For several of the 5–stitch examples, I found it made the most sense (and caused the least amount of strain on the yarn) to manually increase the size of the 5 eyelet stitches by bridging the row prior to making the transfers. (see page 13)

Once the stitches have been transferred to form the eyelets, you need to bring needles back into working position so they can cast on and start knitting again to close or complete the eyelets. You cannot cast on to two or more adjacent empty needles in one pass of the carriage, but you need to close each eyelet over just two rows to avoid laddering. The simplest way to do this is to return the empty needles to working position in two steps. Much like an every—other—needle cast on, you can bring every—other needle to working position, knit one row and then bring the remaining, alternate needles to working position.

I found that the edges of the eyelets were neatest when the first needles returned to working position include the edge needles of the eyelet. For example, for a 3-stitch eyelet, bring the empty 1st and 3rd needles back to working position first, knit one row and then return the 2nd (center needle) to working position to continue knitting. With a 5-stitch eyelet, bring the 1st, 3rd and 5th needles to working position for the first pass of the carriage and then the 2nd and 4th.

This alternate needle, two—row method is the fastest way to complete an eyelet, but there are other methods that may produce a better looking edge or do not rely on having an odd number of needles to work with. You can, of course, create eyelets with any number of stitches if you bridge to cast on with latch tool chaining or e—wrapping.

With an even number of needles, using the every—other—needle method means that there will still be an out—of—work needle at one edge of the eyelet. When you knit the first row, it produces an unnecessarily long float at that edge of the eyelet. Before knitting the next pass of the carriage, the remaining (alternate) needles are brought to working position and the work continues. Unless your design has a reason for allowing that float at the edge of each eyelet, you need to contain it before you continue knitting. There are a couple of ways to do this, but avoiding that extra step to begin with is the main reason I tend to prefer odd numbered eyelets. That said, I have included some even numbered eyelets and their directions detail the methods for eliminating and controlling those unsightly floats.

The shaded transfer rows shown on most of my eyelet variation charts are strictly prep–rows, making the transfers to empty the eyelet needles. Before knitting the next row of the chart, you will need to bring the appropriate needles back to working position to begin closing the eyelets. The carriage does not make a pass until the first half of the empty needles is returned to working position if you are using the EON method. Prep rows are shaded (see pages 20-21 for symbols) and are never knitted or included in the row count. Although my prep row appears at the bottom of some charts, it is assumed that you would have knitted at least one or two rows across all needles before beginning any patterning.

I have used both one—step and two—step transfers throughout this book. The symbols chart on page 19 shows the placement of the doubled stitches in relation to the emptied needles and the text directions also specify when two—step transfers are required.

Whenever samples *specify* 2-step transfers in the directions, it is essential to the final appearance of the pattern. A common 1-step transfer places the transferred stitch on the back of the fabric where it will neither show nor contribute to the pattern; the 2-step method places the transferred stitch(es) on the knit side.

In addition to simple one and two—step decreases, I have also utilized stacked and skipped—stitch decreases, which are also shown on the symbols charts and explained in the accompanying text. These less—common methods contribute to the texture or patterning of the fabric or serve to accent the eyelets themselves.

Two—Stitch Eyelets

E3 bottom STS 5 and 6 are *both* transferred to NDL 4 in the prep row. Before knitting the first row, NDL 5 is returned to WP. Once the row is knitted, the bar below NDL 6 is twisted like an e—wrap and hung onto NDL 6 to complete the eyelet.

E3

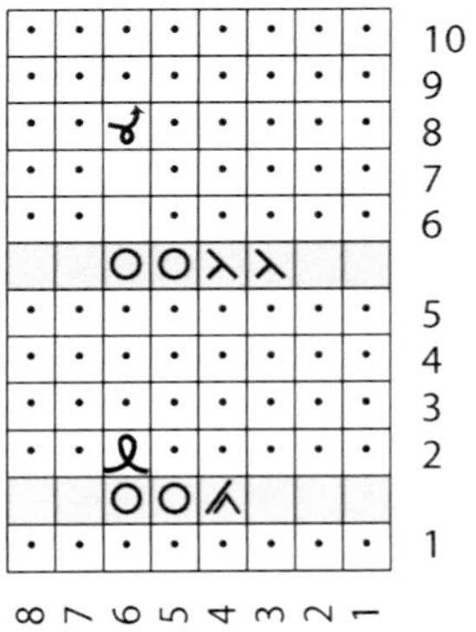

The chart above and the swatch at right show two methods for making and completing a 2—ST eyelet. The bottom eyelet was created by transferring 2 STS to the same NDL and closed with a simple e—wrap. The example at the top was created with a 2—step stacked decrease and completed by the twisted method shown at in E4.

E4A

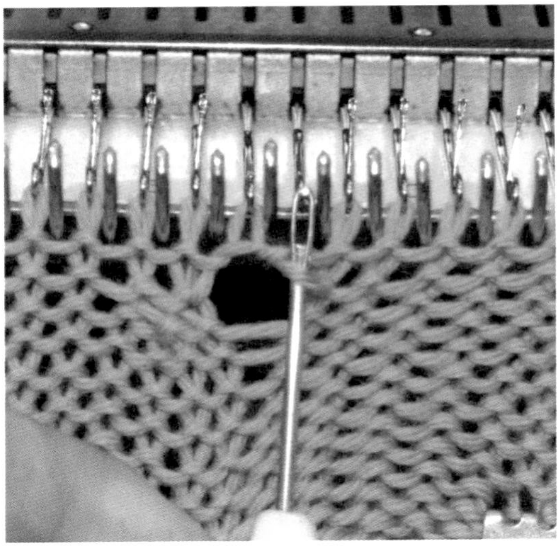

E4B

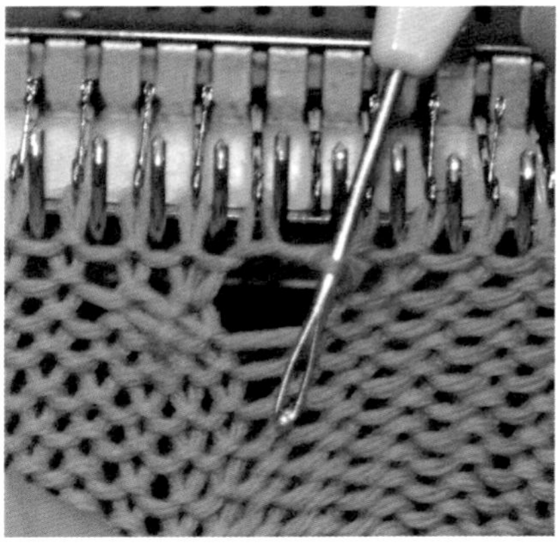

E4 Bring the empty NDL closest to the decreases (NDL 5) to WP and knit 2 rows. Then, as shown in E4a insert the tip of a transfer tool under the first (lowest) bar of the ladder below NDL 6, E4b over the second bar, tipping the tool towards you. Push empty NDL 6 through the back of the ST on the tool (or insert a second transfer tool through the front of the ST, remove the first tool and place the ST on the NDL).

E3 top 2-step, stacked decrease places the transferred STS on the knit side of the fabric where they accent the eyelet. Remove STS 3 and 4 from their NDLS and hold them to the right. Use a second tool to remove STS 5 and 6 from their NDLS then place them on NDLS 3 and 4. Return the STS from the first tool to the same NDLS.

E5

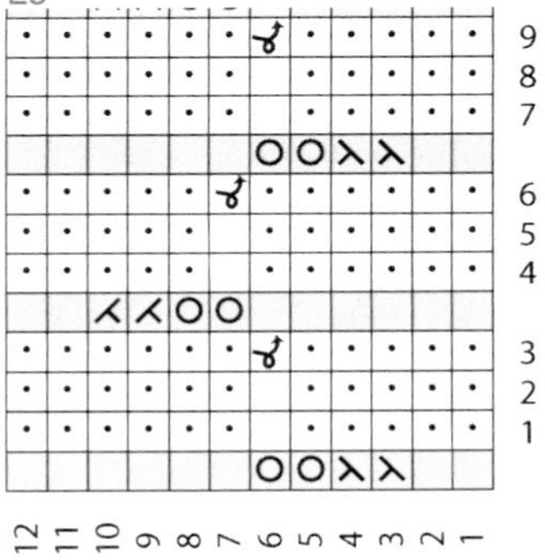

E5

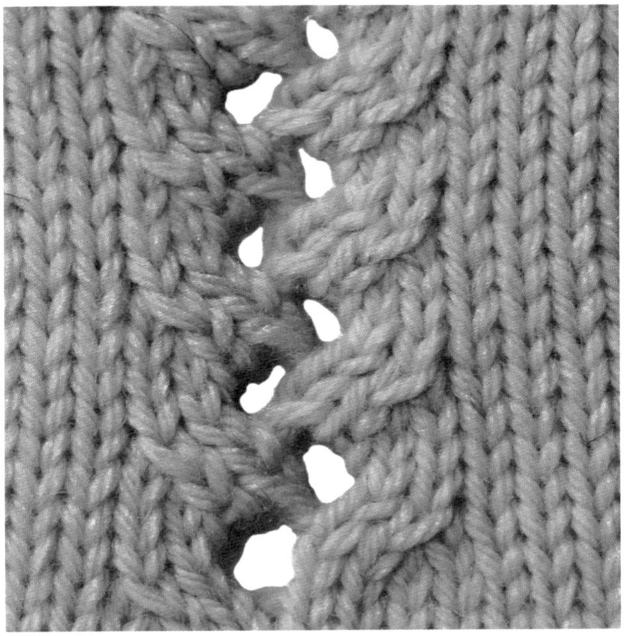

E5This column of fagoted eyelets was worked with 2-ST eyelets, but could just as easily have been worked with any of the larger eyelets that follow. The transfers, which alternate left and right placement, are 2-step transfers, which bring the transferred STS to the knit side of the fabric and create the curving detail at the edges of the column. The empty NDLS are filled as described for E3, with the twisted ladder worked every 3 rows to fill the empty NDL.

E6

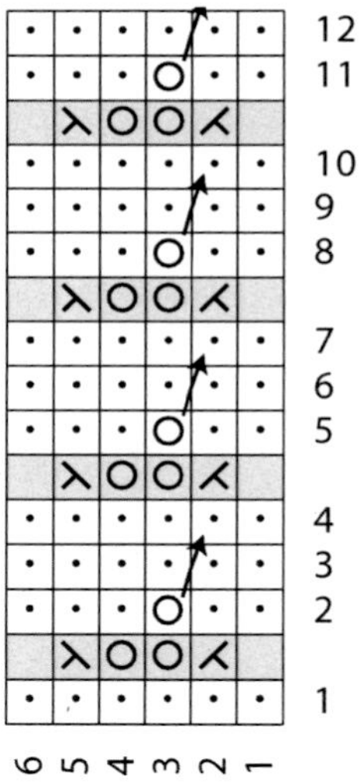

E6

E7

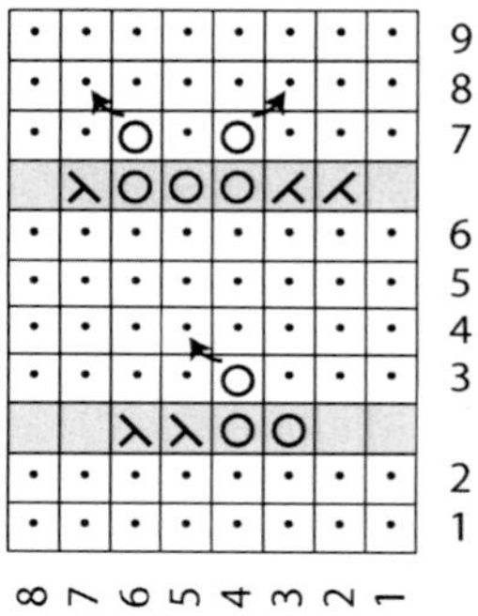

E7

E6 The eyelets at the top of the swatch were worked by transferring one ST to the left and one to the right, then bringing one of the empty NDLS back to WP before knitting the first row. Bring the second empty NDL to WP and knit the second row. Then, pick up the loop/bar that sits across the eyelet and hang it on the adj NDL.

Stacked Transfers

E7 The difference between a 2-ST and a 3-ST eyelet is dramatic and far more pronounced than the typical single—ST eyelet most of us are accustomed to seeing. Both of these eyelets were created with stacked transfers (plus a single transfer for the 3-ST version) and closed with the EON method. The 2-ST eyelet created a float at one edge, which was lifted onto the adj NDL. The 3-ST eyelet was completed in reverse to the norm: I brought the center NDL to WP before knitting the first row, then the two outer NDLS. The resulting floats at each edge were lifted to the adjacent NDLS before knitting the next row.

E8 Two pairs of transfers are stacked on the center two STS of each repeat. That is, two STS from the left (NDLS 7 and 8) and two from the right (NDLS 3 and 4) are placed on the center two NDLS (5 and 6), which each end up holding 3 STS. For each variation, after the decreases are made, bring one of the two empty NDLS at each side of the decrease to WP again and then knit 4 rows. Use a latch tool to reform the short ladder that forms under each empty NDL and then transfer the last ST from the latch tool to the empty NDL.

In the chart, the STS represented by the gray shading are actually the latched up bars of the ladders formed under the NDLS that remained out of work for four rows. For the repeat at left on the chart (needles 12-17) and left on the purl side of the fabric, the NDLS closest to the tripled STS (13 and 16) were returned to WP, while ladders were allowed to form under NDLS 12 and 17. After four rows, the bars were latched up and the STS placed on the empty NDLS above them.

For the example at right on the chart and right on the purl side, the outer NDLS (3 and 8) were returned to WP and the ladders allowed to form underneath NDLS 4 and 7. While there isn't a lot of difference on the knit side of the fabric, this variation creates very different effects on the purl side, which I would probably consider the "right" side for this fabric. Either method is fine as long as you are consistent.

E8

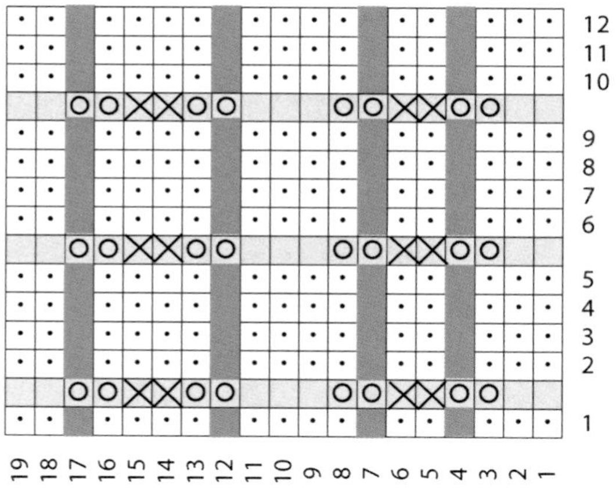

E8 KNIT SIDE

E8 PURL SIDE

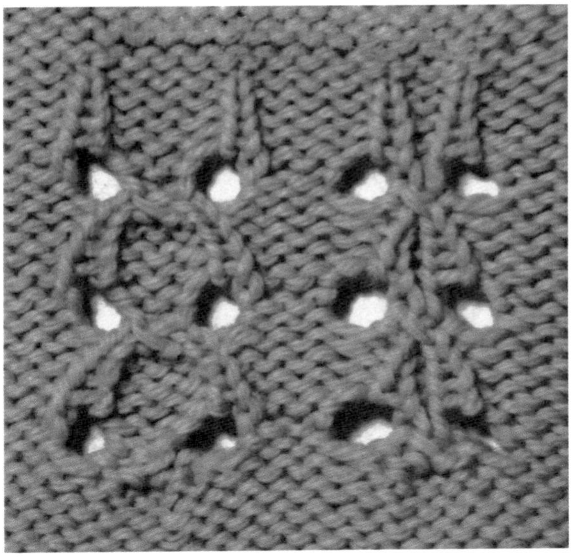

E9

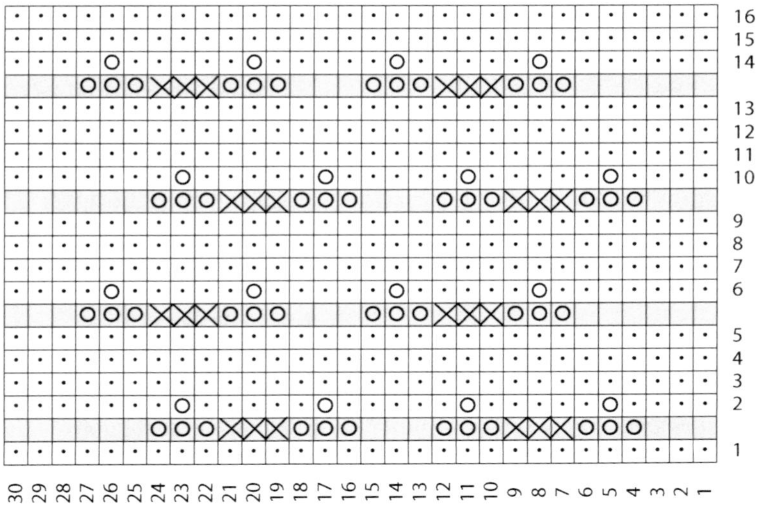

E9

E9 Although this is a 3-ST eyelet fabric, I have included it here because it grew so naturally from the previous examples. Instead of 2-ST stacked transfers, I used a 3-prong tool, which creates larger eyelets. More importantly, it also causes the STS to pull towards each other, adding tension and creating a nubby, very textured fabric. Each eyelet was completed with the EON method and the placement alternates from one repeat to the next.

Note that there are 3 plain STS between all repeats, but that the initial set—up allows for 6 plain STS at the left edge. With the next repeat, when the placement alternates, there are 6 STS at the right. I retained 3 plain edge STS at each side to prevent the eyelets from running off the edge of the fabric. I especially like the opposing angles of the STS in the background fabric and the way the top edges of the eyelets pop forward to create a delicate, popcorn—like surface texture.

E9aThe sweater shown on the next page is a variation on this technique and there is a free pattern ("3-D Nops and Eyelets) available on my web site. It introduces a third placement for the eyelets which adds a subtle zigzag pattern to the overall design of the fabric. I strongly suggest you try working through the example shown above before attempting the sweater pattern because it is easier to keep track of two alternating placements than it is three.

E10 This textured, diagonal fabric is a simple variation on E9. The transfers form both ladders and eyelets at the same time and rather than nops, they create a very raised diagonal.

(Make 2-stitch stacked decreases as shown on the prep row of the chart. Bring the outer empty NDLS in each repeat to WP and knit 1 row. Then bring the remaining empty NDLS to WP and knit 2 rows.)

Repeat from (to) for the length of the fabric, *starting each repeat 2 NDLS further to the right.* Although the pattern repeats progress in one direction, the fabric doesn't bias because the decreases that shape the pattern are worked from both directions. Between the twisted

"Eyelets and Nops" is a free pattern download on my web site. Notice how the pattern causes the lower edges to undulate and the way that the eyelets (and the nops) create a zigzag pattern. This is because the pattern specifies three different placements. It is a bit more complicated and you can certainly knit this sweater with pattern E9.

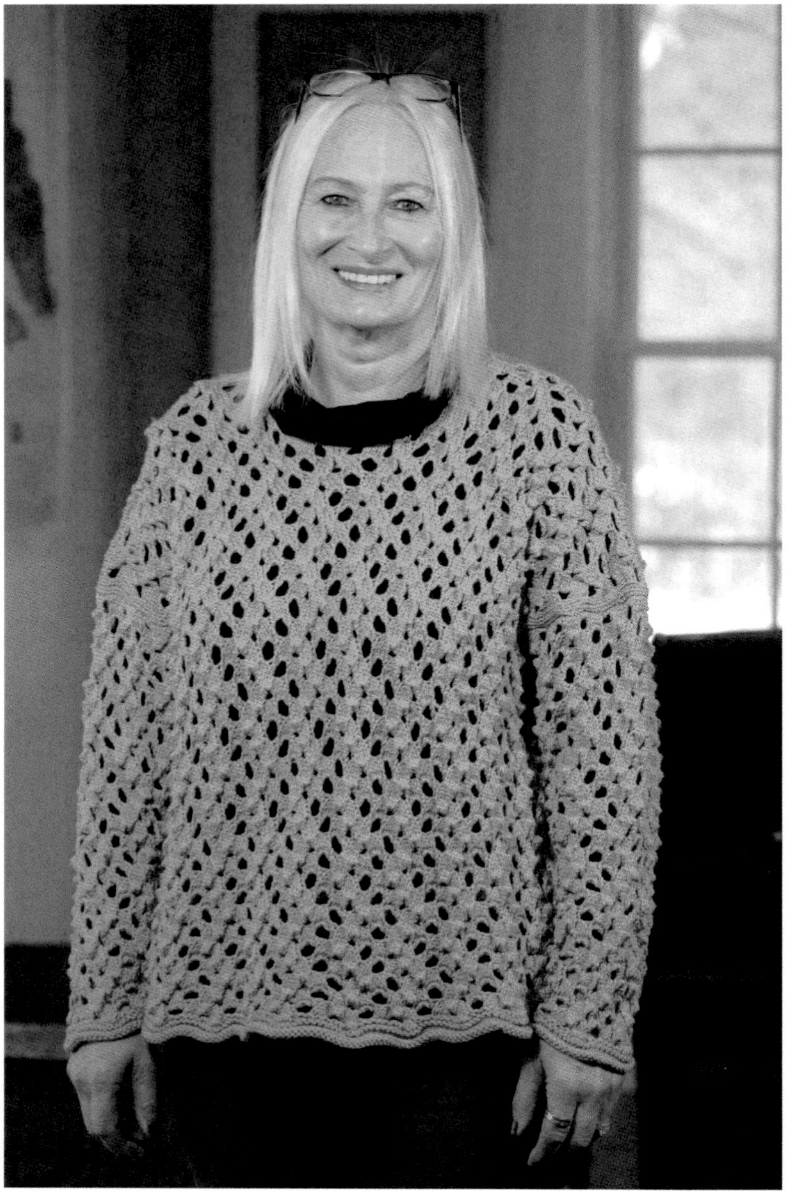

E10

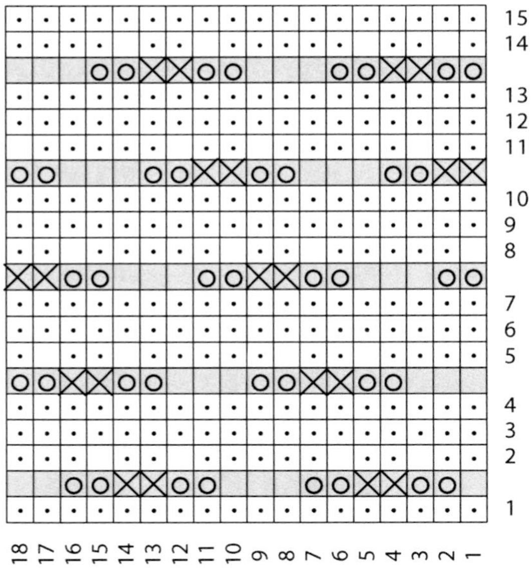

E10

ladder bars, eyelets and the diagonal columns of STS that almost look like cables, there is so much going on in this fabric that it looks more complicated than it is.

E11top uses 2-step decreases. Return NDLS 5 and 7 to WP and knit 2 rows. Reform the 2-bar ladders with the transfer tool as described for sample E4. Note that the C/O edge at the top of this eyelet is much more refined and appears wider than the lower example. The 2-step decrease adds definite interest to the eyelet itself.

E11bottom To make this 4-ST eyelet use a 2-prong transfer tool to move STS 4 and 5 to NDLS 3 and 2; move STS 6 and 7 to NDLS 8 and 9. Bring NDLS 5 and 7 to WP and knit 1 row. Twist the bars below NDLS 4 and 6 like e—wraps and place them on the empty NDLS to complete the eyelets.

E11

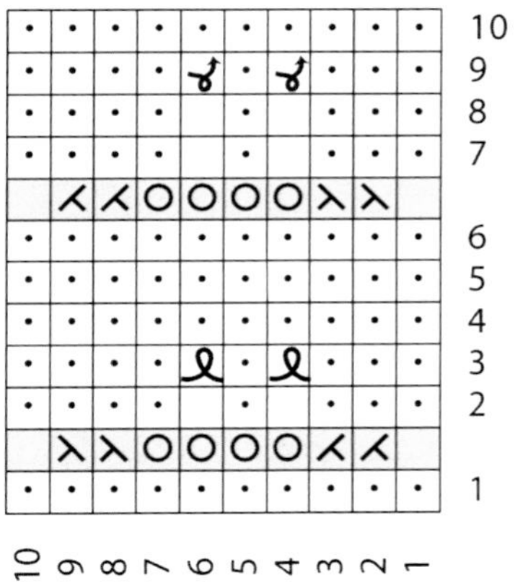

E11

I latched up two ST at each side of the main motif to help it stand out from the background fabric. The 2-step decreases that formed the initial eyelets create the undulating effect at each side. It seems like there is a lot going on here, but if you work your way through the directions, you will find that the transfers and the e—wrapping are the same as earlier swatches. The bridged nops and the lifted STS that anchor them are what create the 3-dimensionality of this fabric. Although there are eyelets underneath each of the nops, they disappear into the fabric and instead of visual impact, offer structural assistance to the texture.

E12

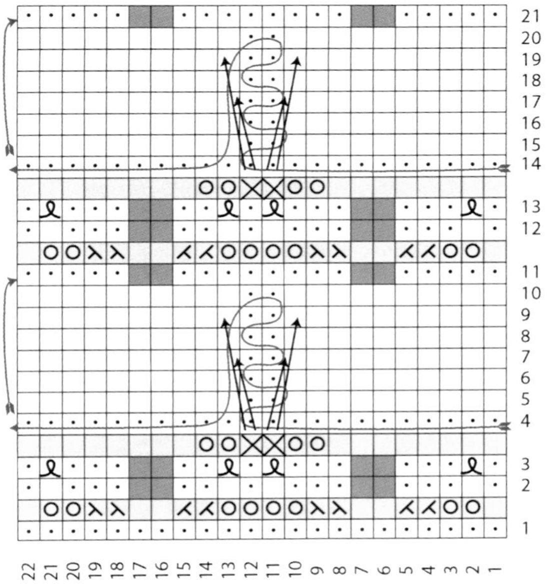

E12 There are two different prep rows used throughout the next fabric. The first prep row shows the 2-step decreases that need to be made for both the central nop motif and the columns of eyelets at left and right. After making the 2-step transfers, bring EON to, knit 1 row and then twist the bars to form e—wraps on the empty NDLS as described for E4.

For the second prep row, make stacked decreases, but do not return any NDLS to WP. Instead, begin with COR, set to hold NDLS in HP and hold all NDLS to the left of the center two NDLS (11 and 12). Knit 1 row. Hold all NDLS to the right of the center two NDLS. Knit 3 rows, ending COR. At the right of center, lift purl bar from first row (below NDL 11) and hang on empty NDL 10. Knit 1 row. COL. Lift the purl bar from first row below NDL 12 and hang it on empty NDL 13. Knit 1 row. COR. Once again, pick up a purl bar from the first row of the nop and hang it on empty NDL 9 and, at the same time, empty NDL 14. Push all NDLS at left to UWP and knit 1 row to left. Continue knitting to the next repeat.

E12

E13 To me, the bridged "sock heel" and pair of eyelets in this sample look like a face with two eyes and a big nose! I could see incorporating the effect for a little whimsy in a kid's intarsia sweater with birds or funny faces or repeating it for an interesting column of texture. Begin by setting the carriage to hold NDLS in HP to work a S/R "heel" over 6 STS as follows: With COR and set to hold NDLS in HP, hold all NDLS to the left of the 6 NDLS to be S/R. Knit 1 row (COL) and hold all NDLS to the right of the same NDLS. *Bring 1 NDL on the side opposite the carriage to HP and knit 1 row.** Repeat * to ** until 1 NDL remains in WP and COR. Then, *push 1 NDL on carriage side to UWP and knit 1 row**, repeating * to ** until 5 NDLS are in WP and COR. Push 6th NDL (at right) to UWP and all NDLS at left to UWP and knit 1 row to the left. Set the carriage to knit all NDLS. Make two 2-stitch eyelets as shown in the next prep row, knit two rows and complete both eyelets.

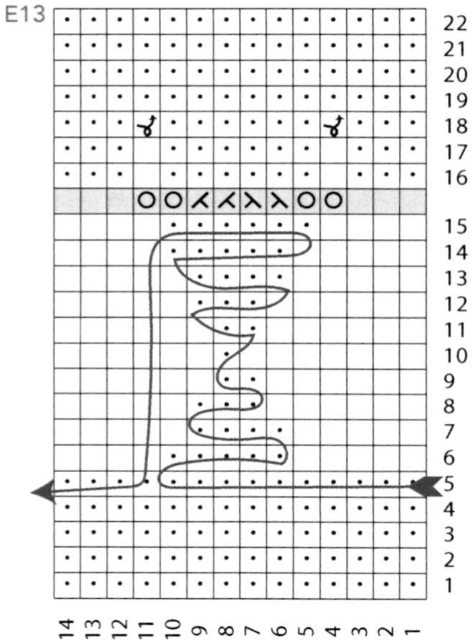

E13

E14 A circle of eyelets surround a 2-stitch nop. The 2-stitch eyelets are completed by bringing the empty NDL closest to the inner edge of the eyelet to WP, knitting 2 rows and then using the transfer tool to

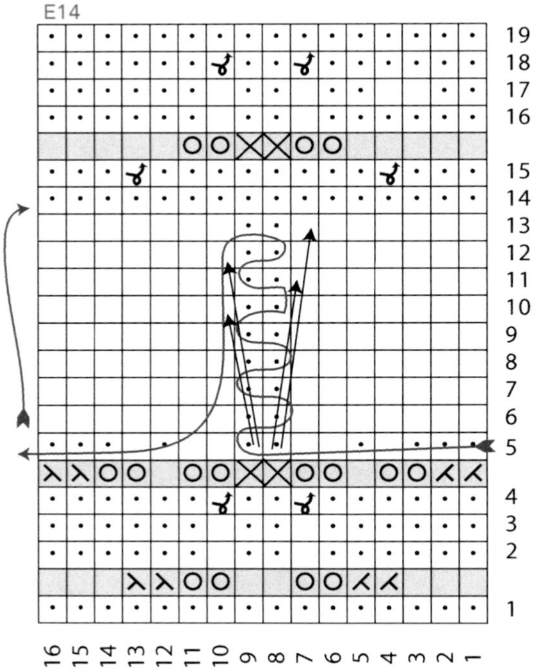

E14

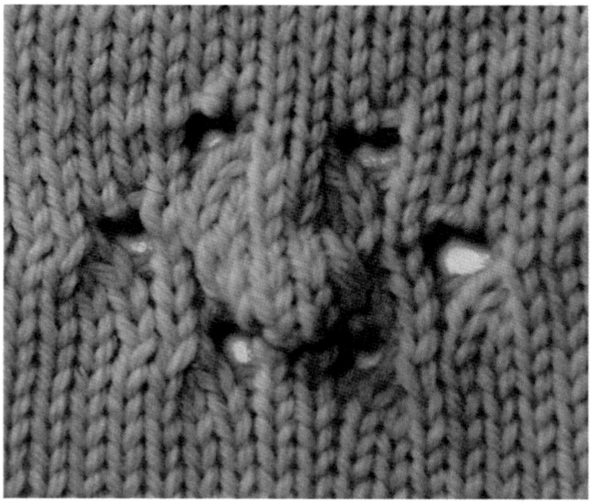

reform the 2-bar ladders as knit STS. Two—step decreases would add texture and accentuate the motif.

E15 This all—over pattern requires transfers for the nops and eyelets to be made in the same prep row. The transfers for the nops are stacked transfers where two STS from the left and two from the right are placed on the same 2 center NDLS; each of those NDLS now holds 3 STS. Bring 1 NDL at each side of the eyelets (not the nops) to WP. Begin knitting the first, bridged row to create the nops as shown by the serpentine blue arrow as follows:

Begin COR, set to hold NDLS in HP. Hold all NDLS to the left of the center 2 nop NDLS and knit 1 row. Hold all NDLS to the right of the center 2 NDLS (11-12). After the 5th row of the nop, lift a purl bump from the back of the ST in the first row of the nop and hang on empty NDL 13. Knit 1 row. Lift a purl bump from the back of the first row of the nop and hang it on the empty NDL 10. Continue, lifting a ST after rows 7 and 8 of the nop to fill the remaining empty NDL at each side. Bridge to the next nop (or end of the row for a single repeat). COL. Knit 1 row, complete the eyelets at each side of the nop with the twisted transfer tool method and then knit 2 more rows. Latch up/reform the STS shown as knit STS on the chart (the single blue stitch between each repeat of

E15

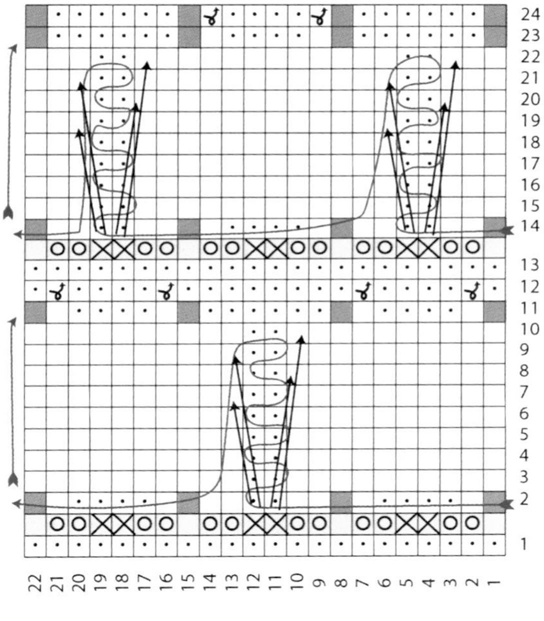

6 NDLS). Repeat, alternating the position of the nops and eyelets. The empty spaces on the chart are the areas that are in hold while the nops are bridged/knitted. They do not represent working NDLS.

E16 Because of the way the transfers are made in this pattern, there is tension on the STS that causes them to separate several rows below. While they are not really ladder bars, they can be treated as such. This fabric is similar to L81 in the ladder chapter. Raise the ST size by 1 or 2 numbers so that you do not put too much strain on the STS.

E16a Knit 6 rows, ending COR and make stacked transfers as shown in row 1 of chart. Bring all NDLS to HP except the first group of 4 NDLS on the carriage side. *Knit 1 row. (Catch the free yarn in the hook of

E15

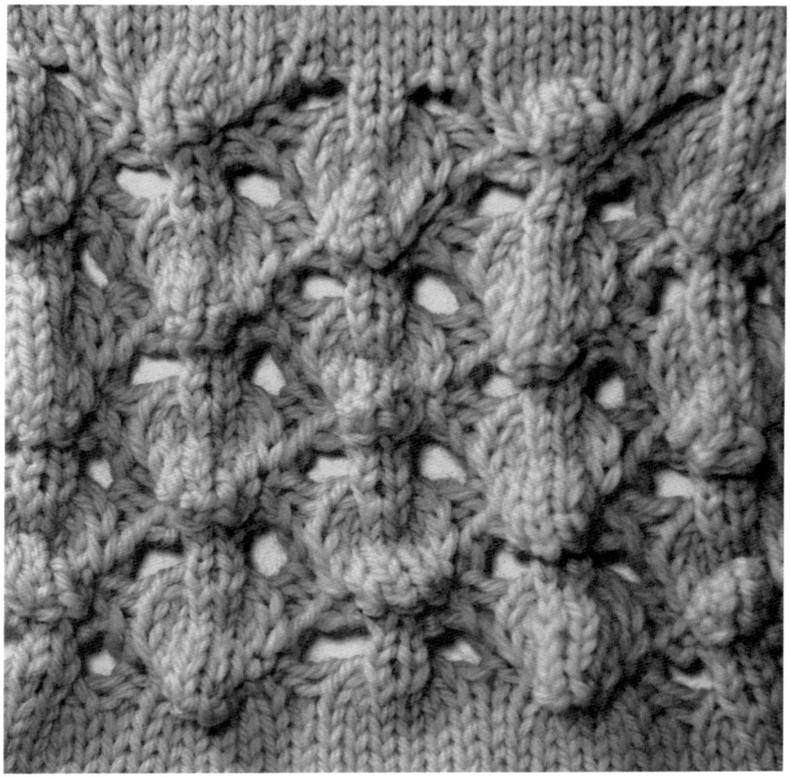

the first empty NDL. Insert a latch tool 3 rows down, under and behind the bars that were formed by transferring the STS to catch a loop of free yarn in the hook of the tool. Pull the loop forward and up and place in the next empty NDL.) twice. Bring all NDLS to HP and return COR. Nudge the next group of 4 HP NDLS at left to UWP** and repeat from * to **.

E16b was worked with 2-step decreases. You could accentuate this effect by knitting fewer rows between repeats. E16c alternates 1 and 2-step decreases with each repeat and the repeats continue to alternate

E16

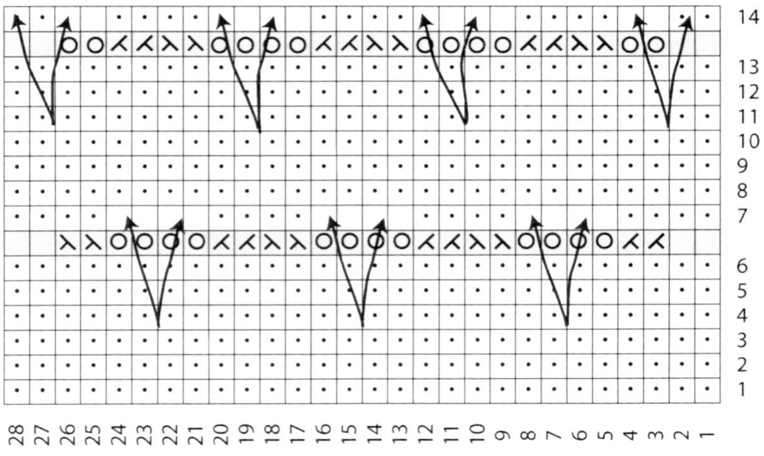

16C

16B

16A

placement. Knitting an even number of rows between repeats allows you to start each repeat on the opposite side, which you can use to keep track of these alternating transfers.

Odd numbered eyelets

There may be times when you must use a 2 or 4-stitch eyelet to work with a specific number of stitches in a pattern or to accommodate other manipulations in the design. Although I used even numbered eyelets for the preceding swatches, these fabrics could just as easily have been knitted with odd numbered eyelets. As I said earlier, I usually find it easier and faster to complete odd—numbered eyelets.

E17 This example shows a 3-stitch eyelet where 2 STS (5 and 6) are transferred to NDLS 3 and 4 at the right and ST 7 is transferred to NDL 8 as shown in the prep row of the chart. Bring NDLS 5 and 7 to WP and knit 1 row. Bring the remaining empty NDL to WP and continue knitting. This is the EON method of filling empty NDLS which eliminates the need to twist or manipulate un—knitted bars to form STS as was necessary for all of the even numbered eyelets.

E18 also utilizes the EON fill method, but the STS are transferred a little differently. In this case, two STS are transferred to the same NDL at right and 1 ST to its own NDL at left.

E19 In the example, the two STS that are transferred to the right (5 and 6) skip NDL 4 and are deposited on NDLS 2 and 3 at right of the eyelet. This kind of a skipped transfer tends to distort the background STS and add to (or perhaps detract from) the fabric.

E20 is also a skipped stitch transfer except that the transfer is worked as a two—step transfer by removing the STS from NDLS 1 and 2 at right, making the transfer and then returning the STS to the same NDLS. This maneuver places the transferred STS on the front (knit) face of the fabric and has more potential for influencing pattern than the previous example.

E21 shows 2 incorrectly formed eyelets, a 2-ST eyelet at right and a 3-ST eyelet at left. When bringing EON to WP for the 3-ST eyelet, the center NDL was brought back *first* and then each of the outer NDLS, which creates slanted floats at each edge of the eyelet — it just isn't as clean. The 2-ST eyelet was cast back on by bringing one of the empty NDLS to WP, knitting 1 row and then bringing the second NDL to WP without any twisting to tighten the bar below. Although these eyelets don't look *awful*, you need to work up a sample incorrectly to appreciate the difference firsthand. In an all—over fabric, these eyelets would look ragged and unfinished. They require further finishing

E21

steps.

E22 These over—sized eyelets were formed by first working a row of single bed drop ST, manually knitting each NDL after passing the yarn around a ruler/gauge (see page 15). Then I transferred groups of 4 STS to the third empty NDL in each group and brought one empty NDL at each side of that NDL to WP before knitting the first row. After bringing the

E22

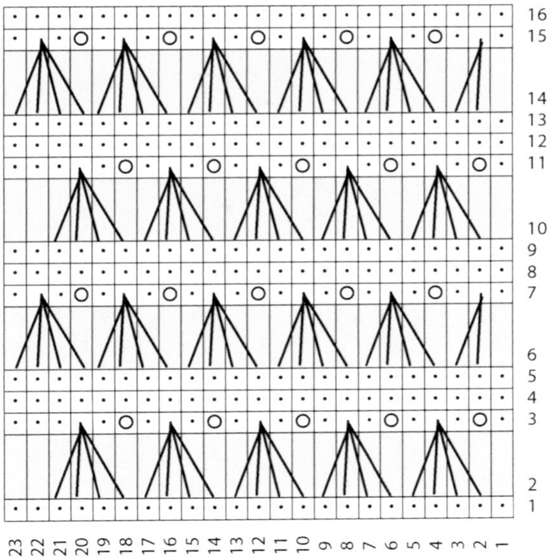

E22

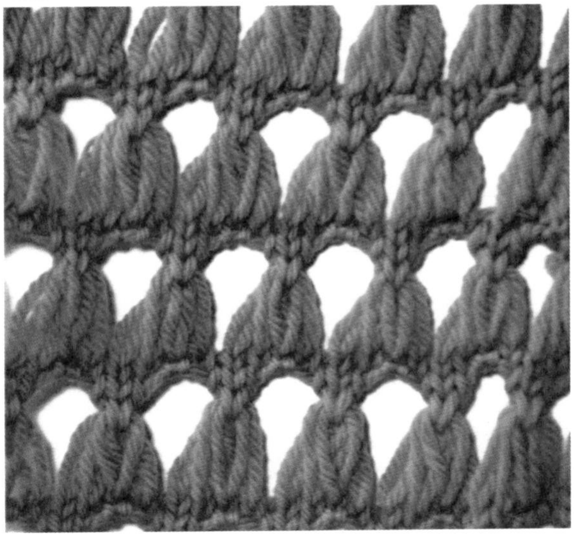

E17

E17

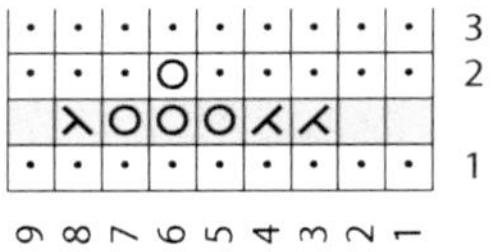

E18

E18

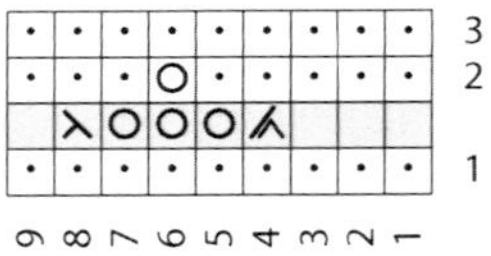

E19

E19

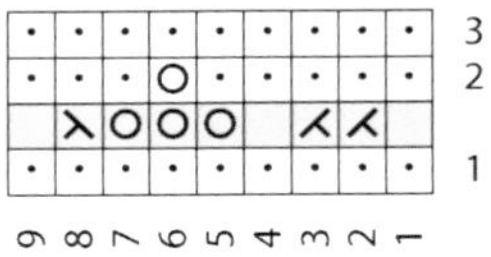

E20

E20

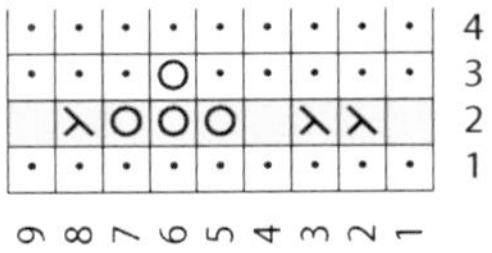

remaining empty NDLS to WP, I knitted 2 more rows and then worked the next row of manual drop ST and alternated the placement of the next repeat. Note that these eyelets were closed using a slight variation on the EON method. Although my example was worked by the single bed method, this fabric would be much faster and easier to knit using double bed drop stitch (see page 11).

E23 is a vertical arrangement of 3-stitch eyelets with three plain STS between the columns of eyelets. I transferred 2 STS to the right and one to the left for the eyelets which were closed with the EON method.

E24 Rather than a vertical arrangement of eyelets, this example illustrates the same 3-ST eyelets with 3 STS between them, worked in a much more interesting and textured alternating arrangement.

E23

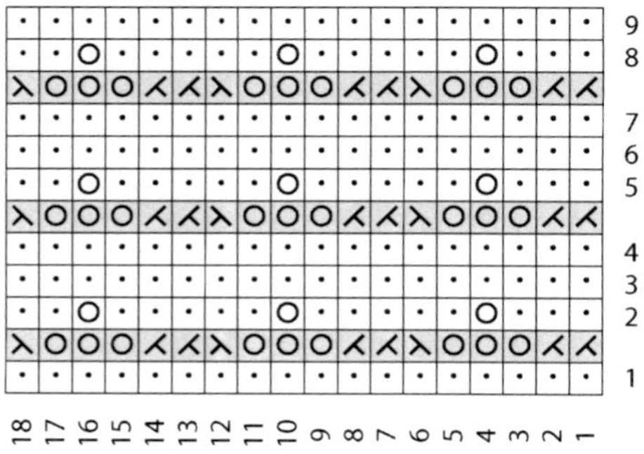

E24

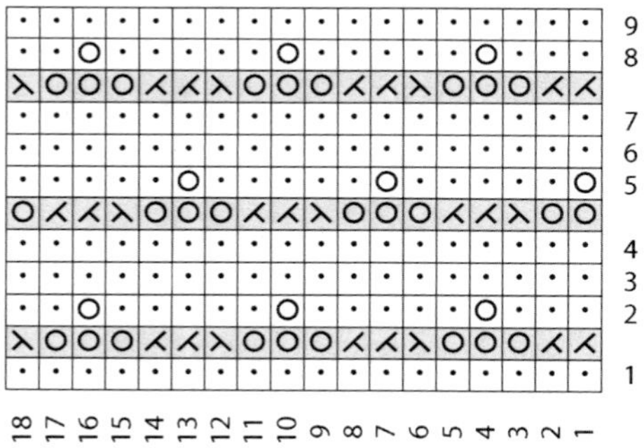

E25

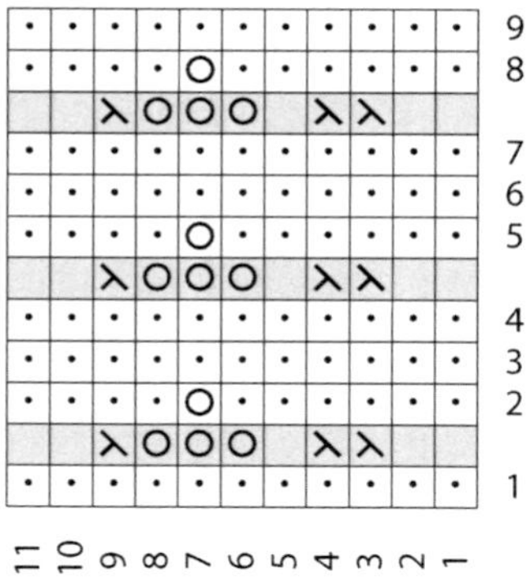

E23

E24

E25

E25 is a further variation of E23, retaining the alternating eyelets, but with 5 STS between them instead of 3 and using skipped transfers. This fabric looks rather flat when compared to the previous example. However, having more STS between the eyelets provides ample space to try 2-step transfers or other manipulations that might add more surface interest to the fabric.

E26 2-step, skipped transfers create extra interest along the edges of this column of STS and could also have been applied to the previous samples.

E27, E28, E29 The eyelets in the next 5 samples were worked with a 3-prong transfer tool. There are no plain STS between the eyelets in E27; one plain ST between the eyelets in E28; and 3 plain STS between the eyelets

E27

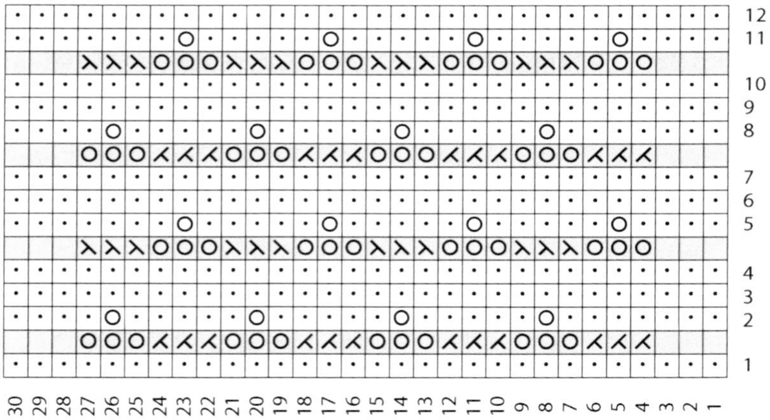

E26

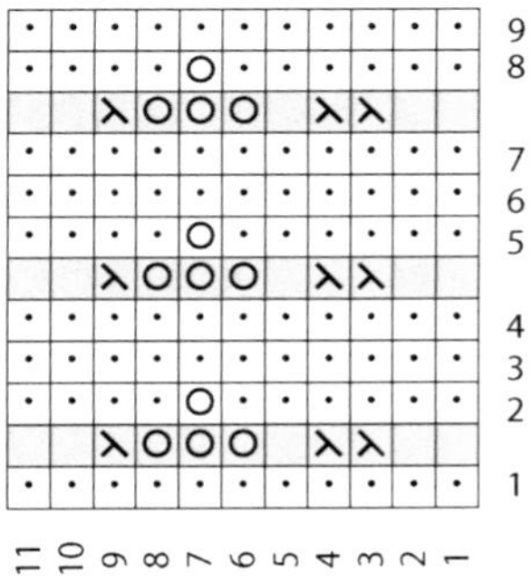

E26

E27

E28

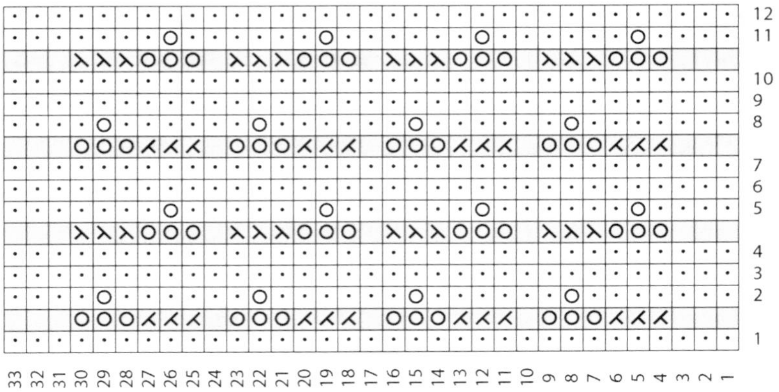

E28

E29

E29

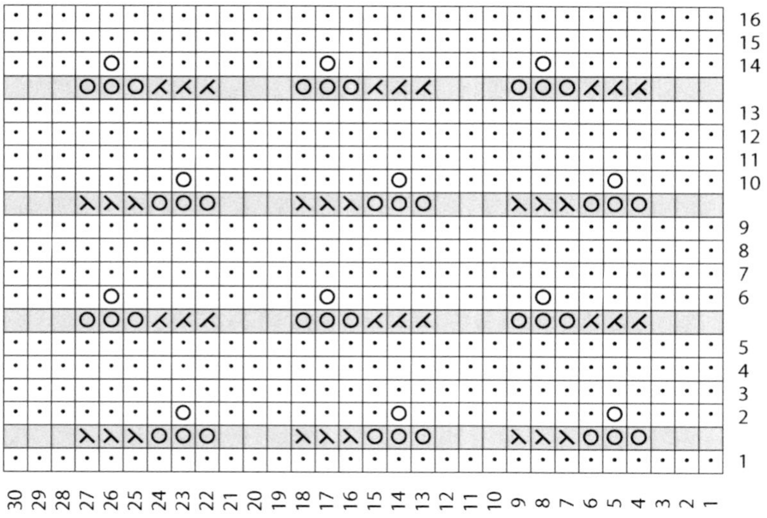

in E29. The eyelets in all 3 samples were closed with the EON method and then followed between alternating repeats by one more row in E27 and E28 and by two more rows in E29. Note that all the eyelets in a single row are transferred in the same direction (in all 3 examples), but that the direction alternates from one repeat to the next. The alternating direction of the transfers contributes to the raised texture.

E30 and 31 These two fabrics are quite similar in that both of them utilize alternating rows of eyelets formed to the left and the right (like the preceding swatches)

E30

E31

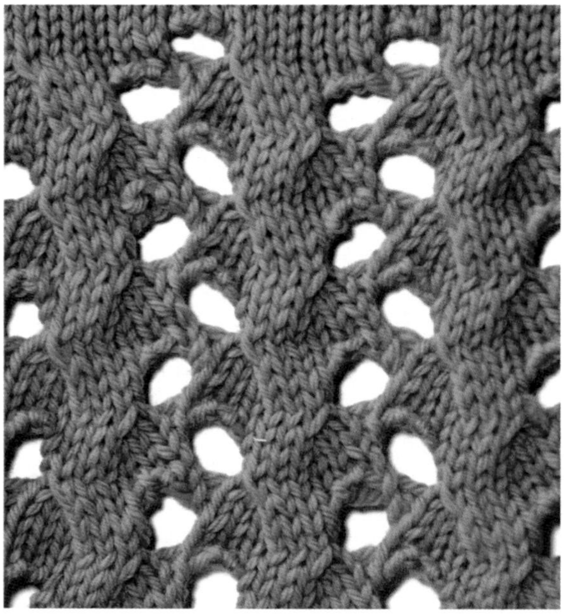

and there are 3 plain STS between all the eyelets. However, both of these fabrics utilize an alternating, rather than vertical, placement of the eyelets.

The background patterning between the eyelets is very different on both swatches. E30was worked with 1-step stacked transfers, while E31 was worked with 2-step, stacked transfers.

E32

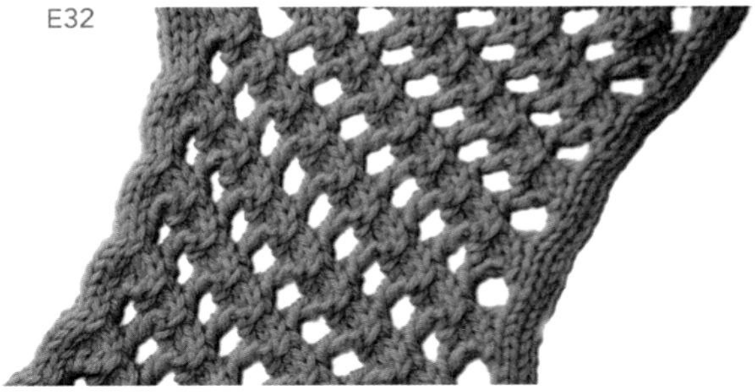

E32 There are no plain STS between the eyelets in this example and from repeat to repeat, the same STS are always transferred to the right. This causes the fabric to bias, which probably renders it useless for all but the most contemporary garments. However, the surface is richly textured and I think it would make a really interesting scarf, shawl or base for a join—as—you—knit fabric.

E33 3-stitch eyelets worked in alternating positions form an open grid. The eyelets were closed with the EON method but I brought the empty center NDL back to WP before knitting the first row. Then I brought the two outer empty NDLS to WP and knitted the next row. This is the reverse of the way the

E33

E30

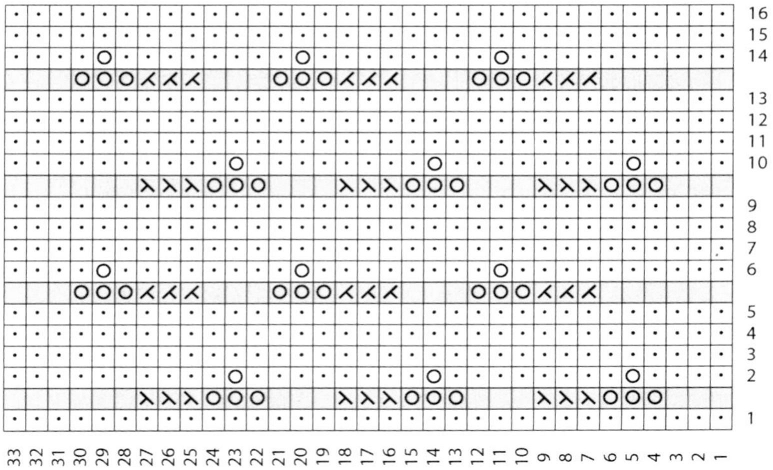

E31

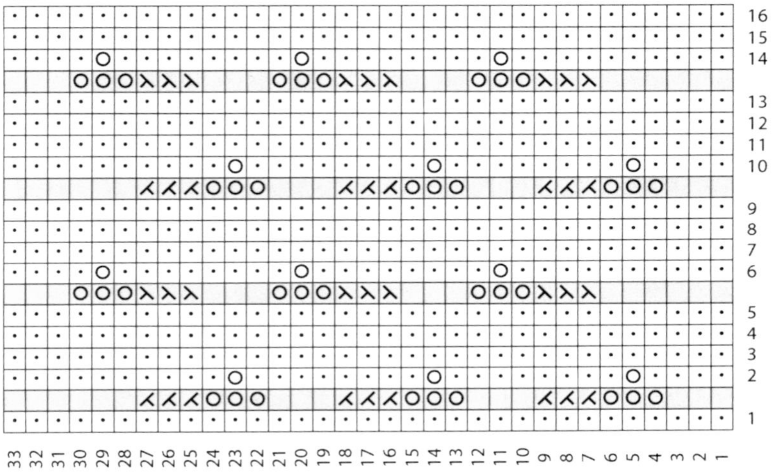

E32

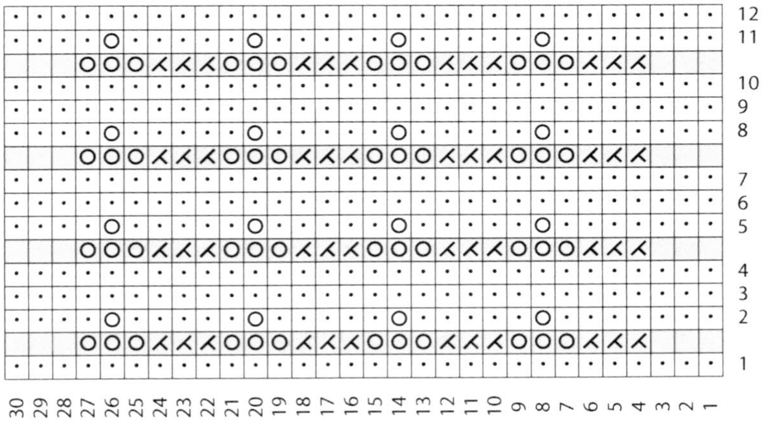

E33

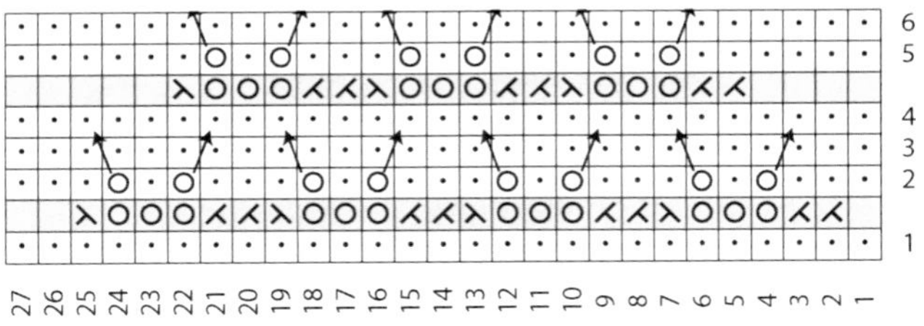

EON method is usually used to close eyelets and leaves a float exposed at each edge of the eyelet. To eliminate those floats, I lifted them onto the NDLS at each edge of the eyelet and knitted 1 more row before alternating the placement for the next repeat. My chart shows all transfers being made in the same direction (two to the right and one to the left), repeat after repeat, but you could alternate them. The lifted STS in this variation add great texture to the open—work grid.

E34This is the most basic 5-ST eyelet. It was worked by transferring 3 STS to the right and 2 to the left with stacked transfers. To C/O with the EON method over two rows, return NDLS 7, 9 and 11 to WP before knitting the first row. Then the remaining empty NDLS are brought to WP to complete the eyelet. Notice that the upper edge of the eyelet tends to curl upward.

There is a free pattern for this worsted weight linen sweater on my web site. Triangular insets/godets at each side seam add fullness to the lower edge (see page 179). I used 5—stitch eyelets here but you can use whatever size you prefer. This garment first apeared in *Machine Knitting Monthly Magazine*.

E35 was worked by bridging to increase the size of the five eyelet STS (7-11) before transferring them all to NDL 12. Beginning with COR set to hold NDLS in HP, hold the five eyelet NDLS and all NDLS to the left of them and knit 1 row. Hold the NDLS just knitted, increase the stitch size to a much larger size and push the five eyelet NDLS to UWP. Knit 1 row and hold the NDLS just knitted. Move COR and change back to the main ST size, return the remaining NDLS at left to UWP and bridge to the end of the row.

Collect all 5 STS from NDLS 7-11 on a single prong transfer tool and move them to NDL 12. Bring NDLS 7, 9 and 11 back to WP and knit 1 row. Bring NDLS 8 and 10 to WP to complete the eyelet with the EON method and continue knitting to the next repeat. Without the bridged row, there would be too much strain on the transferred STS and the separation at the bottom of the eyelet would be very pronounced.

E34, 35, 36

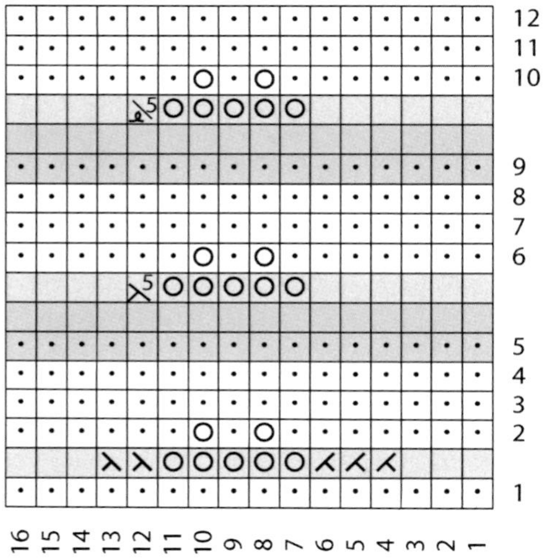

Bottom to top, the charts for e34,35,36 show three possible ways of emptying 5 NDLS to form a giant eyelet. All were completed with the EON method.

E34

E35

E36

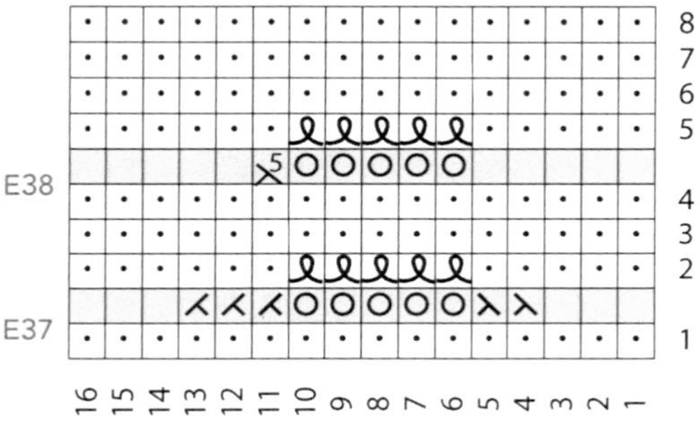

E37

E38

E36 This sample was bridged to manually enlarge the STS, as you would do if you were already working at one of your largest ST sizes. After knitting the first bridge, manually knit each of the eyelet NDLS back to NWP to create the largest STS possible. (See manual bridging on page 8) Remove all five STS on a single—prong transfer tool and twist the tool at least one full rotation before placing these STS on needle 12. Bring NDL 12 to HP to assure that the stitches knit cleanly. Bring three empty EON to WP, knit 1 row and then bring the remaining two empty NDLS to WP to complete the eyelet. The twisted STS at the base of this eyelet begin to add some interesting surface texture to the fabric and seem to balance out the curl at the upper edge.

E37 This sample used 2-step decreases at each edge of the eyelet to place the transferred STS on the knit side of the fabric. This time, however, instead of using the EON method to complete the eyelets, the empty NDLS were immediately cast back on by e—wrapping all five of them mid—row.

First, make the two—step transfers as shown on the prep row and leave all of the empty NDLS in NWP. Next, with COR and set to hold NDLS in HP, hold all NDLS to the left of the eyelet and knit 1 row. Hold the bridge NDLS just knitted. Bring the five empty eyelet NDLS to HP and e—wrap their shafts. Move COR. Nudge all of the NDLS to left of the eyelet to UWP and knit 1 row to left. Set the carriage to knit all NDLS and continue to the next repeat. The e—wrapped NDLS will form a firm upper edge for the eyelet in one row, which also decreases the height of the eyelet and produces a less rounded space.

E38 All 5 of the eyelet STS were moved to the adjacent NDL at left and, like the previous example, the eyelet was closed using bridging to e—wrap.

E39 These four eyelets were all over—twisted by rotating the tool 2 full turns so that the yarn started to kink up on itself. All were completed with the EON method.

Beginning at the bottom of the swatch and the chart, the first eyelet is a 5 ST eyelet where the twisted STS were placed on the 8th NDL. The second eyelet is also a 5 ST eyelet but the twisted STS were returned to the 9th NDL with a 2-step transfer to bring the twisting even more to the knit side. The top two eyelets are 3-stitch eyelets. The first with a 2-step, skipped transfer to place the twisted stitches on the 9th NDL and the second with a 1-step transfer to the 8th NDL.

E41-43 illustrate two transfer methods and two methods of filling the empty NDLS. All transfers were made after crossing the cables and knitting 1 row (which is a variable you can endlessly play with).

E41

E39

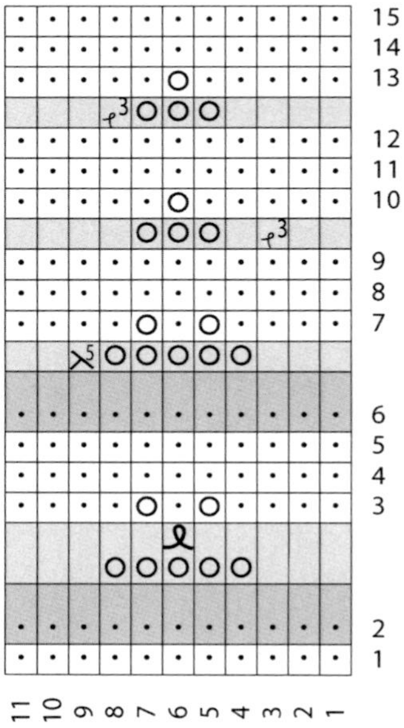

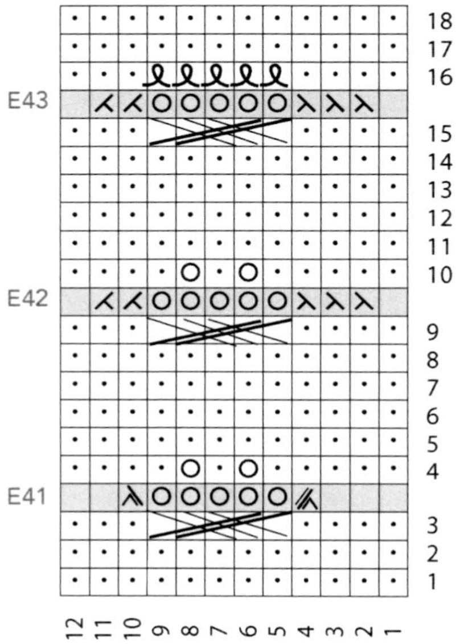

E39

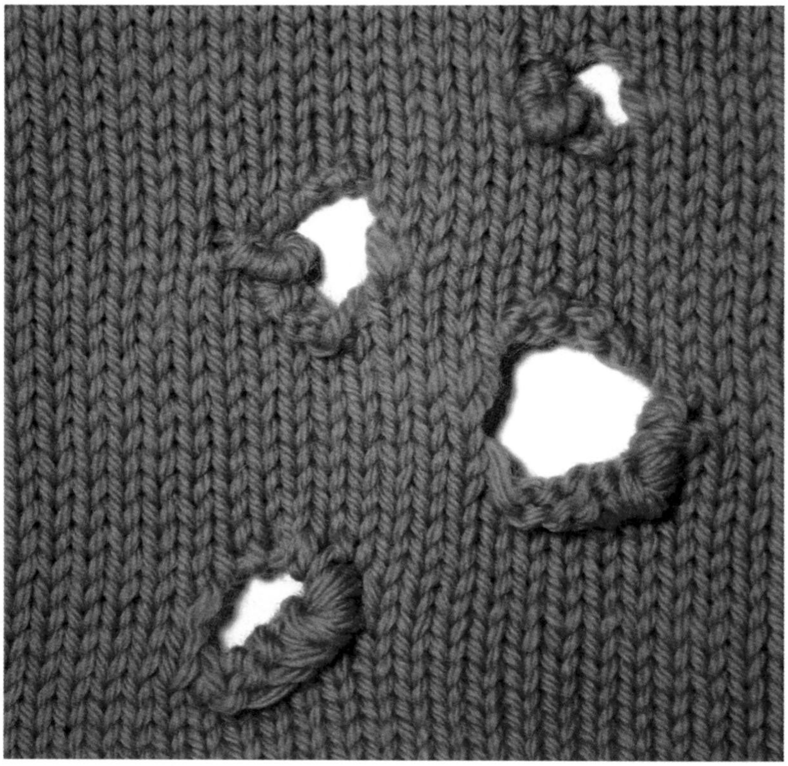

E43

E42

E41 After crossing the cable (3 x 2) and knitting that row, STS 5-7 were transferred to NDL 4 and STS 8 and 9 were transferred to NDL 10. The empty NDLS were cast on with the EON method.

E42 After crossing the cable (3 x 2), 3 STS were transferred to the right and two to the left with 2-step transfers. The eyelet was completed with the EON method.

E43 makes the same transfers as E42, but the row after the transfers was bridged to e—wrap the five empty NDLS. Notice that the eyelets seem a little bit shorter and less open than swatch E42.

On the Edge

In addition to varying the number of STS you use to create eyelets or the number of needles between them, you can also vary the ultimate placement of the eyelets. Rather than placing them in the body of the fabric as I have done so far, the next three examples feature eyelets worked along the edge of the fabric. All 3 examples were worked with 3-ST eyelets, 2 STS from the edge of the fabric. (The differences between them would be even more pronounced with 5-ST eyelets.)

For each of these examples I used a different method to complete each eyelet. The eyelets become slightly

E44

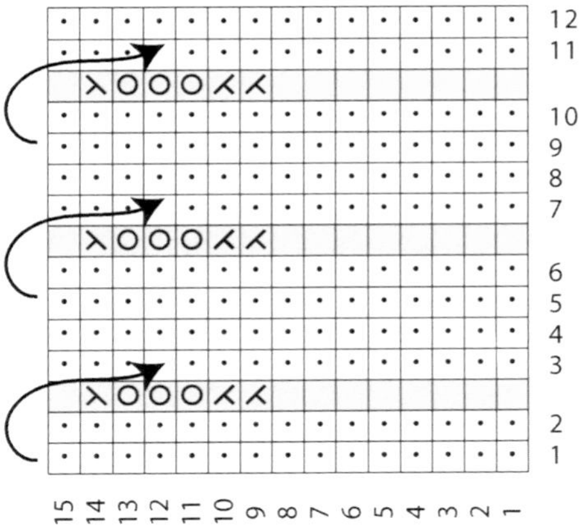

E44

E45

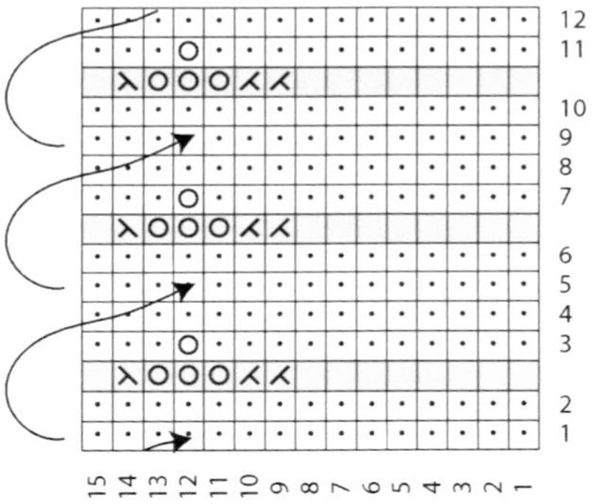

E45

E46

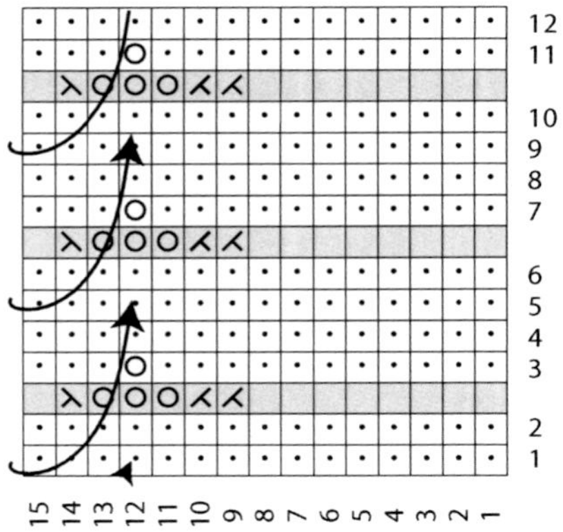

E46

E40

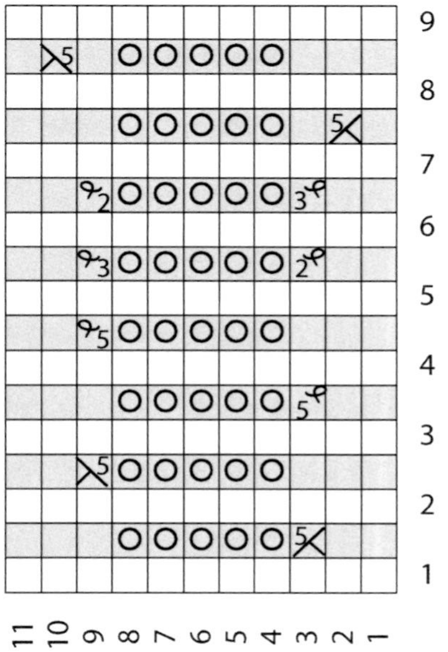

The chart at left, reading from bottom to top, shows several methods for emptying 5 NDLS:

All 5 STS are transferred to a single NDL at right or left.
All five STS have been enlarged by bridging to twist them together and place them on a single NDL at right or left.
Without enlarging the STS, it is possible to twist 2/3 to the right or left and place them on a single NDL.
All five STS, enlarged by bridging, can also be moved with a skipped transfer to left or right. Making this a 2—step transfer would add even more interest to the knit side.

(No Swatch)

more open with each variation, but you might find one method faster or easier to manage than another.

E44 After making the transfers, bring NDLS 11and 13 back to WP then use a transfer tool to lift the edge loop from 2 rows below and hang it on the empty center eyelet NDL. Knit 4 rows and repeat. This method totally closes the eyelet in one row and creates a lovely textured edging.

E45 This eyelet appears a bit more open than the last because I used the EON method to complete the eyelet over two rows before picking up and hanging the edge loop on the center NDL. For variation, you could also hang the edge loop on one of the other NDLS as the eyelet is already closed and not dependent on this loop to complete it.

E46 This last variation is worked like the previous example, completing the eyelet before lifting the edge loop. However, when I lifted the loop from 2 rows blow, I inserted a latch tool through the eyelet and pulled the edge loop through the eyelet from underneath the fabric to hang it on the center NDL. This method added a little more texture to the trim but it also stabilized the edge a lot more, inhibiting lengthwise stretching.

E47 and E48 As a further exploration of location, I worked both a hem and a B/O with giant eyelets. For the hem, E47, I worked an entire row of 3-ST eyelets with 2 STS between them when I reached the halfway depth of my hem. I used the EON method to fill the NDLS and knitted 1 row. Then, I removed the 2 STS between each eyelet on a 2-prong transfer tool which I rotated 360 degrees before replacing the STS on the same NDLS. I used this twisting to help sharpen the edges of the picots.

For the B/O, E48, I also worked 3-ST eyelets with 2 plain STS between them and used the EON method to cast back onto the NDLS. Then I worked a sinker—post B/O to retain a loose edge and manually knitted each of the eyelet STS twice as I worked them off. This added extra length to the B/O at the top of each eyelet and made the edge rounder and more pronounced.

To work a sinker post B/O, transfer each ST to the adj NDL by passing it behind the post and then manually

E47

E48

E49

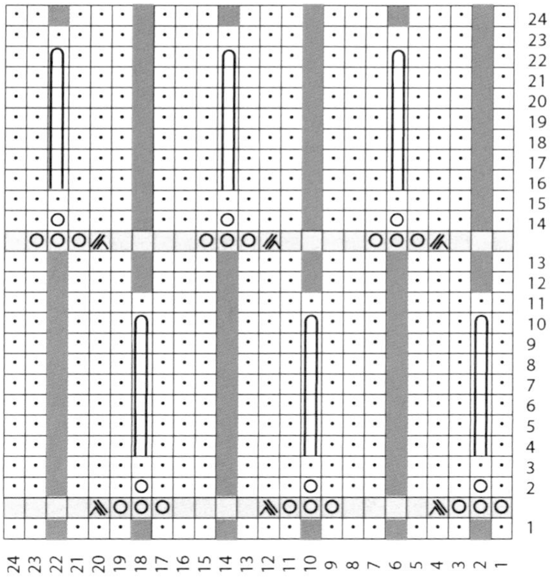

knit the two STS together in the usual way. On machines with flow combs, pass the yarn around the adj empty NDL before knitting the two STS together. This B/O method helps equalize the size of the B/O STS and supports the weight of the entire fabric to the end.

Until now, with just a few exceptions, we've mostly looked at different methods of transferring the STS to form the eyelets and casting on to the empty NDLS to close or complete the eyelets. The following variations can be applied to any size eyelet and, in most instances, you can use whatever closure method you prefer. The actual transfers contribute to the pattern effect so I wouldn't change those. Keep in mind that while my tuck stitch variations are hand—manipulated, you can certainly make use of the automatic patterning features of your machine.

E49

Tucked Eyelets

E49 This swatch features 3-stitch eyelets that are formed by transferring all 3 eyelet STS to the same NDL; alternately to the left or right with each repeat. The repeats themselves also alternate placement on the fabric. The eyelets are completed with the EON cast on method and then the ST above the center of the previous eyelet is placed in HP to tuck for the next 7 rows, then knit for the next 2 rows. Simply nudge the NDLS from HP to UWP so they begin knitting.

The next row is a prep row where transfers are made for the next repeat and the STS indicated by the knit symbols on the chart are reformed. When reforming a column of STS that ends under a newly formed eyelet, transfer the ST from the latch tool to the NDL adj to the empty eyelet NDLS. This latched up column of STS turns left and right, according to the direction of the eyelet transfers and adds visual movement to the swatch.

As with most tuck fabrics, the purl side is the right side. If your machine does easily tuck for 7 rows, knit fewer rows, which will only collapse the scale of the pattern and bring the eyelets closer together. Also, make sure you always keep your weights underneath working needles, not those in HP.

Twisted Eyelets

Traditional twisted ST designs always twist pairs of STS EOR, but there are endless ways to utilize twisted STS for creating texture. In the next three examples, "Rotini" twisted STS, worked three rows after each eyelet is completed, add surface interest to the fabric.

E50

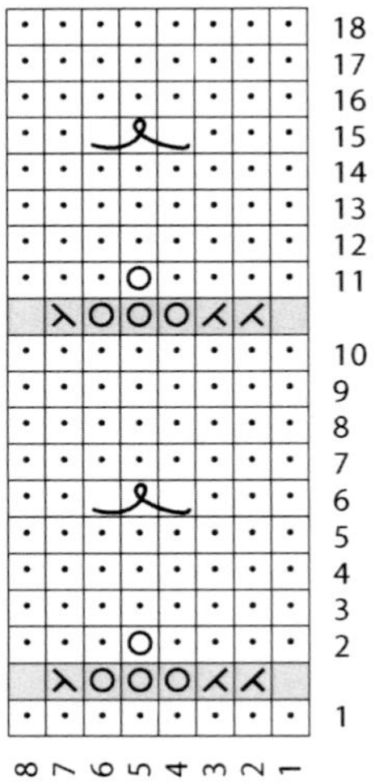

E50

E51

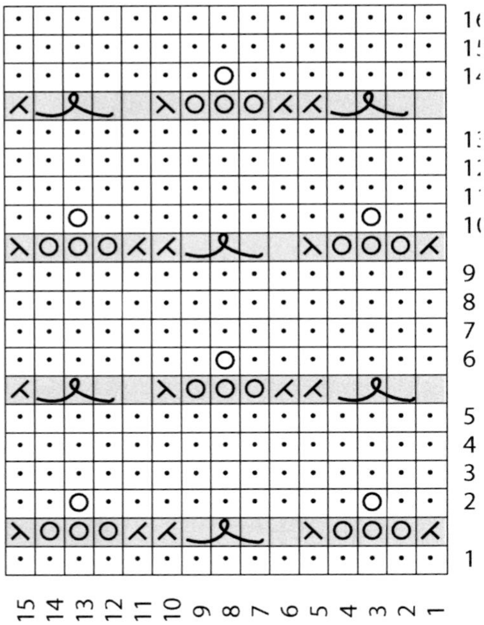

E51

Two STS were transferred to the right and one to the left, then the eyelet closed by the EON method, followed by 2 additional rows.

E50 was worked as a vertical column of eyelets, but E51 utilizes an alternating placement of the eyelets to create pattern.

E51 In the prep rows, the alternate eyelets are formed and the 3 STS above the previous eyelets twisted as follows: Remove the 3 eyelet STS on a 3-prong transfer tool. Insert a second 3-prong transfer tool from back to front of the same STS and remove the first tool. Twist the transfer tool 180 degrees (either direction, but be consistent) and return the STS to their NDLS.

Most twisted ST designs are worked by twisting two STS in this way (2 tool method), emulating hand knit twisted ST patterns. This 3-stitch variation is more textured, though less suitable for traditional twisted ST patterning. You can vary a pattern like this one by alternating the direction you twist from repeat to repeat, but, as always, make sure you take notes and can repeat your experiments later!

E52 The twisted STS in this example are typical 2-stitch twists that "travel" across the fabric by using one of the STS from the previous twist and a new ST for each following twist. The direction of the twists is important here so one of the basic twisted ST rules still applies: twist the transfer tool in the direction the STS are traveling. So, if the stitches are progressing towards the right (as they are on this chart), you need to twist the tool to the right before placing the STS back on the NDLS. Note that the first twists are worked immediately after completing the EON cast on for the

E52

E52

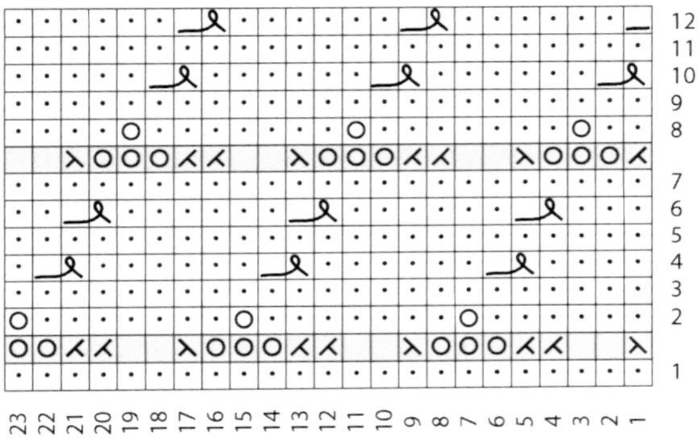

E53

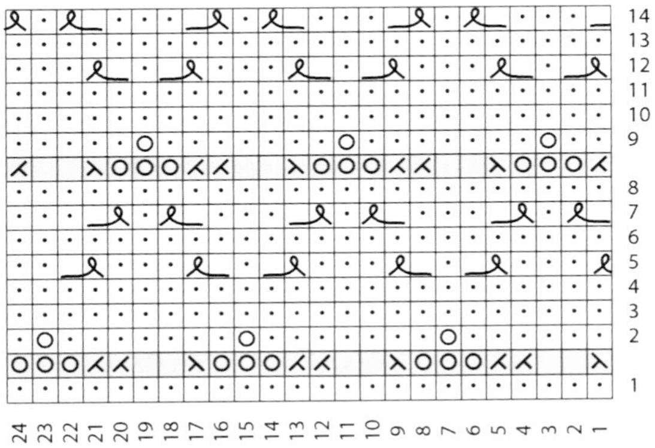

previous row of eyelets. These pairs of STS are twisted exactly as I described above for the 3-stitch twists, but using a pair of 2-prong tools.

E53 The twisted STS in this example form a textural grid of short diagonal lines connecting the eyelets. Pairs of STS are twisted after completing the eyelets with the EON method and then knitting one more row. Note that the STS travel in two directions in each row, slanting towards each other and the center of the next eyelet placement. STS traveling right are twisted to the right; those traveling left are twisted to the left.

E53

Patterns like this can be confusing, so I keep the chart nearby, crossing off each row as it is worked and I always make note of the location of center zero on my chart for a point of reference. While it requires more concentration, I think swatch E53 is far more interesting than E52 because the twisted STS travel in both directions and serve to connect the eyelets.

E54 These twisted STS are not your grandmother's twisted STS! More like twisted STS on steroids, they were all worked after enlarging STS with a row of drop stitch – either manually worked around a gauge or double bed. (See pages 14-15)

Keep in mind that the easiest way to manage such huge STS is to bring their NDLS to HP and then insert a single prong transfer tool through the STS themselves, rather than trying to use it in the conventional way by attaching the tool to each NDL. For these examples, insert the tool through all of the STS as a group and then push the NDLS back to NWP so the STS slide off the NDLS and onto the tool as a group. Keeping a little downward pressure on the STS helps.

The twists at the bottom of the swatch were worked by twisting groups of three enlarged STS two full rotations before returning them to the first NDL in the group and pushing it to HP. Bring the adjacent empty NDL to WP and knit two rows. Complete the eyelet by twisting the bars under the remaining empty NDL.

The second row of twists was worked by removing groups of 5 STS on the tool and twisting it two full rotations before replacing the STS on the center NDL. Then I brought all the NDLS out to HP and e—wrapped every NDL, including those with the twisted STS already on them.

E54

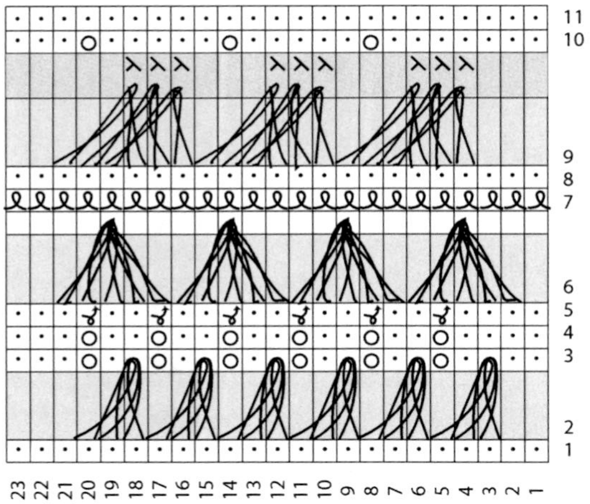

E54

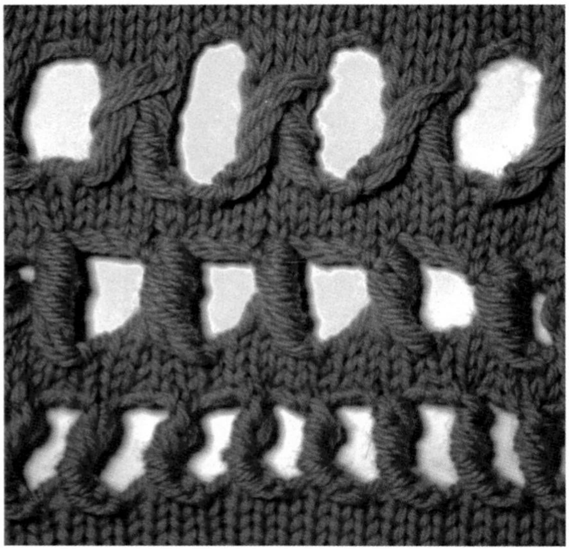

E55

E55

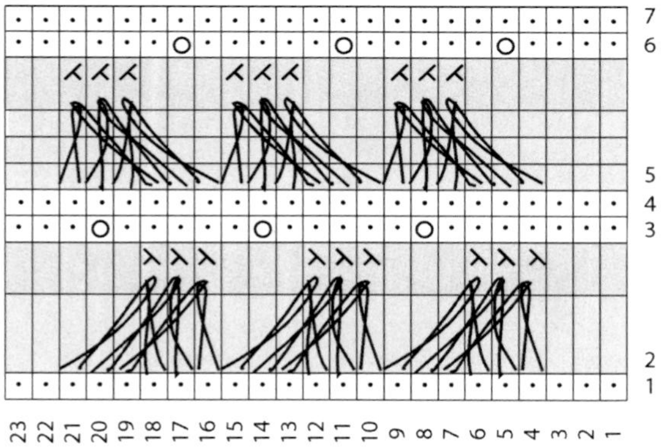

The third row of twists requires alternately twisting groups of three STS in opposite directions.

These eyelets are worked with 2-step twisted transfers as follows: Remove STS 4-6 on a 3-prong transfer tool and hold to the side. Remove STS 7-9 on a second 3-prong tool. Rotate this tool 360°to the right and place the STS on NDLS 4-6. Twist the other tool 360° to the left and place the STS on the same NDLS. Complete the resulting 3-stitch eyelets with the EON method.

E55 This fabric is worked like the last row of twists in the previous example, but the placement of the eyelets, as well as the direction of the twists alternate as shown on the chart.

Skipped Stitch Transfers

Some of the earlier swatches featured skipped transfers, but in the next two examples, the placement of the eyelets shifts one NDL to the right or left (E56) or two NDLS to the right (E57) with each repeat. There are 9 STS between each eyelet in the first example, but only 5 in the second. Both examples utilize just 1 more knitted row after the eyelets are completed with EON. This causes the bars of the ladders that form and connect the eyelets to twist.

E56 In the first example, a single ST is transferred to the left with a 1-step transfer, but the two STS transferred at right are worked as 2-step transfers that skip behind one ST.

This is done by using a 2-prong tool to remove STS 4 and 5 from their NDLS and then using a 2-prong tool to move STS 7 and 8 to NDLS 4 and 5 before replacing the first pair of STS on top of them. The transferred STS pass behind the stitch on NDL 6 and

E56

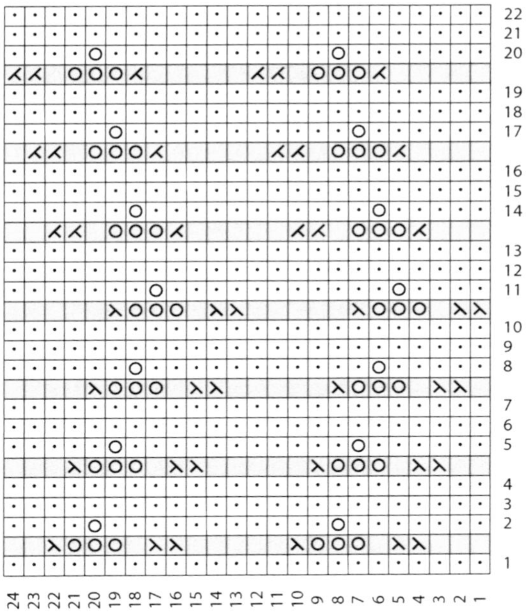

E56

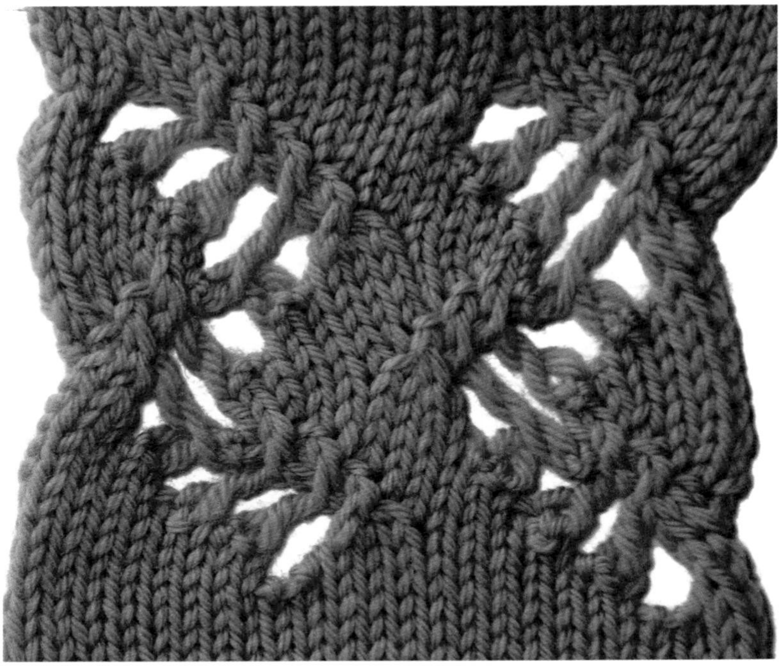

E57

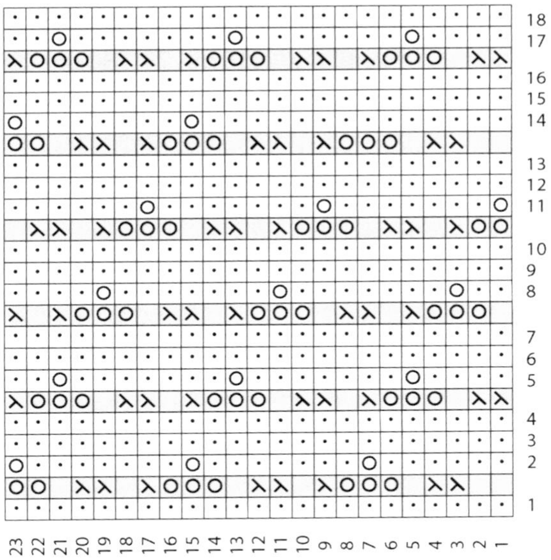

E57

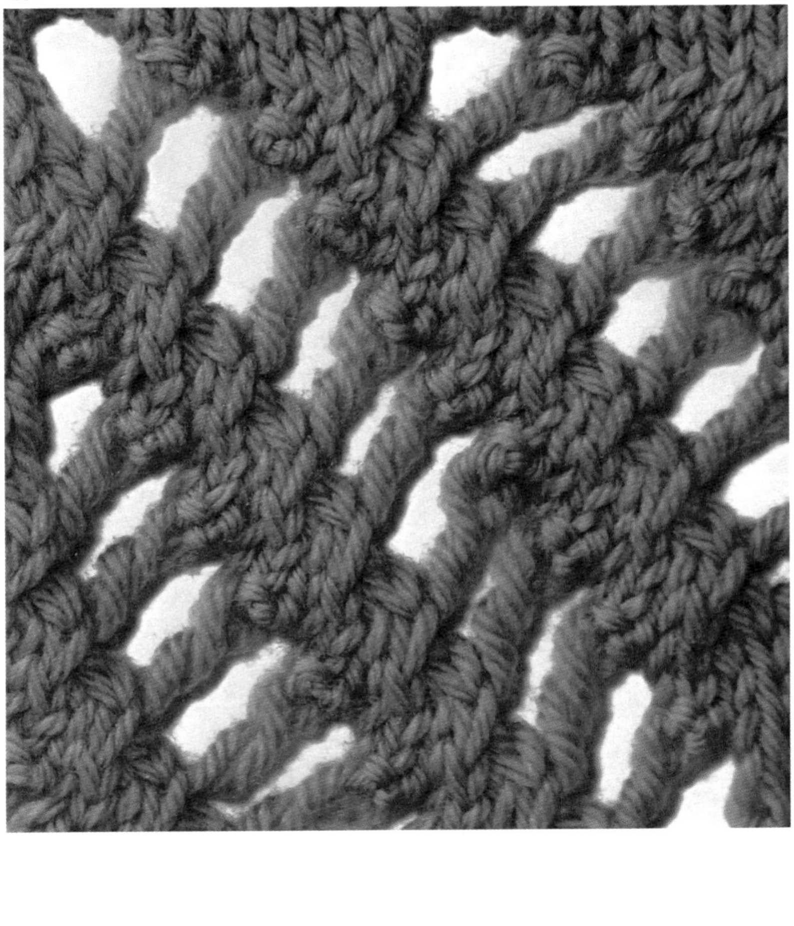

this two—step decrease creates a lovely cabled effect along side the eyelets.

If you work this fabric by removing STS 4-6 on a 3-prong tool, transfer STS 7 and 8 to NDL 4 and 5 and then return 4-6 to their NDLS, you will create an entirely different effect alongside the eyelets.

E57 The second example was worked with both 1 and 2-step transfers, which were worked two STS further to the right with each progressive repeat. That is, STS 6 and 7 were transferred to NDLS 3 and 4 (2-step) and ST 8 to NDL 9 (1-step). However, because all the transfers were made in one direction, the fabric biases, making it unsuitable for most garments. The biasing could be negated by alternating the direction of the transfers within each repeat or by alternating entire repeats. Working the transfers as close to the edge as possible creates a beautiful curved edging that barely curls and makes this fabric particularly appealing for scarves and shawls and creative exploration.

E58

E59

Cabled Eyelets

E58 This sample features 3-stitch eyelets with 5 STS between. All of the cables cross on the second row of the EON cast on for the eyelets (as the last empty NDL is returned to WP) and all of the cables cross in the same direction; you can cross them to the left or to the right, but be consistent throughout the fabric. The placement of the eyelets alternates from one repeat to the next.

5E9 was worked the same as the previous swatch except that the cables all cross to the left in one repeat and then they all cross to the right in the next. They continue to alternate throughout the fabric. The combined alternation of eyelet placement and direction of the crossings is what creates the rich woven cable effect and

E58

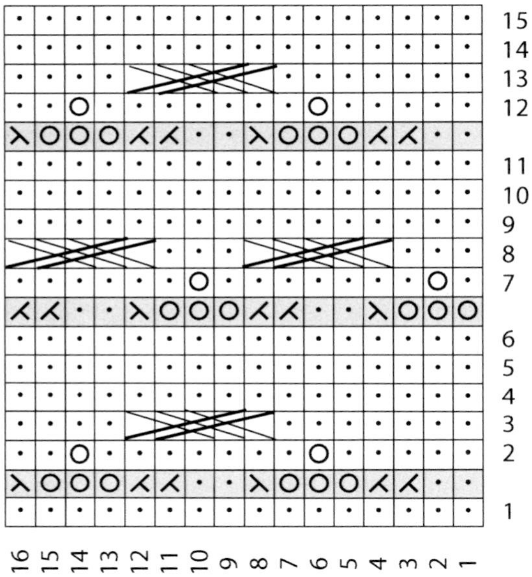

E59

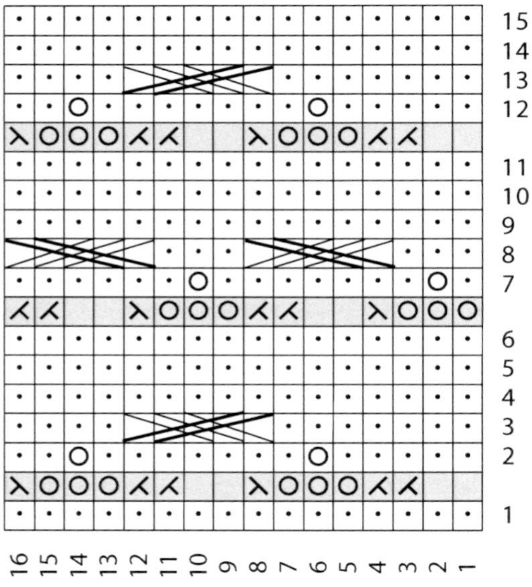

is a very small, though effective, change from the previous swatch. The fabric itself is much more interesting.

Although I worked these last two examples with 3 x 2 cables, you can easily work larger or smaller cables the same way. Although each cable shares 1 ST with the previous repeat, these are not true split pairs.

Pulling Stitches Through Stitches

In Hand—Manipulated Stitches for Machine Knitters, there are several patterns created by pulling stitches through stitches. Most of those, however, do not make the resulting open spaces the focus of the design.

Generally, the easiest way to pull a single ST (or group of STS) through another ST(es) is to use a transfer tool and a latch tool together. The latch tool is inserted through one ST/group of STS to catch the other ST(es), which are then dropped from their NDLS by pushing the NDLS forward and then back so the STS slide over the closed latches and onto the latch tool. The ST(es) on the latch tool are pulled through the other group of STS then replaced on any one of the now—empty NDLS.

You can also remove a group of STS from their NDLS on a transfer tool, place the ST from the latch tool on one of those empty NDLS and then return the STS to their NDLS. There are countless ways you can vary the placement because once a ST has passed through another ST (or group of STS) those STS are secured by the ST passing through them and can be dropped from their NDLS, collected on a single NDL, twisted or transferred.

E60

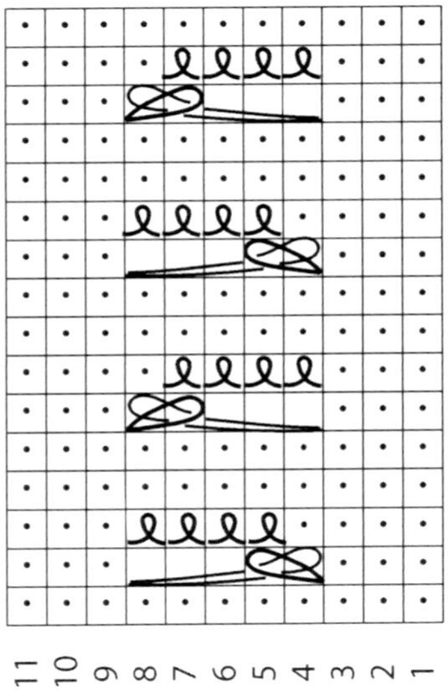

I usually just insert the latch tool through STS while they are still on their NDLS, but you might find it easiest to manage if you first remove the stitches on a transfer tool and then pass the latch tool through them.

Also, I normally pull the NDLS holding the STS that will be collected on the latch tool out to HP so that, once caught by the hook of the tool, I can just push those NDLS back to WP to release the STS on the latch tool.

In short, the STS being pulled through are the ones caught on the latch tool and are usually (though not always) rehung as a group on one NDL, while the STS they are pulled *through* will encircle them and can be dropped from their NDLS because they are secured by the STS passing through them.

E60 shows a single, columnar repeat of a pattern, while E61 is an all—over repeat with just a single ST between repeats. These 3-stitch through 2-stitch maneuvers produced 4-stitch eyelets, completed with e—wraps.

To work this pattern, remove STS 4 and 5 from their NDLS on a single prong transfer tool. Insert a latch tool through these two STS and catch STS 6-8 in the hook of the tool. Release STS 6-8 from their NDLS, pull them through the two STS on the transfer tool and place them all on NDL 4. NDLS 5-8 are empty.

E60

In order to prevent the stitches from tightening and destroying the open effect, I bridged the row before the pattern so I could manually enlarge the five STS in each eyelet group and manually knitted the NDLS all the way back to NWP (page 8).

After completing the bridged row to enlarge the STS and then working the STS through STS patterning across the row, you need to close the eyelets. You could use the EON method, but to produce a crisper, well defined top edge, I chose to bridge and e—wrap the empty NDLS. For the single repeat shown in swatch 60, I bridged up to the eyelet, e—wrapped and then bridged the remainder of the row.

E61 For the next swatch, however, because there is only 1 plain ST between each repeat, I unthreaded the carriage and worked the entire row manually, knitting the single ST at normal size and e—wrapping the empty NDLS. Then I free—passed the carriage to the opposite end of the bed, re—threaded and worked 2 rows over all the NDLS before starting the next repeat.

Please note that for both swatch 60 and 61 I alternated pulling STS through to the right and left from one repeat to the next. All of the repeats in a row are worked the same direction; then the direction alternates for each row of patterning. Patterns like this one are ripe for experimentation and variation by changing the number of plain STS between eyelets or varying the direction of the maneuver.

E61

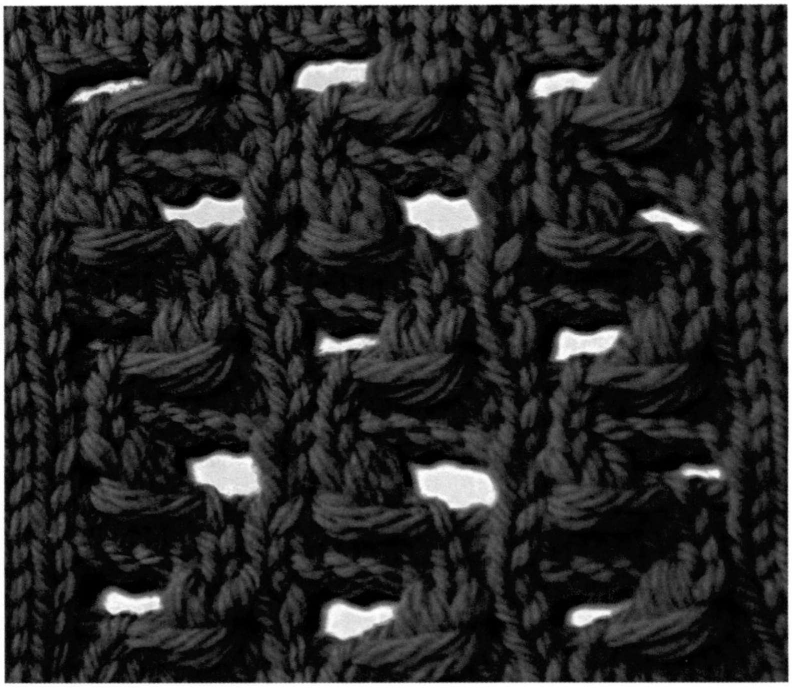

E62

E61

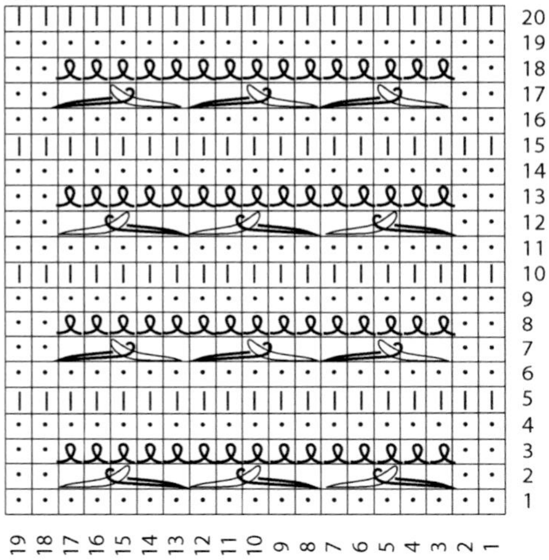

E62

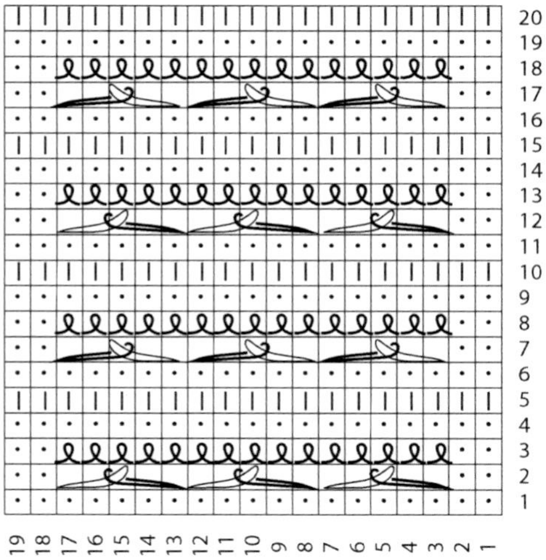

You could also change this pattern by replacing the STS from the transfer tool on a single NDL (instead of just releasing them from their NDLS). In that case, the eyelet would only require casting on three empty NDLS. The open effect would be diminished and you wouldn't see one set of stitches encircling the other but it might produce an entirely new pattern or one that deserves further exploration. With the potential for emptying and then filling 5 NDLS, the possibilities for stitch re—placement are endless.

E62 is a variation on E61. Like that example, the fabric is worked with 5-stitch eyelets, pulling 3 STS through 2, but they are not separated by a single ST. The eyelets and the e—wrap row were worked with bridging. However, after working the next two rows, the work was turned over with a garter bar. Then one more row was knitted and the work was turned again.

This example differs from the previous two samples in the placement of the STS after each manipulation. In the first repeat of E62 you should notice that the three STS on the latch tool were placed on NDL 5, the center NDL of the eyelet. This left NDLS 3 & 4 and 6 & 7 empty. Although you could use the EON method to cast on and close the eyelets, I preferred e—wrapping across all the NDLS, including the central NDL that already held a ST.

These eyelets stack up vertically, though the direction of the maneuver alternates from row to row. In each row, regardless of the direction, the 3 STS that are pulled through the other 2 are placed on the center NDL of each eyelet group, rather than being placed on the left or right—most NDL of the group like the previous examples. The direction of the maneuver is only evident in the direction the groups of STS encircle each other.

With or without the garter turns, you could vary this fabric by pulling 4 STS through a single ST, playing around further with the placement when you return the STS to the NDLS, work more rows of garter ST — or none at all — and experiment with other methods for closing the eyelets instead of e—wrapping.

For a slightly less open look, rather than manually enlarging the STS by knitting them back to NWP, you could use bridging and change the ST size on the ST dial to enlarge the eyelet STS just enough to make them manageable. This should be fine if you are working the rest of the fabric near the middle of the dial, but if you are already knitting on size 8 or 9, you may not see much difference (in terms of ease of manipulation) by working those STS with size 10. On the other hand, you might try working this technique without enlarging the STS at all. The effect will be somewhat less open, but the tension on the STS might create a more textured fabric.

Lastly, If you are comfortable with double bed work, drop stitch (page 11) is definitely the fastest, most streamlined way to work this fabric.

The next two examples (E63 & E64) vary the previous patterns by alternating the direction the STS are worked within each row.

E63 shows two columns of opposing STS through STS. Three STS have been pulled through 2 from each side and deposited on the two adjacent center NDLS. I used bridging to enlarge the STS manually

E63

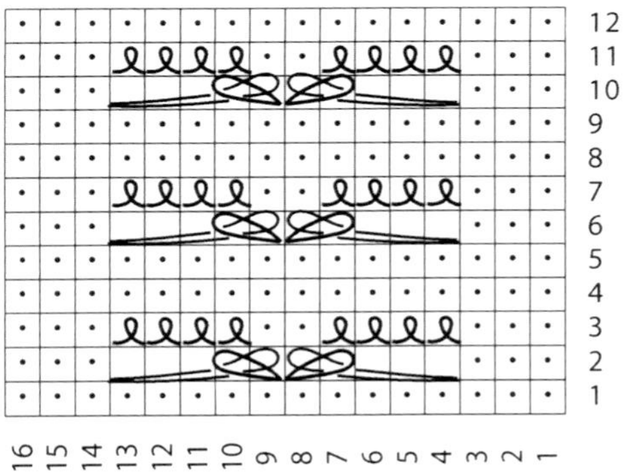

E63

E64

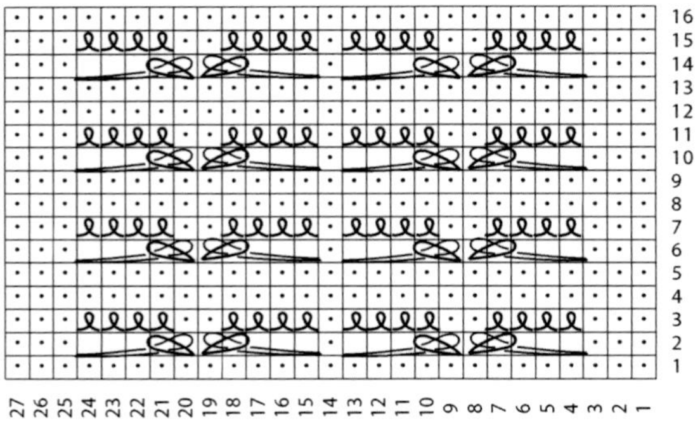

E64

E65

E66

and also to e—wrap the four remaining empty NDLS in each eyelet group. You could vary the number of rows between repeats, add more plain STS between the two halves of the column or reverse the direction of the motion so that the STS are pulled through STS in opposite directions. The pairing is what changes the surface effect of the fabric.

E64 is just an all—over repeat of the previous swatch with one plain ST between each repeat.

E65 and E66 both add traveling STS to the pattern effect employed in the previous swatches. In swatch E65, the STS were returned to the left—most NDL the first time, then the 2nd NDL from the edge, 3rd NDL from the edge, etc until finally they were placed on the right—most NDL of the 5 where I then reversed direction and worked my way back to the left. Although the position changes, it really doesn't create a very strong design feature in the fabric. On a larger scale it might.

E66 was worked with 5 plain STS between repeats. In this case, the 5 NDLS I chose for the eyelets shifted over by one NDL each time and I always pulled the STS through each other and replaced them the same way from repeat to repeat. I never changed direction and you can see what happens to the edges, which is not very satisfactory! Retaining more plain STS at each edge would have eliminated the edge issues just as regularly reversing direction would have eliminated the biasing.

Adding Texture with Nops and Short Rows

In the next group of examples, E67-74, the eyelets take back stage to the textured nops (See page 11). The eyelets provide the give in the base fabric that makes the manipulations possible. Although I have latched up and rehung some STS to help form these textures, the method is very different from the way popcorns are se-

E67

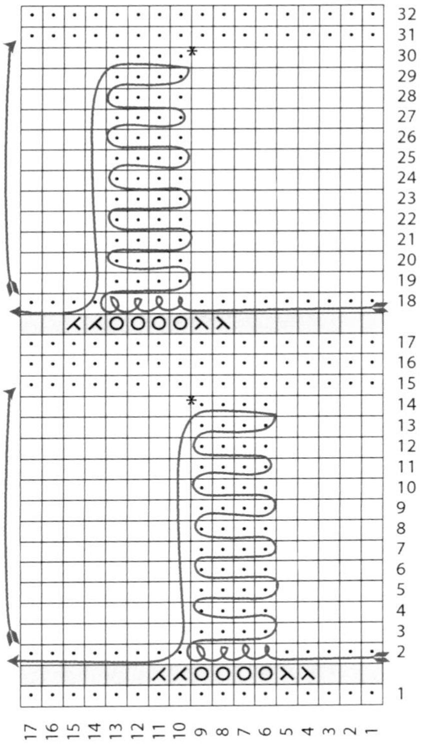

E67

cured with lifted stitches. I love the way these textures sit right up on the surface of the fabrics!

E67 Referring to the prep row, make the first set of transfers to create a 4-stitch eyelet. These 2-step transfers will bring the transferred STS to the knit side.

Begin COR set to hold NDLS in HP for bridging the nops. Hold the four eyelet NDLS and all NDLS to the left of them. Knit 1 row. Hold the bridge NDLS just worked and then e—wrap the four empty eyelet NDLS from right to left and place them in UWP. COL. Knit 11 rows on just these 4 NDLS, ending COR. Use your fingers, a small weight or a transfer tool poked through the fabric to provide tension on these 4 STS so they knit cleanly and do not pop off the NDLS.

You should notice that at the base of the nop, on the left side, the STS below the nop have separated, forming what looks like a short 3-bar ladder. Insert a latch tool into the purl bump of a ST adjacent to the lowest bar and then latch up the ladder and hang the new ST on the left—most nop NDL as shown on the chart at "*". Hold the 4 nop NDLS and return all NDLS to the left of them to UWP to bridge your way out of the row or to the next nop location.

Knit 3 rows over all the NDLS and then repeat, shifting the placement of the eyelet as shown on the chart and, after latching up the short ladder, hanging the new ST on the right—most NDL of the nop. These 2 placements (left and right) are alternated throughout this fabric. You could alter the number of rows between repeats, knit longer or shorter nops or space the eyelets further apart by placing some plain STS between each repeat. Note that in my example, all the nops curl the same direction and that the background STS form a small textured effect because of the 2-step transfers.

E68

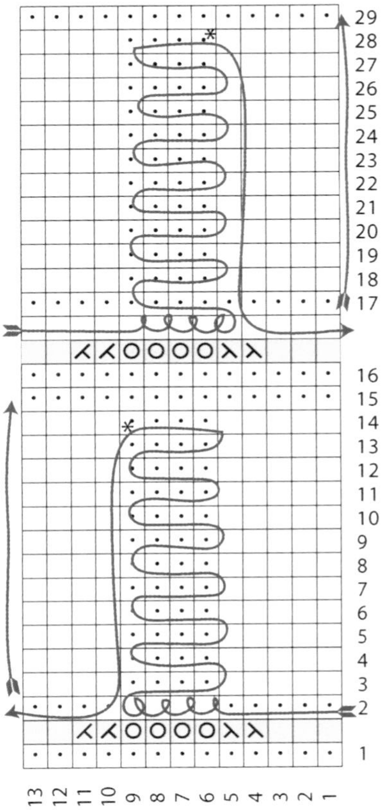

E68

If you lift up each nop, you will find an eyelet hiding behind it.

E68 is worked exactly like #67 except that the eyelets and nops are formed directly above each other from repeat to repeat and the repeats are alternately worked from the left and right side. The new ST formed by latching up the short gap at the bottom is alternately hung on the left or right which, coupled with the vertical placement, causes the nops in this example to curl in opposite directions.

E69 By moving the eyelet to the edge of the fabric, where it is hardly even an eyelet any more, the nops become an edge trim. Notice that while the transfers are still 2-step transfers, the transfers that are worked on the very edge of the fabric actually move two STS to the same NDL so that the edge NDL holds 3 STS.

The trim at the right of the fabric (left on chart) is less curly than the trim at left. This is because the latched up ST was always hung on the innermost NDL of the eyelet group. At the other, curlier edge they were always hung on the second NDL from the edge, which added a little extra tension on the STS. Its not a major difference, but worth noting how the tension on the STS and the ST placement affect the curl of the nops.

If you knit each nop for more than 11 rows, it will affect not only the length of each nop but also the amount of curl. What binds these nops to the fabric is the single BB that runs from the top of each column of 11 rows and bridges to the next group of STS. The more that bar is drawn out, the less the nops curl, unless you add one more step and regularly P/U and hang the BB on an adj NDL.

E69

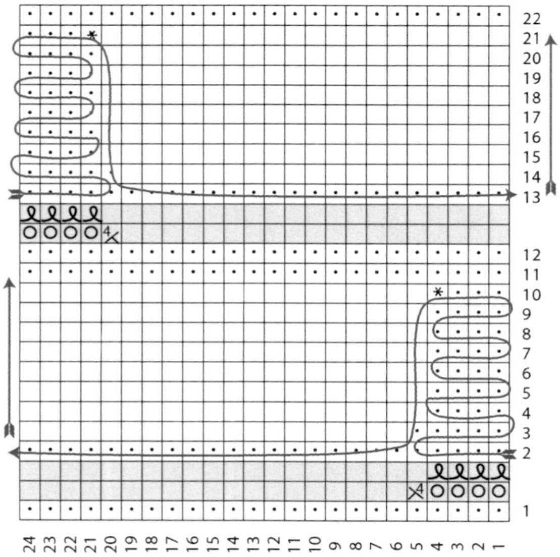

E69

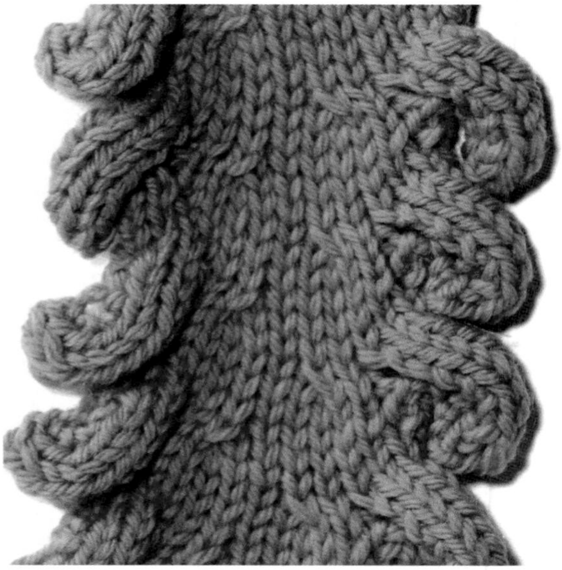

E70

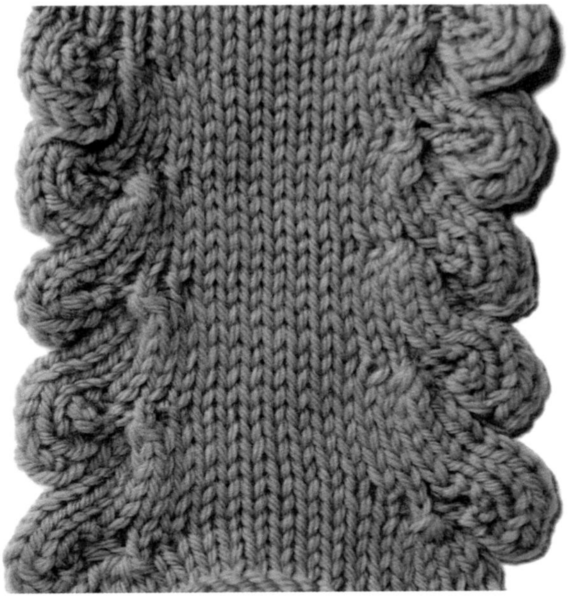

E70 (no chart)This edge trim looks very much like swatch 69 except that the nops are much curlier due to a slightly different construction detail. First of all, the four edge STS are all moved to the fifth NDL from the edge and then the empty NDLS are e—wrapped. All NDLS except the four e—wrapped NDLS and the next two are placed in HP for bridging.

Begin COR. The first row is knitted over the 6 NDLS at the right edge then the left—most NDL of those six is placed in HP when COL. Knit 1 row and hold 1 more NDL at left. Continue knitting on the remaining 4 edge NDLS for 6 more rows then bridge to the opposite side. Latch up the little gap at the left as you did for the previous samples and hang the new stitch on the fourth NDL from the edge as shown on the chart at "*". Knit 2 rows over all NDLS and repeat from the opposite side.

You can vary the number of rows between repeats but because the effect alternates edges, you will always have to knit an even number of rows between repeats in order to alternately work on each edge.

E71 In all of the previous examples, the number of working needles has remained the same. With sample E71 this changes as the nops are used to finish a decreased, shaped edge.

E71

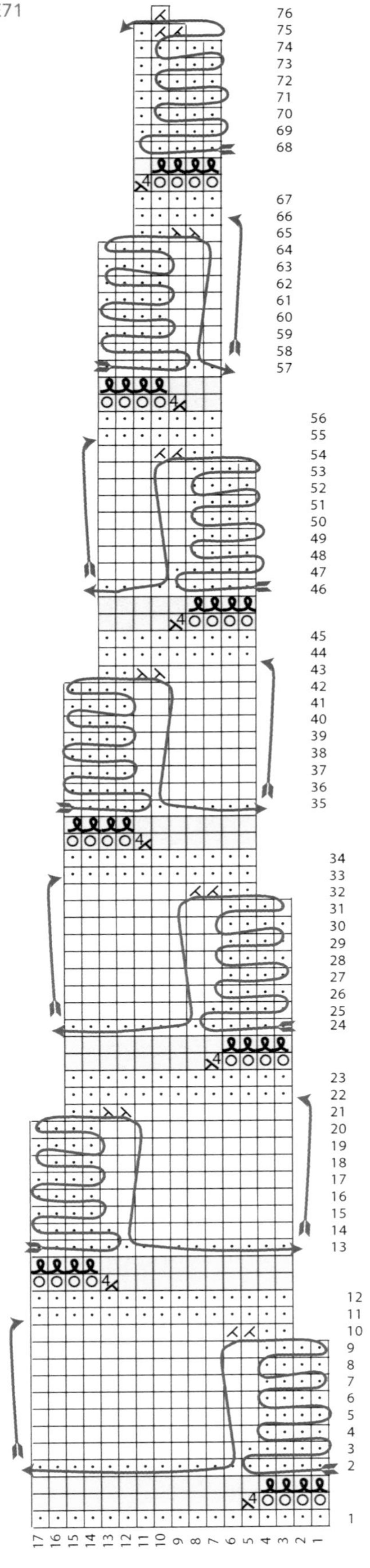

E71

Begin COR to work the two prep rows. Bridge and knit the nop, followed by a 2-step transfer. Move all 4 edge STS over by 2 NDLS. This maneuver decreases the width of the fabric by 2 STS at that edge so place 2 empty NDLS in NWP. Knit 2 rows over all NDLS and begin the next repeat from the left. If you only want to place decreases along one edge of the fabric, work an odd number of rows.

E72 is another nop edging that is knitted and transferred very much like sample E71 except that the work does not decrease and grow narrower. After making an initial 2-stitch transfer (1st and 2nd STS moved to the third NDL), e—wrap the two NDLS you just emptied as well as two extras at the right. At the end of the nop, make a 2-step transfer, moving the 2 edge STS over by two NDLS. Put the two extra, now empty NDLS in NWP.

E73 This last example of a nopped edge is quite similar to sample E70 except that the nops or finger do not curl at all. Begin with the COR and set to hold NDLS in HP. The two prep rows call for transferring the four edge STS to the fifth NDL, then immediately e—wrapping the same, empty NDLS. Knit 8 rows over the four edge NDLS then bridge to the left side. Work 2 rows over all NDLS and then repeat from the left side. There is no latching up bars or lifting STS involved in this variation, which is why the nops don't curl.

E72

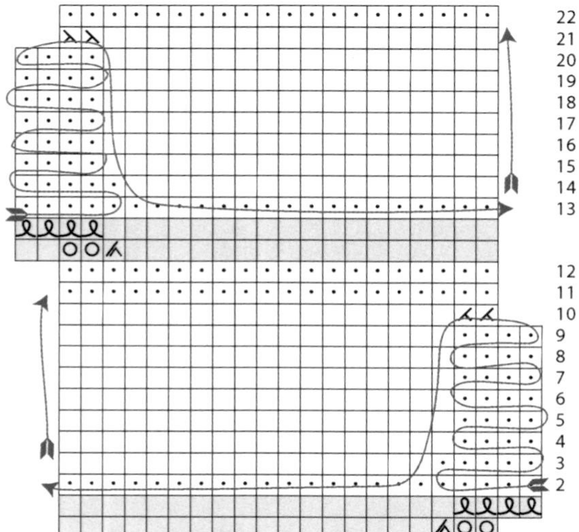

E72

E73

E73

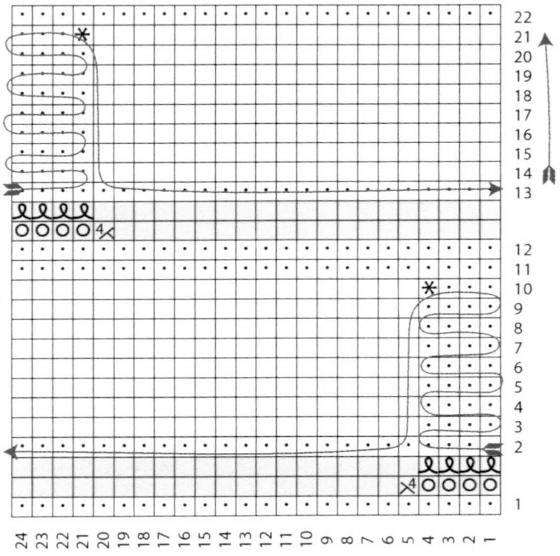

This is a fairly fast edging to execute, but there is a long float on the back that ties each finger to the fabric. I think that this edge might make a good base for rehanging on the machine to work a further, more elaborate edge. Also, worked in narrow, 3-row stripes, the nops would change color and stand out as solid colors along the edge of the striped fabric.

Irregular Surfaces

E74 This fabric is worked as a bridged, S/R fabric on alternate sides to create the zigzag, lightly ruffled edging. Begin COR set to hold needles in HP. Hold all NDLS except the first 2 on the carriage side and knit 2 rows. Transfer ST 3 from HP to the adjacent WP NDL as shown on the chart and place the empty NDL in NWP. Knit 2 rows. Transfer ST 4 to the same WP NDL, place the empty NDL in NWP and knit 2 rows.

E74

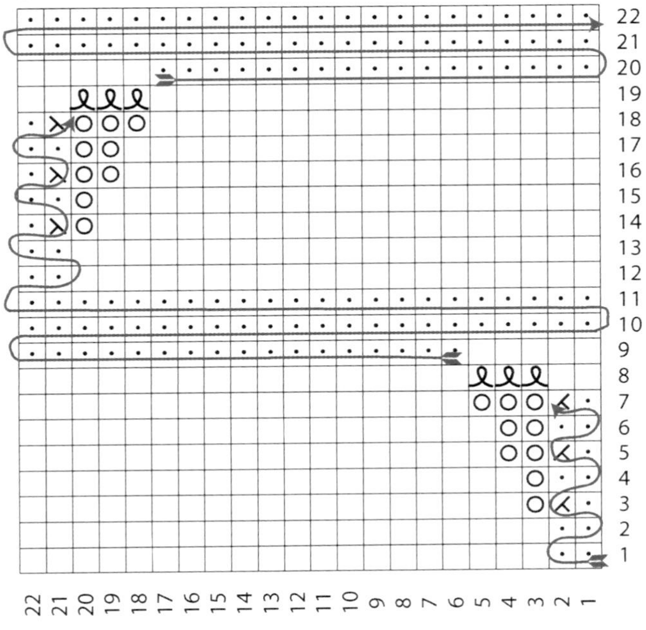

E74

Finally, transfer ST #5 to the same WP NDL and knit just 1 row. COL.

Use the FY to e—wrap NDLS 3-5 from right to left then place NDLS 1-5 in HP (all NDLS are now in HP) and move COR. Push NDL 6 and all NDLS to the left of it to UWP and knit 1 row to the left. Set the carriage to knit all NDLS and knit 2 rows, ending COL.

The next repeat is worked from the left in exactly the same way and the two repeats alternate for the length of the fabric. The extra rows on the edge NDLS, coupled with the eyelet, create the zigzag. You can work more than two edge stitches, but if you use this method in the middle of a fabric, it will distort the fabric.

My finished sample was blocked and steamed and the edges lay flat, but on a larger piece, I think they might tend to roll under. Latching up one or two stitches between the eyelet and the main fabric should counteract this.

This zigzagged edge offers some interesting seaming possibilities for afghans and other large projects. You could fit the zigs of one piece into the zags of the other to butt them up close or you could hold the two pieces wrong sides together and lace a cord or ribbon through the eyelets.

E75 grew out of the zigzag sample. When I moved the eyelets to the center of the fabric, I was, in effect, using 10 STS at each edge instead of 2. I needed to balance out the extra rows initially used to form the eyelets by adding the same number of rows (7) after e—wrapping each eyelet and bridging to the left. Rows 11-17 are the extra rows for the first repeat; rows 30-36 balance the second repeat. The fabric does lay flatter, but there is still some rippling.

At RC 10, the e—wrapped eyelet NDLS and all NDLS to the right of them remain in HP. Bridge to the left. Knit 1 row to the right (RC 12). *Transfer the edge ST to the adjacent working NDL at left and place the empty NDL in HP – not in NWP! Knit 2 rows** and repeat * to **two more times, only knitting 1 row after the last repeat. COL.

E75

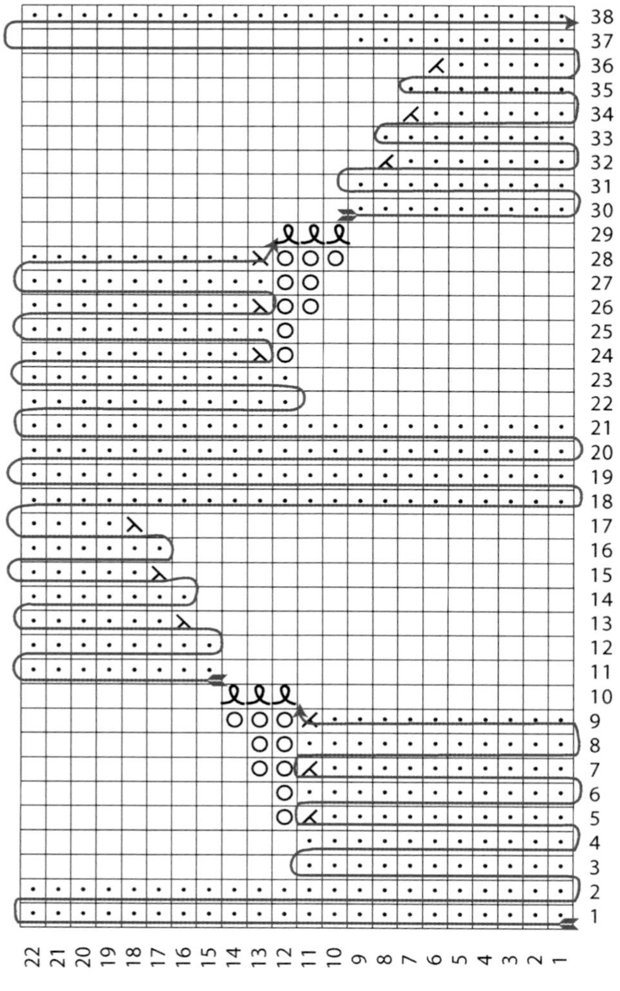

E75

Set the carriage to knit all NDLS and knit 4 rows before beginning the next repeat from the left side. If, for some reason, you prefer to work all the repeats from the same side, simply work an odd number of rows between repeats. You might also want to try working this as an edging just a couple of STS from the edge.

It is interesting to note that the eyelets are formed by transferring STS from HP NDLS to WP NDLS and then placing the empty NDLS in NWP. In contrast, the 7 balancing rows are worked by transferring HP STS to WP NDLS and then placing the empty NDLS in HP.

Because this last maneuver is done on the carriage side, it acts like a wrap. Both of these maneuvers create raised textures and the added rows help to create a balanced, usable fabric. You can knit fewer or more rows between repeats.

I also think that the method of transferring STS and leaving the empty NDLS in HP without having formed eyelets bears further exploration for surface texture. Without having to consider the eyelet or a specific number of rows, you could work these raised ridges anywhere on a fabric by transferring and holding more STS to create a bolder effect. There is bound to be some distortion in the fabric, which is a good reason to vary the direction you work the ridges.

E76 is the result of yet another "what if". It begins exactly like the previous sample, but instead of bridging to the edge of the fabric, I bridged up to the needle where I wanted to begin another eyelet in the same row. When the COR I made both transfers, those creating the ridge for the first eyelet and those to shape the next. There are four rows between repeats and the placement and direction alternate from one repeat to the next.

Try working through E75 before you attempt this one. The bridging is the only difference between the 2 swatches. This fabric is balanced and could be used for garments. The rouched texture is enhanced by eyelets, raised ridges and STS that lie at angles to each other.

E76

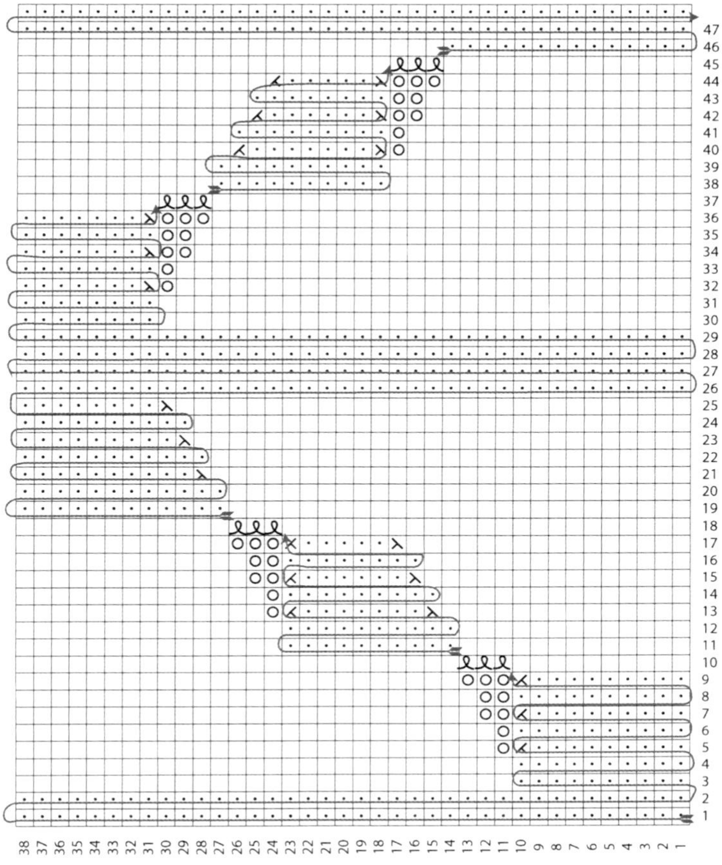

E76

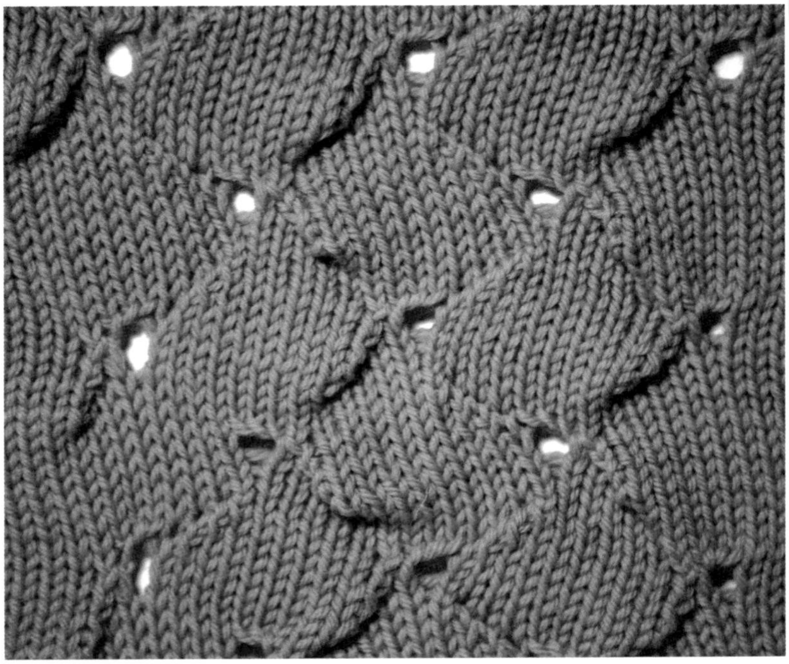

Embellished Eyelets

These join—as—you—knit trims are a fun way to add color or texture to a pre—knitted fabric. I used a variety of methods to embellish 3 and 5-stitch eyelets on this fabric after it was knitted and blocked. The edges of each eyelet were picked up and joined to the trims as I knitted them. I picked up a full stitch from the eyelet edge as I worked my way around each one. The trims all began and ended on waste so that I could invisibly graft the ends together.

E77

Pick up the edge of the eyelet from the outer edge towards the center of the eyelet when you want the knit side of the detail to show.

E78

Pick up the edge of the eyelet from the center outwards when you want the purl side of the trim to show.

How you hold the main fabric as you P/U the edge STS of each eyelet will determine whether you see the knit or the purl side of the trim and whether the trim rolls towards the eyelet or away from it. The right side of the fabric will always face you, but you can P/U the edge of an eyelet by inserting your transfer tool under the edge towards the eyelet E77 or by inserting it under those same STS from the center of the eyelet towards the body of the fabric E78.

The first approach will cause a stockinette band/trim to curl so that the knit side of the trim shows. P/U from the center out will bring the purl side of the trim to the surface (like the large flower on the sample).

E79 The green trim at upper left and the blue at lower left are simply narrow, 5-ST bands of stockinette. The green band rolls inward and the blue rolls out because of the way the eyelet stitches were P/U every 2/R to join the trim to the background fabric.

The purple trim is a bias knitted band where I increased one edge of the band and decreased the other edge by one ST (each edge) every 2/R. I P/U the edge of the eyelet and hung it on the NDL holding the decrease then knitted 2 rows.

The large blue "flower" was worked as a stockinette band 7 STS wide that was shaped with short rows. I used the same trim on E84 where the short rows produced more ruffling because the gores were larger and there were more of them. I wanted the purl side of these trims to show, so hen P/U the edge of the eyelet, I inserted my transfer tool from inside the eyelet towards the body of the fabric. I worked this way so that the fabric would curl back on itself (as it does)) to create an edging.

The green trim adjacent to the large flower is I—cord, which tends to sit closer to the surface of the fabric. This sample shows stockinette, bias, I—cord and short rowed trims, but you can add any of your favorite trims.

Colorful eyelets can be worked on single or double bed fabrics with a second layer peeking through. For heavier yarns, the single bed option produces a lighter weight, more usable fabric. However, for light weight yarns, double bed work opens up all kinds of possibilities.

E79

E80

E81

E80-82 (no chart) are single bed fabrics with pre—knitted patches that were applied to the purl side of the fabric behind each eyelet as I knitted. I tend to think of these more as eyelids than eyelets.

First I pre—knitted pieces 7 STS wide and 8 rows long, beginning and ending each on waste to preserve the live STS. When I reached the point where I wanted to create a backed opening in the main fabric, I folded back the waste on one end of a patch and rehung the STS on the NDLS where I planned to make my eyelet. You can decide whether you want to see the knit or the purl side of the patch showing through the eyelet and should re—hang accordingly.

E82

E83

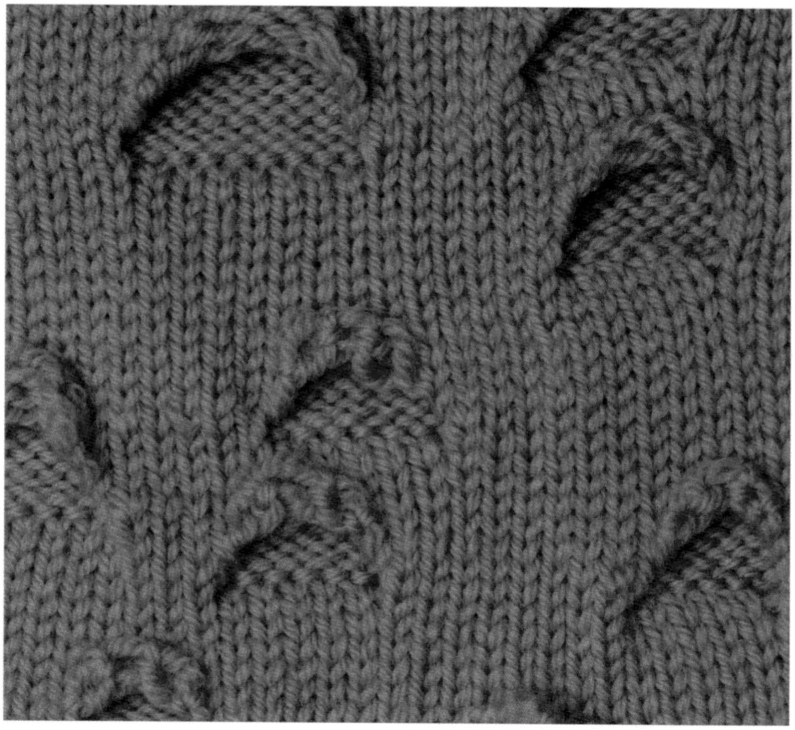

Once my patch STS were hung on the NDLS, I bridged the next row to enlarge the center five of the seven STS where I hung the patch, knitting the eyelet and the patch STS together and loosely enough to easily B/O with a latch tool. Bridge to the end of the row and then B/O the enlarged STS, chaining one ST through the next then hang the last ST from the tool on an adj NDL.

To C/O the five empty NDLS, you can use the EON method as I did in the first two examples 80 and 81) or you can use the latch tool or e—wrap method as I did in the bottom example (E82) After closing the eyelet, *knit 2 rows and then use a transfer tool to P/U and hang a loop from each edge of the patch on the NDL at each side of the eyelet.** Repeat from * to ** a second time. This will ensure that the two fabrics do not separate at the edges.

After the 6th row, fold back the scrap knitting on the top of the patch and hang those STS on the NDLS so that the top of the eyelet does not separate from the eyelet. You may prefer not to hang the top edges of the

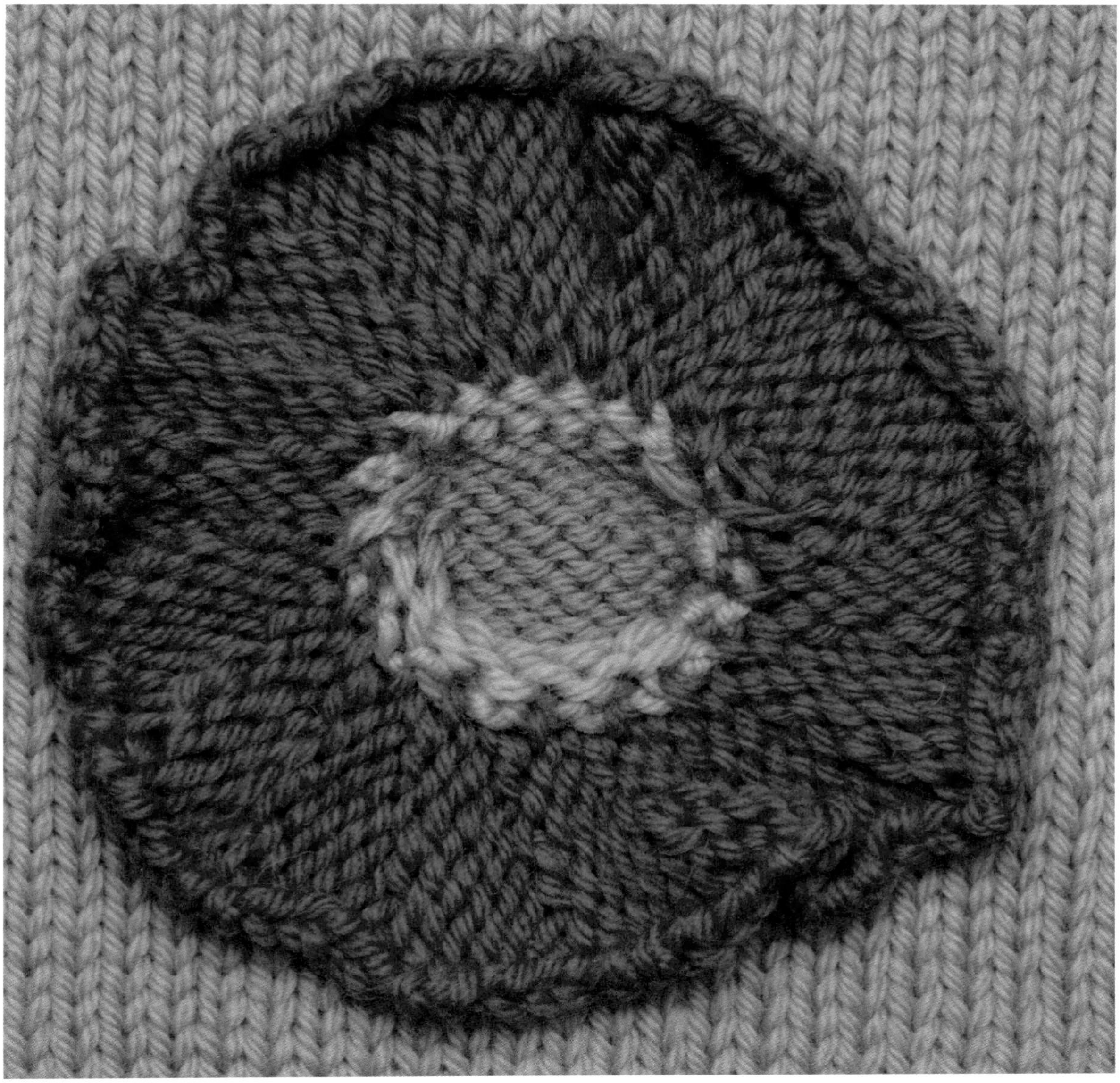

E84 I applied a patch to the back of this fabric while I knitted and then afterwards I worked a short rowed ruffle around the finished eyelet.

patches because it does tend to show a bit. In that case make sure you knit the patches with either a closed cast on or a bound off edge and knit those swatches for 10-12 rows so that they end well above the top edge of the eyelet. You should also repeat the * to ** directions a couple more times to secure the side edges. Even if the eyelets gape a bit, the patches will be long enough to look like a continuous layer behind the main fabric. If however, they are too short or not secured at the sides, you will see gaps.

E83 With a double bed machine and much finer yarns, these eyelids are a snap to knit. With the beds in full pitch, set the carriages for circular knitting. Make eyelets any size you want by transferring main bed STS to the ribber (or visa versa). Over the next 2 main bed rows, work the EON method to close the tops of the eyelets. You can also bridge and e—wrap or use a latch tool cast on, but you need to make sure the ribber bed does not knit at all. Otherwise, there will be extra rows on the ribber and the two layers will not align. Note that the ribber STS appear as purls in the eyelets.

If you also have a color changer, you can work each layer in a different color. To do that, instead of working circular, you need to knit two or four rows of a color on each bed. The fabrics will only be joined together at the base of each eyelet so you will need to find other ways to bind the two layers together. The simplest way to do this is to randomly pick up the purl bar of a main bed ST and hang it on the opposite ribber needle.

LADDERS

LADDERS ARE FORMED by columns of un—knitted "bars" of yarn that pass under needles in non—working position. They can be planned and specifically placed or they can occur accidentally when, for example, you have made a lace transfer and forgotten to return the empty needle to working position.

When directions call for reforming or latching up a dropped stitch, they usually refer to manipulating the ladder that forms when a stitch drops down and un—knits. Dropped stitches that occur accidentally are usually latched up from the knit side to restore the fabric structure, while planned ladders may be reformed in more decorative and unusual ways.

Deliberate ladders are familiar to most machine knitters for creating ease along side cables or, in the absence of a ribber, for working mock rib. Both of those suggest that ladders are utilitarian effects that may not have much decorative value on their own. However, you will discover that ladders offer all kinds of creative possibilities for open fabrics when you apply some of the "what ifs" and begin to play with their size, placement and shapes.

Mock ribbing is usually worked with a fairly tight stitch size on alternating arrangements of working and non—working needles. While mock rib does tend to pull a fabric in and give bands and edgings some shape, it is not elastic like a true ribbing. However, it is often quite effective when used as an all—over fabric treatment and offers a good alternative to plain stockinette for yarns that have pronounced texture and will retain the open ladders.

As for leaving ladders along—side cables, they have never been my method of choice for easing cable crossings. I find that, unless the yarn is very textured, such ladders tend to spread into the adjacent stitches and lose definition. Occasionally I use ladders to help cross wide cables, but I always go back afterwards to latch up and eliminate those ladders by reforming them as purl stitches alongside the cables.

There are two ways to create ladders you plan to reform later. Leaving an empty needle in non—working position produces a fairly narrow ladder. If you decide to latch up the bars of that ladder, the stitches it forms are likely to be somewhat tighter and more difficult to manage than the other stitches in the fabric.

If instead, however, you allow the empty needle to cast on and continue knitting until you drop it later on, when you reform the bars of *that* ladder, the stitches will be the same size as those formed by the other needles in working position. You could also leave two (or three) empty needles, but only allow one of them to cast on and knit. In that case, the stitches that you reform after dropping that ladder will be larger and looser than those in working position and may offer some contrast in scale or new opportunities for experimentation. (See pages 11-16 for drop stitch information).

The important thing to keep in mind here is that whether you place needles out of work or allow them to cast on, knit and drop, even simple ladders offer lots of possibilities for manipulating stitch size and spacing right in the middle of a fabric. These ladders affect vertical columns of stitches, rather than horizontal rows, while offering new possibilities for exploration and exploitation. They may also form the basis for more involved patterns.

In a few of the examples that follow, the ladders themselves take a back seat to the resulting texture or patterning and may not even be obvious at first glance. Similar to using a ladder alongside a wide cable to facilitate crossing, some ladders are used simply to support or produce other effects.

Please note that, when possible, I have tried to show two repeats horizontally and vertically for each pattern so that you can see how the repeats connect. I did not mark the individual repeats. Also, although I did allow a couple of examples to repeat right to the edges of the sample either to illustrate a decorative effect or a distracting one, most of the patterns retain at least 2 or 3 plain stitches at each edge of the fabric. Some patterns also show half—repeats at the edges and, where possible, that is often the best solution to dealing with fabric edges and large repeats.

The first row of most charts shows all transfers or other maneuvers only to show the connection between the last and first rows of the chart when repeating. Always begin these fabrics with at least one plain row. It may not be possible to make specific manipulations in the very first row because they may be dependent on the preceding row as the pattern repeats.

Sometimes the ladders that you create look great while the fabric is still on the machine, but once the stitches are no longer under any tension from being stretched across the bed, the ladders start to close in. Each bar of the ladder is absorbed by its neighboring stitches and as the ladders disappear, the adjoining stitches may become looser than the other stitches in the row. When ladders are not stable, open effects are easily lost. Stability is important and I'll explain a number of ways to make sure that your ladders are open when removed from the machine and remain so even after a garment has been washed or worn many times.

Functionality differs enormously from person to person and when you plan to wear something, rather than drape it across a window. Please keep in mind that the width of a ladder, relative to the number of empty needles that formed it, varies greatly when you compare standard gauge and bulky fabrics and that an effect that may be totally non—functional on a bulky machine might work out just fine on a standard gauge. Similarly, methods that would be tedious to do on standard gauge may be more practical to do on a mid or bulky gauge machine.

Ladder Basics

Beginning and Ending Ladders

In the eyelet chapter we explored a number of ways to transfer stitches to nearby needles and to use bridging for casting on and binding off in the middle of a row. All of that information can be applied to beginning and ending ladders as well.

Narrow ladders are much easier to form than very wide or extreme ladders because you can usually just transfer a stitch to an adjacent needle, place the empty needle in non—working position and continue knitting. Although you can also opt to leave some needles in non—working position when you cast on, with many fabrics you will probably find that this produces a sloppy lower edge. For that reason, I almost always cast on with waste yarn and, after knitting 8-10 rows and hanging some claw weights, knit 1 (or more) row with my main yarn and then transfer stitches as needed. That step is understood on most of the charts that follow.

If your ladders begin after just one row at the lower edge, it often doesn't matter how you begin them. The transfers will probably disappear into a band or trim. If, however, you want to introduce wide ladders mid—garment or after more than a few rows from the bottom edge, you will probably find that they look best when the bottom of each ladder is formed by binding off, rather than transferring, specific stitches. This almost always requires bridging in order to use the free yarn mid—row. If the stitches are very large, the yarn quite stretchy or there are only a few stitches involved, you may be able to use a latch tool to bind off without any bridging, but I usually find that it is worth the few extra minutes to bridge.

At the other end of things, depending on the location in a garment or the fabric's ultimate use, you can end some ladders by using the EON method I described in the previous chapter for completing eyelets. In other cases, you will find it necessary to bridge and cast on stitches mid—row. (see pg 11). You can use whatever bind offs or cast ons you prefer and may want to match the two by using, for example, a latch tool method to begin and to end the same ladder. The charts and directions for each of the examples will illustrate the beginning and/or ending of the ladders only where it is important to the overall effect or structure.

Ladder Specifics

Initially I tried to divide these ladder designs into very narrow categories, but the more I experimented, the more I found that the categories overlapped or weren't as clearly defined as I had first thought. In spite of that, I hope I have divided them into related groups, beginning with some fairly basic ladders.

From there, they branch out to effects based on traveling, transferred, rehung and lifted stitches; to shaped, cabled and short rowed ladders. There's a group that are as much eyelets as they are ladders, some double bed ladders and some that include simple patterning. Sometimes I grouped several samples together when each grew directly out of the previous example and I felt it would help you to follow my thinking to see how an idea developed. Although I focused on hand manipulated patterning for a few patterned ladder samples, you may find that some of these patterns can be adapted to punch card or electronic machines to minimize the hand—manipulations.

Basic Ladders

L1 The first sample and chart show four different ladders created by NDLS in NWP and drop stitch. Remember that while the knit side of the fabric faces you in the photographs, the charts always indicate the purl

L1
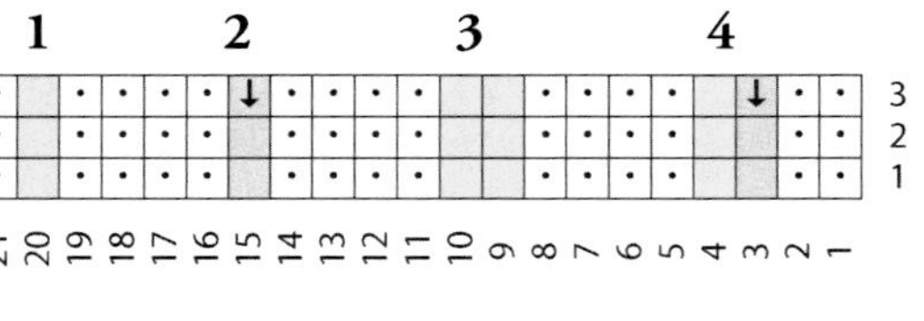

L1

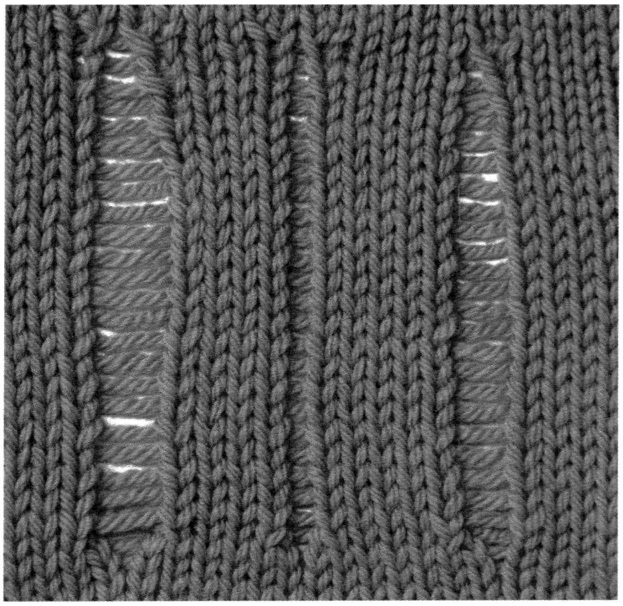

L2

side and are reversed left and right. The ladder formed over NDL 20 is barely visible and, in fact, looks more like a defective NDL track than a ladder. It was created by transferring ST 20 to an adj NDL then leaving the empty NDL in NWP and is not shown in the photo.

The second ladder was formed by transferring ST 15 to an adj NDL, then returning the empty NDL to WP. At the end of the knitting, the STS were dropped from NDL 15 to create a somewhat wider, more noticeable ladder.

The third ladder was formed by transferring STS 9 and 10 to adj NDLS and leaving the emptied NDLS in NWP. This ladder is wider than the first, but not as wide as the second. The fourth ladder was formed by transferring STS from NDLS 3 and 4 to adj NDLS, placing NDL 4 in NWP and NDL 3 in WP. Later, the STS were dropped from NDL 3, creating the widest ladder of the four.

L2 (no chart) shows one method of stabilizing a ladder so that it doesn't close in on itself later on. At the beginning of the ladder, 2 STS were transferred to adj NDLS. After a number of rows, one of the empty NDLS was brought back to work by making a full—fashioned increase, which positions the increase 1 ST from the edge of the ladder and helps to keep it open.

L3

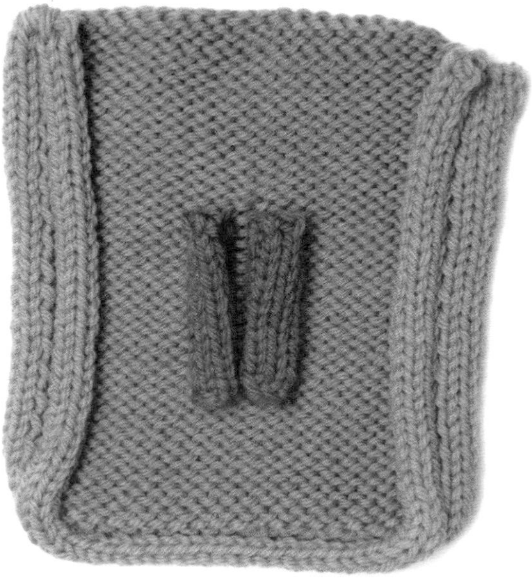

Join—as—you—Knit Ladders

L3 Ladders can be used for attaching join—as—you—knit edgings and trims quickly and easily because you don't need to poke around or guess where to insert your transfer tool to pick up the edge. The green border on and the small blue square at the center of the swatch were pre—knitted as strips with 4 STS on either side of a 2-ST ladder. I calculated the length of the edging strip based on my gauge and I tagged the corner points on the strip so I didn't have to count or improvise when re—hanging it on the machine.

The center of the strip acts as the C/O edge of the swatch. With the purl side of the strip facing me, I folded it in half lengthwise (along the ladder) and, working between the corner tags on the strip, hung 3 out of every 4 ladder bars across the required number of NDLS. The 3:4 ratio accounts for the difference in ST and row gauges.

Then, as I knitted the swatch, I P/U a ladder bar at each side and hung it on the edge NDL. I P/U one bar each side, E/R because I was joining rows to rows. You could also P/U every—other—bar of the ladder every A/R, depending on the gauge of your fabric. Just be consistent.

The patch at the center of the fabric was applied to the purl side of the fabric by P/U 1 ladder bar E/R and hanging it on the same NDL each time. Placing the patch on the knit side would require some fairly clumsy manipulations, removing STS from their NDLS to work underneath the fabric. It isn't impossible, but neither is it very practical.

To apply strips like this to the knit side of the fabric, do so after the fabric is removed from the machine by P/U knit STS from the fabric and hanging them on the ladder NDLS as you knit the patch or strip.

While I applied both the edging and the patch along straight lines, you can also let strips and shapes meander across the surface of the fabric by hanging the ladder bars on different NDLS. It is always a good idea to plan and chart out samples like that in advance.

L4 The band across the bottom of the next sample was pre—knitted and hung across the NDLS to act as the C/O edge. In this case, an 8-NDL ladder was bordered by 4 STS at each side. The piece was knitted a multiple of 6 rows and bound off at the correct length, leaving a 12" tail.

With the purl side of the band facing you, use a crochet hook or a latch tool to chain groups of three ladder bars through the next three and then secure the last with the yarn tail. The tripled strands assure that the chaining stands out and creates an over—sized effect in the band. To hang the band on the machine, work with the knit side of the band facing you to pick up three out of every four stitches along the back edge of one of the curled edges of the trim.

Needle—Woven Ladders

L5 and L6 Ladders often form the base for needle woven accents like this plaid. The original swatch was knitted with a couple of 2-NDL ladders as well as some well—spaced rows knitted at ST size 10. You can also use drop ST to create large, weavable rows of STS.

This is an excellent way to use up left over bits of yarn and to utilize yarns that may be too heavy to knit on your machine. Just remember that the larger the weaving yarn, the wider the ladders (and the looser the enlarged rows) need to be to accommodate them.

Begin by blocking the laddered fabric. I find it easiest to work with the purl side of the fabric facing me and my weaving yarns threaded through a blunt tapestry needle to avoid splitting the STS. When you weave over one, under one, the ladder bars will probably show (as they do in my example). However, if you work over two and under two the weaving yarn packs closer together and covers the ladders as it does in the square woven ladder on page 93.

L4

L5

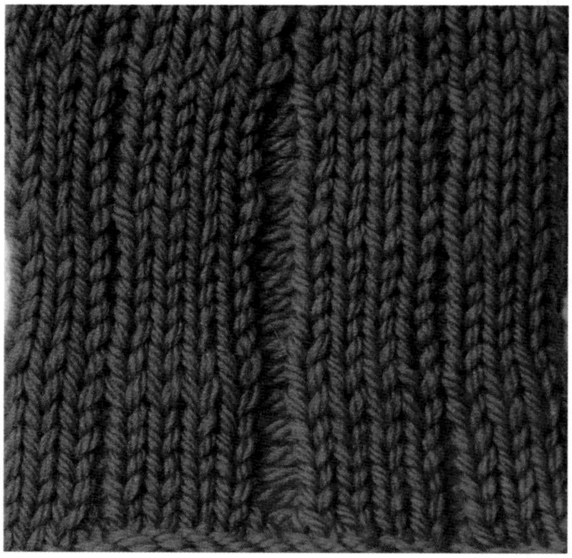

L6

Stabilized Ladders

L7 shows a pair of stabilized ladders. Each of these ladders was created by transferring the 4th and 5th STS to the 6th NDL, then bringing the 5th NDL back to WP. Needle 5 was allowed to knit for 2 rows, then dropped. The enlarged STS were caught on a transfer tool from behind and then the tool was twisted to the right (or left) to form an e—wrap, which was deposited on the adj NDL at right (or left). The direction you twist is less important than being consistent about it unless you plan to alternate throughout. If you chose to stabilize a narrow, 2-stitch ladder like this one without using drop stitch first, the shorter bars will probably close up the ladder and create a vertical crease instead.

L7

L8 shows the same kind of twisted STS technique to stabilize the ladders, but it requires a pair of transfer tools to work a 2-step decrease. First use a 2-prong tool to remove 2 STS from their NDLS along one edge of the ladder. Use a single prong tool to twist the ladder bars and place them on the second empty NDL from the edge before replacing the 2 STS on their NDLS. This 2-step approach places the twists on the knit side of the fabric, instead of hiding them on the back.

L8

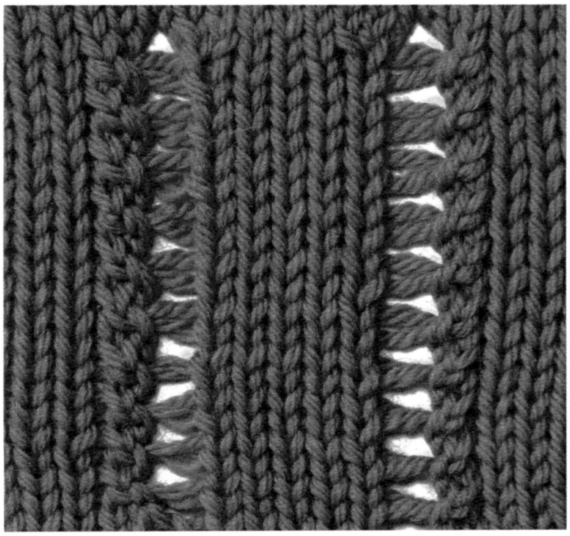

L9 The base and top of this wide ladder were worked by bridging and B/O and C/O 5 STS. The decorative, stabilizing effect was worked as follows: Knit 2 rows. Lift the first (lowest) bar of the ladder onto the first WP NDL at right. Knit 1 row and then lift the next bar from the bottom onto the first WP NDL at left. Continue lifting the lowest bar of the ladder after each knitted row, alternating left and right sides. I find it helpful to coordinate the carriage side to the lifting left or right. To work a larger version of this effect, you can lift two bars after every two knitted rows, beginning the sequence after the first four rows.

L9

L10

L11

L12

Ladder Fringes

L10 To knit fringe on the side of a scarf or other item, C/O the required number of NDLS. Skip the next 30-40 NDLS on the carriage side and C/O 2 more NDLS. Knit 1 row and then skip 30-40 NDLS at the second side and C/O 2 more NDLS.

Knit the entire scarf and B/O all of the STS *except* the extra 2 STS at each side. Let these STS drop and then ravel the loops at each side edge, catching them on a dowel or hand knitting needle so you can pull them taut as you block the scarf. With plain fringes, the edge STS usually lose their definition and start to spread. To avoid this, you need to either knot or twist the fringes in groups.

To twist the fringe, hold groups of 3 (for example) strands of yarn in each hand and separately twist both groups to the right until they are tightly over—twisted and start to kink up on themselves. Hold the two twisted groups *together* and twist to the left. Tie a knot in the end to secure. After the item is washed or steamed you can probably trim off the knots as the twist should be set by the finishing. For very wide pieces that use most of the needles on the bed, you can still create extra length at the sides by using drop stitch to enlarge the ladders.

L11 In addition to fringing the side edges, you can also use fringe to join pieces of fabric together. In that case, when twisting the fringes (or leaving them loose) tie knots close to the base fabric to ensure a secure join.

L12 is also a fringed sample, but the fringe is part of a unique B/O method. Knit the required number of rows for your scarf (etc) and end COL. Drop the ST size by two numbers. At the right edge, skip 10 NDLS and then bring 1 NDL to WP. Knit 1 row. COR. Bring 1 more NDL to WP at right so there are 2 WP NDLS and 10 empty NDLS between them and the edge of the fabric. Set the carriage to hold and bring all NDLS to HP *except* the two extra NDLS at right and the first NDL on the right of the main knitting. These are the only 3 NDLS in WP.

[*Move the 2nd scarf ST to the 1st scarf NDL and knit 2 rows. Move the 3rd scarf ST to the first scarf NDL and knit 2 rows. To fill the resulting gap between the WP and HP NDLS, move the ST on the first NDL of the main knitting over by one NDL to the left and at the same time move the two fringe NDLS over to the left, thus maintaining the 10 NWP NDL spacing between them and the edge of the main knitting.** Repeat * to ** once. Then move both the 2nd and 3rd STS to the 1st NDL and knit 2 rows.] Repeat [to] until all of the STS have been B/O. Twist, knot or braid the fringes to secure.
To work this kind of fringe on both ends of a scarf, begin the scarf on waste yarn. Complete the scarf and the B/O fringe. Then, rehang the starting STS and work the B/O method again.

L13 is also a fringe bind off, but it secures the fringes in a way that does not require knotting or twisting to finish them. Set up and begin as for the previous sample with 10 NWP NDLS between the edge of the scarf and the fringing NDLS. All NDLS except the two extra NDLS and the 1st ST on the right are in HP.

Stitches are always transferred to the first scarf NDL at the right and the empty NDLS placed in NWP as follows: *Use a single—prong transfer tool to remove the 3rd scarf ST and place it on the 1st scarf NDL. Knit 2 rows. Move the 4th scarf ST to the first scarf NDL and knit 2 rows. Move all STS to the left, maintaining the 10 empty NWP NDLS between the scarf and the fringe NDLS. Move the 3rd ST to the first scarf NDL and knit 2 rows. Then move the 2nd scarf ST to the first scarf NDL and knit 2 rows. Shift STS as necessary to close the gap and maintain fringe spacing.** Repeat * to ** until all STS are B/O.

L13

L14 and L15 Loop—to—loop joinings have always been a popular way of creating huge afghans from narrower panels and can also be used to join garment sections.

Knit two pieces, one fringed on the left and the other on the right. Depending on your yarn and how open you want the joining to be, you can vary the number of ladder NDLS to suit your taste. For example, in these swatches, I only skipped two NWP NDLS before adding a single fringe NDL.

Knit the desired length and then B/O all STS *except* the single fringe ST. Knit the second piece with the fringe on the opposite side. Ravel the loops (do not cut them) and block the pieces. I usually insert a blocking wire through the loops to tame them as I steam the pieces.

To join: Lay the two pieces side by side and crochet two loops from the left hand piece through two loops of the right piece. Work from side to side, chaining the loops and taking care to always insert the crochet hook the same way.

The decorative edge along the edges of the ladders of the 2-color swatch was created by working a twisted stitch every other row on the fringed edge of the fabric.

L14

L15

Laced Ladders

L16 Ladder bars of various widths are perfect for lacing ribbons or decorative yarns through. They also provide an excellent base for crochet, decorative trims or structural additions.

L17 You can gather a scarf by lacing a double strand of yarn through a ladder running down the center as long as you have allowed extra length. You should knit the scarf at least twice as long as you want it to be once gathered.

L16

L17

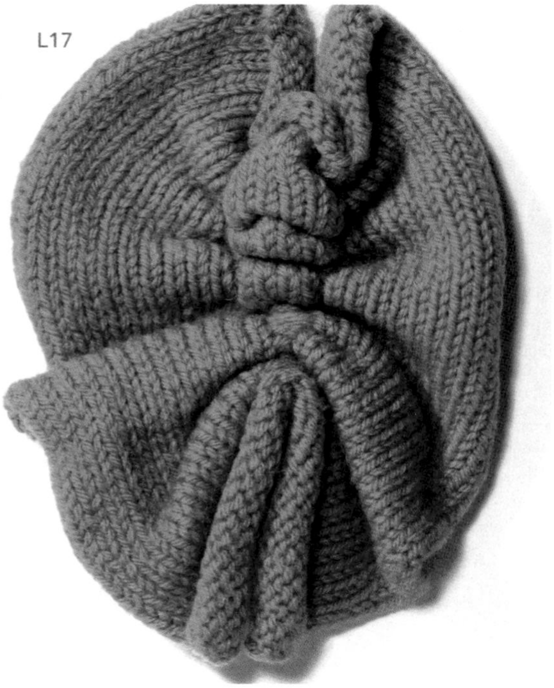

Ladders Formed by Transferring Stitches

There are samples throughout this book that rely on transferred stitches, but the following ladder fabrics were worked *primarily* by transferring stitches. In many instances, the transfers serve two purposes. First and foremost they shift the position or width of the nearby ladder. They may also serve to stabilize the ladders.

L18 is a simple mesh created on a framework of two WP NDLS alternating with two NWP NDLS. The transfers were made every 3rd row and alternate left and right as shown on the chart. The empty NDLS remain in WP after making the transfers so that they cast back on and begin knitting immediately. They do *not* form eyelets. Specifically, in row 1 the ST on NDL 6 is transferred to NDL 5 and NDL 6 remains in WP, which is why it shows a purl stitch, rather than an eyelet symbol in that space.

This is an extremely stable mesh. The proportion of NDLS in WP to those in NWP is about equal so the fabric looks well balanced. You can also work a version of this fabric with wider ladders, which will change that proportion and create a totally different look.

L19 has 3-ST ladders alternating with columns of STS that change from three to one STS wide. The transfers are made every 3/R in each alternate repeat and are paired with increases in the companion repeat. The increases are accomplished in the simplest way by

L18

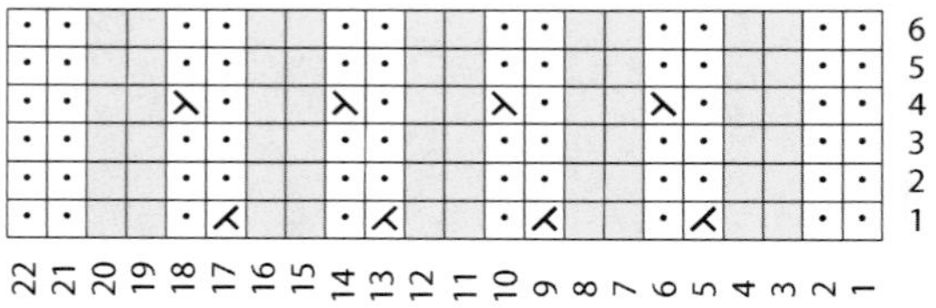

L18

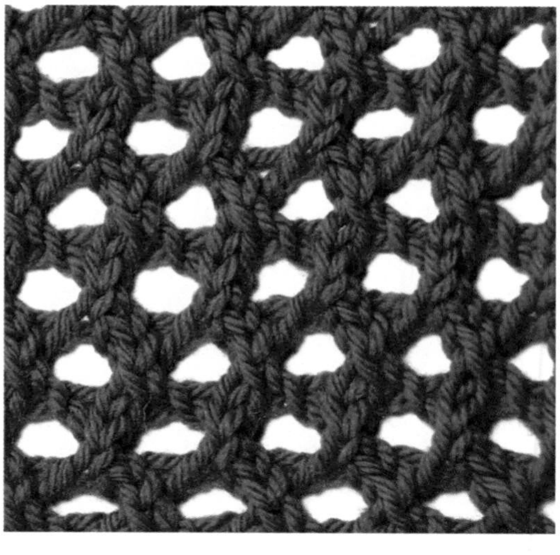

L19

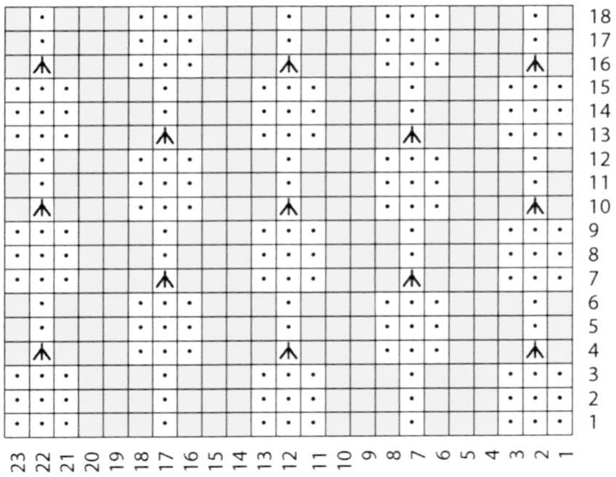

L20

bringing an empty NDL from NWP to WP. Before knitting row 4, for example, STS 1 and 3 are transferred to NDL 2 and NDLS 6 and 8 are moved from NWP to WP. L20 is a slightly larger version of the same pattern arrangement.

L21

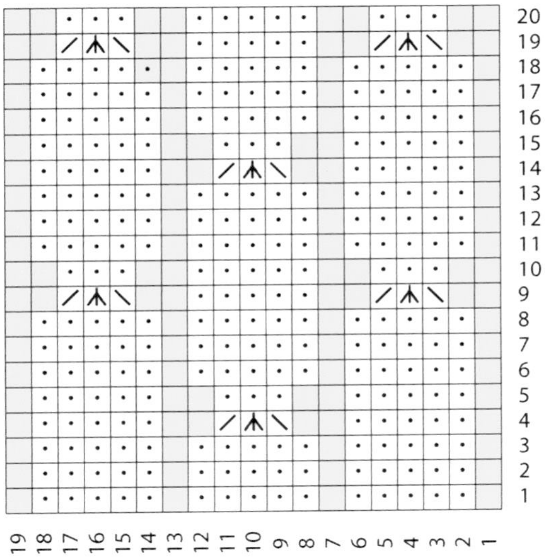

L19

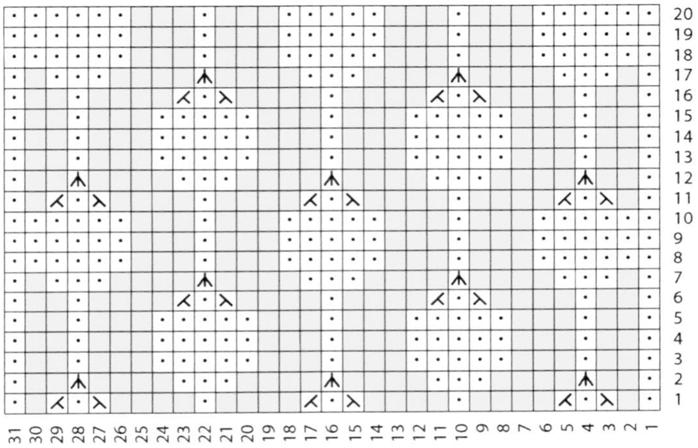

L20

L21 features single ST ladders,with transfers made every 5th row. Use a 2-prong transfer tool to move STS 8 and 9 one NDL to the left. Then move STS 11 and 12 one NDL to the right. There are 3 STS on NDL 10, the center NDL, Knit 2 rows before moving the empty 8th and 12th NDLS back into WP. That delay creates the slightly zigzagged effect in the ladders.

L21

L22 has single NDL ladders and lozenges of 3STS forming between them as they shift. Before knitting row 2, transfer the ST from NDL 2 to NDL 3 and the ST from NDL 6 to NDL 5. Before row 3, transfer the STS from NDLS 3 and 5 to NDL 4 and bring the empty 9th and 11th NDLS to WP.

The transfers in L23 are skipped transfers, as are the cable crossings. In row 2, the cables are formed by using a pair of single—prong transfer tools to cross STS 8 and 10 behind ST 9, which remains on its NDL. If you look at the cable crossings on the fabric, you will notice that the 9th ST continues straight up the fabric, uninterrupted, and the STS are crossed behind it. Rather than a cabled effect, the STS appear "tied".

At row 6 (and every 6th row thereafter), STS 2 and 8 are transferred across the ladder to NDLS 4 and 6 to create the alternation in the pattern as the placement of single STS and groups of 3 STS shift. In the next repeat, STS 6 and 12 are transferred across the ladder to NDLS 8 and 10.

L22

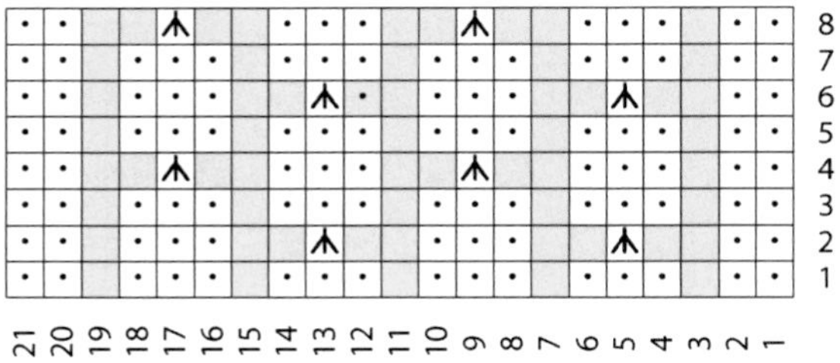

L22

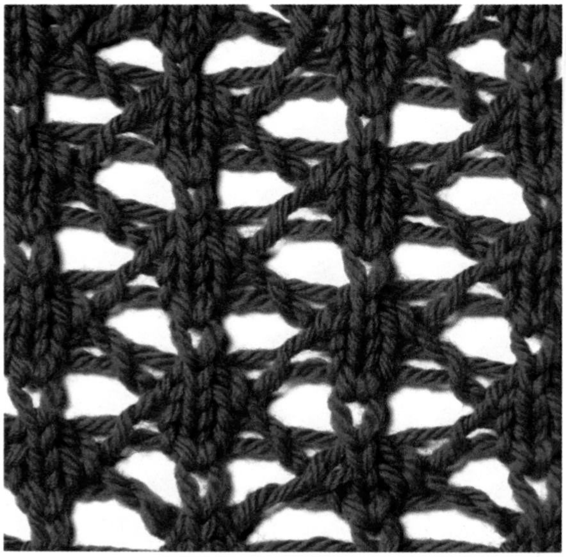

L23

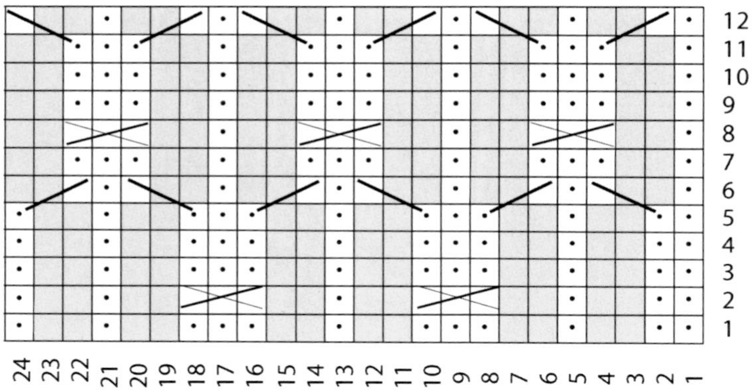

L23

L24

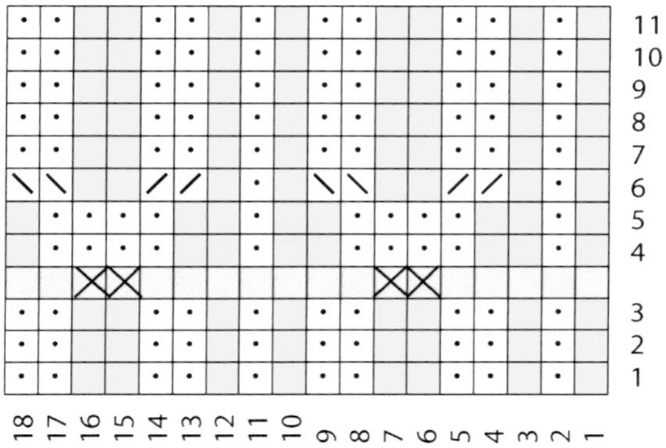

L24

L25

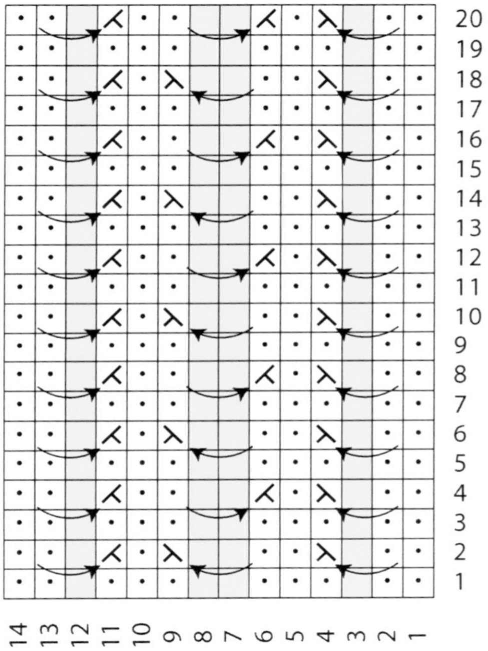

L25

L24 includes a prep (non—knitted) row after row 3 on the chart. Before knitting the 4th (and every following 10th row), make a stacked decrease by moving STS 4 and 5 and STS 8 and 9 to NDLS 6 and 7. Bring NDLS 5 and 8 to WP before knitting the next 2 rows. Before knitting row 6, move STS 5 and 6 to NDLS 5 and 4 and STS 7 and 8 to NDLS 8 and 9.

This pattern always repeats on the same NDLS, rather than alternating placement. The stacked decreases make a very stable fabric and the ladders that result from the transfers create a pattern of eyelet—like spaces alongside. In fact, at first glance this looks more like an eyelet pattern than one created by ladders.

L25 utilizes skipped transfers. The STS that form the columns at either side of the swatch are always transferred to the left or right. The transfers in the center alternate left and right, crossing over a 2-NDL ladder, which causes a zigzag arrangement of the resulting eyelet effect. The emptied NDLS remain in WP so that they C/O and continue knitting.

Because these are all 1-step transfers where the transferred STS remain on the purl side of the fabric, the transfers themselves don't contribute much to the knit surface of the fabric, though they do stabilize the open spaces. You could, of course, work 2-step transfers instead to add some interest along side the ladders.

L26 is decorative and at first glance looks as though there must be some cables or twisted STS. The effect is, in fact, created by transferring STS behind adjacent STS to bring ladder NDLS back to work. For example, before knitting row 3, transfer ST 3 to the empty NDL 1, passing behind the ST on NDL 2. Then put NDL 3 in NWP. Move ST 6 to NDL 8, passing behind ST 7 and then put NDL 6 in NWP.

This is a single tool version of twisted STS and the mesh it creates is extremely stable. To create an even more open fabric, you could start with wider ladders and continue moving the STS towards each other until they meet, then reverse direction. This fabric looks more complicated than it is, but this is an extremely fast method to execute.

L27 These staggered ladders are shaped by twisted STS (or 1x1 cables), making full fashioned transfers at the same time. Remove 2 STS on a 2-prong tool, insert a

L26

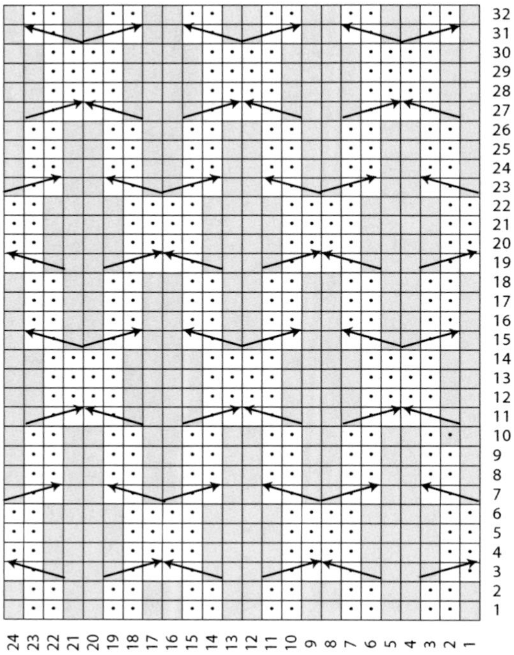

L27

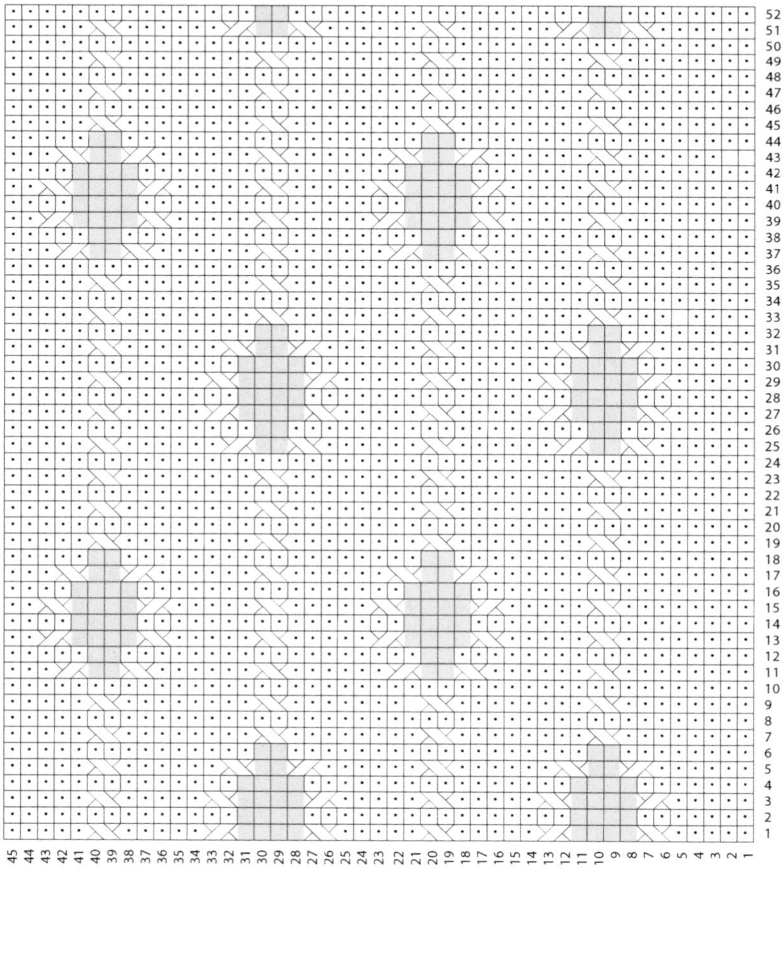

L26

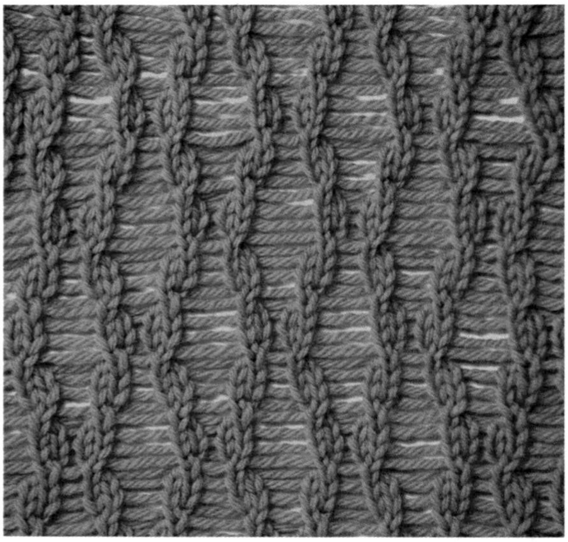

L27

second tool from above and remove the first tool. Rotate the tool holding the STS in the direction the STS are traveling (i.e. the direction the ladder is widening) and then replace the STS on one of the empty NDLS and the next adjacent NDL that already holds a ST. Place the remaining empty NDL in NWP.

When closing shapes, increase by making a twisted ST towards the center of the shape and replacing the 2 STS on the next empty NDL and the last one holding a ST. Fill the empty NDL created by the movement by P/U the purl bar of either adj ST. Be consistent from one P/U to the next. That is, always P/U the purl bump from the adj, plain ST or from the base of the twisted ST. You could also choose to just bring the empty NDL to WP and let it cast on and begin knitting, forming an eyelet alongside the twist. Depending on the number of plain STS between repeats, this might be a nice addition — or a sorry distraction so do a sample to compare the two effects.

L28 (chart only) is an old favorite of mine, Peacock Tails. The differences between these samples is the number of plain STS between each repeat and the number of plain rows knitted after each repeat. L28 has 5 plain STS between repeats and 2 rows after completing the eyelets.

At the start of each pattern repeat, there is a prep row. Transfer STS 3, 4, 5 and STS 7, 8, 9 to NDL 6. Before knitting the next row, bring the empty 3rd and 9th NDLS to WP. There are 7 STS on the 6th NDL so bring it to HP to make sure it knits cleanly. Knit the first row and then bring the next 2 empty NDLS to WP and knit 1 row. Bring the last 2 empty NDLS to WP and knit 4 rows to begin the next repeat with the motifs alternating position.

Note that the chart shows a half repeat at the edges of the second repeat. Also, although most machines actually *will* knit the 7 STS on the center NDL of each repeat, if your machine balks at the prospect, leave those NDLS in HP (do not set the carriage to knit them back) when knitting the first row and then just hand knit each NDL before continuing.

L29

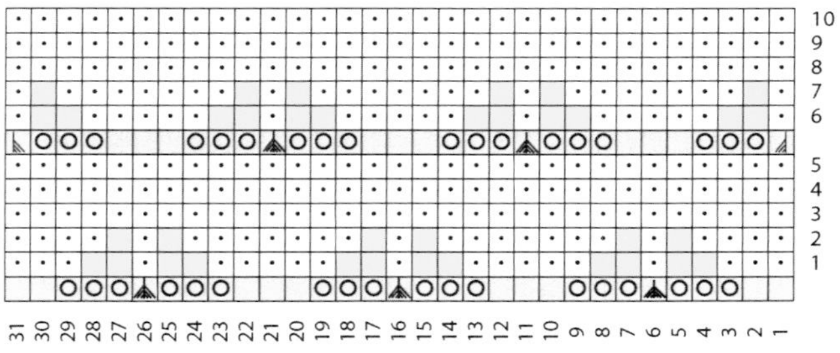

L28

With fewer rows between repeats, the fabric is very open, with the lozenges of STS smaller and only connected by a few STS. Its an effect that I like for mohair where the texture helps to fill the empty spaces. It also uses a whole lot less yarn.

L29-31The next three examples were knitted with only 1 ST between each pattern repeat. L29 has 2 rows at the end of each repeat (1 row to complete the C/O plus 1 more row), L30 has 3 rows and L31 has 4 rows.

L30

L31

L32

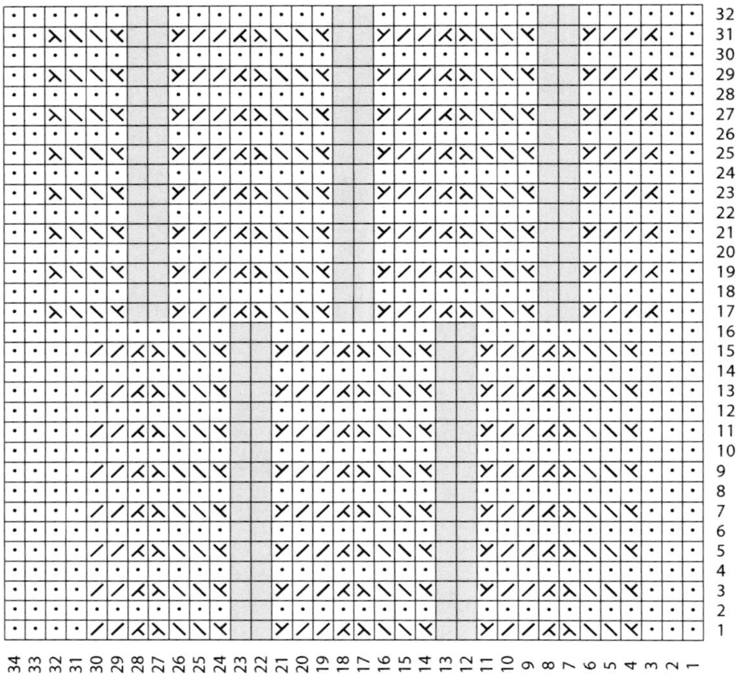

L32

The ladders in L32 almost disappear into the fabric, but they contribute to the patterning and to the drape of the fabric. The pattern on the chart shows alternating placement of the 16 row repeats, but you can knit fewer or more rows.

The 3 STS at each edge of the ladders are moved away from the ladder with a 3-prong tool. Before knitting the next 2 rows, make a ST on the emptied NDL by P/U the purl bar of the adj ST. The width of the ladder is unchanged by the transfers, but they contribute to the full fashioned detailing that defines this pattern. Although you can easily work this pattern with wider ladders, they may spread as this method does not stabilize them. Note that the ladder bars lie straight across the spaces in pairs.

L33 is very similar to L32 with some differences. First of all, the 3-ST transfers are made to the left/right on *alternate* rows, not all at the same time. Secondly, the NDLS emptied by the transfers immediately return to WP to C/O and start knitting. It is not necessary to P/U the purl bars of adjacent STS as was done in the previous example. The ladder bars twist, creating open, lacy lozenges in the fabric. Last of all, these repeats are only 10 rows, rather than 16. The chart shows a partial repeat only to illustrate the alternating transfers.

L33

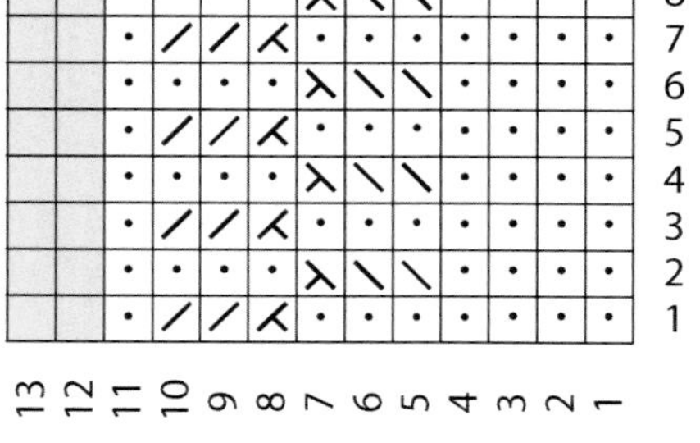

L33

Traveling Ladders

Traveling ladders are formed when the stitches that define them are continuously shifted one or more needles to the left (or right) every so many rows. Those transfers may occur every row, every other row or every three or more rows and depending on the desired result, the transfers may also be made at very irregular intervals.

L34 features a single ST that travels back and forth across the ladder every 2 rows, shaping the ladder as triangles at each side. The ladder was started by transferring 2 STS to NDL 10 and 2 STS to NDL 5; you could also bridge to B/O those STS. It was ended by bridging and e—wrapping the empty NDLS.

There is no decreasing or increasing involved here. When the ST is transferred to an adjacent empty NDL, the NDL it was transferred from is placed in NWP to become part of the ladder. At each side of the traveling ST, the ladder grows from a single NDL to 4 NDLS wide and then reduces back down to a single NDL. As the triangle ladder at one side grows wider, the one on the other side narrows.

The traveling STS are stabilized by making half—transfers at rows 10 and 12, etc. To make a half—transfer at row 10, the ST that was on NDL 9 was only partially transferred to NDL 10. One leg of the ST is caught by NDL 10 while the other leg remains on NDL 9.

L34

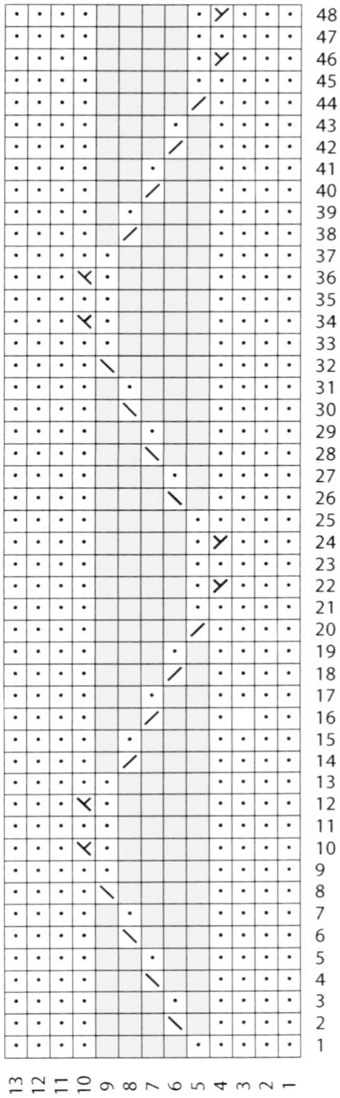

L34

L35

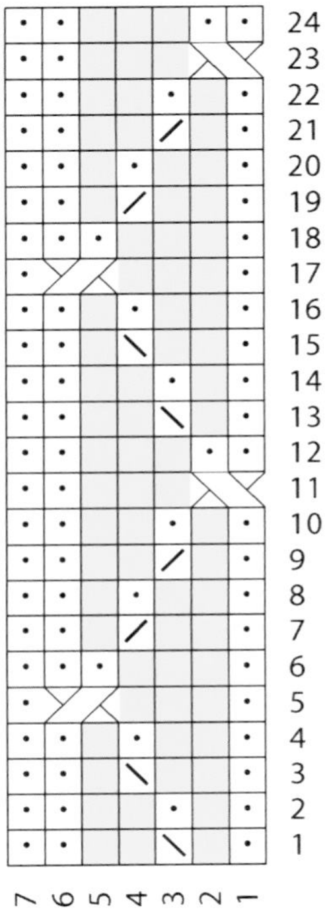

L35

L35 also features a single traveling ST that forms two triangular ladders that increase and decrease in width as the single ST zigzags back and forth. A traveling ST can be stabilized by crossing/twisting it with the edge ST as shown on the chart or by pulling one ST through the other as seen on the fabric.

L36 illustrates yet another way of stabilizing a ladder by twisting the pair of STS that travel back and forth. Just remember that when the STS travel left, you must twist the tool to the left; when traveling right, twist to the right.

Each time the pair of twisted STS is replaced on the NDLS, they are placed 1 NDL closer to the edge towards which they are traveling, leaving a wider ladder behind. To stabilize this ladder, at each edge make two twists — one in the old direction and the next in the

L36

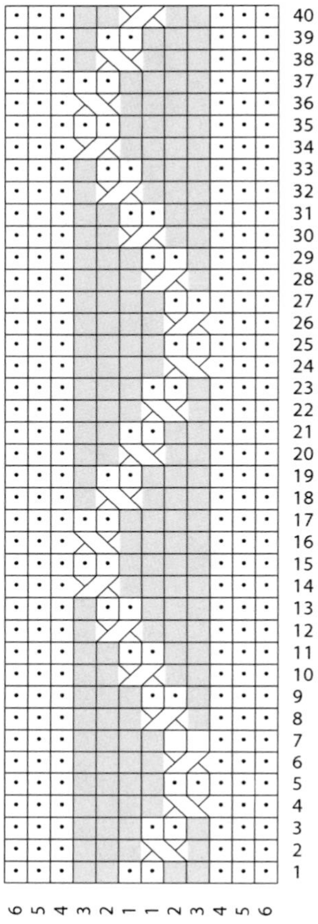

L36

L37

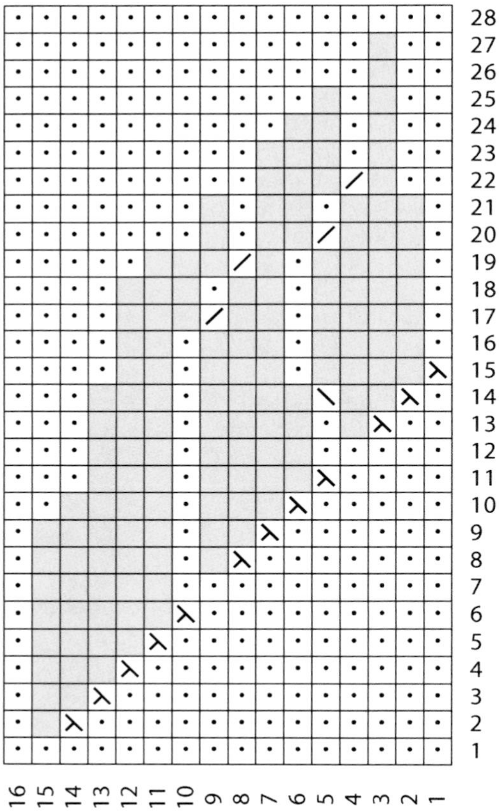

L37

new direction the STS will begin traveling. Also, P/U the purl bar from the plain (untwisted) row between the two edge twists (row 5, for example) and hang it on the NDL at the edge of the ladder.

L37 is an abstract leaf shaped by traveling ladders and STS. It begins with a single NDL (15) in NWP and then the ladder increases in width as adj STS are decreased with 2-step, full fashioned decreases. The decreases are worked E/R and maintain the same ST on the front of the fabric, creating the strong line that accents the lower edge of the leaf.

While the lower edge of the leaf is shaped by the 2-step decreases, there are also some plain traveling stitches in rows 14, 17, 19, 20 and 22. The empty ladder NDLS were brought back to WP sporadically. When done every row, the ladder bars are straight, but will twist whenever there are two rows knitted after bringing an empty NDL to WP. This is important to remember moving forward to more complex designs.

Rather than just diving in, abstract shapes like this one should be planned in advance in order to guarantee that the shape will turn out somewhat as expected.

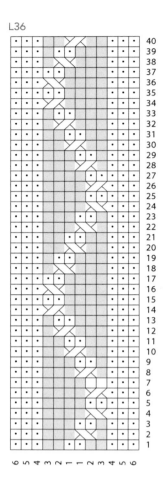

L38a, b, c The bars of the ladders in these 3 examples are very different due to the way that the STS travel and form the ladders. In the first example L38a , I made a simple decrease and brought an empty NDL to WP to C/O every row. These bars are straight and almost vertical. The second example L38b was worked the same way, except A/R instead of E/R. These bars are twisted and nearly vertical.

L38A

L38B

38C

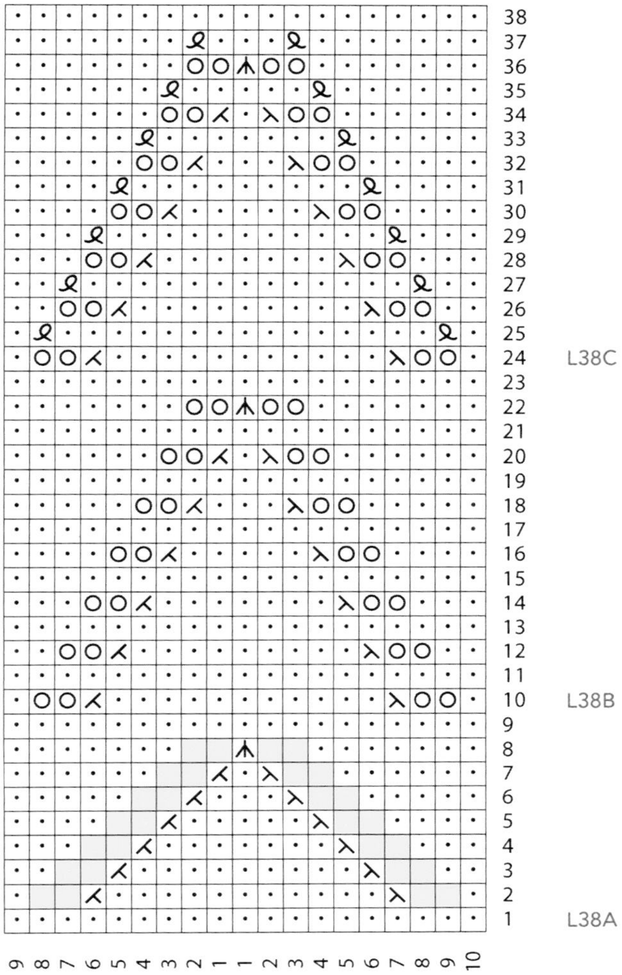

In the third example L38c I worked a twisted ST A/R to accomplish the increase, rather than letting the empty NDL C/O. The twisted ST was formed from the top bar of the ladder below the NDL. These bars are straight, paired and more horizontal.

Note that the outer edges of each of the ladders in L38c appears slightly different because The bar/tool was twisted to the right for both of them. This means that as the fabric faces you, the edge of the right ladder is correct according to the rules for twisted STS: always twist the tool in the direction the STS are traveling. That edge has a neatly "stitched" look to it. The outer edges of both the left and right ladders would look like this if the tool had been twisted to the left for the ladder traveling left and to the right for the ladder traveling to the right.

On the other hand, if you like the way the outer edge of the left ladder looks, you would accomplish this on both ladders by twisting the tool in the opposite direction the ladders are traveling. While this is not standard, neither is it necessarily incorrect as long as you are aware of it and in control at all times. Consistency is key here.

L39 adds a vertical ladder between the two traveling ladders and a small, wider ladder at the top so that the end effect is that of a dragonfly. The sample was worked from the chart with simple 1-step decreases, but 2-step decreases would create a sharper line along the edge of the wings. All of the increases were made by bringing an empty NDL to WP and because the increases were made A/R, the bars of the ladders are twisted.

L40 is a very common traveling ladder design that looks more complicated than it is. Begin by making transfers at row 3, moving ST 4 to NDL 3 (for example). Then make a lifted increase on NDL 7 by P/U the purl bar from the adj ST. Lifted increases make the mesh more stable than just bringing the empty NDL into WP, allowing it to C/O. While a simple increase is certainly faster, it may not hold up over time unless your yarn is very textured. My chart shows simple decreases, but be aware that a 2-step decrease would better accent the edges of the traveling STS.

For designs like this one, always work partial repeats as close to the edge as possible while maintaining a 2-ST edge. Even then, the edge of this fabric is somewhat irregular. For a straighter edge, maintain an even wider border of plain STS.

L39

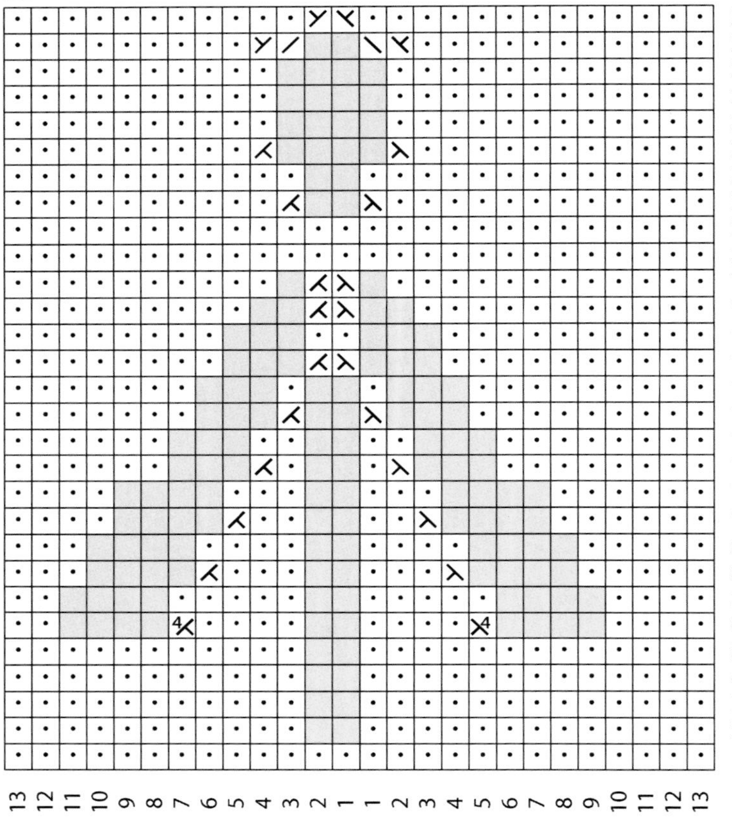

L40

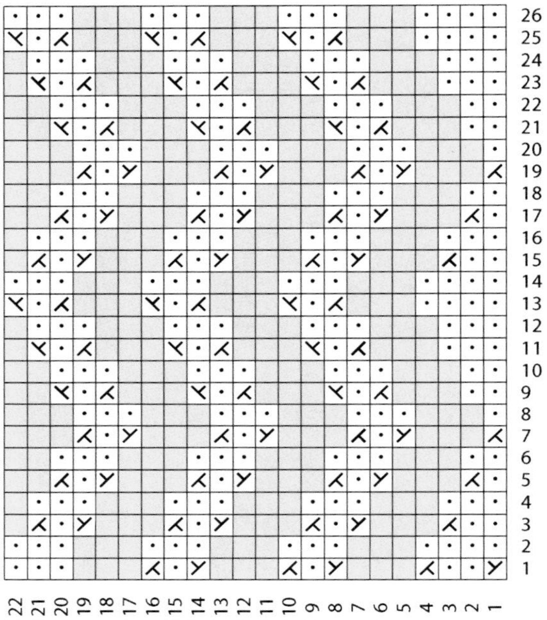

L39

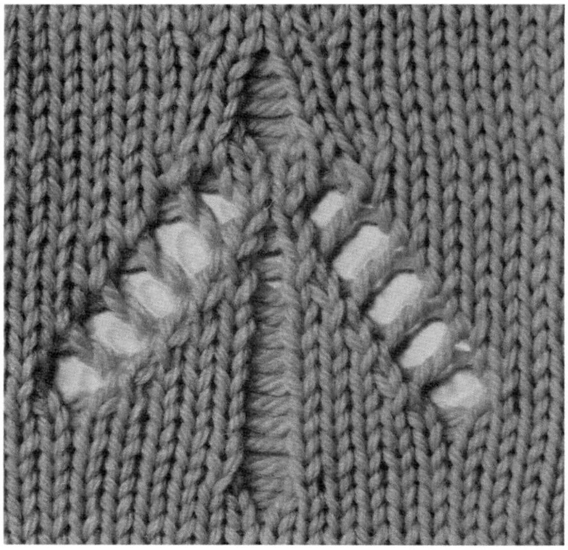

L40

L41

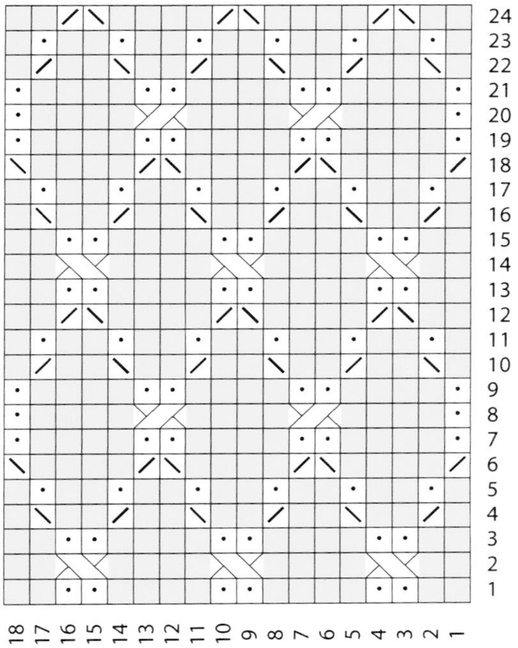

L41

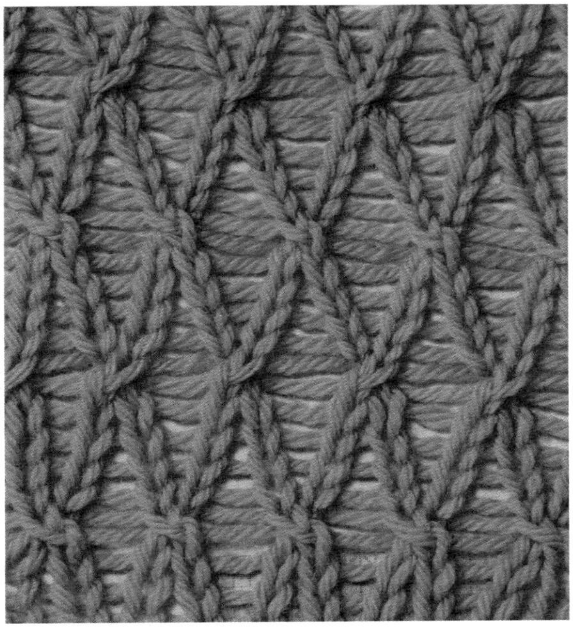

L41 employs 1x1 cables or twisted STS to stabilize the mesh. I chose to alternate the direction of the twist/crossing as the placement alternates to create a subtle woven look for the lines of traveling STS, but you can also cross all of them in the same direction.

The STS travel singly, moving over by 1 NDL. Then each pairs off with a ST that traveled from the opposite direction. Look at row 4 on the chart. ST 4 has been transferred to NDL 5 (towards the left) and ST 9 has been transferred to NDL 8 (to the right). They remain in this position for row 5, but prior to knitting row 6, they each move over by 1 more NDL which pairs them and prior to knitting row 8 they cross or twist. After row 9 the STS split off and travel singly in the opposite direction.

When the STS travel to the edges of the fabric, if there are not enough STS to cross cables, just maintain their position and resume traveling back when the direction changes again. With this design, you can maintain a single edge ST — or many — that never travels or crosses.

The next four samples are variations on a theme, with slight changes from one to the next. L42 is worked on columns of 4 WP NDLS alternating with 4 ST ladders.

L42

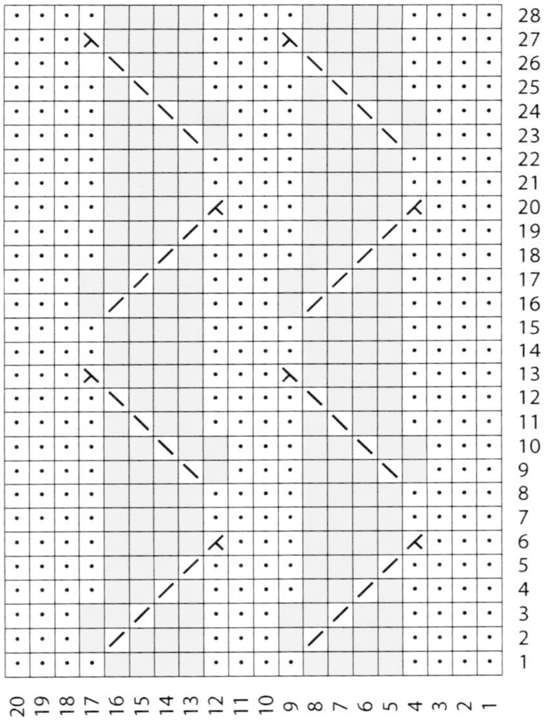

L42

The STS travel every row and the first ST that travels leaves an empty NDL that remains in NWP for the next 2 rows as shown in rows 2 and 3 at STS 9 and 17. Prior to row 4, the empty 9th NDL is returned to WP and continues knitting.

At row 6 the traveling ST is deposited on NDL 4 and then rows 7 and 8 are knitted with no travelers. At row 9 the next repeat begins, reversing direction. The undulating effect is created because of the way the NDLS are brought back into WP.

L43 is very similar in that the stitches travel back and forth through the ladders, but there are only 2 STS between ladders and, more importantly, the empty 7th NDL remains in WP when the ST transfers to NDL 6 before knitting row 2. It C/O immediately and forms a pronounced eyelet that adds to the lacy effect.

L44 takes the previous swatch one step further. First of all, the STS only travel in one direction, not back and forth. Secondly, the traveling STS begin by making a full—fashioned increase, P/U the purl bar of an adjacent ST and hang it on the empty NDL to the right of it. In row 2, for example, the purl bar of ST 9 is used to make a ST on NDL 8.

L45 creates the traveling ST in the same way as the previous swatch, by P/U the purl bar of an adj ST and hanging it on the empty NDL. The spacing is the same, alternating 4 NWP ladder NDLS with 2 WP NDLS. In this example, however, the STS branch towards each other instead of traveling in the same direction or zigzagging back and forth.

L46 This last variation creates a diamond effect in the fabric by reversing every alternate repeat.

L43

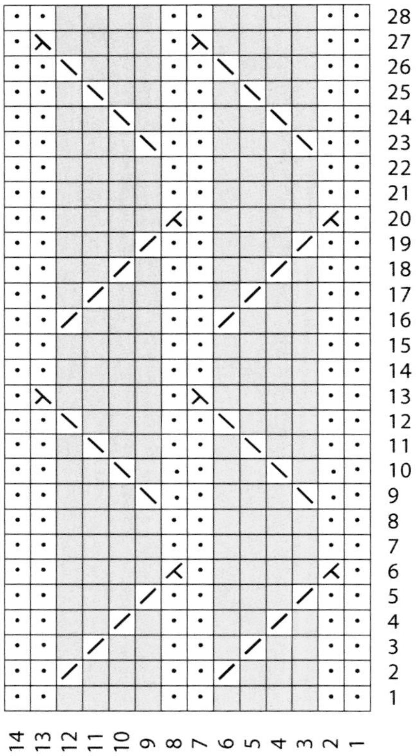

L44

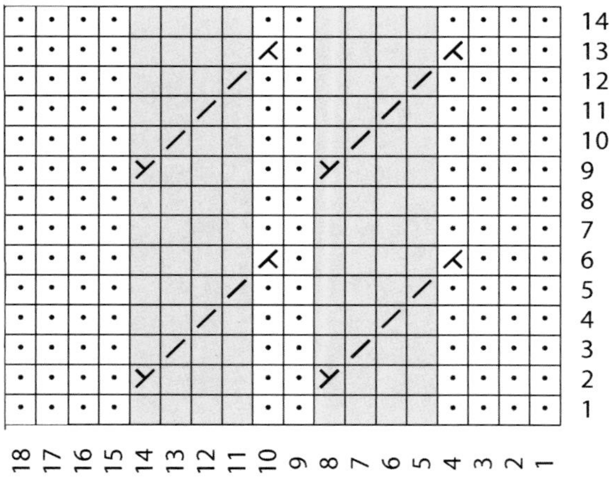

L45

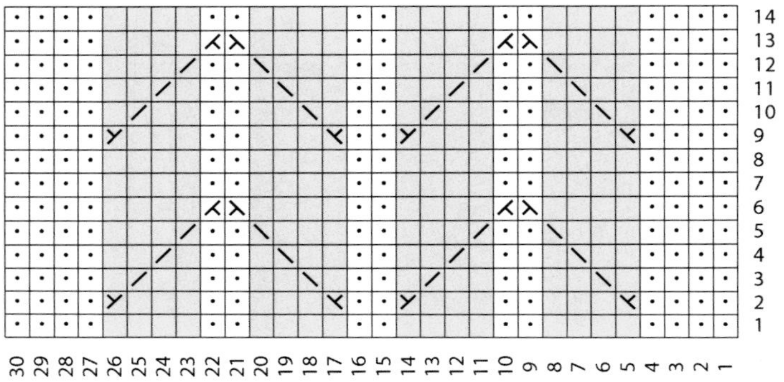

L46

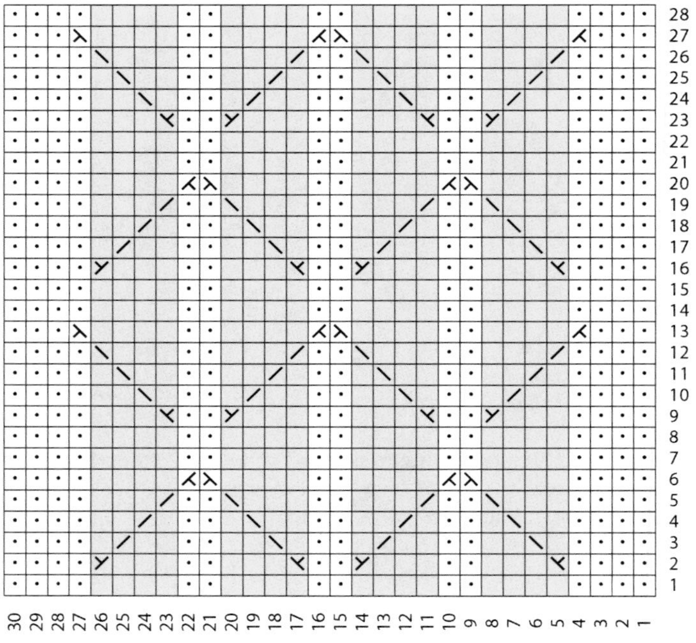

L43

L45

L44

L46

L47

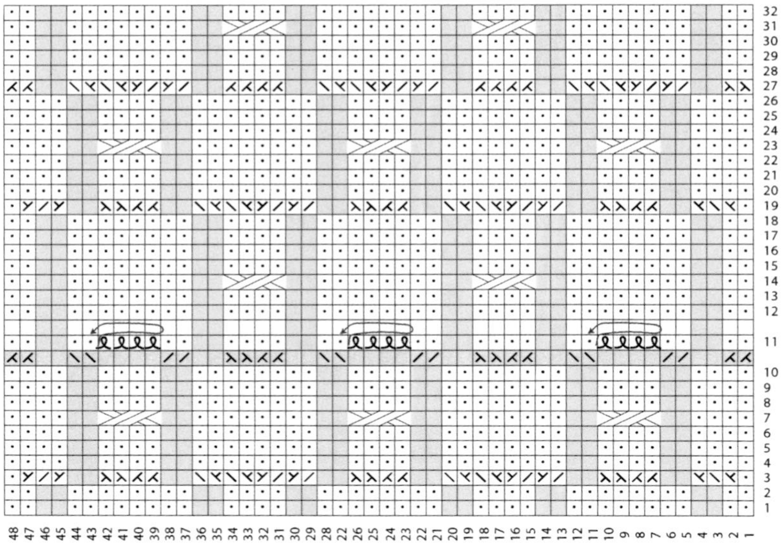

L47

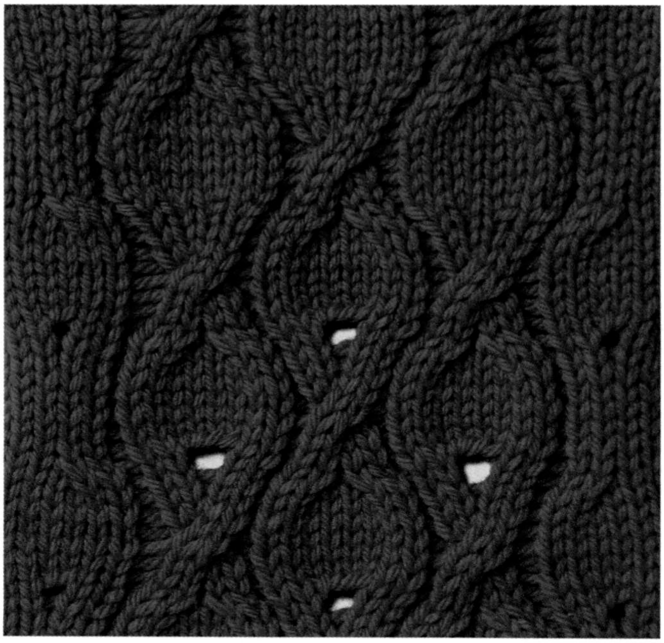

L48

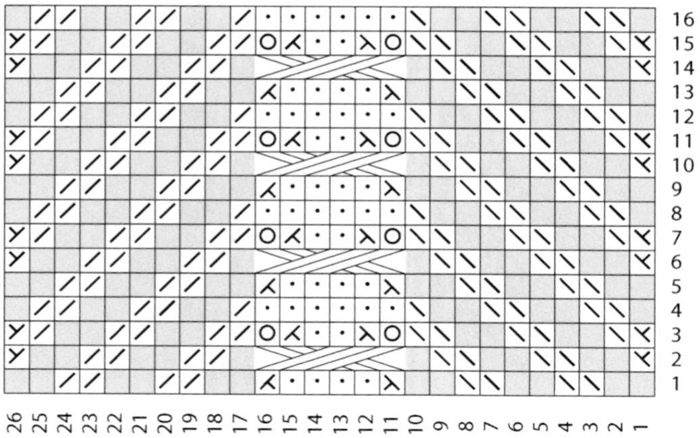

The ladders in L47 undulate around the cabled lozenges formed by the working NDLS. The decreases on NDLS 7-10 in row 3 and all prep rows are 2-step, stacked decreases worked as follows: With a 2-prong transfer too, move STS 7 and 8 to NDLS 5 and 6 and then move all of the STS back to NDLS 7 and 8. Work the other decreases in this row the same way to keep the outer STS on the front of the fabric as the STS travel towards each other.

In rows 3, 19 and 27, the empty NDLS are filled as follows: STS 15 - 18 are spread out over NDLS 13-20 by moving 1 ST to NDLS 13, 15, 18 and 20 and then P/U the purl bar of these STS to fill the remaining empty NDLS. If you prefer to form eyelets instead, proceed as shown on row 11 where the row is bridged in order to use the free yarn to e—wrap all 4 empty NDLS.

L48

The medallions formed by the traveling STS and cables are a great place to add popcorns or other lace transfers. If you replace the 2-step transfers with 1-step transfers, the effect will change totally.

I think that the panel shown on L48 would be fabulous at the center back or front of a garment where the lower edge would add interest to the shape. Although the lower edge drops down measurably, the other rows in the fabric are not distorted as a result. At the edges of the traveling ladders, you need to maintain plain border STS by making a new ST at each edge as shown on STS 1 and 26 on the chart.

Each pair of traveling STS begins with full—fashioned increases at the edges and although I transferred the STS every row, you could work a faster version by transferring them on A/R. Note that prior to knitting the row after each cabled row that the outer ST at each side of the cable (STS 11 & 16) is transferred to the adjacent NDL with the empty NDL left in WP to create an eyelet. The eyelet helps accentuate the cable column. All of the cables cross the same direction.

Drop Stitch Ladders

L49 These zigzagging ladders were created with traveling drop ST. To begin this fabric, C/O all NDLS and then make the decreases shown in row 1, bringing both empty NDLS to WP so they knit for 2 rows. For row 3, move ST 6 to NDL 7 and then move all STS from NDLS 7-9 to the right. This is a 2-step full—fashioned decrease. There should be 2 STS on NDL 6, 1 ST on NDLS 7 & 8 and the empty NDL 9 remains in WP to C/O and begin knitting. Knit 2 rows.

Continue making decreases A/R and note the change of direction at row 9. The shaded ST should be dropped every 10 rows to create the main ladders. The eyelets along side will form a secondary ladder effect that alternates sides with the change of direction.

If you do not want the eyelets, you can P/U the purl bar of an adj ST to fill the empty NDL. Also, note that the decrease at row 9 is simply for the eyelet. There are no other transfers.

L49

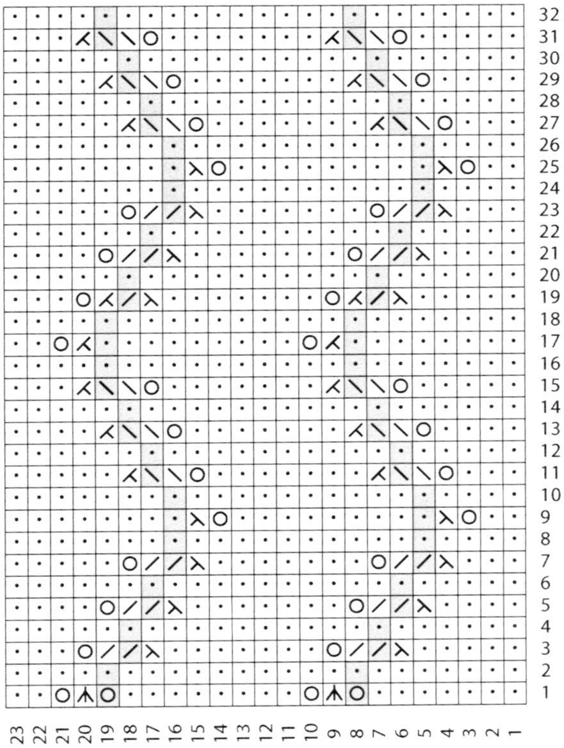

L50 also uses drop ST to create more open ladders. Begin this fabric with 5 WP NDLS alternating with 1 NWP NDL. On the chart, NDLS 1, 7, etc. are in NWP. Bring the empty NDLS back to WP. Knit 2 rows.

Move ST 5 to NDL 6 and move both STS back to NDL 5. NDL 6 is empty but remains in WP. Drop the

L49

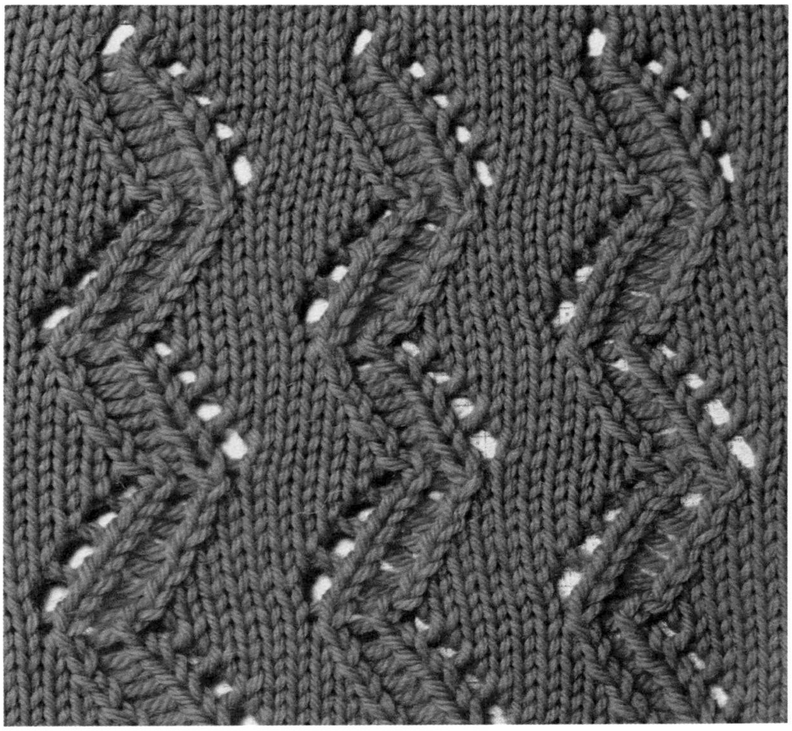

L50

L50

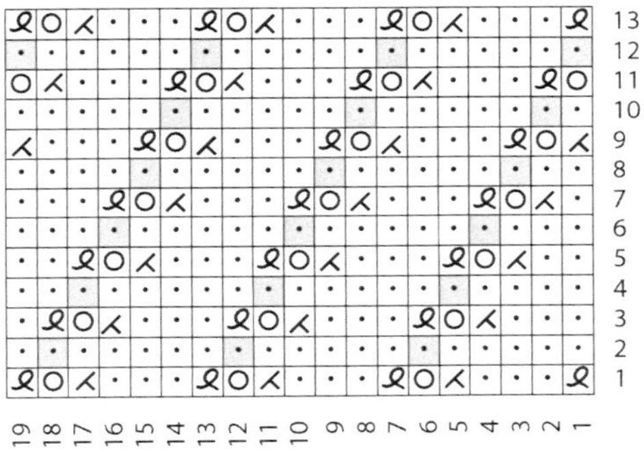

L51

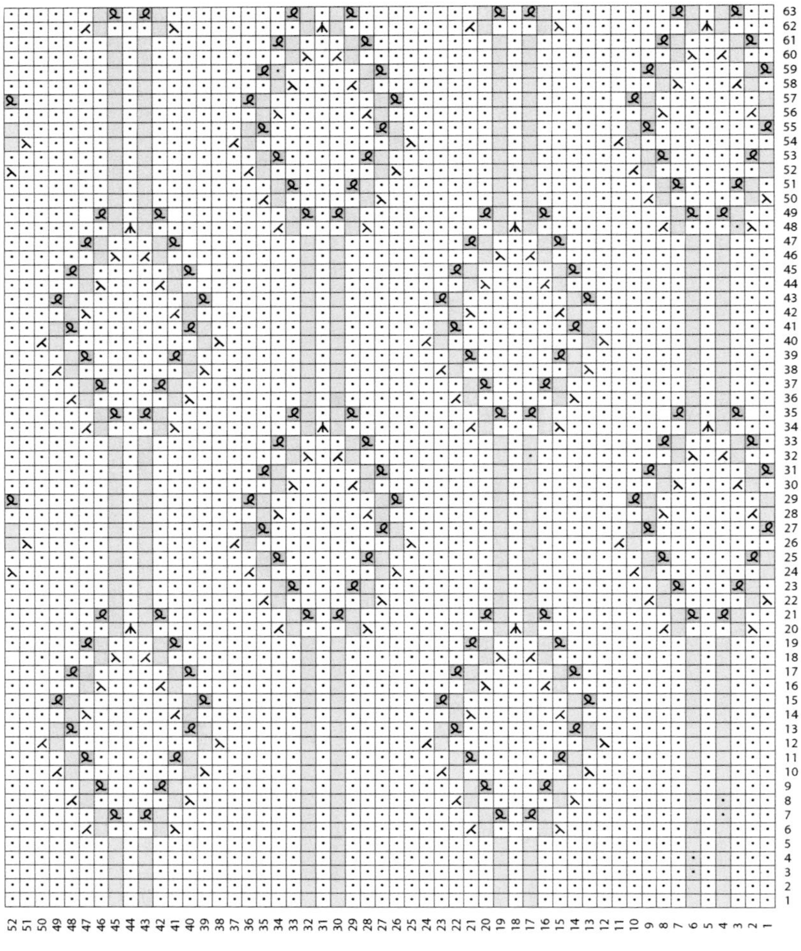

L51

ST from NDLS 1, 7, 14, etc, and twist the top bar of the 2-bar ladder. To twist the bar, insert a single prong transfer tool from above, catching just the top bar of the ladder and twist to the right (direction you are traveling) to form an e—wrap. Replace this e—wrap on the same NDL. Knit 2 rows.

*Move ST 4 to NDL 5 then move both STS back to NDL 4, leaving the empty NDL in WP. Drop the STS from NDL 6 and twist just the top bar of the ladder before replacing it on the same NDL. Knit 2 rows.**

Continue repeating this sequence * to **, always moving 1 NDL to the right with each repeat as shown on the chart. The 2-step decreases are what creates the sharp line along side the ladder. Note that the bars of the ladder are parallel and untwisted because of the drop stitch and twisted e—wrap.

Twisted Fills

L51 features paired single NDL ladders that are spaced 10 NDLS apart, with 1 NDL between each pair. The widening and narrowing that creates the diamonds alternates between pairs of ladders as shown on the chart.

All of the decreases shown on the chart are 2-step decreases and all of the increases are accomplished with twisted e—wraps like L50. In this case there are no dropped STS involved so the ladders are much narrower and less obvious. They do, however, help the diamonds stand out from the background fabric.

Remember that all of the e—wrap twists should not be twisted the same direction. When traveling left, twist left and when traveling right, twist to the right. The 2-step decreases create a sharp line at the base of the diamonds where it widens and at the top of the inner diamond where it narrows.

The decreases and increases are worked on alternate rows. For example, prior to knitting row 6, make 2-step transfers at NDLS 15 and 21, leaving empty NDLS 16 and 20 in NWP and at the same time, bring NDLS 17 and 19 to WP. Knit 1 row. Drop the STS from NDLS 17 and 19, twist and replace on their NDLS and knit 1 row. Make the transfers for row 8 and continue this alternation of transfers and twists. Pay special attention to the rows where the decreases and twists change direction to narrow the diamonds.

L52 The traveling ladders in this sample are stabilized by twisted ladder bars that are hung on the empty NDL above left or right, depending on the direction the ladders are traveling. Again, always twist in the direction the ladder is traveling because the twist contributes to the appearance of the edge STS.

L52

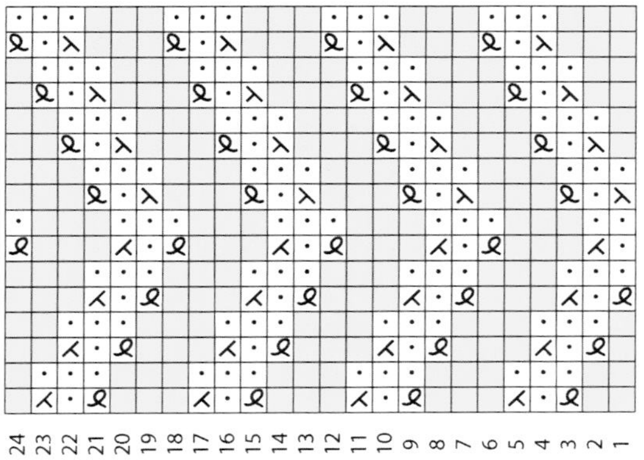

L52

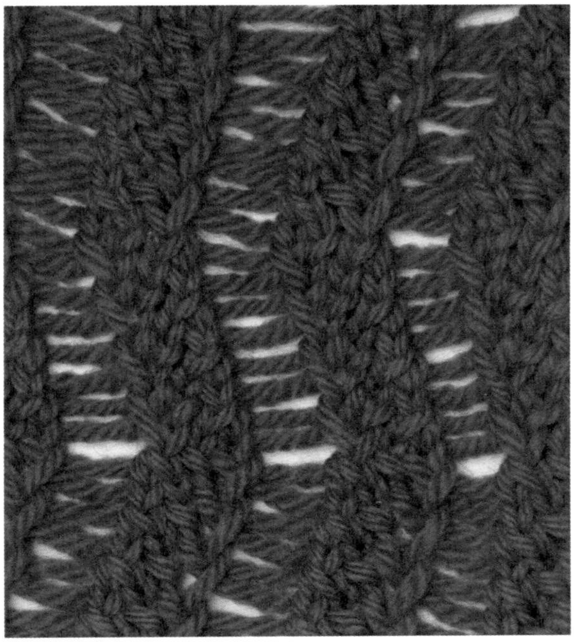

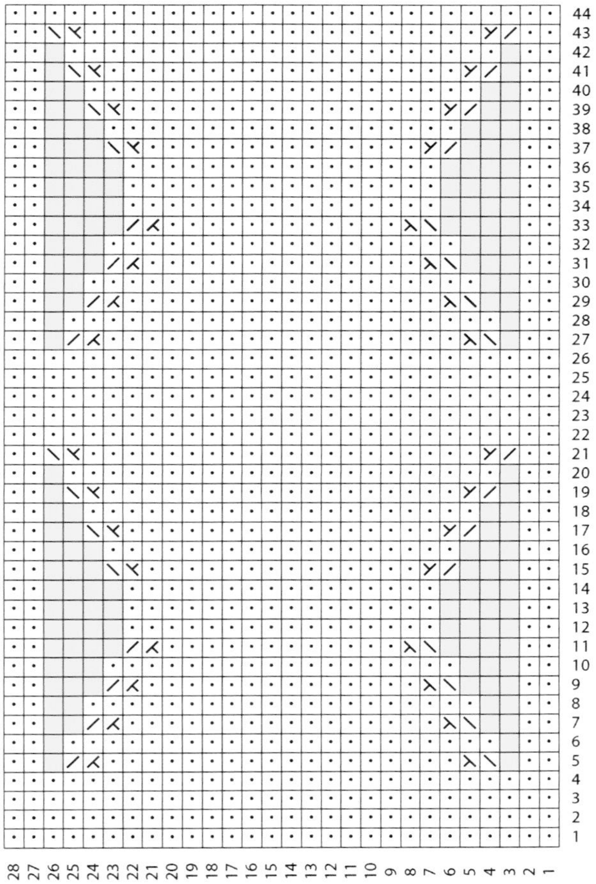

L53

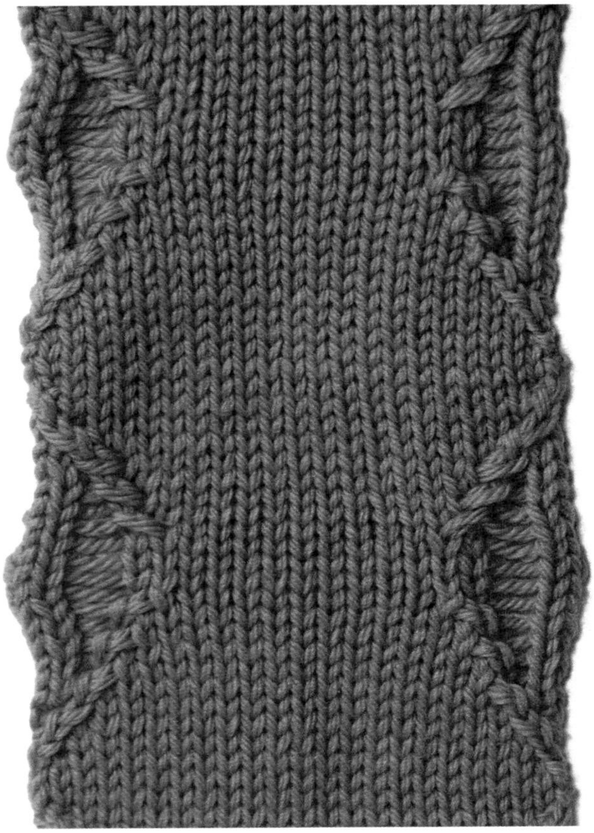

L53

In row 3, for example, transfer ST 5 to NDL 4 and at the same time, make a twisted increase on NDL 8 to maintain the ladder width. When twisting, you can twist one or both ladder bars, but be consistent throughout the fabric. My sample was worked with regular, 1-step decreases, but you can work 2-step decreases to accent the zigzagging STS.

These last two examples of traveling STS create triangular ladders along the edge of a fabric. Please note that although the chart shows regular full—fashioned decreases to shape the ladders, if you look at the samples themselves, you will see that I actually used twisted full—fashioned decreases for a more decorative edge.

L53 As with all twisted ST patterns, it is essential that you twist in the direction the STS are traveling. I worked these twisted decreases as follows: In row 5, remove STS 3 & 4 on a 2-prong transfer tool. Insert a second tool through the same STS from above and remove the first tool. Rotate the tool 180° to replace the STS on NDLS 4 & 5. NDL 3 remains empty in NWP

L54

if you want a less open ladder or in WP if you decide to use drop stitch for a more open look. Either is fine, but be consistent.

If using drop ST, make sure you do the dropping before increasing to close the shape. At row 15 of the chart, you would drop the STS from NDL 6 before making the increase and then knit 2 rows.

This method will create a lovely, nearly—non—roll edging for a scarf. You can also use it for a lower band by working a narrow piece and re—hanging it on the machine. L54 was worked over a total of 8 NDLS with a 24 row repeat. When rehanging a band like this for a C/O edge remember that ST and row gauges are seldom the same. It is common to rehang just 3 out of every 4 rows over the required number of NDLS. Allow for this in your initial calculations so you know how long to knit the band. You can adjust the band to fit the width requirements by working half repeats at each end or by changing the number of plain rows between ladder shaping.

L55

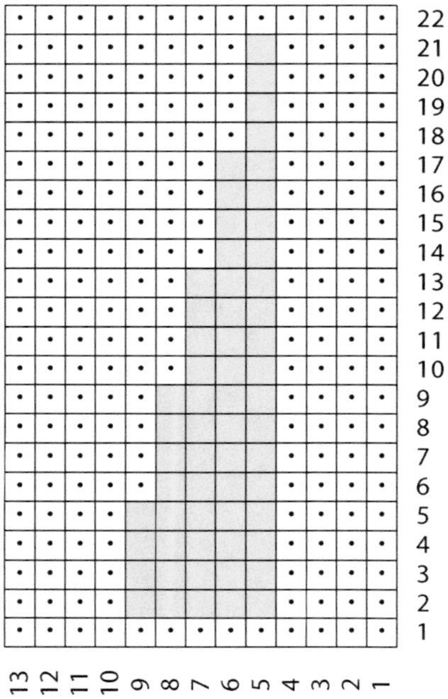

Shaped Ladders

Remember that when ladder NDLS are brought to WP, one at a time, every so—many rows, the resulting bars are always going to twist because of the way the empty NDL begins to form STS. When a ladder is closed with full fashioned increases, the ladders remain straight and parallel.

L55 was bridged and B/O to create a 5-NDL ladder. The first 4 bars of the ladder are straight and untwisted because no new NDLS have been brought into WP. The triangle narrows each time an empty NDL is brought into WP and allowed to C/O and begin knitting. Needles brought into work this way will always create crossed/twisted ladders.

L55

L56 grows from a single empty NDL to 5 empty NDLS at the widest point. All of the decreases used to widen the ladder every 3/R are 2-step transfers, which creates a strong linear affect along side the ladder as it widens. For a steeper angle, you could work 4 or 5 rows between transfers; for a flatter angle, the transfers could be made E/R or A/R. These ladder bars are straight and parallel because the ladder was shaped just be decreases — no new NDLS were brought into WP.

In order to stabilize the ladder once it was 5-NDLS wide, I made 2-step transfers at rows 14, 17 and 20 and 1-step transfers for the remainder of the rows, immediately returning the empty NDL to WP to continue knitting. The top of the ladder was completed with bridged e—wrapping.

Note that in the upper portion of the swatch the ladders are twisted, due to the way the NDLS were brought back to WP after making each transfer. In essence, the edge ST changed and had to be C/O.

The ladders in the next 2 swatches begin with bridged, B/O lower edges and are shaped by increases to narrow and close the shapes. L57 bottom was shaped with 2-prong full—fashioned increases every 4/R. Although I chose to lift the purl bump from an adjacent NDL to prevent an eyelet, you could also just bring the empty NDLS to WP and allow them to C/O so that there would be a trace line of eyelets along side the slanted edge of the triangle.

L57 top was closed by making lifted increases onto the empty NDL every 4/R. In this case, the edge ST was moved 1 NDL inwards and the empty NDL filled by P/U the adjacent purl bump. Because the increases both placed a ST on the next empty NDL of the ladder and made the increase between it and the body of the fabric, the bars of the ladder remain straight and parallel.

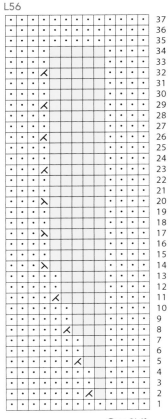

L57 TOP

L57

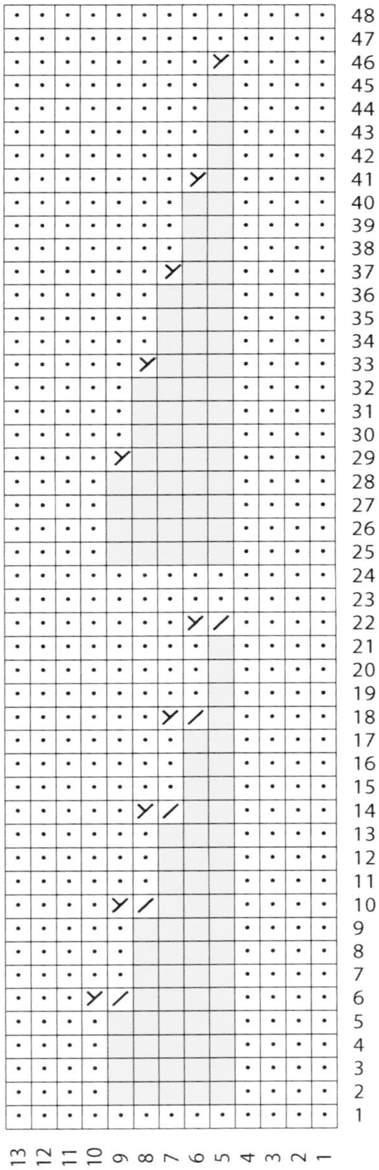

L57 BOTTOM

L56

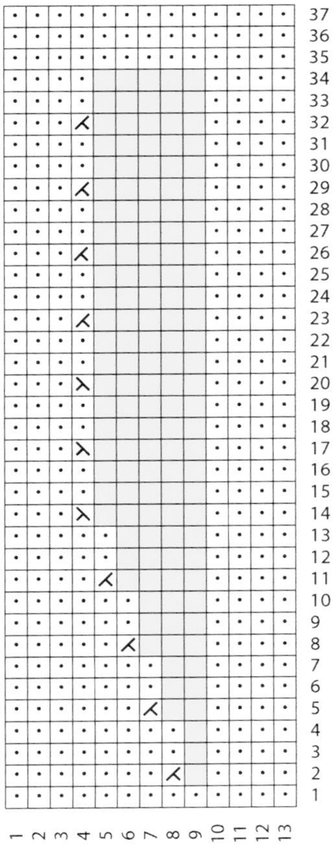

L56

L58 Careful placement of increases and decreases can create ladders that echo fairly specific shapes like flowers and leaves and geometrics. This little leaf—shaped ladder utilizes double, 2-step decreases that create an especially strong line along the edge of the shape. To begin the ladder, remove ST 5 on a single—prong tool and hold to the side. Next move ST 6 to NDL 7 and then move both STS to NDL 5. Finally, replace the 5th ST on top of the other two so that there are 3 STS on this NDL and NDLS 6 & 7 are empty. All of the increases are made by bringing an empty NDL to WP. However, because I brought an empty NDL to WP every row (rather than A/R), the ladder bars remain parallel and do not twist as they would have if I had brought a NDL to WP A/R.

L59 These triangular shapes begin with bridged B/O. The empty NDLS are brought to WP at left and right of the shape A/R so the bars of the ladders twist, creating an interesting lacy pattern within each shape.

L59

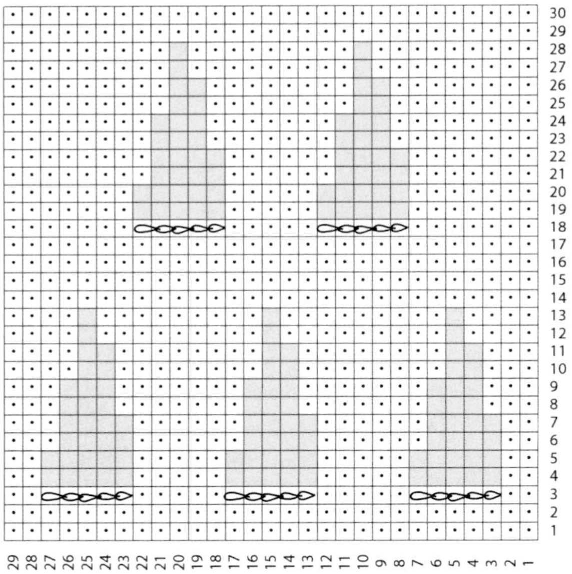

L58

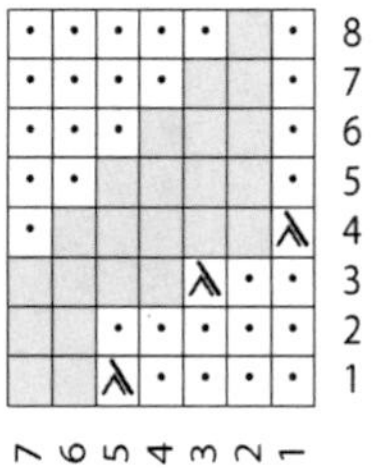

L58

L59

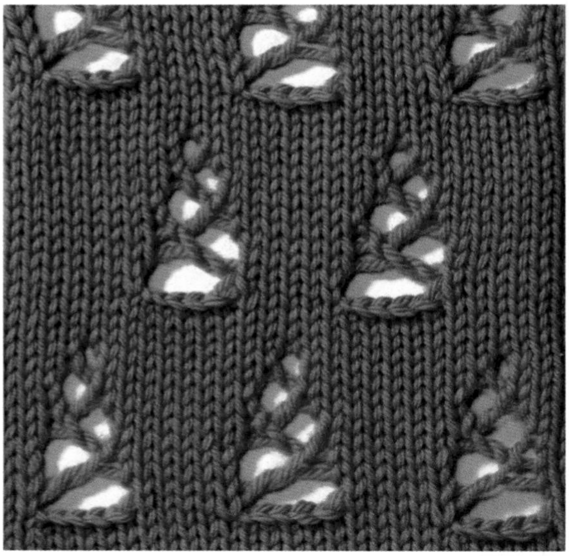

L60

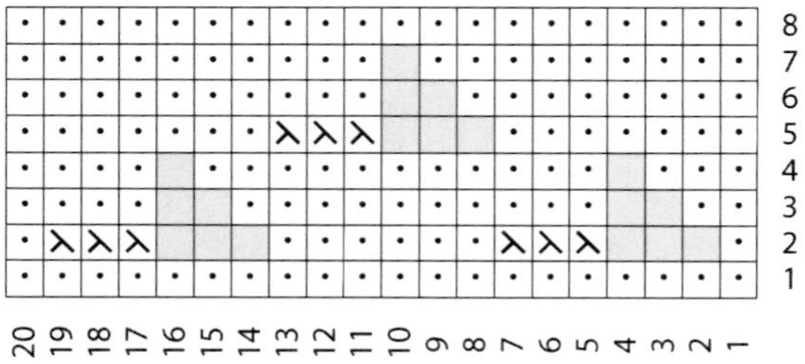

L60

L60 These tiny ladders resemble eyelets, but on closer examination you will see that there is a short, slanted ladder above each one. The ladders were all started by making a 3-prong stacked decrease that adds some curved texture to the surface. Then I brought 1 empty NDL back to WP on the right of the ladders, E/R.

L61 looks more complicated than it is. It begins with an 8-stitch ladder on either side of 3 WP NDLS. The ladders narrow and widen as a result of the STS traveling back and forth. The eyelets were created as part of full fashioned shaping where I did not P/U the purl bump of the adjacent STS. Instead, the empty NDLS were allowed to C/O and knit

Large shaped ladders are perfect for needle weaving. The weaving is worked after the fabric has been knitted and blocked and allows you to use yarns that your machine might not accommodate to create colorful,

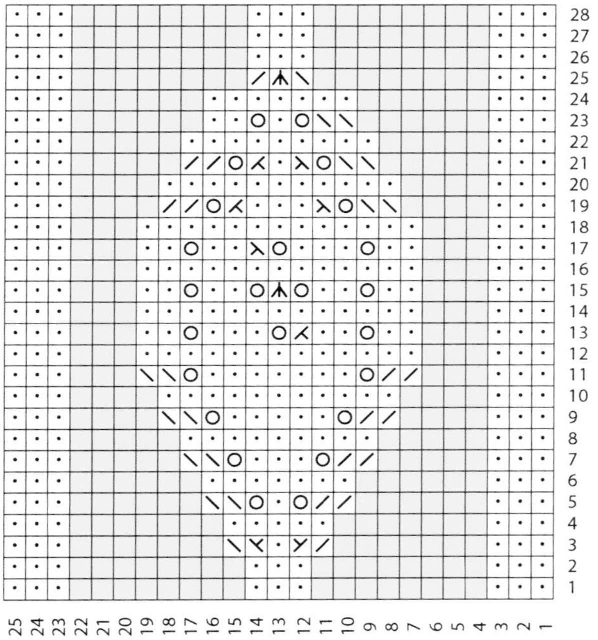

L61

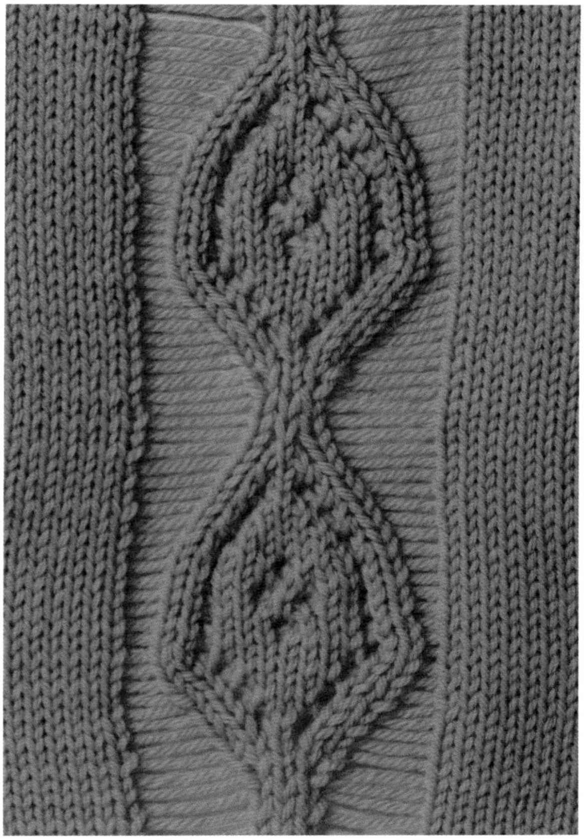

L61

intarsia-like designs. In the chart L62 note that the base for each of the shapes has been bridged and B/O to create as straight an edge as possible. While the circle and the triangle were further shaped with increasing/decreasing, the top of the square required bridging to C/O a straight edge. Full fashioned shaping will increase the stability of these large ladders.

L62

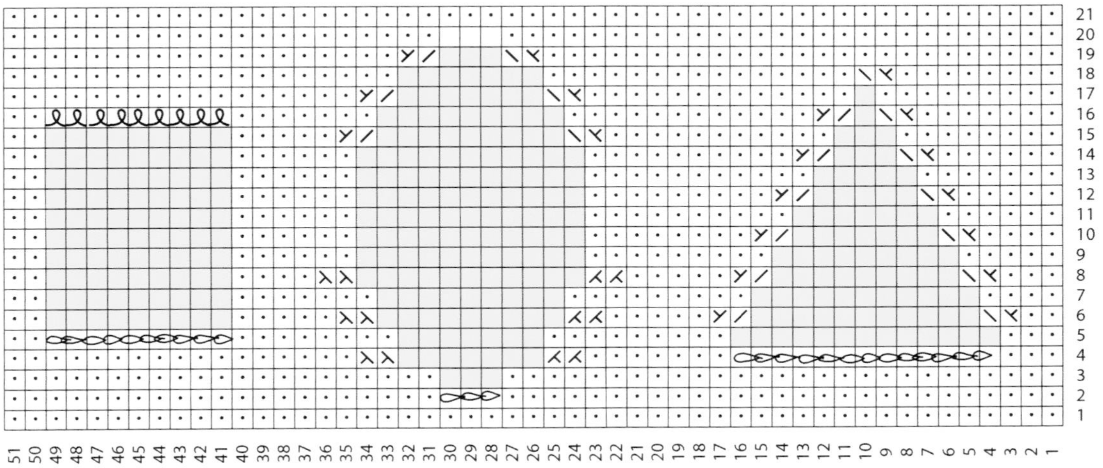

L62A

L62B

L62C

L63

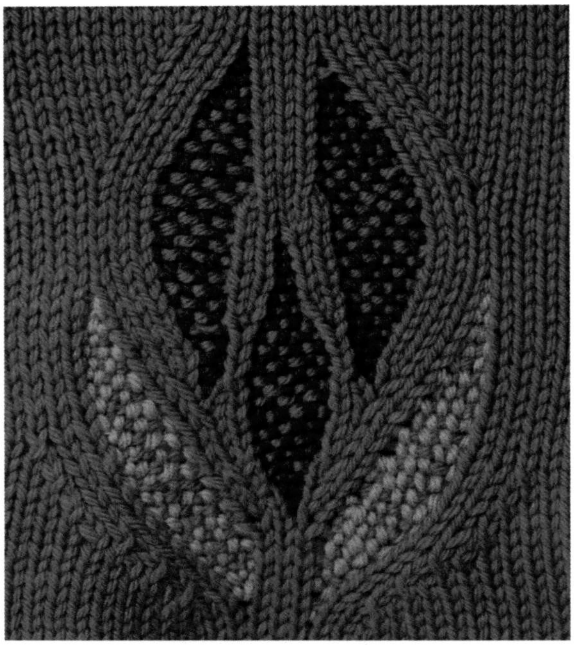

L63

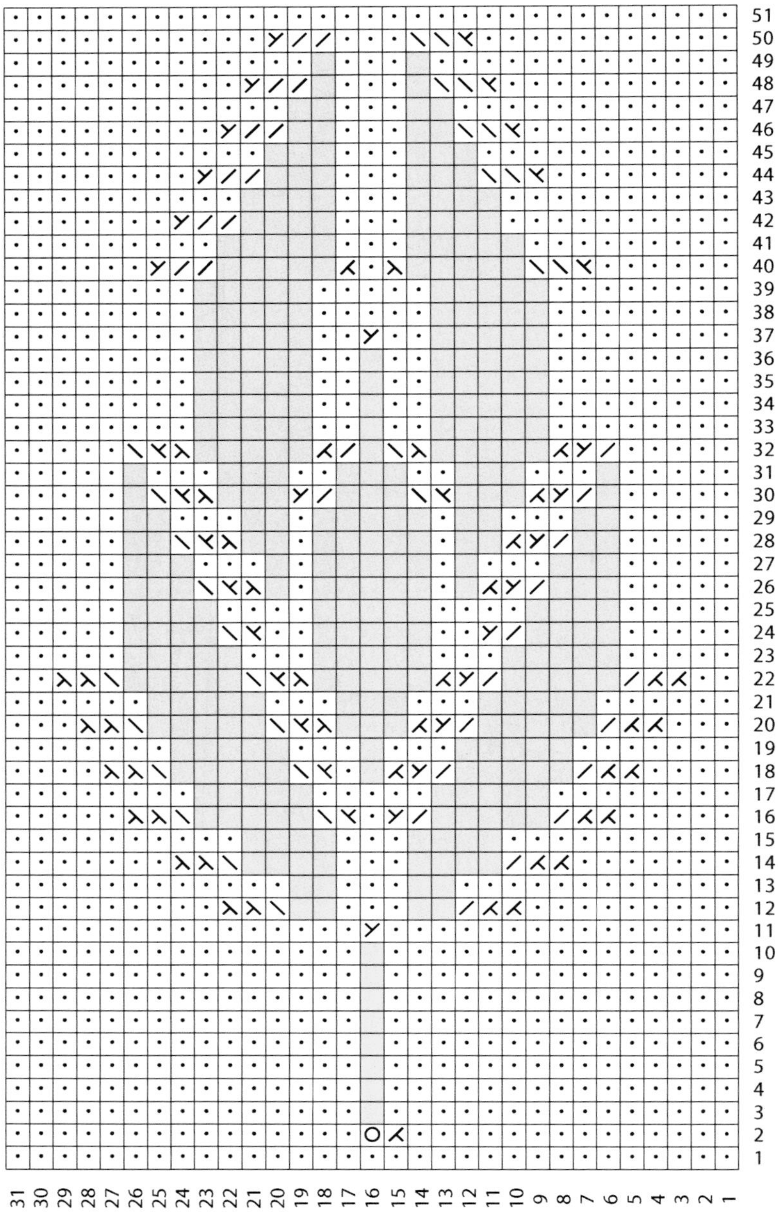

L63 is also a NDL woven ladder and features a somewhat more complex arrangement of increases and decreases to create this "tulip" shape. If you compare the needle weaving on this sample to the square, you should see that the bars of the ladder are more visible in the flower than in the square. This is because I worked weaving over/under two bars at a time for the square, while the flower shape was worked over/under one bar at a time. Either is correct, depending on how much of the color of the ladder bars you want showing.

When I work each row of the needle weaving, the ladder bars act like warp threads on a loom so it is important that they lie flat and easy to see. You must block this fabric before you start weaving. Also, I always catch the upper/lower edges of the ladder before I reverse to weave the next row to avoid any gaps or separations along the edges.

L64

L64

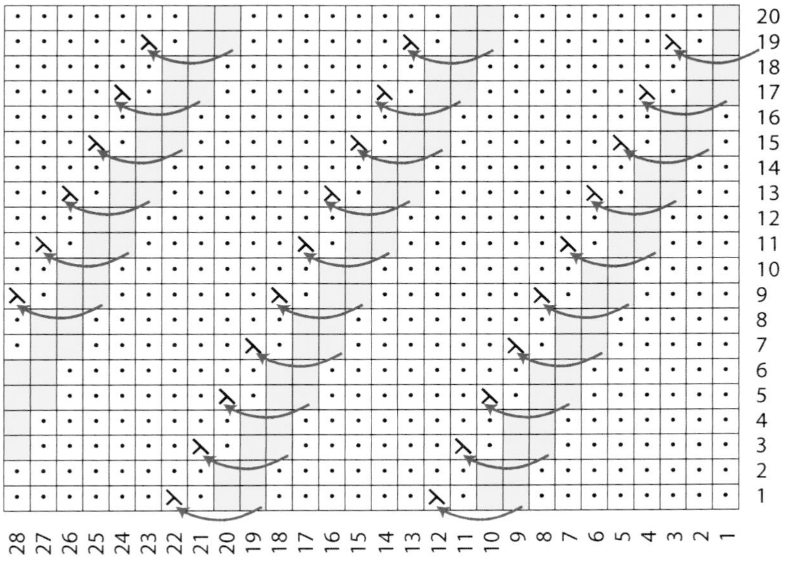

L65

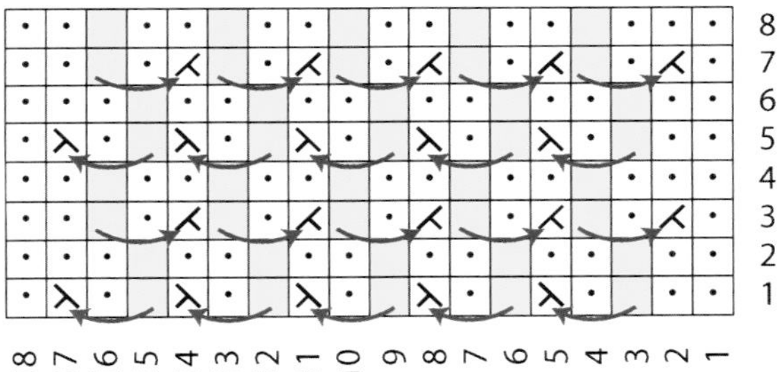

Lifted Ladders

You can lift ladder bars or STS along side of them to create wonderful, textured fabrics with open spaces.

L64 Although (on the chart) the ladder travels to the right, the lifting is done to the left. Begin with 9 NDLS in WP and 1 NDL in NWP. Knit 1 row. Work the skipped transfers as follows: Prior to knitting row 1, Transfer ST 9 to NDL 12 and place the empty NDL in NWP, where it will remain for the next four rows. Knit 2 rows. Transfer NDL 8 to NDL 11 and at the same time bring NDL 10 to WP. Knit 2 rows.

L65 is similar to the preceding sample except that the placement is alternated throughout, forming an all—over grid rather than individual traveling ladders. Because of the way this mesh is stabilized, this fabric would be very suitable for string bags and similar projects.

C/O all NDLS. Prior to knitting row 1, transfer ST 3 to NDL 5 and place the empty NDL in NWP. Knit 2 rows. Then, bring the empty NDL to WP and at the same time make the second set of transfers by moving ST 4 to NDL 2. Knit 2 rows and then continue alternating for the remainder of the fabric.

L65

L66 a, b, c are variations on a theme that illustrate how placement affects patterns. The first, sample L66a, was worked from the chart that shows 5 WP NDLS between each 3 NDL ladder and 5 rows between repeats. Because it was important for the base of each ladder to be perfectly straight and flat, I bridged row 2 to do a latch tool B/O to begin each ladder. After 8 rows I used a latch tool to reach behind the ladder, catch the top bar and pull it down and up, depositing it on the center NDL of each ladder. Then the empty NDLS on each side of it were returned to WP and 5 row knitted to the beginning of the next, alternate pattern.

L66

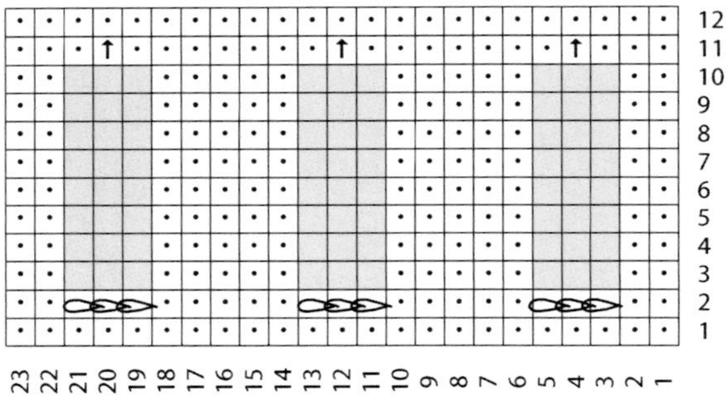

L66A

L66b was worked the same way except that both the knitted sections and the ladders were worked over 5 NDLS. After hanging the lifted ladder bar on the center NDL, bring NDLS 1 and 5 in each group to WP and knit 1 row. Then bring the remaining empty NDLS to WP and knit 1 more row (*). Knit 5 rows.

L66c which is probably the most interesting of the swatches was also worked over 5 WP NDLS alternating with 5 NWP NDLS but there were no extra rows knitted between repeats. Instead, begin the next repeat immediately at (*) in L66b.

L66B

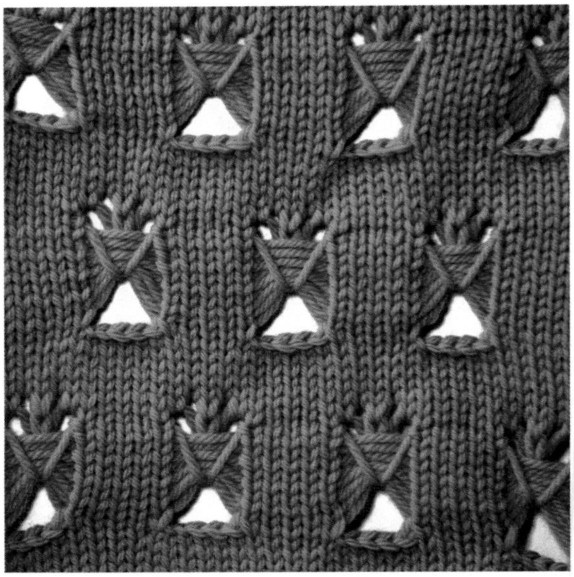

L66C

Varying the number of WP or NWP NDLS and changing the number of ladder bars or rows between repeats can alter this pattern in many ways. For example, to take this last variation one step further, you could begin the alternate repeats half way through the first so that they overlap lengthwise.

L67A, B, C The next 3 samples were based on the same chart. For the first, transfer STS as shown on row 2 of the chart then knit 2 rows. Bring NDLS 3 & 5 to WP and knit 1 row then bring the remaining empty NDL (4) to WP and knit 2 rows. Drop the STS from NDLS 3, 4 & 5 and insert a transfer tool from the bottom of the ladder, under just the first 2 bars of the ladder, then over the third bar to pull it down and through towards

L67

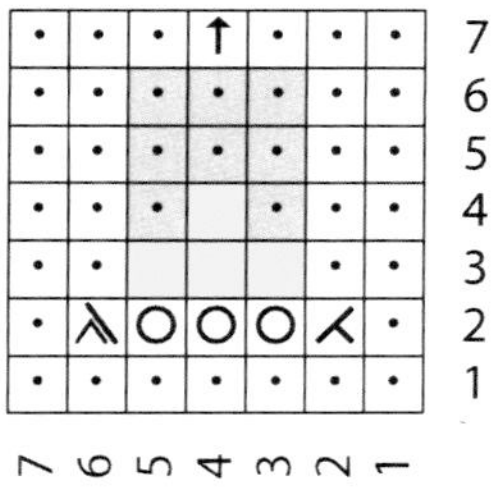

L67A

you. Twist the tool either left or right to replace the ST on the center NDL. Bring the empty NDLS to WP and knit 2 rows.

L67b shows slightly longer ladders (4 bars/rows) with the repeats shifting over by 1 NDL each time for an interesting all over design. I worked 3 repeats in each direction before reversing direction to avoid biasing the fabric.

L67c the ladder is knitted for 4 rows before lifting the bars and — as clumsy as it was — I inserted the transfer tool from bottom to top, under the four bars and then over the one formed on the 6th row of the chart. I tipped the tool down and lifted the last loop up to the front. Then I pinched the loop with my fingers, removed it from the tool and reached the tool under again to catch the loop for a second time and pull it through to the front. The end result is sort of a double lifting that more clearly defines the top of the resulting open spaces. There were 4 rows knitted between each repeat at left, but only 2 rows at right.

L67B

L67C

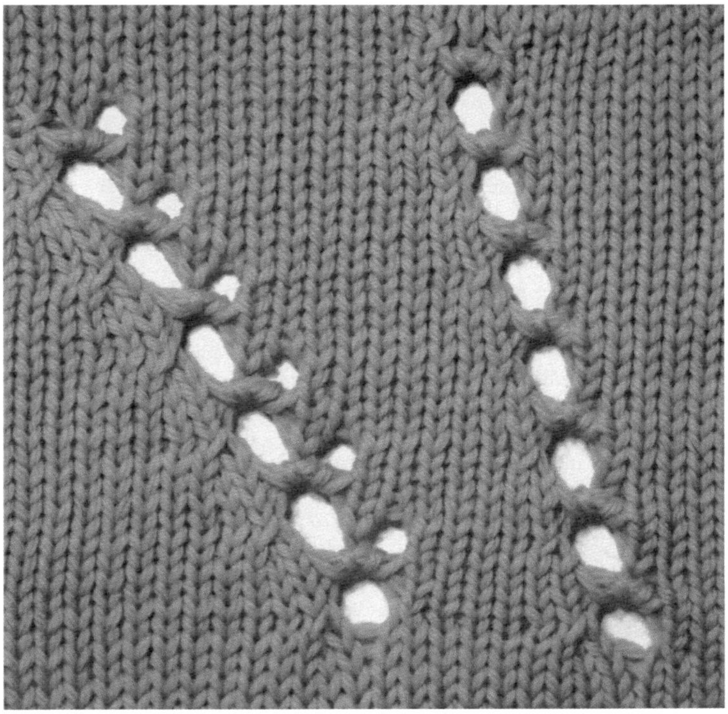

L68 FRONT

L68 BACK

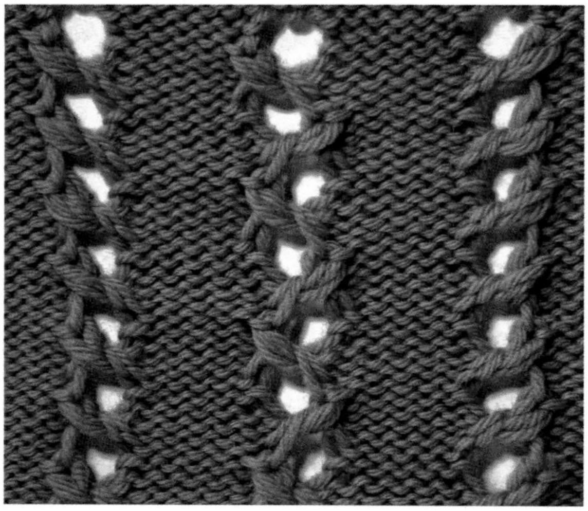

L68 was worked the same way as the previous examples. However, as seen on the back of the fabric, the bars of the left ladder were always hung on the adj WP NDL at left; the ladders on the right of the swatch were always hung on the adj right NDL and the column at center alternated left and right each time. These are subtle differences that would matter if this technique were worked with other pattern effects — or if you inadvertently switched mid—fabric.

L69 is a simple rouching pattern where the first 2 bars of a continuous ladder are lifted every 5/R and hung on either the first adj NDL at left or right. The STS zigzag across the fabric as a result. You can vary the number of STS, the width of the ladder, the frequency at which the ladder bars are lifted or the NDLS to which they are lifted.

L70 and L71 These sweet little hearts were inspired by one of the Stoll fabrics. I included both of the charts here because I like the way the two sizes compliment each other. At the base of the larger heart, I crossed a 1x1 cable to keep the "v" from separating. You could also cross a 1x1 cable behind a center stitch.

L69

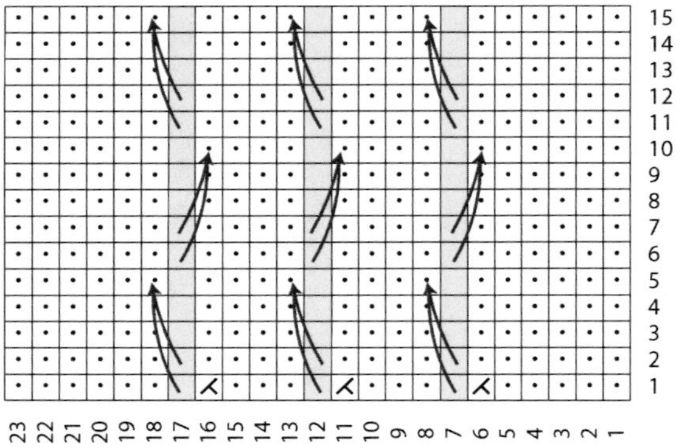

L69

The hearts are shaped with full fashioned decreases. Use bridging to C/O the empty NDLS as follows: at row 14 with COR, lift all of the ladder bars onto the center NDL (10) and bring the NDL to HP. Set the carriage to hold NDLS in HP and hold all NDLS except the first 4 on the right. Knit 5 rows, ending COL. Use the FY to e—wrap NDLS 5-11, knitting back all the loops on the center NDL as you do so. Hold all NDLS except NDLS 9-11. Knit 2 rows and then, with COL, e—wrap NDLS 12-15. Hold all NDLS and move COR. Move NDLS 16-19 to UWP and knit 5 rows over those NDLS, ending COL. Set carriage to knit all NDLS back from HP and continue working over all NDLS.

L70

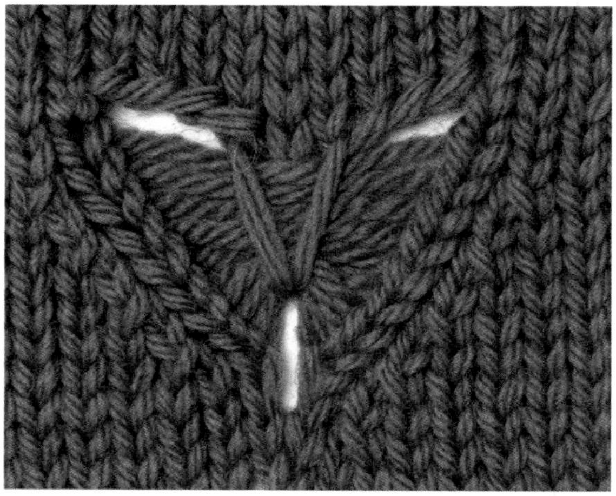

L70

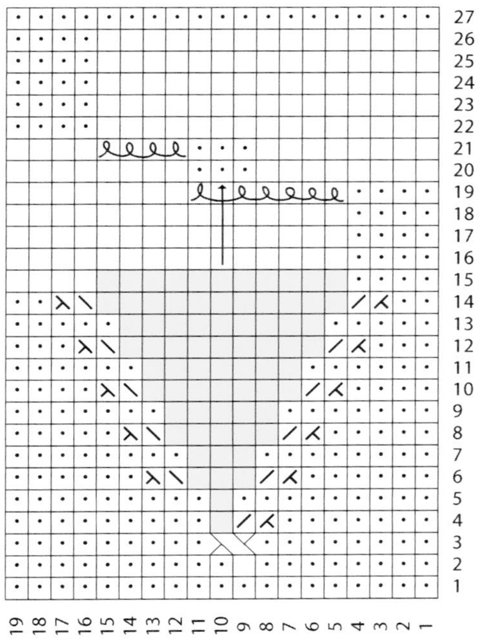

The smaller hearts are worked the same way as the previous example, just on fewer NDLS for a more delicate look. The chart has not been expanded to show the bridging, but this heart would also be bridged like the previous example. You could use the EON method to fill the tops of the hearts, but the shape will not be as clearly defined.

L72

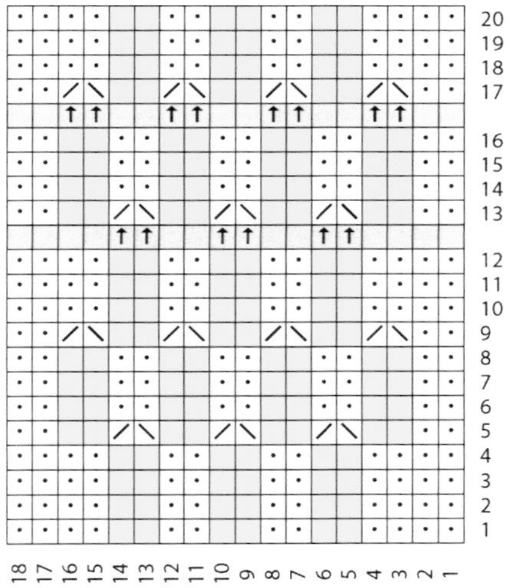

L71

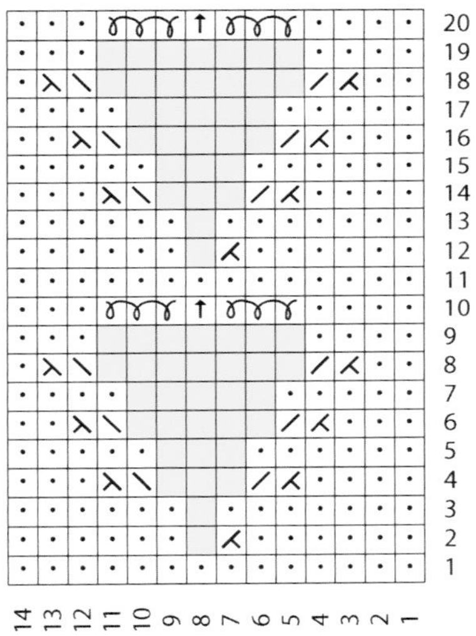

L72

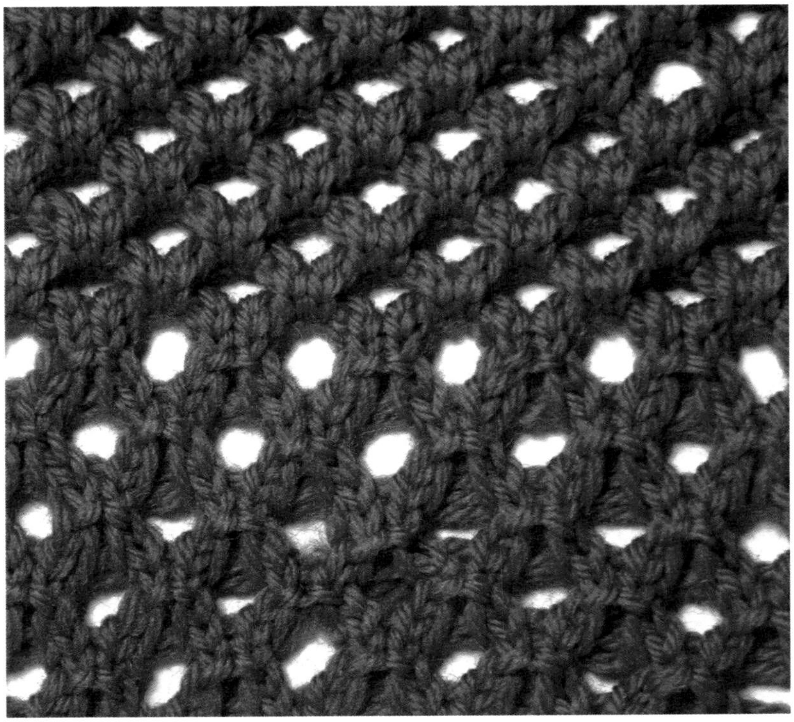

L71

L72 illustrates 2 variations on the same design. For L72 bottom, arrange NDLS as shown and knit 4 rows. Split the pairs of working STS and move them towards each other. That is, move ST 4 to NDL 5 and ST 7 to NDL 6. Use a 2-prong tool to lift all 4 ladder bars onto

L73

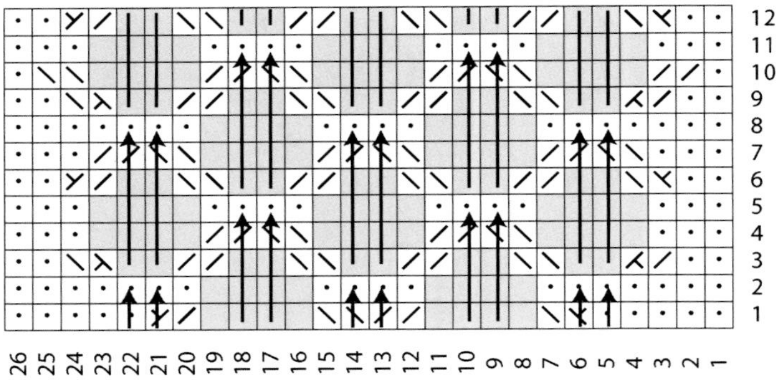

L74

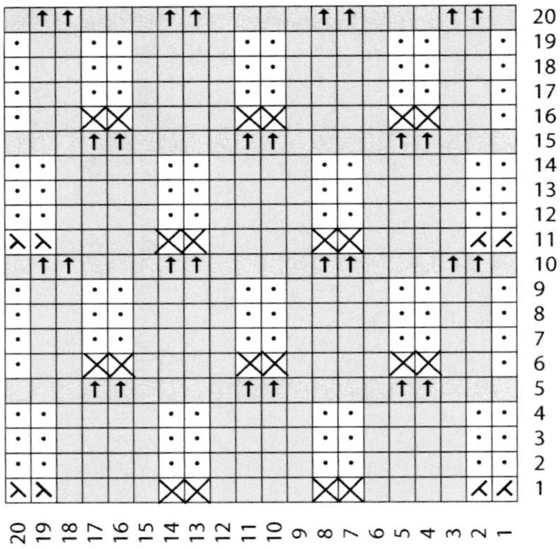

L73

L74

NDLS 5 & 6. With the carriage set to knit NDLS back from HP, repeat, alternating the placement. L72 top produces a more dense mesh because the ladder bars are lifted before shifting the working STS.

L73 utilizes wider groups of WP NDLS and ladders. Knit 2 rows then use a 2-prong tool to move pairs of STS as shown on row 3 of the chart: move STS 6 and 7 to NDLS 7 and 8 and STS 12 and 13 to NDLS 12 and

11. Knit 1 row. Move STS once more and then lift the 4 ladder bars below. It will be necessary to make some actual increases and decreases on the edges of the fabric.

L74 was inspired by one of the Stoll fabrics and is just a larger version of L72. Begin COR and make stacked decreases as shown on the chart to establish the pattern. There are 3 STS on each of the working NDLS with 4 empty NWP NDLS between them. Knit 4 rows.

*Use a 2-prong tool to lift all 4 ladder bars onto the empty 2 center NDLS and bring them to WP. Next, move the STS from the next WP NDLS at left and right of each group onto these same 2 NDLS (i.e. ST 2 to NDL 4 in row 6). Knit 4 rows.** Repeat * to * lifting, shifting STS over to alternate the placement and knitting 4 rows.

L75 is a decorative effect that might look great as a single vertical or as a repeating motif. Arrange the NDLS as shown on the chart and knit 1 row. Bring NDL 6 to WP and knit 1 row. Bring NDLS 5 & 7 to WP and knit 4 rows.

This unusual cable variation crosses a group of twisted ladder bars with 3 STS as follows: Drop the STS from NDLS 5, 6, 7. Collect all of the ladder bars on a single—prong transfer tool and rotate the tool 180° clock—wise (to the right). Remove STS 8, 9, 10 on a 3-prong tool and then cross the first half of the cable so the twisted STS return first to NDL 10. Replace the other 3 STS on their original NDLS(8, 9, 10).

Next drop the STS from NDLS 14, 15, 16 and collect them on a second tool by inserting the tool behind the bars from above and then rotate the tool 180° counter clock—wise (to the left). Remove STS 11, 12, 13 on a 3-prong tool and cross the second half of this cable so that the twisted STS return to NDL 11 before replacing the other STS on NDLS 11, 12, 13.

L75

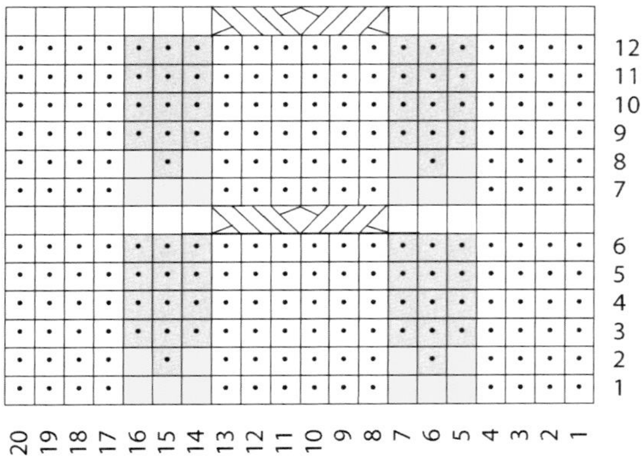

L76

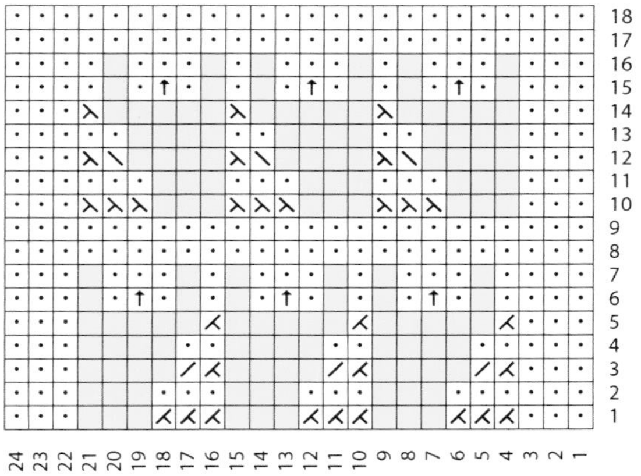

L75

L76

L77

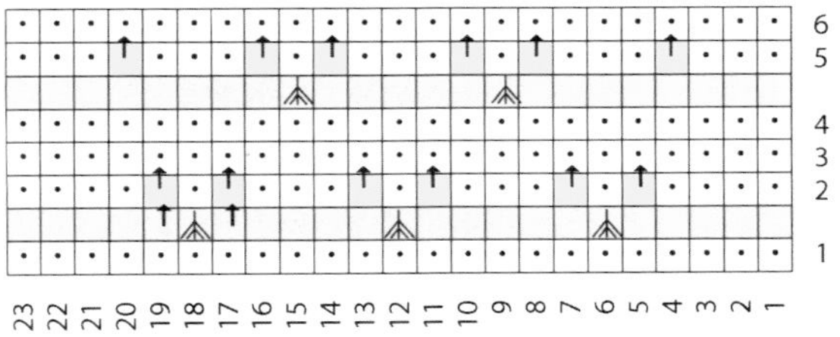

L77

L76 requires a fairly wide plain border at each side because, as you can see from the photograph, both edges are irregular and different from each other. The ladders are increased as shown on the chart and then, prior to knitting row 6 the ladder bars are lifted. Insert a latch tool under all 5 bars, from bottom to top, and catch the top (5th) bar of the ladder in the hook of the tool. Pull this bar down and towards you and then hang the loop on the center (7th) empty NDL. Bring NDLS 6 and 8 to WP and knit 2 rows. Then bring NDLS 5 and 9 to WP and knit 2 more rows. Repeat as shown. These repeats are not evenly staggered so pay attention as you begin each new repeat just 1 NDL to the left or right of the previous repeat.

L77 is a small repeating pattern where 2 STS from left and right are transferred to the same center NDL. Then, bring NDLS 4 and 8 to WP and knit 1 row. Lift the ladders below onto NDLS 5 and 7 and knit to rows to the next, staggered repeat.

L78 features a much wider ladder, along with some tuck STS in the sections between. You can work the tuck

L78

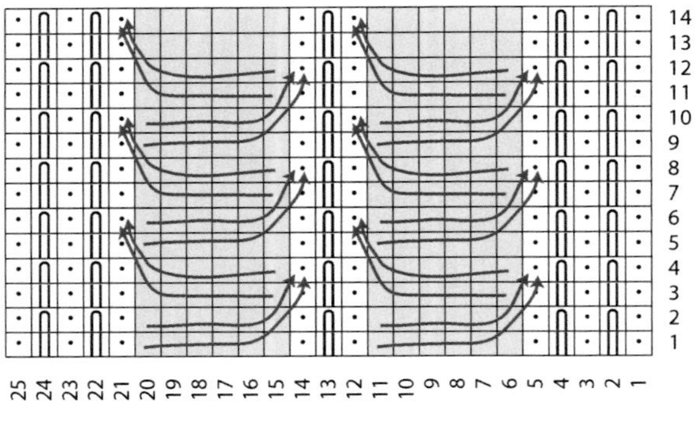

L78

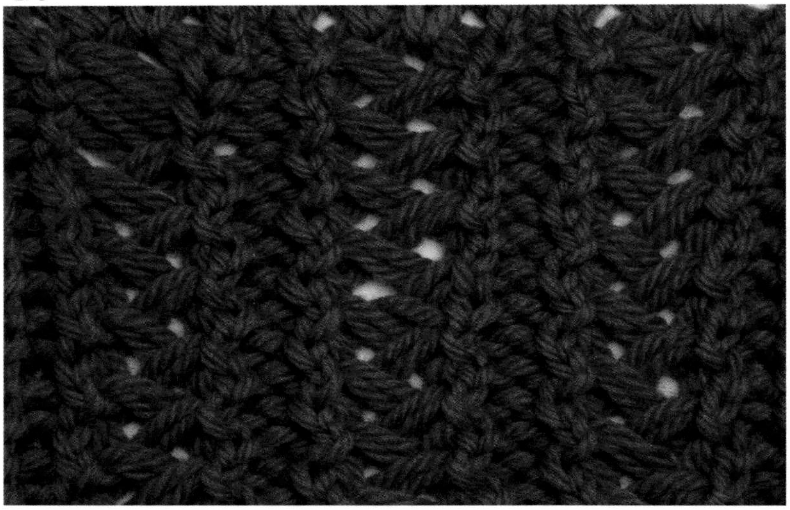

L79

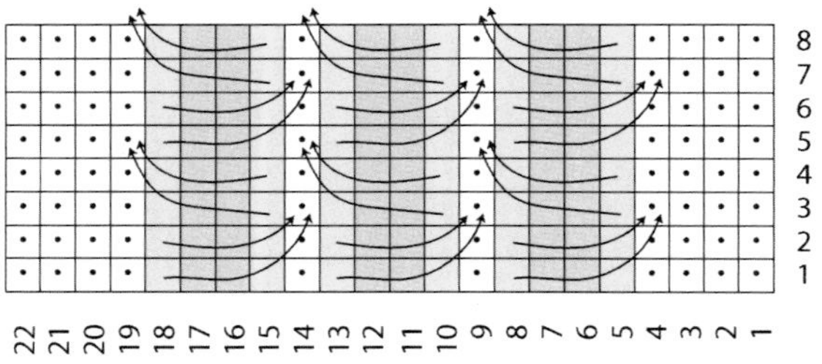

L79

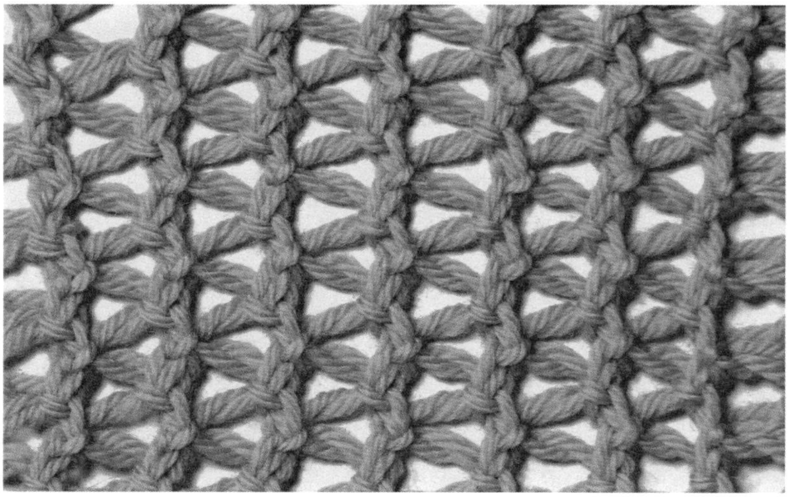

manually or with automatic selection. Arrange the NDLS as shown and knit 4 rows. Lift only the bottom 2 ladder bars to the first WP NDL at the right of the ladder. Knit 2 rows and then lift the lowest 2 bars to the left.

Lifting 3 bars every 3 rows might make it easier to keep track of what you are doing because you can coordinate the direction of the lifting to which side the carriage is on. This might cause some distortion in the fabric so knit a large enough sample swatch to evaluate it.

L79 For this example, the center two NDLS of each ladder are allowed to knit and then drop to create longer bars. Every 2 rows, drop the center two ladder STS and lift both bars to the first adjacent NDL at left or right, alternating sides each time. Bring one of the NDLS back to work before knitting each of the next 2 rows, then drop them both for the next repeat. Without the ease provided by the drop stitch, this is a very difficult fabric to knit. You could also drop more than 2 STS by bringing NDLS 5 and 7 to WP before the first row and the remaining 2 (or 1) NDLS before the last. Try working this fabric with as few drops as possible because if the ladders are *too* loose, you lose the structure and definition of the fabric.

L80 alternates 5 ST ladders with a single ST between them. Knit 6 rows and lift all 6 ladder bars onto NDL

L80

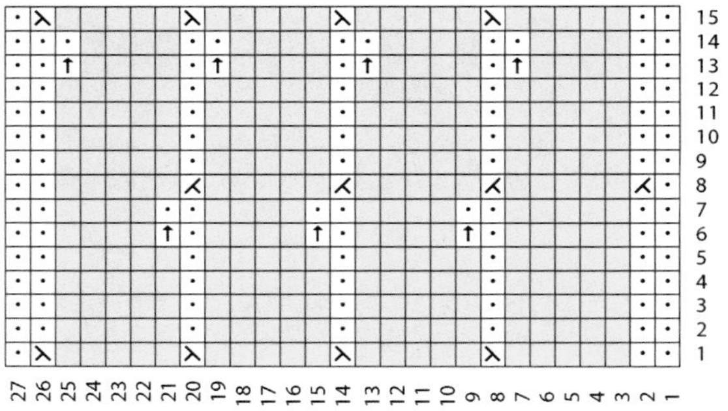

L80

9 and then knit 1 more row. Transfer the ST from NDL 9 to NDL 8 and knit 6 rows. Repeat the lifting and transferring, alternating left and right sides for the lifting as shown on the chart. By working even numbers of rows for the ladders and then a single row to complete each repeat, the carriage will alternately be on the left or right which you can use as a guide to which side to lift towards. If you bring the NDLS to HP before lifting the ladders, it makes it easier to manage all the bars. You must alternate sides for the lifting or this fabric will bias.

L81 These ladders are lifted to C/O the empty NDLS. Begin COR. (Make all decreases as shown on chart and knit 2 rows) 4 times, placing empty NDLS in NWP and ending COR. There are 8 ladder bars between each working group of NDLS. Hold all NDLS except the first group on the right.

*Working right to left, alternately fill the empty NDLS by catching a loop of the FY then passing a latch tool behind the 8 bars to catch a loop of the FY, pulling it down and up to place this new loop on the next empty NDL. Bring all NDLS to HP and move COR. Nudge the next group of HP NDLS into UWP** and repeat * to ** to the end of the row. COL. Knit 2 rows to begin next repeat from the left, alternating the placement of the repeats and the direction of the transfers.

L81

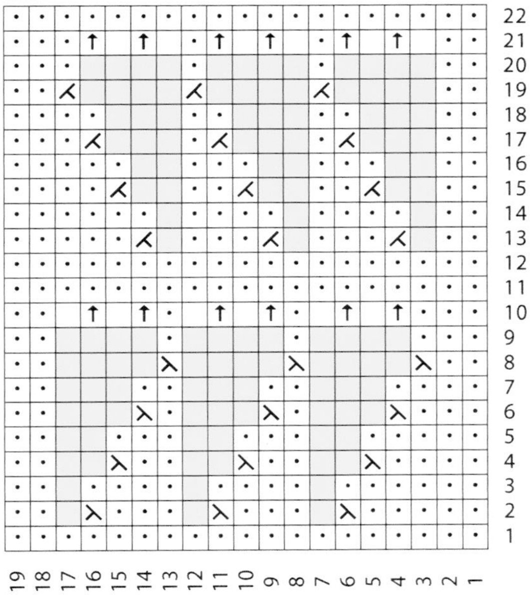

The edges of this fabric will be scalloped and irregular. When there are only 1 or 2 edge STS it is easier to just manually knit them from HP to WP. You might find that 2-step decreases create a sharper edge along each triangle. The purl side of is quite attractive, making this fabric suitable for projects where both sides of the fabric will show. This method of lifting ladder bars is similar to swatch E16 in the eyelet chapter.

L81

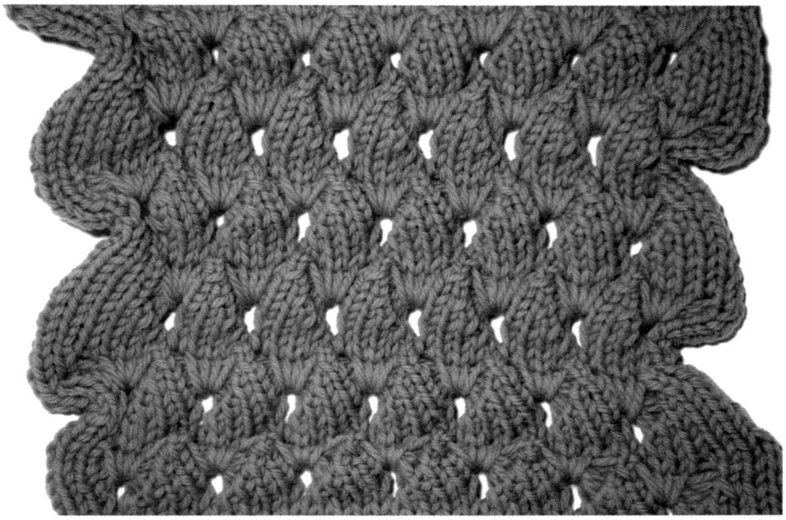

L82-L84 create neat little triangles of STS with inverted triangular ladders. L82 does not include any lifting at all, but it served as the basis for the other two samples so I have included it here.

L82

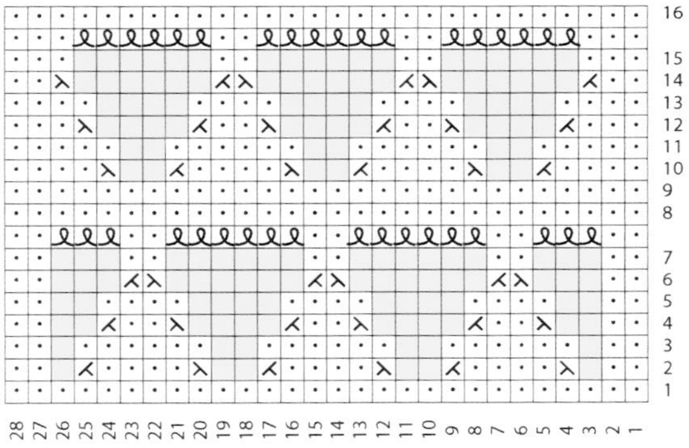

L82

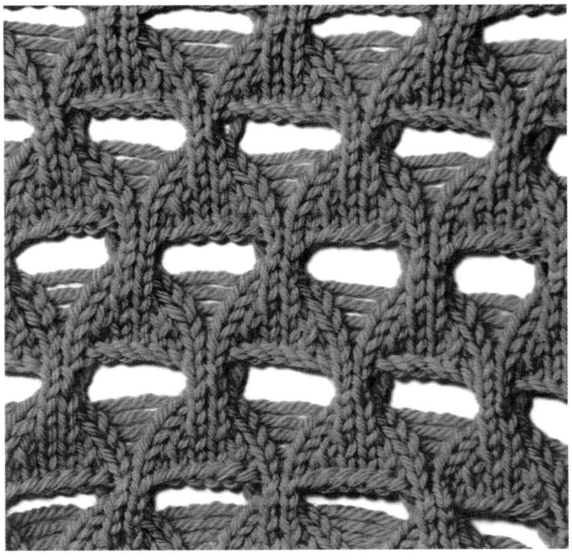

L82 is worked with staggered repeats and simple decreases. At the end of each repeat, the last row is bridged to e—wrap the empty NDLS. For a faster method, you could eliminate the bridging and just e—wrap the entire row, including the NDLS that already hold STS. This is a good pattern for working half—repeats right out to the edges, but I would still retain 2 plain STS at each edge. Also, note that the shapes reduce down to a pair of STS that, in turn, become the outer STS of the next repeat which is why this pattern has such a continuous, fluid look to it.

L83 is very similar to L82 except that the pattern reduces down to a single, central ST rather than a pair of STS and the repeats are directly above each other, rather than staggered. The real difference is that the 6 empty NDLS at the end of each repeat are C/O by lifting the last two ladder bars to fill them. After row 6, use a transfer tool to lift the second ladder bar from the top onto the 2nd and every alt empty NDL in each group as shown on the chart. Then insert the tool under the bar you just lifted to lift the first ladder bar onto the remaining, alt empty NDLS. Reaching behind the first lifted ladder to lift the second adds a twist to the bars that neatens the cast on, while eliminating the need for bridging. Knit 2 rows across all NDLS and then work the next repeat directly above the last.

L83

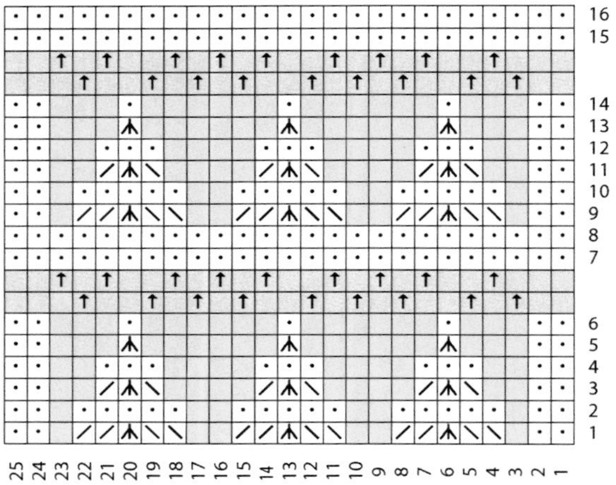

L83

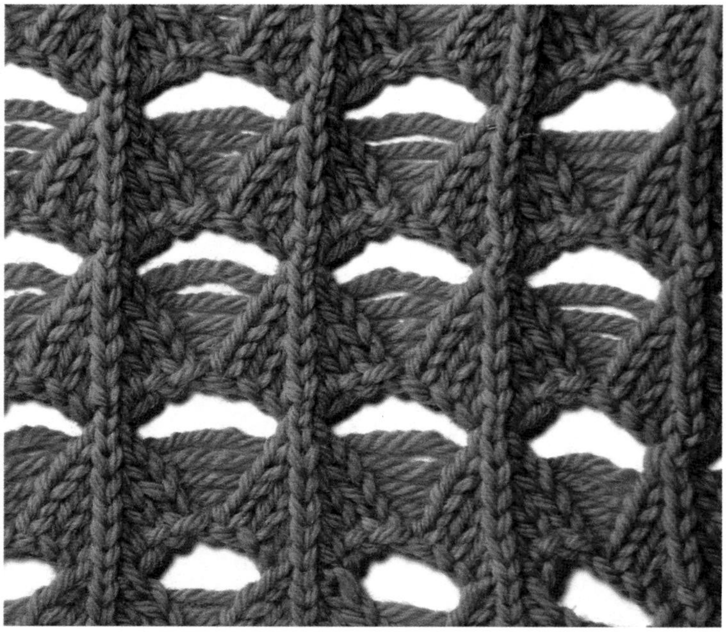

L84

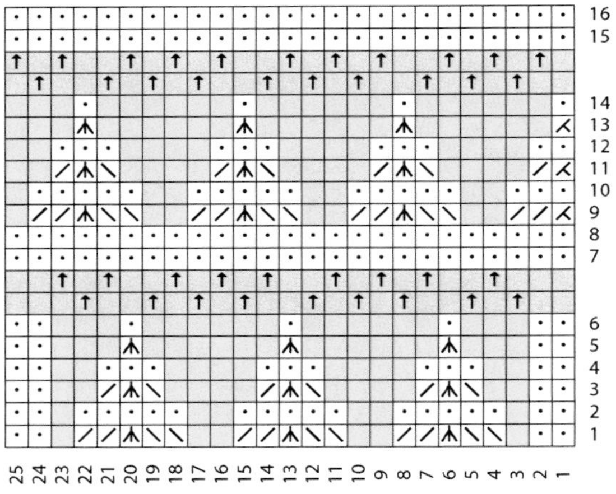

L84

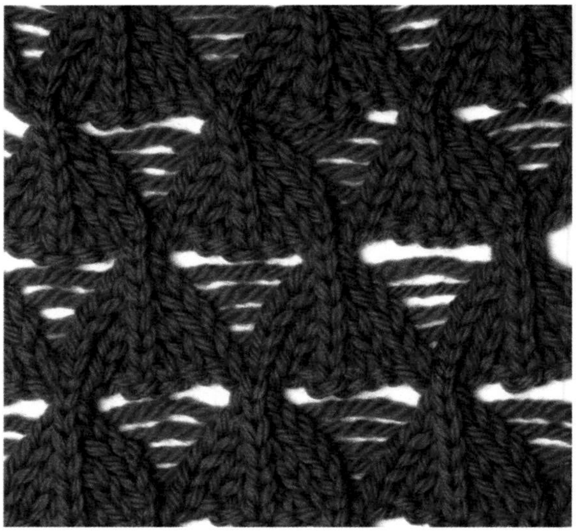

L84 is worked exactly like L83 except that the repeats are staggered, rather than stacked vertically. Note that these repeats are actually offset by 1 NDL and not centered. Instead, the central ST becomes the edge ST of the next repeat, alt to the left and right.

L85 The next lifted ladder is used to create individual rosettes, suitable for joining as an afghan or pillow cover. The fabric is thick and probably not suitable for garments when worked on a midgauge or bulky machine. Standard gauge rosettes should be more appropriate for wearables, but do a couple of samples first to make sure.

L85

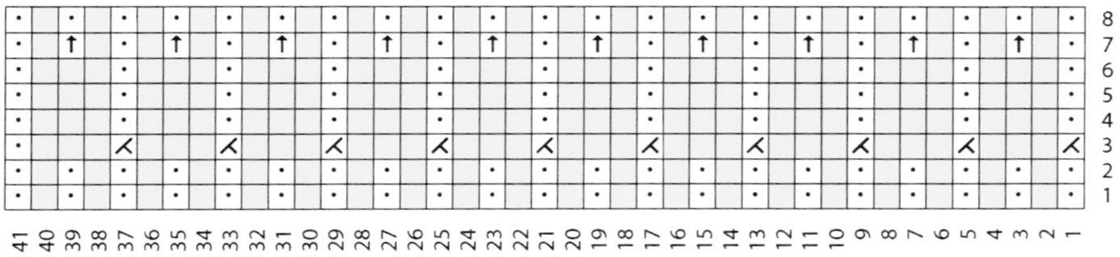

L85

L85a This giant "pigtail" was worked over 150 NDLS and *not* seamed. Smaller versions might make an interesting fringe for a scarf or blanket.

L86

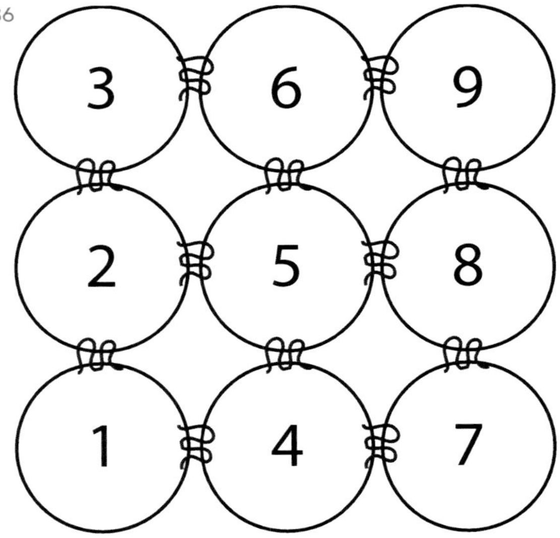

*Bring 41 NDLS to HP and, leaving a 10" tail at left, work latch tool C/O, left to right. Slip the last ST from the tool to the edge NDL. Starting with the 2nd NDL from the left edge, push EON back to NWP, dropping the chaining from those NDLS but retaining it on the others.**

Knit 2 rows and hang claw weights. Transfer EOS to the adjacent NDL and put the empty NDLS in NWP. Knit 4 rows. Lift the 4 ladder bars onto the middle NWP NDL in each group. Bring the NDLS to HP and set the carriage to knit NDLS back to WP. Knit 2 rows.

Cut the yarn, use yarn NDL and gather off the STS, running the yarn through the STS twice for added strength and security. Use this end or the beginning tail to sew a short seam on the side to close the shape.

L86 To join rosettes for a continuous fabric: Work *to **. P/U the purl loops from the first 2 rows (after the chain C/O) of the previous rosette at each side of the rosette's seam and hang on NDLS 1 and 3. Complete the second rosette. Repeat for the length of a strip.

To join a second strip, rehang the side edge of the first rosette when C/O the first rosette of the 2nd strip. For the next and following rosettes in the 2nd strip, after C/O from * to **, hang 2 purl bars from the previous rosette on NDLS 1 and 3. Then hang 2 purl bars from the side of the second rosette on the first strip on NDLS 9 and 13. Complete the rosette. Repeat the side and end joinings for the remaining strips.

Rehung Ladders

L87 is what I think of as "free spirit knitting." I began by knitting a 10 ST wide strip with a ladder and an occasional cable crossing, closing up the ladders and narrowing the strip as I worked. Then, when there were only a couple of STS remaining on the machine, I P/U the side of the strip and hung it over about 20 needles and worked some more cables and ladders for a dozen or so rows.

L87

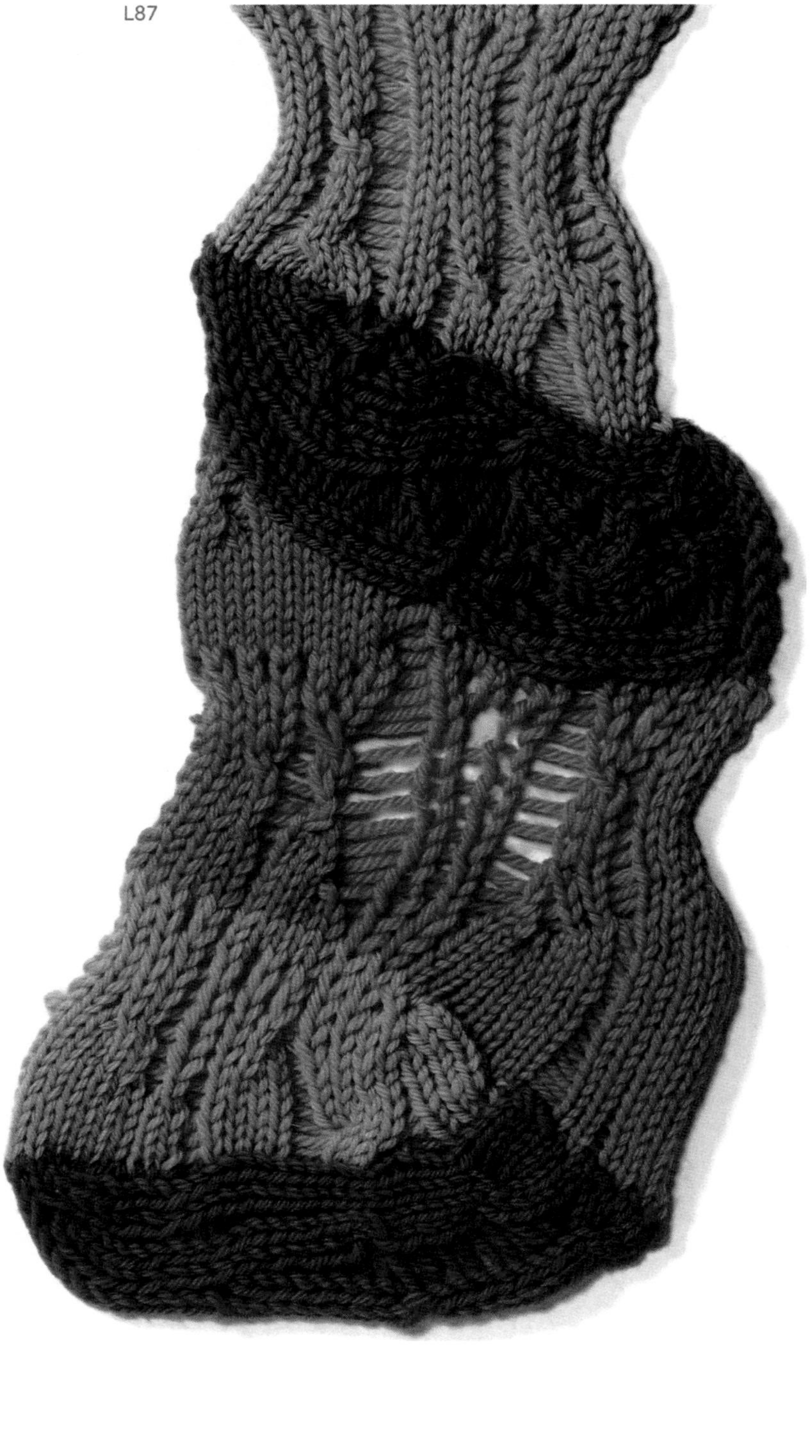

When I changed color for the third section, I continued on those NDLS and also picked up the C/O edge of the first section and worked all 28 STS for another 20 rows or so, making decreases and cables whenever it occurred to me to further shape and contort the ladders. I scrapped off the piece to get a good look at it and then I C/O a new piece over about a dozen NDLS and made some transfers to create more erratic ladders.

As I worked this section, I hung the live STS from the last section onto the NDLS to join the two. After I bound off the last few STS in that section, I rehung the edge of the 4th section to begin the last section of the piece.

Long story short: As much as I would like to give you specific directions for this piece, it just isn't possible. In fact, I think that row by row directions would make it all much harder than it is.

I will tell you to tighten up your stitch size a number or two and to think about incorporating lots of color changes, short rows, cables, transfers and lifted stitches to accent the ladders. And, while this is definitely a free wheeling way to work, do give yourself some guidelines as to how wide or long you want the piece to be and keep it in mind when you start rehanging sections.

L87A

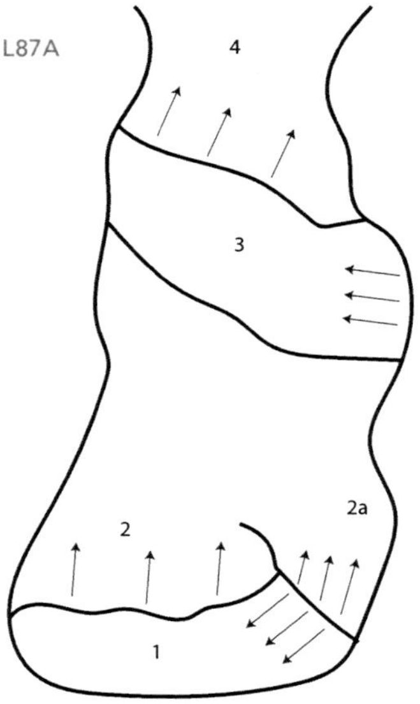

L87a I began section 1 with about 10 STS and randomly created ladders and crossed cables. When the piece was as long as I wanted, I reduced the STS by half and then P/U and rehung the edge of section 1 to begin section 2. When I completed the light blue portion, I P/U the beginning end of section 1, changed color and knitted the rest of section 2. I S/O the piece and then C/O to knit section 3, joining the live STS from section 2 as I worked. Once all of the STS were P/U, I B/O section 3. Lastly I P/U and rehung the edge of section 3 to knit the fourth and last section. The random ladders, twists and cables were help break the surface of the fabric and add textural interest. You could continue, P/U any of the edges to increase the length or width of the fabric.

L88

L88 I think that knotted ladders make a great edging for all kinds of projects and they couldn't be easier to do! They are knit similar to the fringes on page 70.

With waste yarn, Cast on 4 NDLS, leave 6 - 8 NDLS in NWP and C/O 1 more NDL.

You must knit 12 rows to complete each knot. Knit the strip as long as you need it and then B/O the group of 4 STS. Drop the ST from the single NDL and ravel the ST to free the individual loops. Steaming the strip will make it easier to handle and when you do so, insert a blocking wire through all the loops so you have something to pin down as you work. The 4 ST border will curl towards the knots, making a great edging.

Loosely knot 3 x 3 loops and then rehang the loops on the machine by one of these methods (or one you think of on your own!) Rehang 1 loop on every NDL, skipping 1 NDL in WP between every group of 3 loops. Rehang them on EON, which spreads them out and is less dense so the edging is softer.

How you decide to hang the strip will depend on your gauge and garment style. You may need to double up some stitches or loops to make the strip fit the garment or you might have to adapt your pattern to work with the 6 loops that complete each knot. You could change the proportion by leaving fewer or more NDLS in NWP between the four edge NDLS and the single fringing NDL. Instead of knotting 3x3 loops, you could do 4x4 or 2x2 or a mixture of them all. Just remember that you need to knit your strip with enough loops to account for the number of STS you need to C/O to begin your project.

L89A

# of 20 row repeats for strip	***# of loops to hang***	***Actual # of NDLS***	***Difference between loops and NDLS***
2	**20**	**17**	**3**
3	**30**	**25**	**5**
4	**40**	**33**	**7**
5	**50**	**41**	**9**

L89 is one of the fabric trims that the clever knitters at The Silver Reed Institute developed back in the 80's. Their version was another fringe—type strip, rehung as a lower edge. In this case, the loops are woven as they are rehung. I worked with the technique, then stretched it a bit further for a join—as—you—knit edging up the sides as shown in L90 and a separate strip to graft to the end so that it could be used as an edging all around an afghan or similar project.

L88

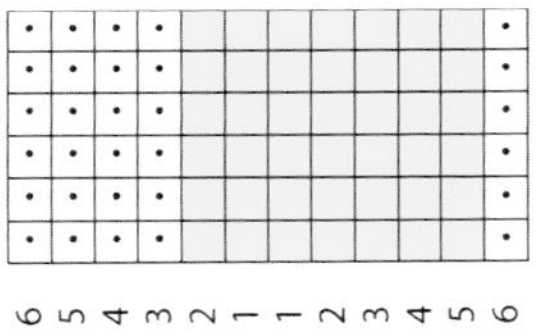

L89

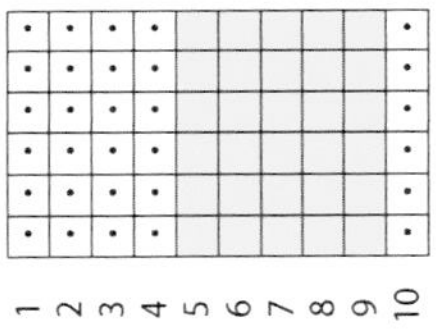

L89

L90

Like the previous example, you need to figure how long to knit your strips so that they can be hung sideways on the machine for the beginning edge. For L90, the strips up the side are completed in advance and worked row for row the same as the main fabric because you'll join rows to rows. Chart L89a should help you plan.

First you need to knit the strips. C/O 4 NDLS, skip over 5 in NWP and C/O 1 more as shown on the chart below.. The 4 STS at one edge will roll and look like an I—cord edging along the trim; the single ST is dropped to form the weaving loops.

You will need 10 loops for each repeat of the woven border, which translates to 20 rows. Because I usually double the center loops and the edge loops, this eventually translates to 9 NDLS per repeat when rehanging the loops on the machine. You can, of course, skip a NDL here or there or double additional loops to fit the exact number of NDLS you need to C/O for a specific project.

As a general rule, if you plan to double the middle and ending STS of each repeat to avoid gaps in the border you will have fewer NDLS than loops. You can use the chart above as a guide and extend the math to the number of repeats you need — with each additional repeat, there will be 2 fewer NDLS.

For a practice piece like L90, I suggest proceeding as follows: First, knit 4 pieces , 60 rows each. B/O the 4 edge STS. Ravel the single ST at the other edge and as you do so, catch the loops on a blocking wire or straight knitting NDL that you can use to tension the loops as you steam them. Next, each of the strips needs to be woven. Three of them will be woven, their loops rehung on the machine as you do so and then those pieces will be scrapped off for later use. The fourth strip will be woven, hung on the NDLS and remain there to begin the work.

L91a To weave each of the pieces: With the knit side of the strip facing you:

> Hang the 6th loop on the 1st NDL at the far right
> Hang the 7th loop on the 2nd NDL from the end
> Hang the 8th loop on the 3rd NDL from the end
> Hang the 9th loop on the 4th NDL from the end
> Hang the 10th loop on the 5th NDL from the end.

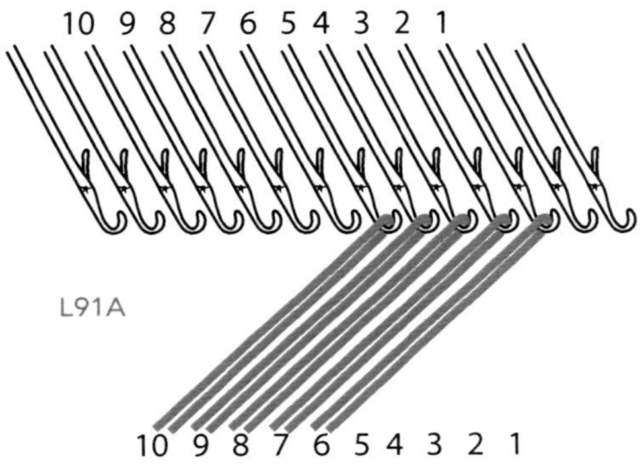

L91A

L91b Next, retaining a little tension on the 5 loops on the NDLS, insert a latch tool through them, weaving over and under each pairs of strands. Catch the very first loop of the strip in the hook, pull it through and hang it on the 5th NDL along with the 10th loop. This is the middle of the first repeat and the doubling will prevent a gap.

Re—insert the tool through the loops again, weaving over and under the alternate pairs. Catch the 2nd loop from the strip in the hook, pull it through and hang it on the 6th NDL. Continue weaving over and under and pulling loops through to hang on the next empty NDL until 10 of the first loops are hung over *9 NDLS,* with 2 loops hung on the middle (5th) NDL. L91B

Begin the next repeat, by hanging the last 5 loops on NDLS 9 - 13. NDL 9 already holds the last ST of the previous repeat and the doubling here is to prevent a gap from one repeat to the next. Then weave the first 5 loops of that repeat through the first 5 loops, hanging them on NDLS 13 - 17. Once again, the center NDL (# 13) will hold 2 loops.

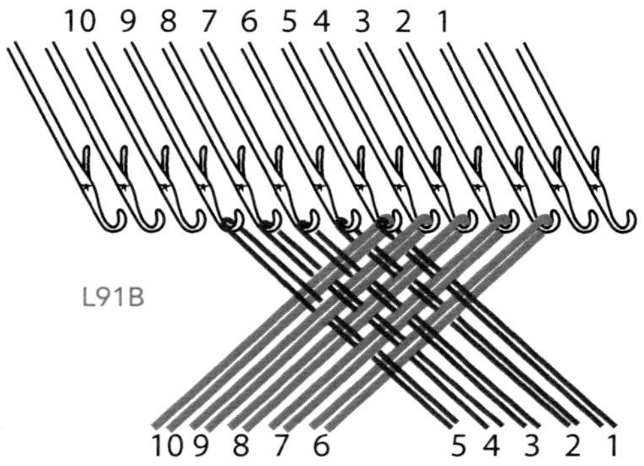

L91B

Continue hanging remaining repeats, doubling the 1st loop of one repeat with the last loop of the previous repeat and doubling at center.

When all 17 loops have been woven and hung you should have three distinct, woven sections. S/O all 17 loops and set aside. Repeat for two more sections. Press the waste knitting to prevent it from raveling as you handle the strips later.

After hanging and weaving the 4th strip, leave it on the machine to begin knitting the main fabric in the same or a contrasting color. You will join one of the other 3 strips at each edge of the work, A/R with the knit side of the strip facing you so that it can roll towards the knit side later on. Fold the waste under so you can clearly see the STS/loops of the strip.

*Knit 2 rows. Use a single—prong transfer tool to lift the first loop from the strip onto the edge NDL, pulling the NDL out to HP as you do so. Repeat for the second side with a separate strip.** Repeat * to ** until you reach the end of the knitting and the end of the strips. S/O the fabric, leaving a long tail.

Lay the main knitting and the last strip flat on a table, with the waste knitting folded back out of the way and graft the last strip to the live STS of the fabric. I usually find it is easiest for me to graft with the purl sides facing me, but you may want to work with the knit sides up and that is fine.

Instead of doubling the center and ending loops on the NDLS, you could also try just crossing them like a cable. To do that, you would hang the last loop of the first repeat on the 10th NDL and the first loop from the next repeat on the 9th NDL. This little 1 x 1 cable will help reduce the gap between sections. Concessions like this may be necessary if you are trying to make the edging fit a specific number of NDLS.

Instead of separate side strips, you might also be able to work one very long piece, hang the center portion for the C/O edge and then join the remainder of the strip at each edge of the knitting. With careful figuring, you would also be able to include the ending section so that the trim is fully continuous.

L92 These pansies couldn't be easier to knit and while I used them as an edging for an afghan sample, you could also use them to embellish a sweater or other project.

To knit each individual pansy: C/O 35 NDLS with waste yarn and then change to MC. Begin COR and knit 8 rows. Make decreases as shown in row 9 to reduce each group of working NDLS from 5 to 3. Knit 5 rows. Make decreases to reduce each group of 3 STS to a single ST. Move these single STS closer together so there are only 3 empty NDLS between each one. You can use a garter bar or just move them over in a couple of steps with a transfer tool. Knit 1 row, ending COR.

Unthread the carriage. Place first NDL at right in HP. *Insert a latch tool over the first 3 ladder bars at left of this NDL and then under the remaining bars. Catch the free yarn from the carriage in the hook of the tool and pull the tool down and towards you. Let the ST slide over and behind the latch. Catch the FY in the hook of the tool again and pull through snuggly to form a ST. Put this new ST on the next WP NDL at left and then use the FY to knit those 2 STS together. Bring that NDL to HP.** Repeat * to ** for the remaining STS. Cut the yarn, leaving a 24" tail. Thread a yarn NDL and gather off all 6 remaining STS, passing the yarn through the STS a second time and tying off snuggly on the back of the work.

To use multiple pansies for an edging, rehang each one over 19 NDLS by P/U a full ST along the upper edge, with the wrong side of the piece facing you. When you reach the center of a pansy, skip 1 NDL (do not hang an edge ST), but do bring the NDL to WP so it C/O when you begin knitting. This will provide a little ease at the center of each flower so they lie flat.

L93 The large, single flower was worked very much like the pansies, but was worked over a total of 143 NDLS as follows: With waste yarn, beginning on the left end of the bed, set the NDLS to (7 NDLS WP then 5 in NWP) 4 times, ending with 7 WP NDLS for a total of 55 NDLS (WP and NWP) in this section (A).

Then, for section B, set the NDLS (5 NWP NDLS followed by 5 WP NDLS) 5 times, ending with 5 NWP NDLS for a total of 55 NDLS in this section. Lastly, set the NDLS (3 WP NDLS then 3 NWP NDLS) 6 times, ending with 3 WP NDLS for section C.

C/O with waste and knit some rows before changing to MC. COR. Change to the MC and e—wrap the same NDLS from left to right. Knit 5 rows, ending COL. Working just in section C, bring the latch tool up behind all the bars in the first ladder at right, holding the tool so that the hook is facing you. Catch the top 3 bars in the hook of the tool. Pull the tool down then forward, towards you. Lift this tuck onto the NDL above and place the NDL in HP. Set carriage to hold NDLS in HP.

L92

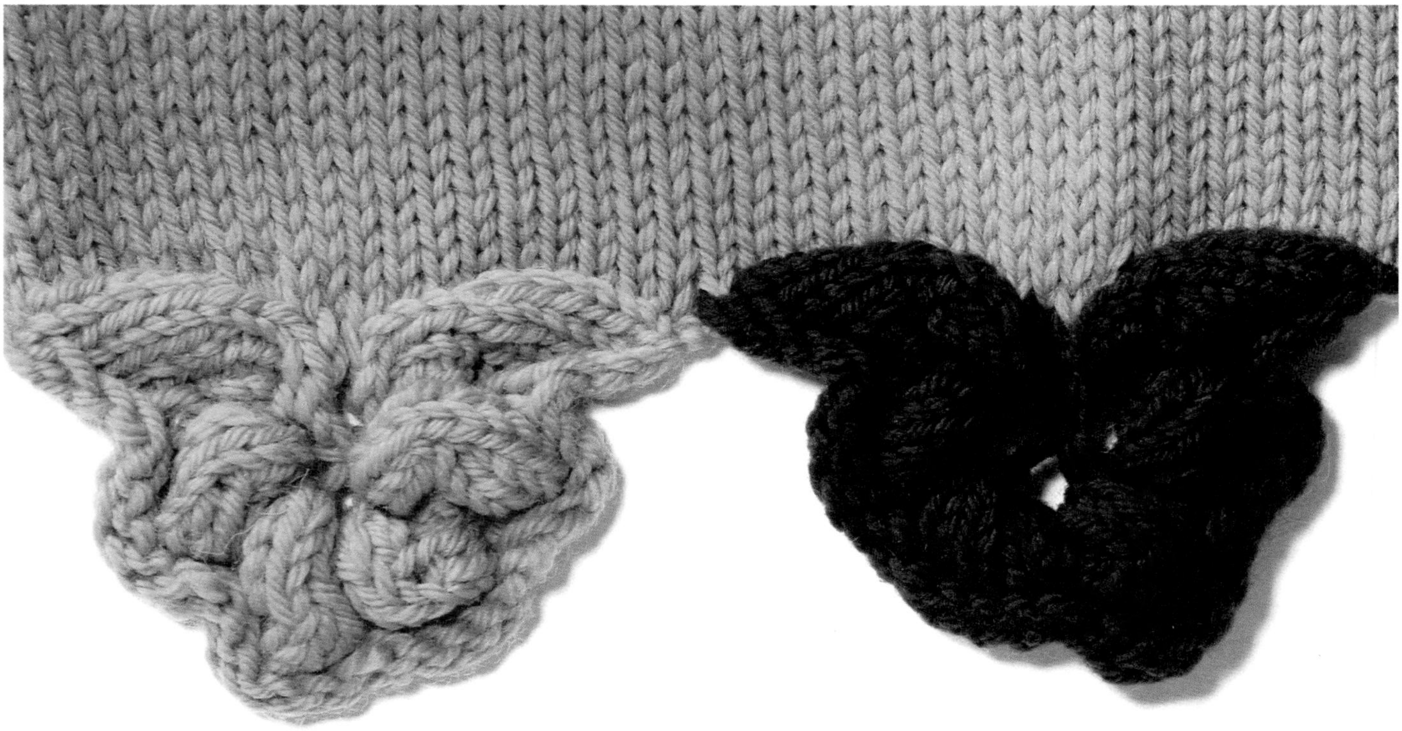

Knit 4 rows on the remaining NDLS. Working on just the NDLS in section B, lift all 5 ladder bars onto the NDL above. Work all ladders in group B then make decreases to reduce from 5 STS to 3 in each group. Knit 2 rows and then reduce each group in section B from 3 NDLS to 1 and place those NDLS in HP.

Reduce the groups in section C from 7 STS to 5 and knit 2 rows. Reduce each group from 5 to 3 STS and knit 2 rows. Finally, reduce each group down to 1 NDL. Set carriage to knit NDLS back from HP and knit 2 rows across all NDLS. Cut the yarn, leaving a long enough tail to gather off the STS, passing the yarn through all the STS a second time to secure. The smaller section, C, will stack up on top of B and A. Work the end into the back of the piece.

L93

L92

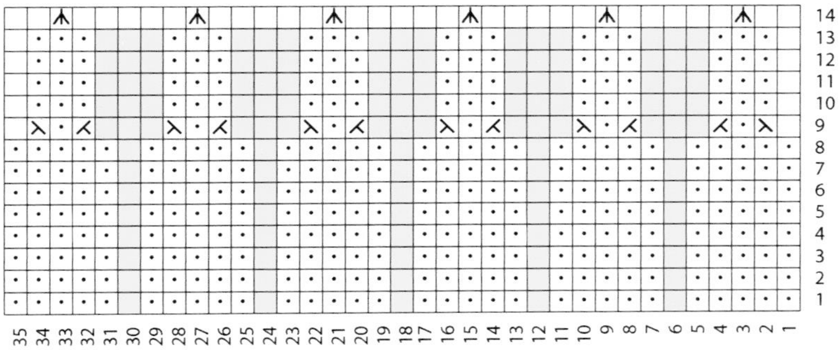

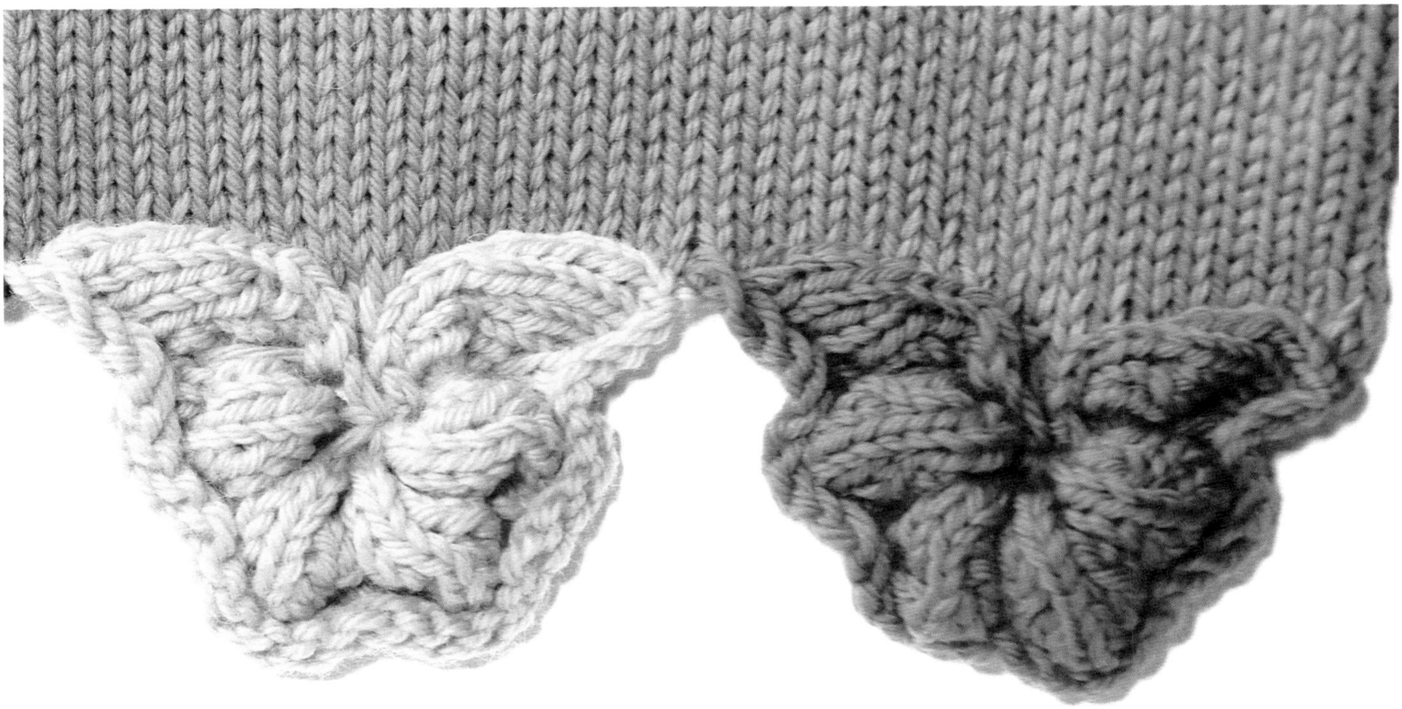

Winged Ladders

L94 The last rehung ladder fabric is one of my favorites because it is so versatile and so easy to do. The original trim was developed at the Silver Knitting Institute back in the 90's. They showed it as an edging on one side of a fabric. I immediately began working it on both sides to produce a nearly non—roll edging on stockinette scarves and such. This technique was included in the Studio Tips & Techniques #9, which is available on my web site. I have dubbed it the "Winged Ladder Trim" because of the way the trim attaches at each side.

To work this trim at both edges, C/O enough NDLS for your scarf or project, reserving 6 extra NDLS at each edge for the trim. Begin with waste knitting and then change to the MC and knit 2 rows, ending COR with the carriage set to knit all NDLS.

*On the carriage side (right), skip the first 3 NWP NDLS adj to the fabric, e—wrap C/O the next 3 NDLS and bring them to HP. Knit 1 row to the left. On the carriage side (left this time), skip 3 NDLS adj to the fabric , e—wrap the next 3 NDLS and bring them to HP. Knit 5 (or 7) rows, ending COR.

On the right edge only, use a 3-prong tool to remove the 3 STS from the NDLS you previously e—wrapped and replace the STS on the first 3 NDLS at the right

L94

L94 Every 6/R move the STS from the A to the C NDLS and then e—wrap the empty NDLS as described in the text. The B NDLS remain empty throughout.

on the main fabric. There are 2 STS on each of those NDLS so bring them to HP so they knit cleanly.. Before knitting the next row, e—wrap the same three NDLS and bring them to HP. Knit 1 row to the left.

On the left edge, use the 3-prong tool to remove the 3 STS from the previously e—wrapped NDLS and replace them on the first 3 NDLS at the left of the main fabric and bring those NDLS to HP. Immediately e—wrap the same 3 NDLS and knit 5 rows, ending COR. **

Repeat * to ** for the length of the fabric. You can try leaving more than 3 empty NDLS between the "wing" and the main fabric, but unless your yarn is fuzzy and textured, it is apt to look rather stringy. If you have a 4-prong tool, (or are willing to use two 2-prong tools together) you can also try e—wrapping 4 extra NDLS at each side, rather than 3. Depending on the gauge of your machine and the size and character of the yarn, you may want to knit more than 5 (or 7) rows between repeats. Watch your weights!

Winged Ladder Cast On Edge

After a while I realized that I could pre—knit bands to rehang for a C/O edge by working an ultra—narrow "main fabric" to attach the trim to. Because the winged trim is 3 STS wide, I needed 3 NDLS to transfer them to after each repeat so it was clear that the narrowest trim I could knit was 9 NDLS wide (3 WP, 3 NWP and 3 WP NDLS).

C/O 6 NDLS as shown in the diagram L95. Specifically, C/O 3 NDLS (section A), skip 3 NDLS in NWP (B) and C/O 3 more NDLS (C). Change to the MC and *knit 6 rows. Transfer the 3 STS from A to C. Immediately e—wrap C/O the same 3 NDLS** and repeat * to ** until the piece is long enough to rehang sideways across the NDLS to act as the lower edge of your garment. Each repeat of the edging will rehang on approximately 6 NDLS.

Winged Ladder B/O

Once I figured out how to add the effect to the lower edge, I decided to forge ahead and work out a B/O method so that I could, essentially, apply this winged ladder affect on all four sides of an afghan or other project.

Initially, I dealt with B/O by S/O the last row of my project. Then I worked a band like the C/O band above and P/U 1 ST from the garment scrap E/R or EOR. That method evolved into a true B/O, which eventually gave birth to the fabric.

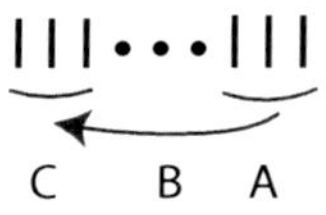

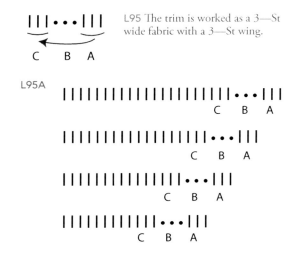

L95 The trim is worked as a 3—St wide fabric with a 3—St wing.

L95A

|||||||||||||||||||||•••|||
C B A

|||||||||||||||||•••|||
C B A

|||||||||||||||•••|||
C B A

||||||||||||•••|||
C B A

Winged Ladder Fabric

After a while I had one of those "Eureka!" moments when I realized that I could create an entire fabric of winged ladders. The method allows you to use up all those little odd bits of yarn you have been saving and it is one of those projects you can take off the machine on a safety pin at the end of each band to return to another time.

L95a To begin, knit the first band of the fabric by C/O a multiple of 3 STS with waste yarn. Knit some rows, ending COL then change to the main yarn, knit 1 row ending COR. Set the carriage to hold NDLS in HP and hold all NDLS except the first 3 NDLS on the carriage side. Skip the next 3 NDLS in NWP and e—wrap the next 3 NDLS.

*Knit 6 rows, ending COR. Remove the 3 STS from the A NDLS, move them to NDLS C and then move all 6 STS to NDLS B. There are 2 STS on each of the 3 B NDLS. The C NDLS are empty and the A NDLS are now in NWP.** Move the next group of NDLS at left into UWP and repeat * to **. With each repeat of the directions, you are B/O 3 STS And A, B and C shift 3 NDLS to the left as shown on the NDL chart. When you get to the last group of 3, you can B/O all 3 doubled STS or you can leave them on their NDLS to begin the next repeat from the left end of the bed. You can also remove them on a ST holder and set the work aside for another day.

To re—cap, you will C/O a multiple of 3 STS and immediately proceeded to bind them off, down to the last 3 STS. For the fabric, rehang the edge of this first band and start again, but keep in mind that you can also use this method to B/O any fabric.

To work the next band of the technique, rehang the edge of the previous band with the wrong side facing you, over the exact same number of NDLS you began with. To do this, either (consistently!) P/U above the STS 95b or above the ladders 95c, but not both because the fabric will grow wider and wider. However, if you want to increase the width of the fabric, this might be a way to do so.

Note that you only e—wrap the 3 extra NDLS for the very first repeat in a row to prevent the fabric from narrowing each time you start another band. You can work the bands from either the left or the right or you can alternate left and right as I did in my example at L97.

95b Use a 3—prong tool to P/U just 3 STS from the edge of the previous strip directly over the knitted portion below. Skip the adj laddered area and make the next and all following P/U over the knitted portions only.

95c You could also choose to P/U from the edge of the previous strip directly over the laddered portions as shown below. The fabric is apt to be a little less stretchy and may even narrow a bit as the laddered portion contributes more give than does the knitted portion and P/U this edge confines it some.

L96 The applied winged ladder trim was worked after the fabric was complete. I knitted the trim over 6 NDLS (3 WP/3NW-P/3WP) and P/U a ST from the surface of the fabric A/R twice and then 3/R to prevent it from rippling. This would make a great edging alongside a button band on a cardigan.

There is a definite right and wrong side to the way the band attaches to the surface of the fabric . To match the application on both fronts of a cardigan, for example, P/U the first from bottom to top and the second from top to bottom. Also, I find that the join is less bulky if I only P/U a half ST, rather than a whole ST from the surface of the fabric.

L97 If you look at the multi—colored sample you will see that the effect zigzags back and forth while the solid blue version L98 is more horizontal. The multi—colored example was worked as I described above, but the solid example was worked with 2-step transfers. To do this, transfer the 3 STS from A to the C NDLS and then move all the STS to B. It is definitely more work and I personally prefer the look of the simpler method.

Even though the fabric looks narrow when hung on the NDLS, the resulting fabric expands greatly because of the ladders. The sweater at L99 was worked with a worsted weight yarn (all my Noro yarn leftovers) on a midgauge machine. I cast on a total of only 75 STS and the sweater measures 24" across, so you can see that this is a great way to get as large a sweater as you want with relatively few NDLS.

Gauging a fabric like this is different than working with stockinette or tuck stitch. You need to do a fairly large swatch and then measure how many inches each *repeat* equals. In short, plan out your sweater by the number of repeats both widthwise and lengthwise, rather than the usual STS and rows per inch.

To shape the armhole of a sweater, you can skip a group or two when you rehang the body of the sweater so that instead of continuing to rehang 25 groups of 3, for example, you would only rehang 23 groups.

To divide a neckline, only rehang half of the previous band to work one side at a time. You can add some shaping by reducing the number of repeats you hang each time. I reduced and shaped the neckband on my sweater by P/U a little differently. Rather than P/U 3 STS from the next 3 groups I rehung, I averaged it out and picked up just 2 STS from each of the 3 groups, which still retained my multiples of 3 rule and helped to make a more gradual curve than skipping an entire group of 3.

L97 FRONT

L97 BACK

L98

You can work these bands as wide as you want to by working down to the last 6 STS (3 WP/3NW-P/3WP), removing them from the machine and replacing them at the end of the opposite end of the bed and adding more STS. For an afghan, start with a couple of separate pieces of waste knitting that each end with 1 row of the MC. Hang the first piece on the machine and work the B/O down to the last 6 STS on the left. Then move those STS to the right end of the bed to make room for hanging the next pre—knit piece and continue working across those STS. Once you've established the width of the final piece by adding these pre—knitted sections, you will be able to continue working the whole fabric by hanging as many STS as you can fit, moving those to the edge of the bed and hanging some more.

I think this is a really fabulous afghan stitch. You don't need very much of any yarn to work a whole band — or even a partial band — of any color. Also, I think it is a real plus that you can work one band at a time, remove the last 6 STS on a holder and put the project away for a day so it doesn't tie up the machine.

To shape a triangular piece of fabric, I would simply P/U 1 less section from each end of the last band. You could create a triangular shawl (probably standard gauge) or you could work and afghan or other large project in triangles to join together later.

Sleeves will require some extra figuring to avoid stair—stepped edges and although I opted for ribbed sleeves on my garment, I don't think it would be impossible to work them in pattern. Just remember that you *always* need multiples of 3 to work with and that simply eliminating a group at each edge will produce stair steps.

The better alternative is to average out the decreasing as I indicated for the neckline. The only downside to this is that it will shift the pattern. If you limit the averaging to the 3 edge groups and you should be fine

L99 was knitted with all my leftover bits of several Noro yarns over the years. They were all too precious to throw away and they finally came in handy!

Cabled Ladders

While a ladder alongside a wide cable will definitely add some ease to the crossing, ladders can also be used to create cabled fabrics with better drape. Occasionally a ladder's ease will be absorbed into the cable stitches and barely show at all; other times they create a more open fabric.

L100

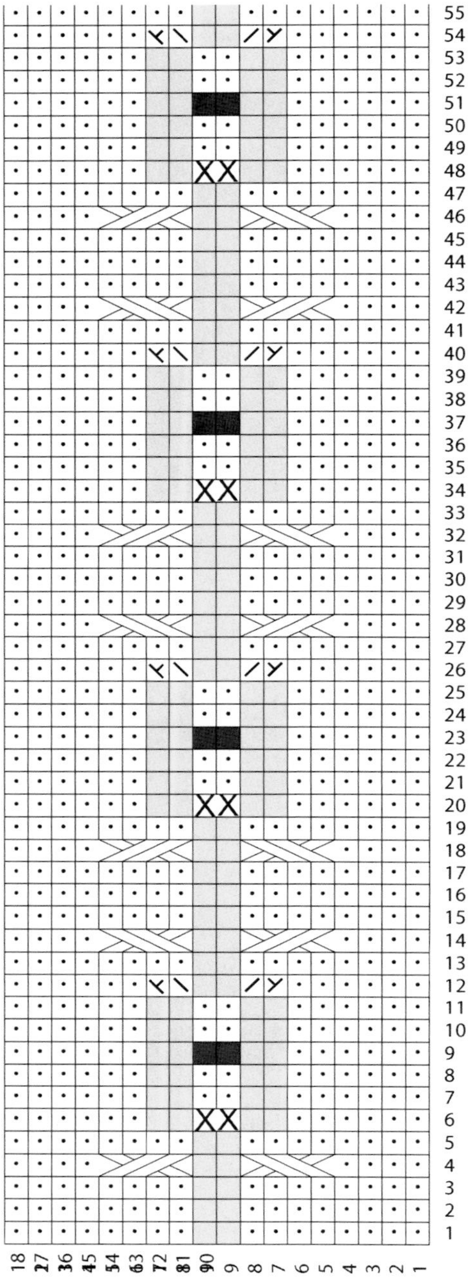

L100 and L101 show 2 different arrangements of cable crossings in relation to the accompanying ladders. Although I also included some popcorns on these samples, that effect is optional.

L100 is a single column of cables and ladders. There are some standard cable crosses at row 4, but after the 5th row I made stacked transfers by moving STS 7 and 8 and 11 and 12 to NDLS 9 and 10. Prior to knitting row 12, the ladders shift back to the center by making full fashioned increases at either side to shift the STS and to fill 2 of the empty NDLS. Move ST 9 one NDL to the right to NDL 8 and lift the purl bar to make a ST on NDL 7. Make an increase at the left the same way so that the ladder is on NDLS 9 and 10.

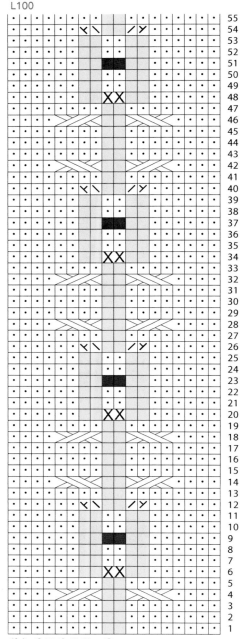

L100

L101 is the exact same column of ladders and cables, side by side. It may be difficult to cross two cables right next to each other on rows 4, 14, 18 and 28. If so, use drop ST to provide the ease by bringing one of the nearby ladder NDLS to WP the row before crossing,

L101

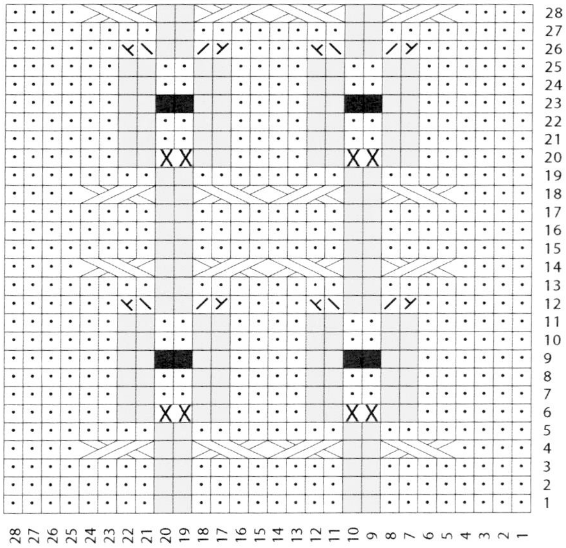

L101

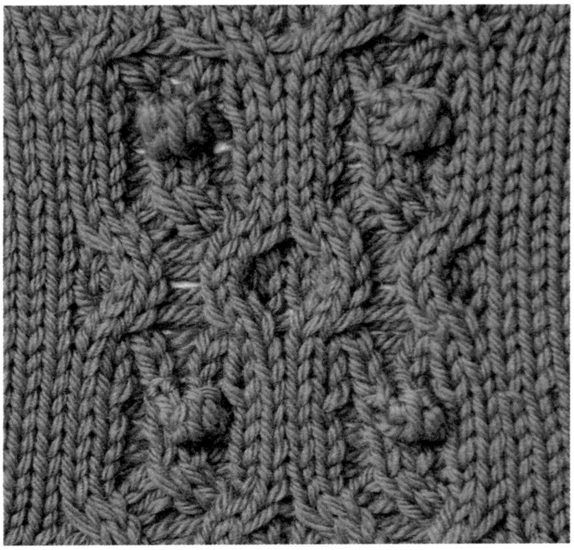

L102

then drop the ST from that NDL and place it in NWP. You could also offset the columns by 7 rows to create an alternating pattern.

L102 combines traveling STS and ladders to highlight this cable pattern. These traveling STS are a little bit different from some of those we looked at earlier because only half of the STS move. The rest stay right where they are and later *appear* to have moved because of the tension on the STS. The cables provide stability for this open fabric and the alternating direction of the cable crosses creates a woven effect.

Because these STS travel in pairs, you can accentuate the woven look even more by crossing the STS in a way that closely interweaves all of the intersection points. The chart L102a shows how to do this. (no photo)

L102

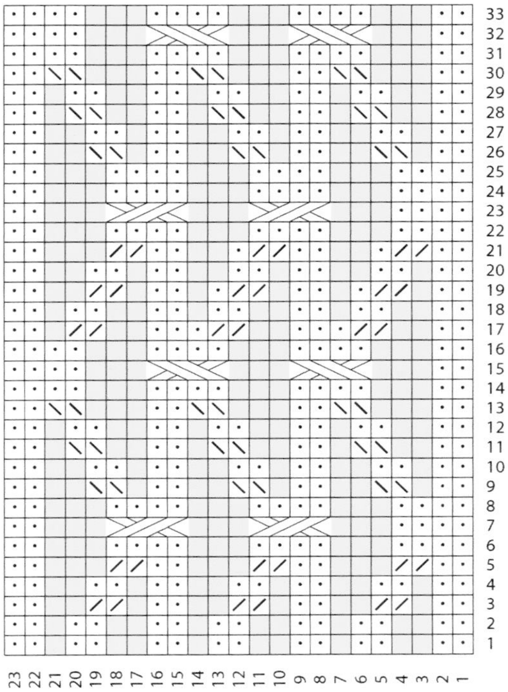

L102A

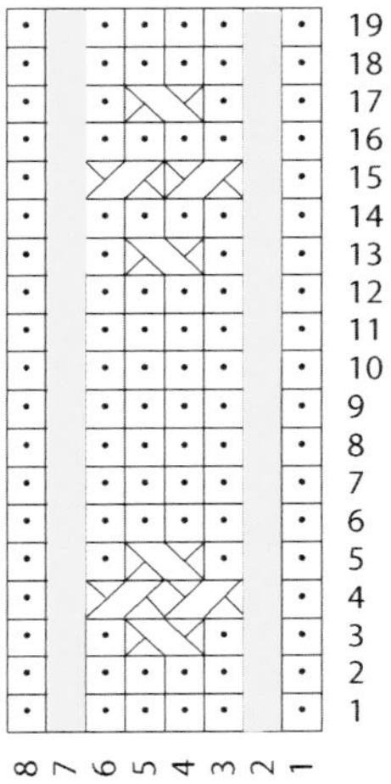

The fabric at right is one of Jo Bee's samples and allows the ladders to take center stage over the cables. Most of my samples that follow are a bit more restrained, but I have to admit a strong attraction to the motion and detail in this example.

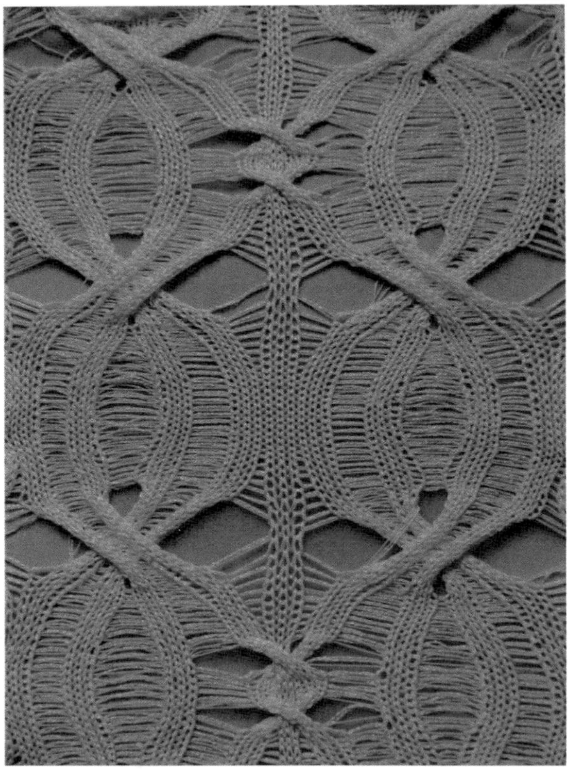

L103

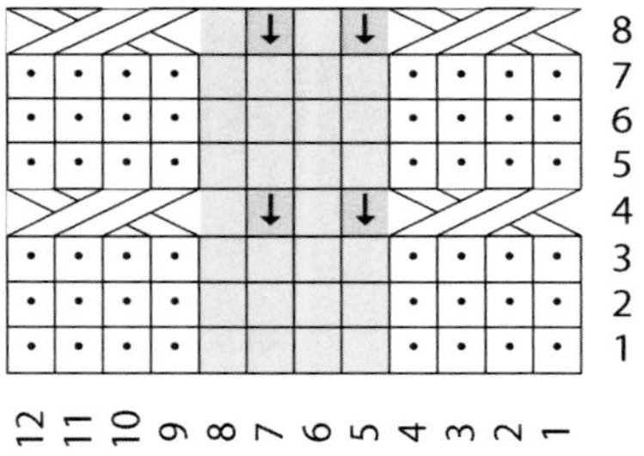

L103 This fabric forms a lovely cabled,non—roll edge.

L103 looks like a simple pattern of cables and wide open ladders, but it can be tricky to knit because the cables are all crossed at the same time and may be tight and difficult to cross.

To make it easier, bring two of the ladder NDLS to WP the row before the cable crossings, allow those NDLS to C/O and then drop their loops before crossing the cables. You could also ease the crossings by alternating the crossings so that every—other column crosses alternately with the other. The cables will totally stabilize these ladders and you should work this pattern right out to the edges of the fabric, with a cable on each selvage.

L104 is another cable pattern that requires drop ST to provide ease for the crossings. Knit 3 rows then bring the empty 3 and 4 (etc) NDLS to WP and knit 1 more row. Drop the STS from those NDLS and return them to NWP. Cross STS 8, 9, 10 with STS 13, 14, 15, shifting them 1 NDL towards each other so that NDLS 7 and 8 and 15 and 16 are empty, placed in NWP to form the next ladder. At the edges, you will need to cross partial cables, though in most fabrics, I would reserve a couple of plain edge STS to avoid this.

L104

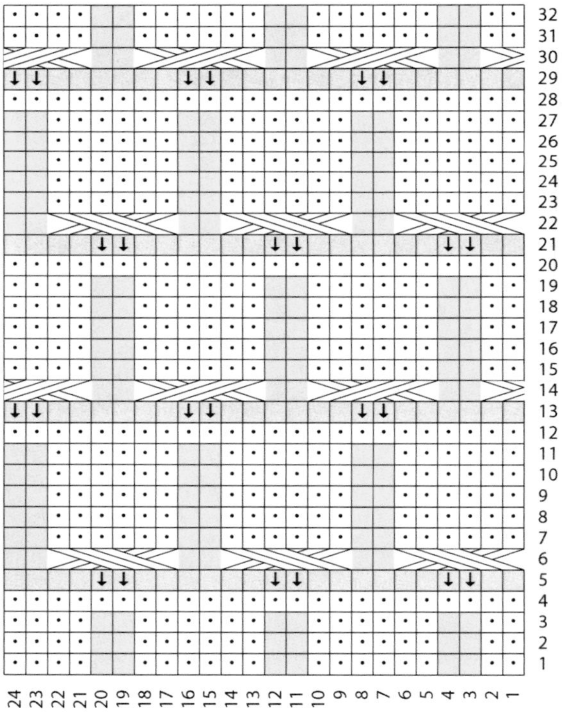

Because this is a woven cable, the "pairs" (in this case groups of 3 STS) of STS are split from crossing to crossing and the crossings alternate direction throughout the fabric. Without the ladders, a fully woven cable fabric by machine is very difficult to knit. The ladders create enough ease to make the crossings and also lend some openness and drape to the fabric.

L104

L105

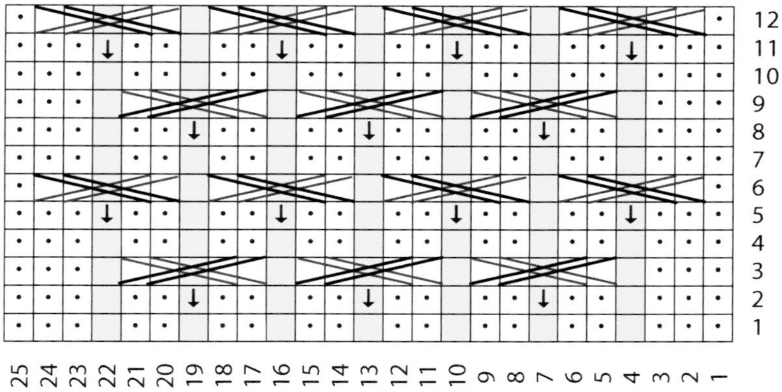

L105

L105 is another example of woven cables that result from splitting pairs and alternating the direction of the crosses. In this example, however, the cables cross behind the ladders, which provide considerable ease and drape to the fabric.

After each cable crossing, the ladder NDLS are brought back to WP, allowed to C/O and then dropped prior to crossing the next group of cables. I worked 3 rows after each crossing because an odd number of rows allows you to coordinate the direction of the cable crossings to the carriage side.

Note that I only worked drop ST on the ladders directly under the cables, but you may find that you get more ease for crossing by dropping the ladders between the cables and, for resistant yarns, you may want to drop all the ladder STS prior to each crossing. A lot will depend on the yarn you choose.

L106

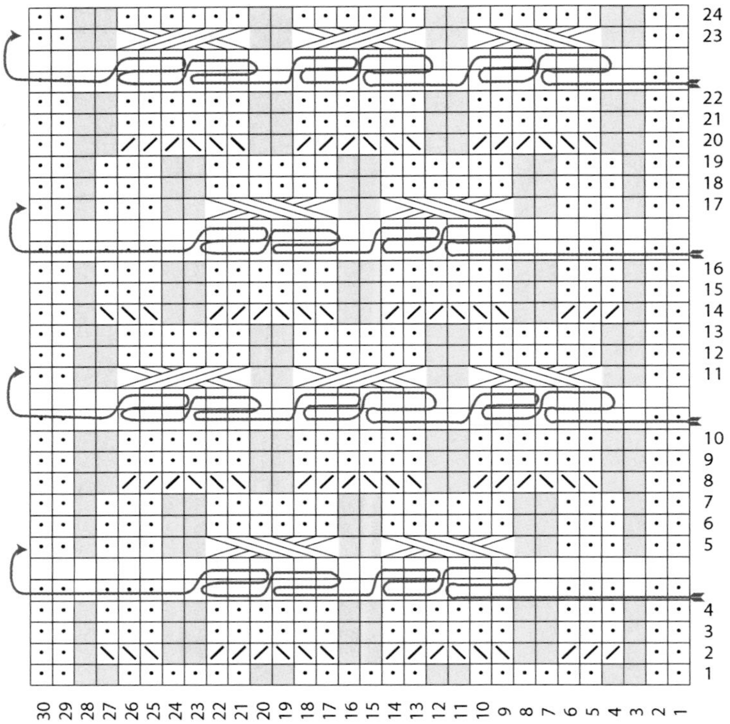

L106

Rather than relying on drop stitch for ease, the next two samples utilize bridging to add extra rows on the cable NDLS. Both of these examples are woven cables so, once again, they "split pairs" prior to each crossing and the direction of the crossings alternates throughout. L106 adds 2 extra rows to each half of the cables, while L107 adds 6 extra rows to each half of the cable.

Adding 6 extra rows to each half of the cable introduces a very long float or BB on the back of the cable that must be avoided when you cross the STS so that it is not trapped on the knit side of the fabric.

L107

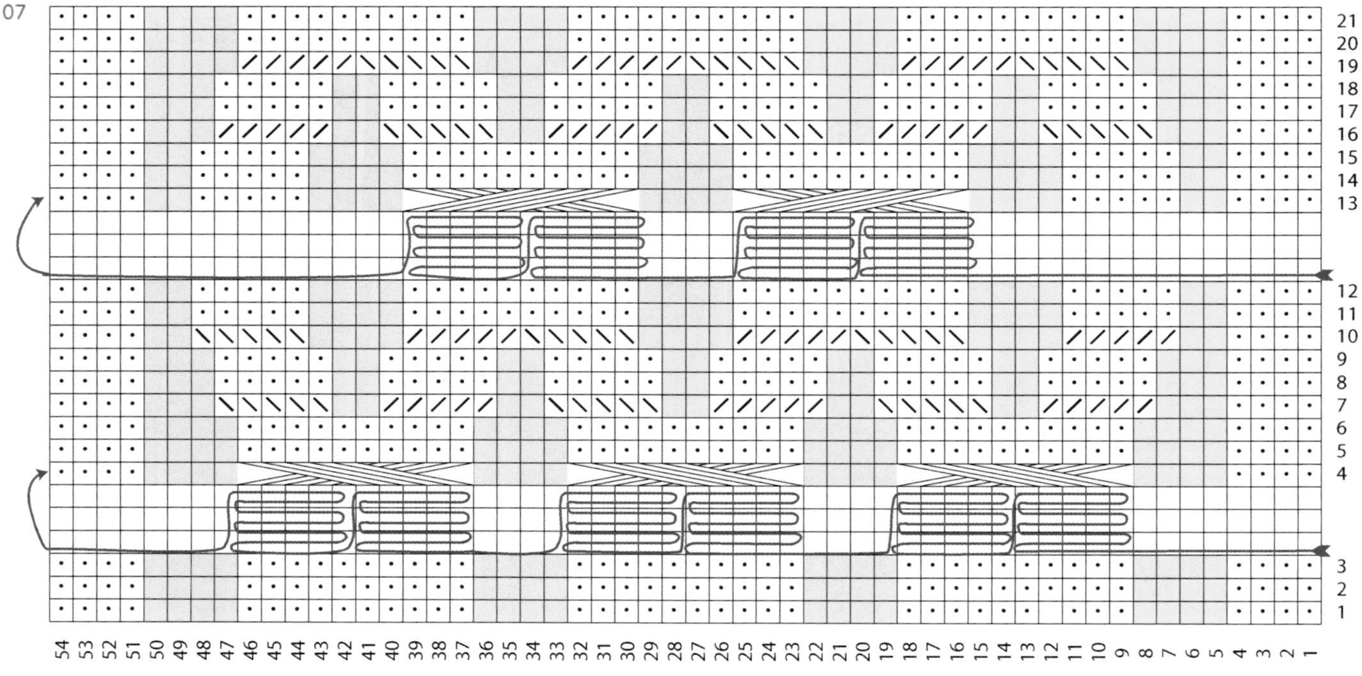

When bridging starts on the right as shown on the chart and the cables first cross right to left and then left to right, there is no BB to worry about. However, when crossing the alternate cables, the second tool must pass under the BB (which is easy to see) which is the case with the cables in row 4, but not in row 14.

After crossing all the cables in row 4, *knit 3 rows. Begin (as shown in row 7), moving groups of 5 STS to the left or right by one NDL** twice. The previous ladders narrow as the new ones are created. After row 12, repeat the bridging and, when crossing the cables, reverse the direction of the crossings

L108 is modeled after one of the Stoll fabrics. There are two slightly different effects here. The ladder in the center of the cables at left in the photo (right on the chart) has parallel, straight bars; the bars of the ladder in the pattern on the right of the photo (left on the chart) appear twisted. The difference is caused simply by which NDLS return to work first. You'll also find that these are not your average cable crossings.

Look at row 1. There are two cable crosses shown, both at the right of their ladders. They are 2 x 3 cables, where STS 6 & 7 cross in front of STS 3, 4, 5 and are placed on NDLS 3 & 4. STS 3, 4 & 5 then return to their original NDLS so that, in some ways, this is more of a 2-step decrease than a cable. The ladder NDLS are always empty and in NWP after each crossing.

How the ladder NDLS return to WP has a direct affect on the formation of the ladders between the cable crossings. Look closely at row 2 and you will see that at the right, NDL 6, which is closest to the cable, is brought back to WP first and then NDL 7 in the next row. At the left example, however, NDL 18 returns to WP first and then 17 in the next row. To put it another way, in the example at right, the empty NDL closest to the cable return to WP first while in the left example, it is the empty NDL further from the cable.

L108

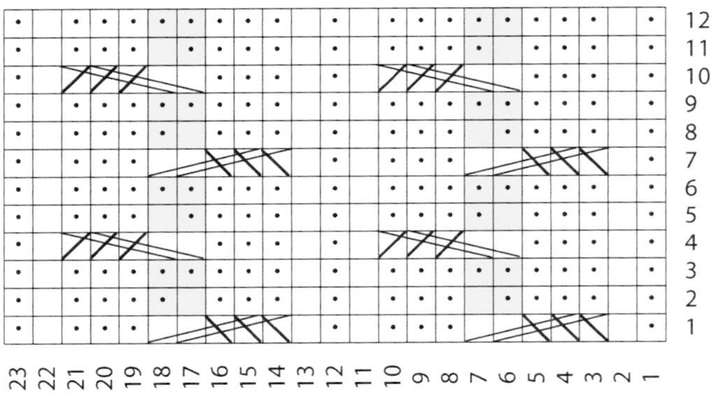

L107

In short, when the empty NDL closest to the cable always comes to WP first, the bars of the ladder will be parallel and untwisted. When the further NDL returns first, the bars of the ladders will twist. This is a very small detail, but one that makes a huge difference in the final pattern. You must be consistent throughout because one wrong move will show!

L108

L109 This last cabled ladder fabric was also inspired by a Stoll fabric. It could be knitted as intarsia, Fair Isle or 2-color slip on a manual machine as shown on the chart.

This is a 2-color version of L103, where the ladder bars between the cables are two colors. The ladders and/or the cable groups can be wider (i.e. 3x3 cables instead of 2x2). All of these ladders cross the same direction — though they don't have to and you have the option of latching up the ladders in one color or two.

If you decide to select the needles electronically or with a punch card, make sure you include the ladders in your design. My sample was knitted with manual selection for slip ST. *For the first 2 rows, I knitted NDLS 3, 4 and 9, 10 with the lighter color, slipping NDLS 5, 6 and 11, 12, while also passing by the ladder NDLS (yellow). The darker color knits the next two rows, slipping the NDLS knitted in the first 2 rows and bypassing the ladder NDLS again.** Repeat from * to ** and then cross the cables.

Once the cables cross, the colors change position. For manual selection, you should select accordingly. For punch card or electronics you can use the same design card but just change the color order, knitting the dark color first and then the lighter one. Whichever method you use, the effect is dependent on the placement of the colors, which alternates with each cable crossing.

L109

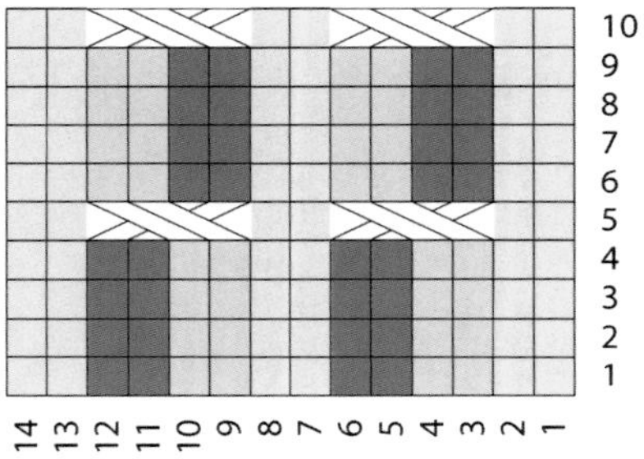

L109

Eyelet Ladders

This next group of samples are hybrids that look like ladders but are actually formed by eyelet—type transfers. I debated whether to include them in the eyelet chapter, based on structure or the ladder section based on appearance and ladders won out.

L110 The 2-step transfers in this fabric move 1 NDL to the right every two rows and produce a strong line of STS at the edge of each ladde. Otherwise these are fairly standard eyelets where the empty NDL remains in WP to C/O with the next pass of the carriage.

L111 This pattern appeared in an old, 1950's machine knitting pattern collection. It intrigued me because the effect is identical to an elaborate fabric I studied in the Stoll archives. Although this is an all—over pattern where the progression of the design moves from left to right, because the decreases are made from both right and left, the fabric does not bias as you would expect from looking at the chart.

This pattern is unusual in that the transfers are made E/R, rather than A/R, which is more common for lace patterns. As a result, the diagonals created by the trans-

L110

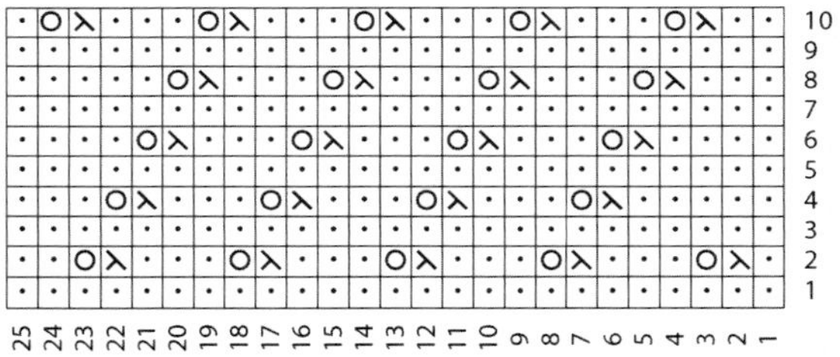

L110

L111

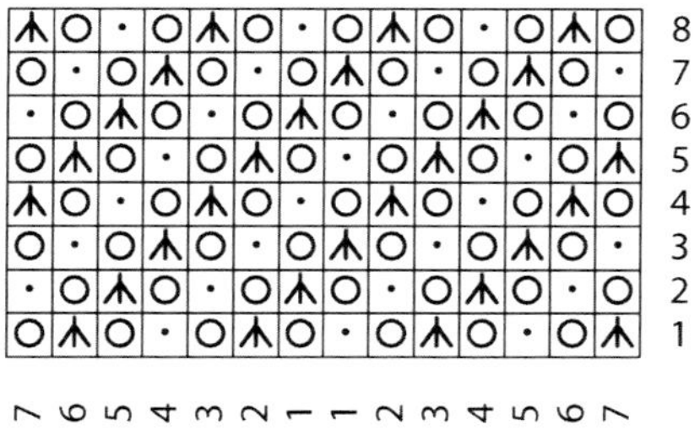

L111

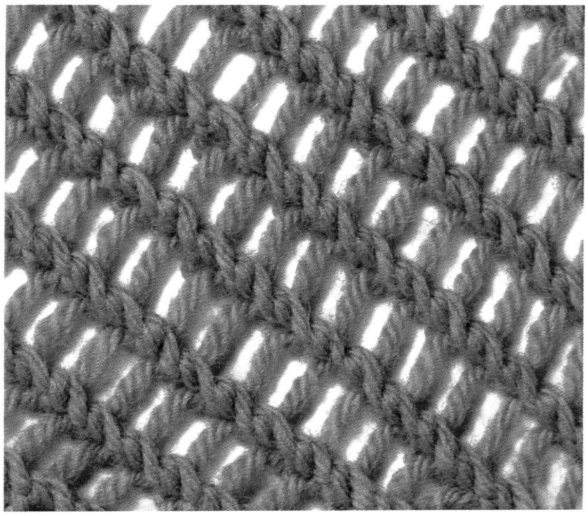

fers is raised and twisted; the ladder bars are single, parallel strands. This fabric is extremely stable and can be worked right out to the edges of the fabric.

With some advance planning, the same transfers can be used to create open motifs on a plain background as shown in L112. Note that the edge transfers are single transfers.

L112

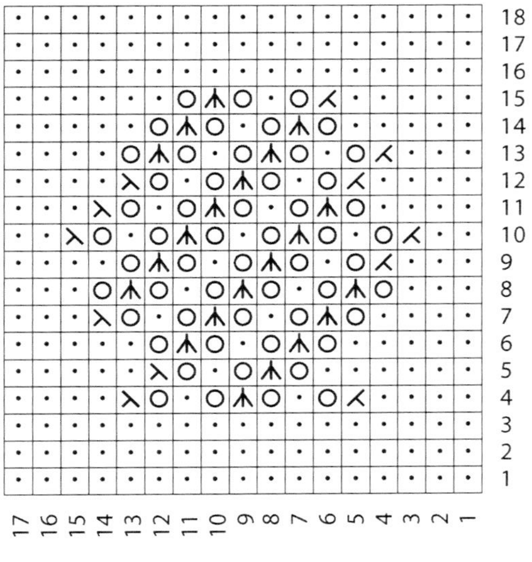

L112

L113 Simple 1-step decreases in a small, all—over repeat create an open, mesh—like fabric where the eyelets actually create continuous ladders. Once again, the transfers were worked E/R, rather than the usual A/R. This fabric could be opened up even more by working a single eyelet on the center ST of each lozenge (i.e. ST 4 in row 4).

L113

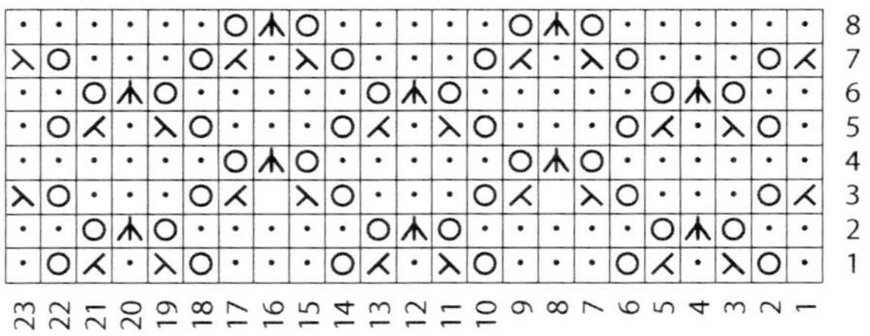

L113

L114

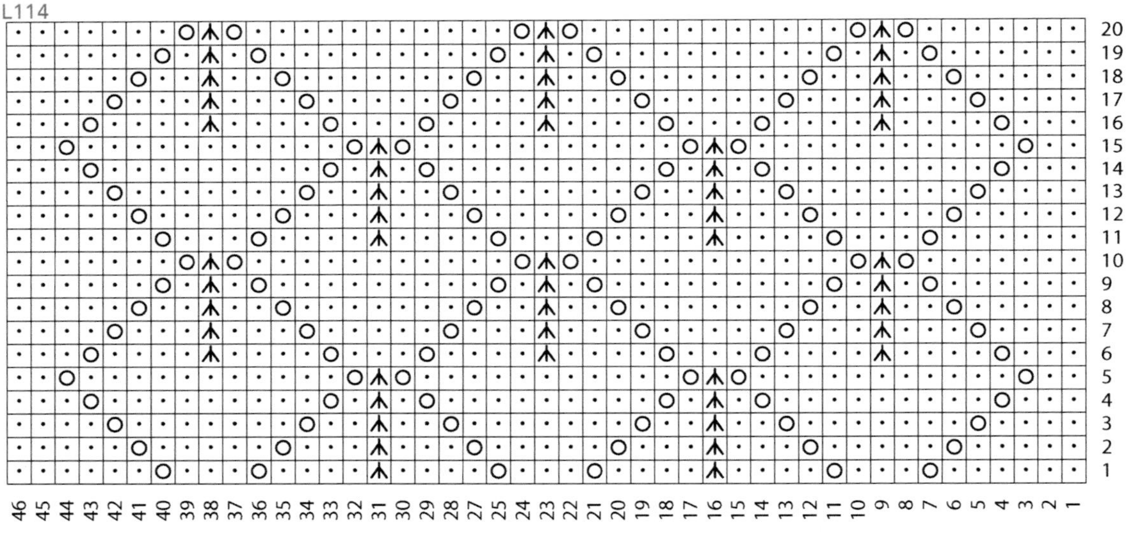

L114 The transfer rows alternate with a plain row throughout, rather than E/R as shown on the chart. By working the transfers A/R, the repeat becomes 20 rows, rather than 10. The ladder bars are twisted and the vertical accent at the center of each repeat is isolated.

L115 The decreases were made E/R, as shown on the chart so the ladder bars are straight and single. The vertical accent seems more continuous from one repeat to the next.

L116 These transfers were worked E/R with 2 plain rows added after rows 5 and 10 tso the repeat becomes 14 rows, rather than 10. These ladders are also straight and untwisted.

L114

The next 3 samples, L114 - L116 were all worked from the same chart with some slight variations. I think it is interesting that each of these variations totally changes the character of the fabric and the design.

L117 The transfers were made E/R as shown on the chart, with the eyelets shifting over by 1 NDL each time. Every 10 rows, the pattern changed direction to avoid biasing. The decreases were all worked as 1-step full fashioned decreases with a 3-prong tool, which helps create the raised, decorative surface of this fabric.

L115

L116

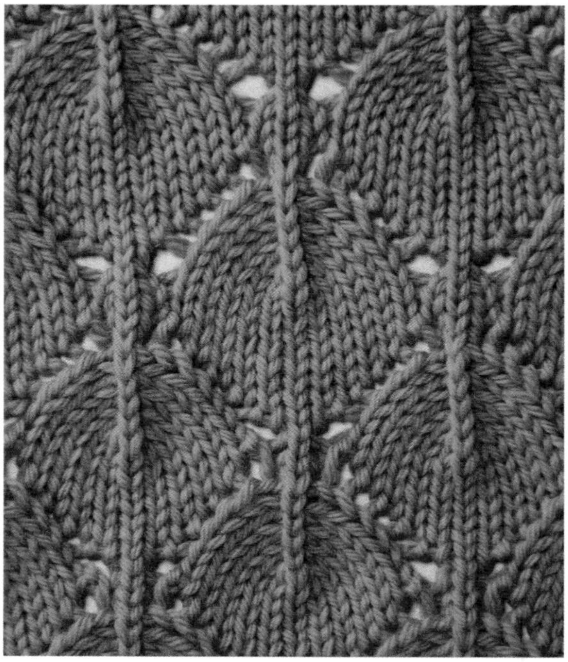

The edges of this fabric are quite irregular and the effect shifts from side to side as the direction of the pattern alternates. While this would not be a problem (and may even add interest) for a scarf or shawl, it would probably limit the fabric's use for garments unless you want to engineer a complex closure for a cardigan. Otherwise, I recommend leaving a fairly wide (4-6 ST) stockinette edge at each side.

You could vary this pattern further by making wider full fashioned decreases, increasing the number of plain STS between each repeat or working fewer repeats in each direction. The latter may also solve some of the zigzag edge issues. I alternated the direction of the pattern to avoid biasing, but a biased fabric can sometimes make an excellent scarf or the base for a join—as—you—knit fabric.

The next 3 samples include some actual ladders along with the eyelet transfers. L118 uses the ladders to create divisions between the diamond patterns created by the eyelets. The chart indicates A/R transfers, which produces the twisted ladder bars that outline the diamonds. You could also work the transfers E/R for a smaller pattern where the bars would remain straight. Although the chart shows 1-step decreases, 2-step decreases will create a sharper line around the diamonds. Designs like this are perfect for lacing ribbons through the ladders.

L119 These ladders shift with the transfers so there are never 2 empty NDLS side by side. The more open diagonals in this fabric are, in fact, created by the eyelets.

L117

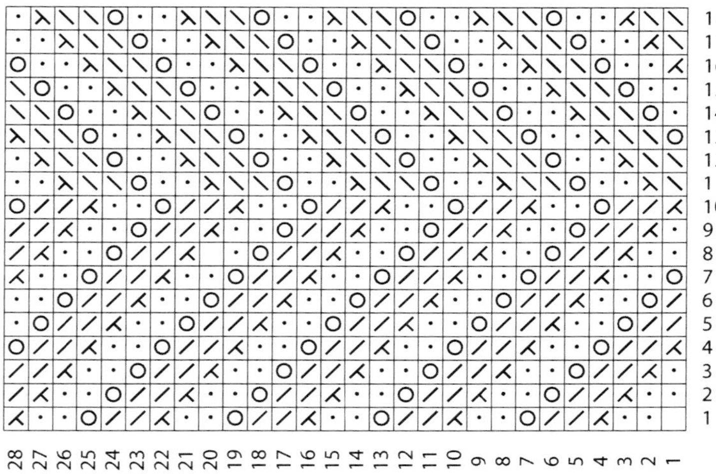

L117

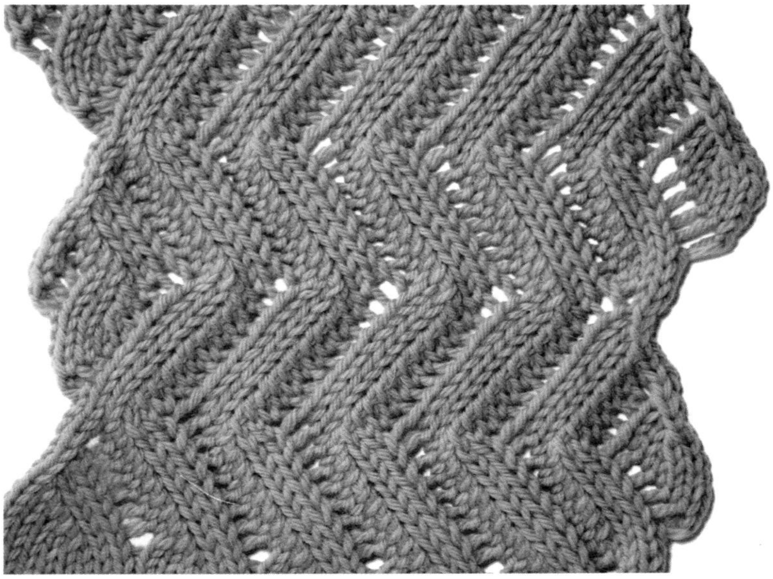

L118

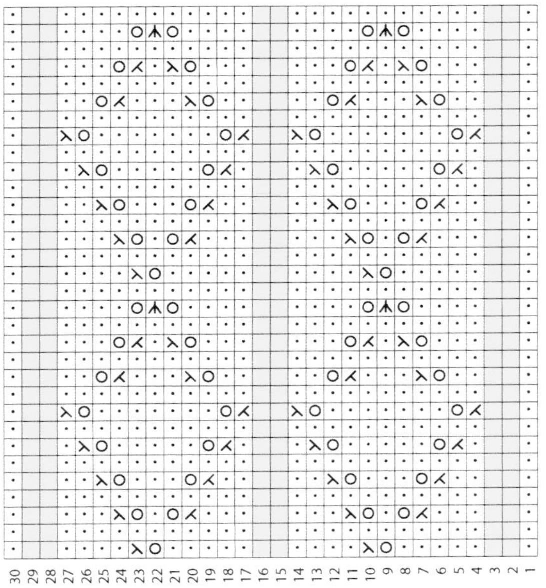

L118

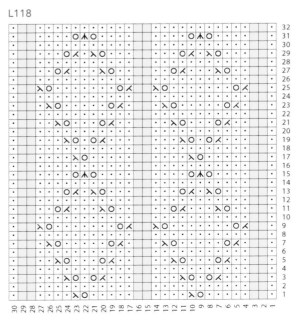

L119

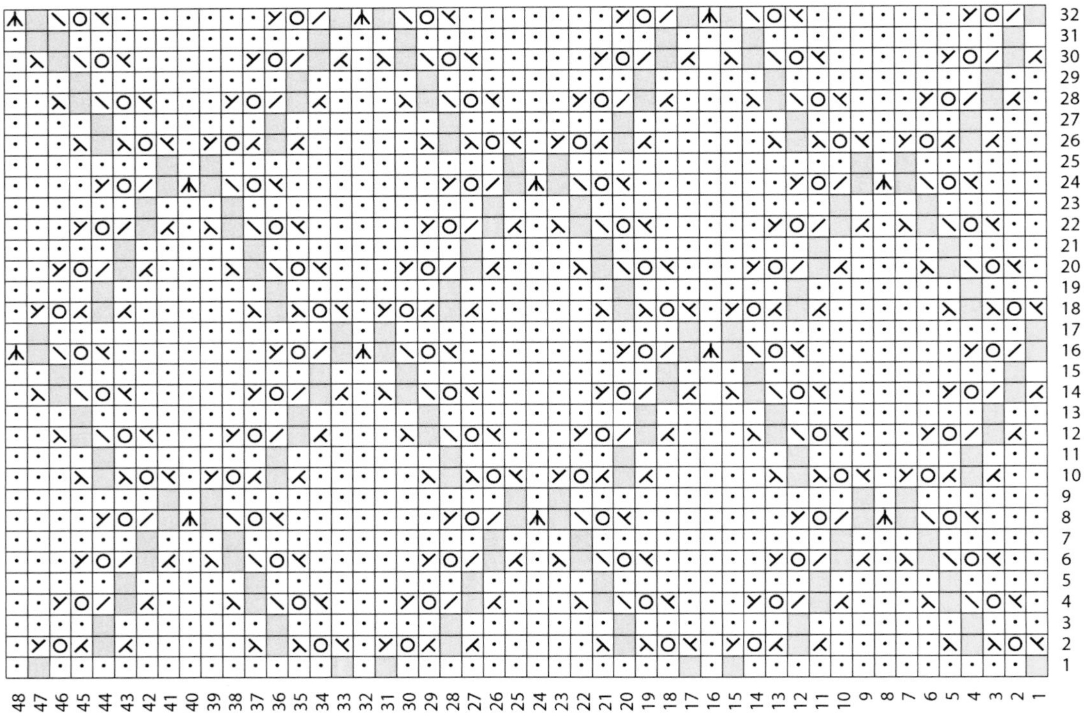

L119

The ladders are much more subtle and simply outline and accent the decreases, much as purl STS would do.

Row 1 on the chart shows the tops of some ladders as they would appear in repeat. To begin the fabric, just knit row 1 across all NDLS. For row 2, push NDLS 2 and 4 to HP and use a 3-prong transfer tool to remove these 2 STS from their NDLS. Push the empty NDLS to NWP and shift the tool over by 1 NDL to replace the STS on NDLS 3 and 5. Repeat for other pairs across the row to create both the beginning of a ladder and eyelet. Bring only the eyelet NDLS to WP and knit 2 rows.

Using a 3-prong tool to remove the 2 STS in HP is easier and faster than making separate transfers. Just be sure to place the empty NDLS in NWP and then only bring back to WP the eyelet NDL, not the ladder.

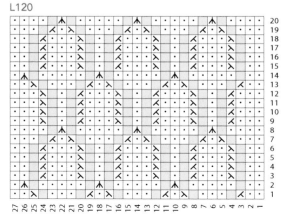

L120

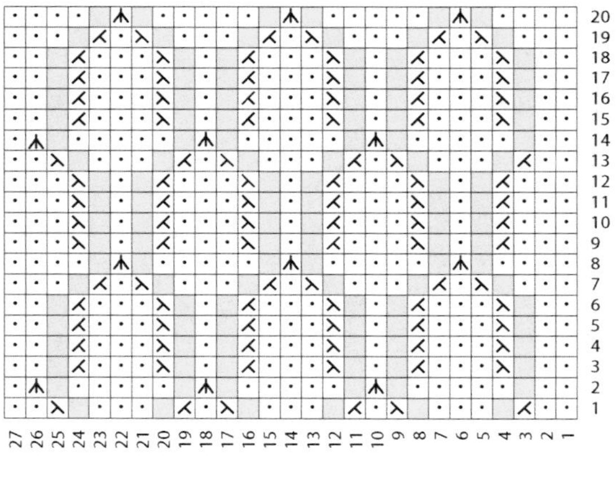

Row 4 push NDLS 3 & 5 to HP, remove the STS on a 3-prong tool and replace them on NDLS 4 & 6. Make a ST on NDL 2 by P/U the purl bar of the adjacent ST on NDL 1.

Continue working the traveling STS and eyelets and making STS as required through row 9 of the chart. Row 10 is worked like row 2, making 2 decreases to begin the next traveling ladders/eyelets. I added bridged popcorns to the last row of each repeat (not shown on chart) and you could also introduce eyelets or other textures to the plain STS at the center of each diamond. Note that the ladder jumps from the left side of the transfers in one repeat to the right side of the next.

L120 The last eyelet/ladder hybrid is another 1950's pattern that creates ladder effects with eyelet transfers E/R. This sample was worked with 1-step decreases, but 2-step would define the edges of the lozenges even more. For a larger (i.e. faster to knit) pattern, you could also increase the size of the stockinette lozenges. The ladders in this fabric are single and untwisted and the fabric has great depth and texture as a result.

L120

Patterned Ladders

The next group of samples combine ladders with various kinds of patterning and may give you some ideas to explore further. The first two samples L121 and L122 originally came from Silver Reed and combine 2-row stripes with ladders, drop stitch and reformed stitches.

L121

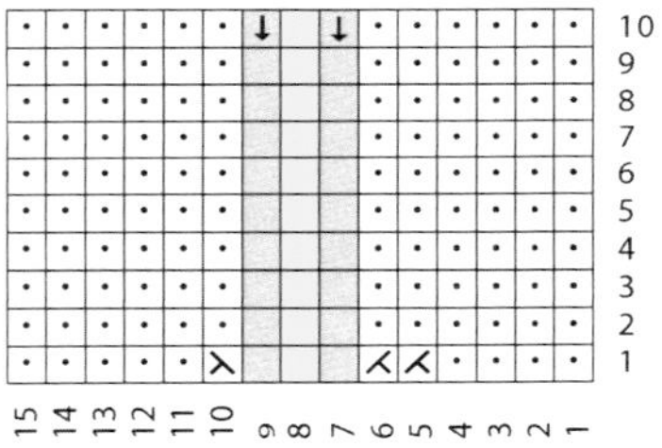

L121 shows three large—scale reformed tuck STS against a striped background. Begin by transferring STS 7 - 9 to adjacent empty NDLS, leaving the empty 7th and 9th NDLS in WP. E/10 rows, drop the STS from NDLS 7 and 9 and reform as a single ST in tuck. Pass the latch tool under the first 4 bars of the ladder (2 green and 2 blue), catching only the top 2 bars in the hook and pull towards you. Pass the tool under the next 4 bars and, again, just catch the top 2 bars in the hook of the tool. You should only latch the bars of one color or the other while the unlatched color forms the tucks that lay over the reformed STS.

L121

You can vary which color shows as the reformed ST by starting t latch up with either the 1st or 2nd pair of bars. Latch up after every 10 rows or so and leave the STS in the hook of the tool (if there is only one column of STS). When there are several columns of STS to latch up, I use a long double pointed or circular hand knitting NDL as a ST holder.

Bring the same 2 empty NDLS to WP so they begin knitting again and can be dropped and reformed after the next 10 rows. You can work more than 10 rows before dropping, but they may be clumsy to manage if you wait too long.

L122 In the second example of this technique, the reformed STS travel from right to left by making a decrease at the right of the ladder and allowing the empty NDL at left to remain in WP and C/O again. When the ladder STS are dropped, they will drop at an angle. Note that both the chart and the fabric show the effect

L122

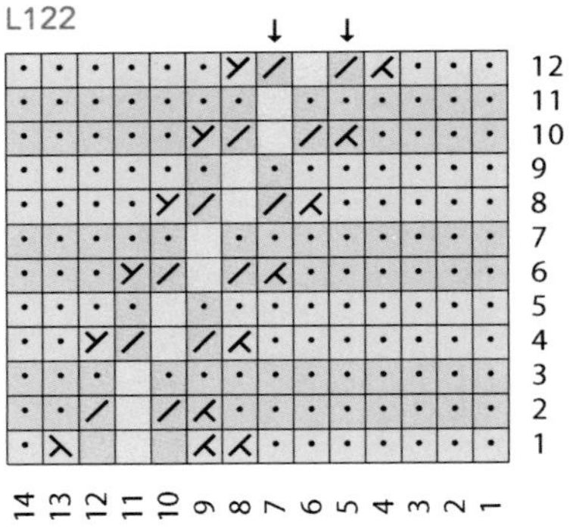

L123

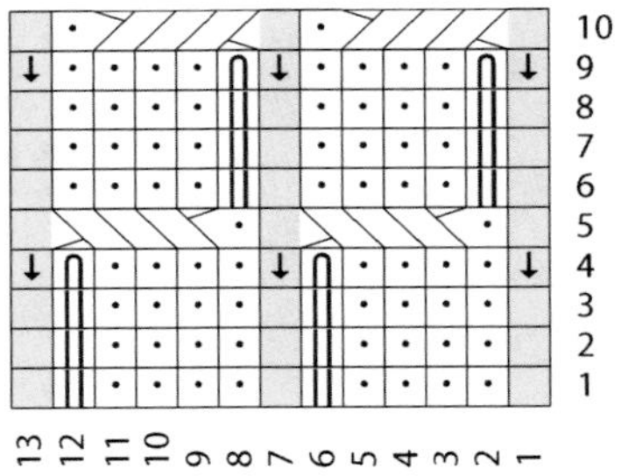

L123

L122

slanting from left to right because the chart represents the purl side of the fabric and this is a purl side effect.

L123 was also a Silver Institute design from the 90's. It combines tuck (through HP), ladders, drop ST and 1 x 3 cables all in a single fabric!

To begin, transfer every 7th ST to an adjacent NDL to create the ladders. Leave the empty ladder NDLS in WP so they will C/O and begin knitting again. Set the carriage to hold NDLS in HP. Hold NDL 6 and every 7th NDL from there and knit 3 rows. Nudge the NDLS back from HP to UWP and knit 1 row. Drop the STS from the ladder NDLS.

Next, remove the 6th ST on a single—prong tool and STS 3, 4 & 5 on a 3-prong tool. Cross the cables, returning the single ST to NDL 3 and crossing the other 3 STS behind it to NDLS 4, 5 & 6. The single ST is meant to show on the knit side of the fabric.

For the next alternating repeat, hold NDL 2 and every 7th NDL and repeat the process, crossing the next cable with STS 2, 3 & 4 behind ST 1. Note that there is always one NDL in each group of 5 that is not included in the cable. Although you can program a punch card/electronic machine to do the tucking, you still need to manually drop the ladder every 5 rows. If your machine balks at tucking for 4 rows, you could shorten the pattern by one row and tuck 3 rows instead.

While the ladders run straight through the fabric, the position of the tuck STS and the cable crosses alternate with each repeat. Unlike most tuck fabrics, the knit side is the right side of this fabric.

L124 The last tuck sample is similar to some of the lifted ST patterns, but uses HP rather than lifting the ladder bars. Prior to knitting the first row, set the carriage to hold NDLS in HP and bring NDLS 4, 8, 12, etc. to HP and knit 2 rows. Transfer STS 2, 6, 10, etc to the adj NDL at right. Then push the NDLS in HP to UWP and at the same time push NDLS 3, 7, 11, to HP. Knit 2 rows. Continue making transfers, returning NDLS from HP to UWP and pushing the adjacent NDLS to HP A/R. It sounds more complicated than it is and once you begin you will get into a rhythm!

To reverse the direction of the design to the left, make the last transfer to the right and bring the NDLS just emptied out to HP — not the NDLS adj to the ones returning to UWP as in previous repeats. See row 11 on the chart. Once the direction is reversed, continue making transfers and moving NDLS in and out of HP and UWP as before.

On a punch card or electronic machine, you can program the machine for tuck instead of using HP. This is well worth doing if you plan to knit a large project with this ST. The combination of lifted and transferred STS makes the texture of this fabric very dimensional.

L124

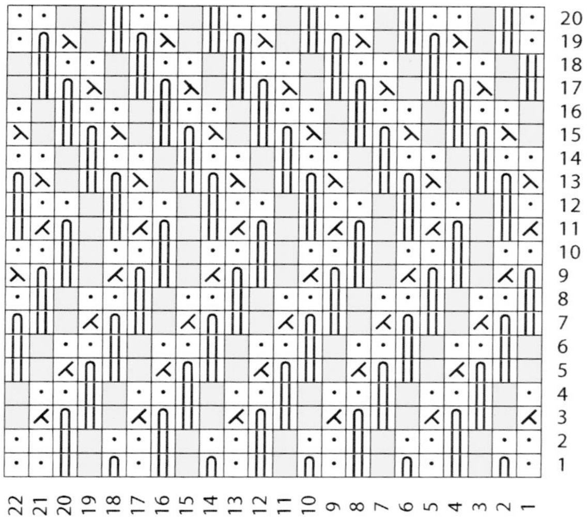

L124

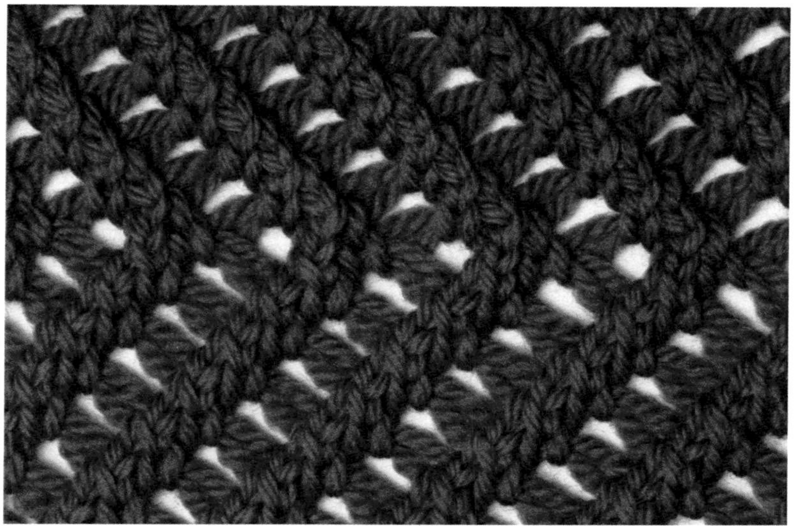

L125

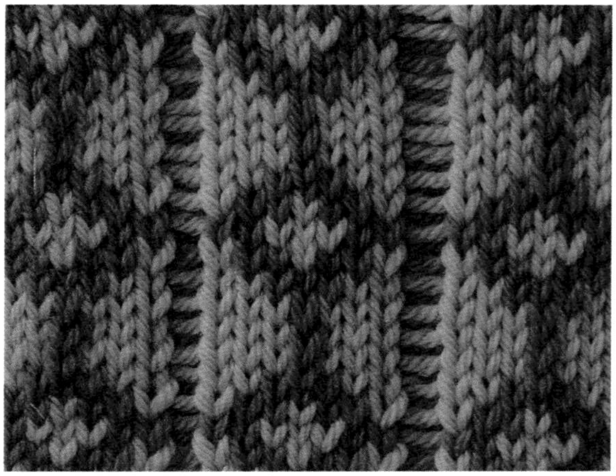

L126

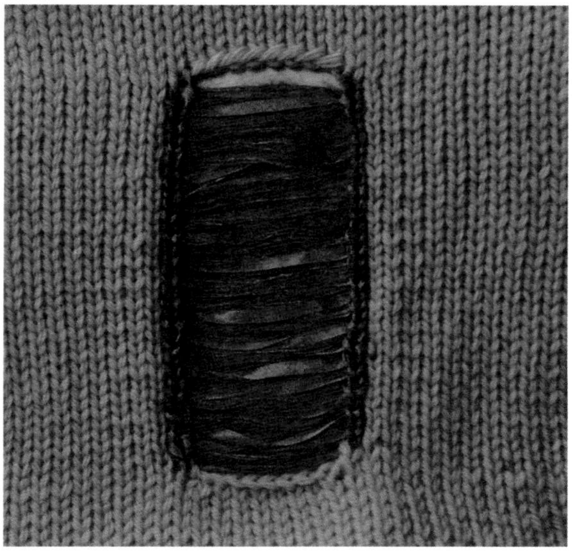

L125 There is no end to the possibilities of creating ladders between Fair Isle motifs. The ladders can remain as ladders or be reformed in one color or the other, but I would add drop ST to the equation to prevent reformed ladders from shortening the fabric. If you program a machine for automatic patterning, remember to allow for the empty, non—patterning NDLS.

L127

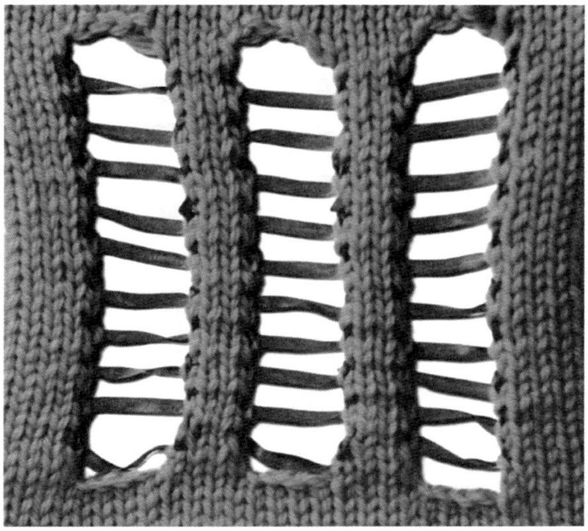

Intarsia Ladders

All of these intarsia swatches were inspired by fabrics in the Stoll archives. In L126, the mohair/ribbon knitted every row, crossing between NDLS with the smooth background yarn in the usual way. In L127, the ribbon only knitted every 4/R to create very open ladders.

L128 was worked with 2-ST ladders on NDLS 4 & 5, 12 & 13, 20 & 21, 28 & 29 and 36 & 37 as shown on the chart by horizontal lines running across those colored squares to indicate the color each ladder should be. The yarns, carried on 5 separate bobbins, do not twist or cross as they meet, which is unusual for intarsia

L128

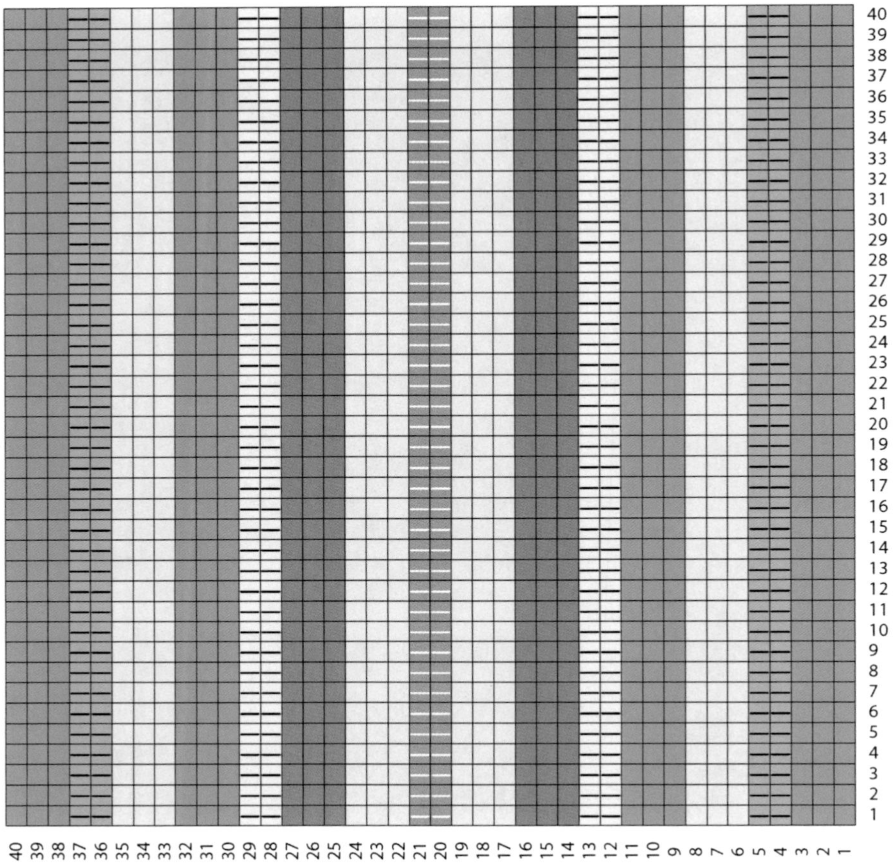

L128

knitting. Instead they almost weave through each other on the back side of the fabric, skipping over NWP NDLS to knit more than one column of STS.

A single dark green bobbin was used to knit NDLS 1 - 3 and then 9 - 11, by—passing NDLS 4 - 8. It knitted back and forth only on NDLS 1 - 11 throughout the fabric.

A light green bobbin knitted NDLS 6 - 8, by—passed the next 8 NDLS (dark green stripe, ladder and blue stripe) then knitted NDLS 17 - 19. In the same way, the blue bobbin that knits NDLS 14 - 16 by—passed the next 8 NDLS to knit NDLS 25 - 27.

A 2nd light green bobbin knitted NDLS 22 - 24 and by—passed the next 8 NDLS to knit NDLS 33 - 35. Finally, a 2nd dark green bobbin finished each row by knitting NDLS 30- 32 and 38 - 40, skipping past the 8 NDLS between.

Whenever one of the bobbins by—passes a group of NDLS, it floats behind STS of a different color and is visible as the ladder bars under NWP NDLS. This is a very stable fabric, defined by ladders that appear to zigzag back and forth rather than pairing or twisting.

L129 First of all, please note that the yellow areas on this chart still represent ladders, not yellow bobbins. The green border of STS that outline the motif on this sample is actually the same width/number of NDLS throughout. What changes is the width of the ladders at the center of the shape and, as a result, the background area.

I used full fashioned increases (rows 3, 5, 7, 9) and 2-step decreases (rows 13, 15, 17, 19) to move the green STS. At the same time, I worked this fabric like

129

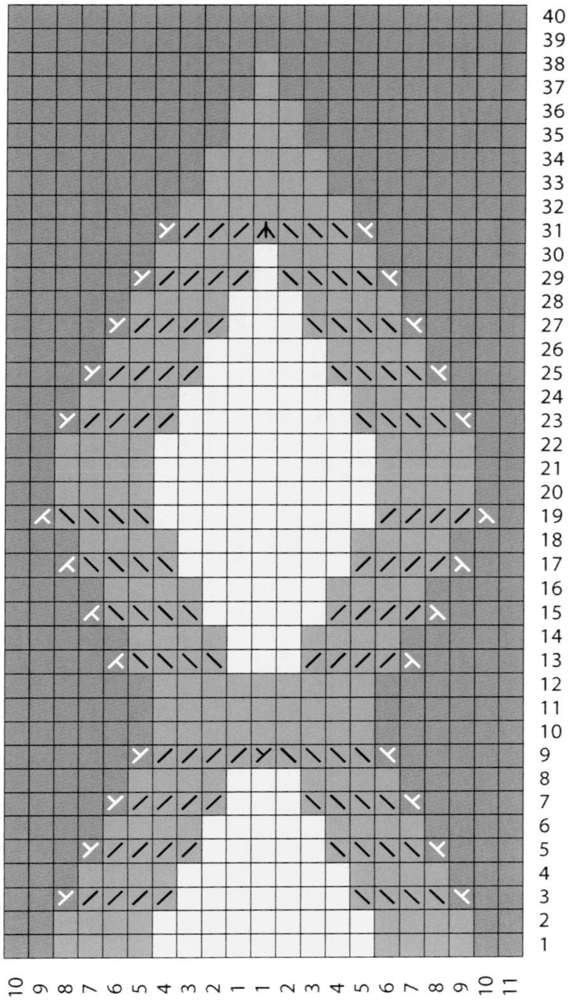

129

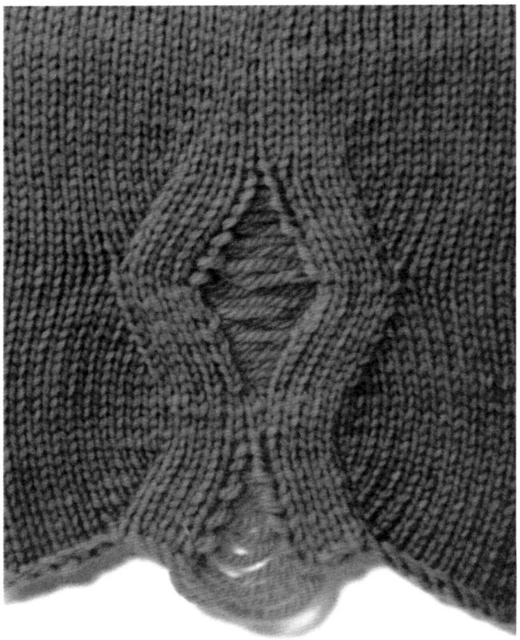

a regular intarsia fabric, selecting additional or fewer NDLS per color to shape the areas without ladders. See rows 10 - 12 and 32 - 38.

Modular Ladders

I dedicated a whole chapter of my last book, Hand Knits by Machine, to modular knitting so will not provide detailed directions here. I have included these 2 samples for inspirational purposes only and highly recommend that you are comfortable with basic modular methods before introducing a ladder to the mix.

L130 added a 2-stitch ladder at the center of each segment, with the decreases along each edge of the ladder as shown on the chart. The ladder opens up and softens the drape of this fabric.

L131 is an example of entrelac, knitted in one color, with 2-stitch ladders between them. Each section of this entrelac was knitted over a width of 7 NDLS, which includes the 2 ladder NDLS, which are positioned 1 St from the edge of each repeat. So, the first group of 7 NDLS is NDL 1 - 7 and the next runs from NDL 8 to 14.

L130

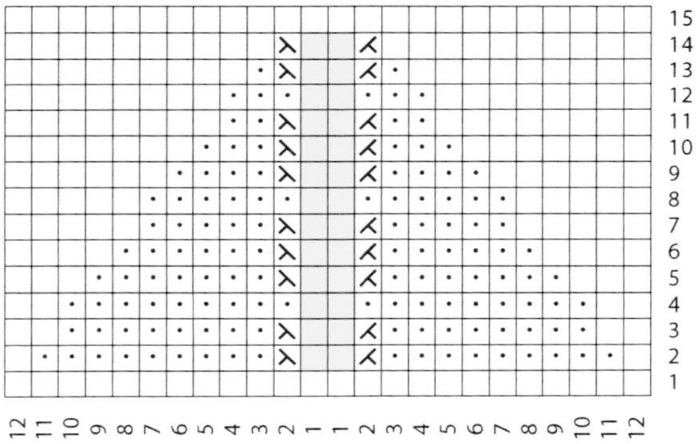

L130

L131

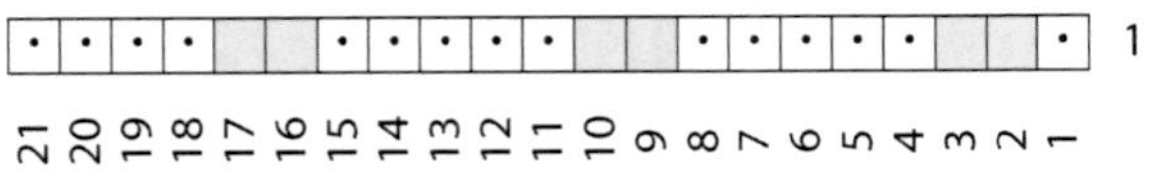

L131

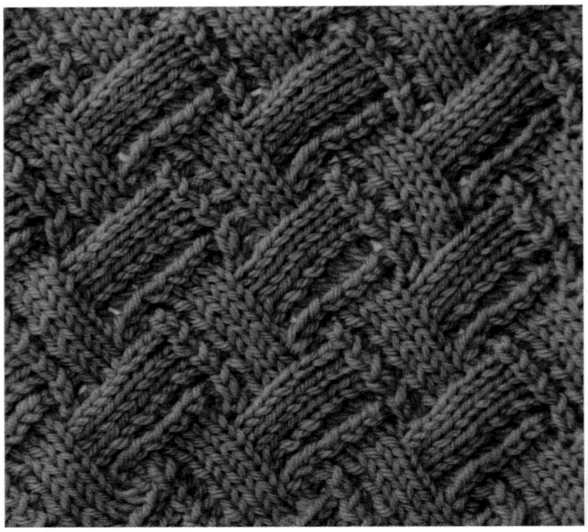

You must maintain this ladder when shifting STS over to fill empty NDLS and when P/U the edge of one section to knit the next. The ladders add a nice open quality to this fabric but they also increase the woven effect because the eye sees groups of 3 STS interweaving throughout the fabric as well as single STS that parallel them.

Bridged Ladders

The next group of samples are all extremely open and, in spite of that, fully stable. While some of them might be suitable for garments as shown, others may require modification or reduction in the number of NDLS worked in each group. Several of these samples look very similar, but there are subtle differences in construction or scale.

L132

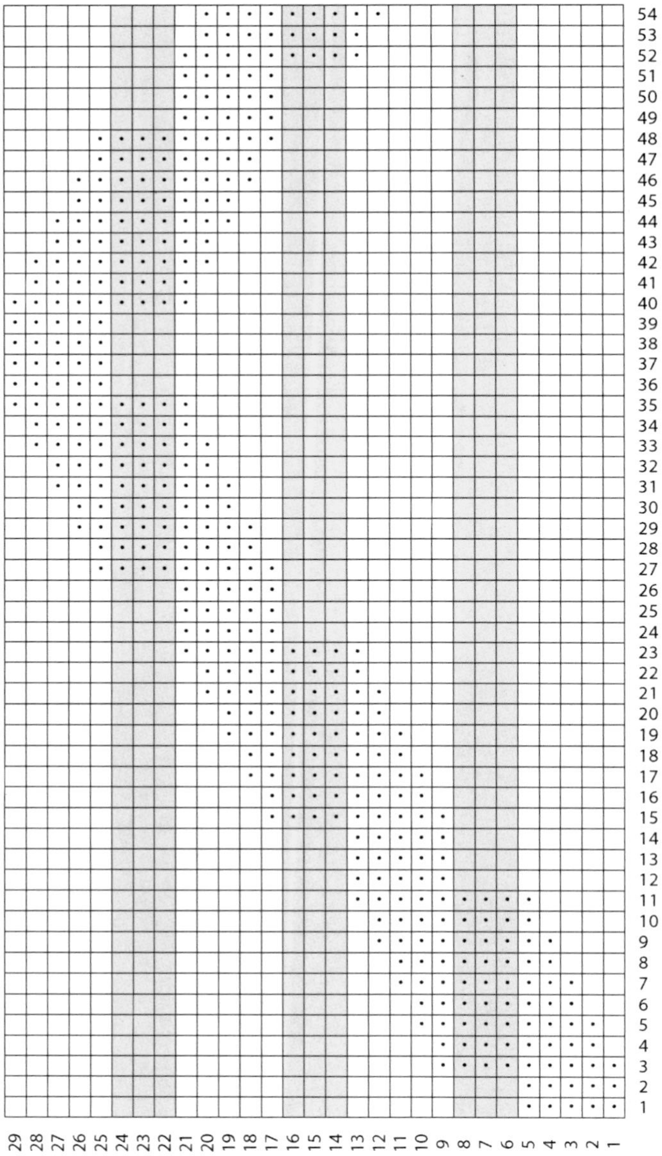

These charts tend to be lengthy so that I can illustrate full repeats and avoid second guessing as to what to do next. On all of these charts, the yellow spaces still indicate ladders and NDLS in NWP. The empty, white squares indicate NDLS in HP. These are NDLS that *do* have STS on them, not empty NDLS. The dots indicate purl STS on WP NDLS and are the only ones that should be knitting on any given row. Ladder NDLS always remain in NWP unless you are instructed otherwise. SO, when directions say to put all NDLS in HP, those directions apply only to WP NDLS and not to those in NWP. This is a slightly different charting format than I use throughout this book, but there is just too much short rowing in all of these fabrics to depend

L132

on red and blue arrows. Please rely equally on the charts and text directions for working all of these samples.

L132 C/O and knit at least 1 row of the MC over the NDL arrangement shown on the chart: 5 NDLS in WP, alternating with 3 empty NDLS in NWP. Begin COR, set to hold NDLS in HP. Hold all NDLS except the first 5 on the carriage side. Knit 2 rows.

*Move 1 NDL at left to UWP and knit 1 row. Hold 1 NDL at right and knit 1 row.** Repeat * to ** until all 5 NDLS in the leftmost group on the bed are in WP. Knit 4 rows and then repeat in reverse direction.

The quality of the yarn makes a huge difference in the final result with this pattern. Springier, loftier yarns will produce a more 3-D fabric. There are endless possibilities for this pattern by varying the width of the working NDL groups or the ladders.

L133 Begin COR set to hold NDLS in HP. The ladder NDLS remain in NWP throughout. Hold all NDLS except the first 2 on the carriage side. *Knit 2 rows. (Return 1 NDL at left to UWP, knit 1 row) twice. COR and RC 4.(Hold 1 NDL at left, knit 1 row) twice. COR and RC 6.

Move 2 NDLS at left to UWP and knit 1 row. Hold the 2 NDLS at right and knit 1 row.** RC 8. Only NDLS 5 & 6 are in WP when ending this first section. Repeat * to ** for the width of the fabric. This fabric can be varied by changing the set up with more NDLS in WP, wider ladders or by knitting additional rows on each section before bridging to the next. L134 The ladders seem to disappear into this fabric so that undulating columns of STS divide giant eyelets.

L135 This is one of the fastest bridged ladders to knit because no individual NDLS are moved to HP. They always move as groups of 3. Begin COR set to hold NDLS in HP. Hold all NDLS except the first 3 on the carriage side.

L133

L133

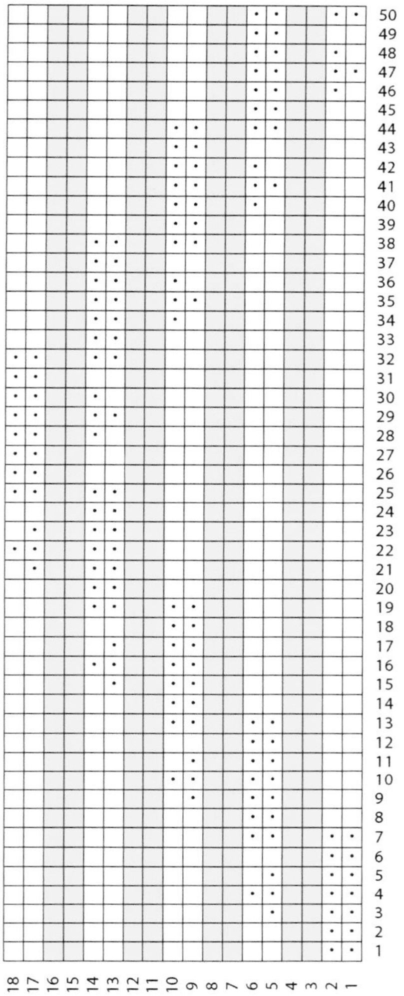

L134

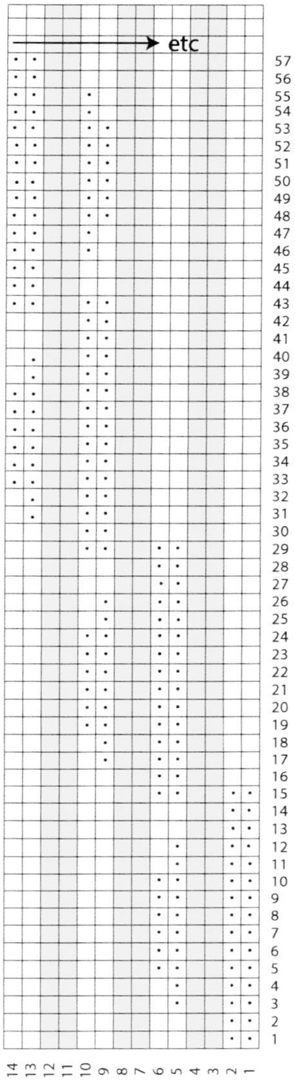

L134

L135

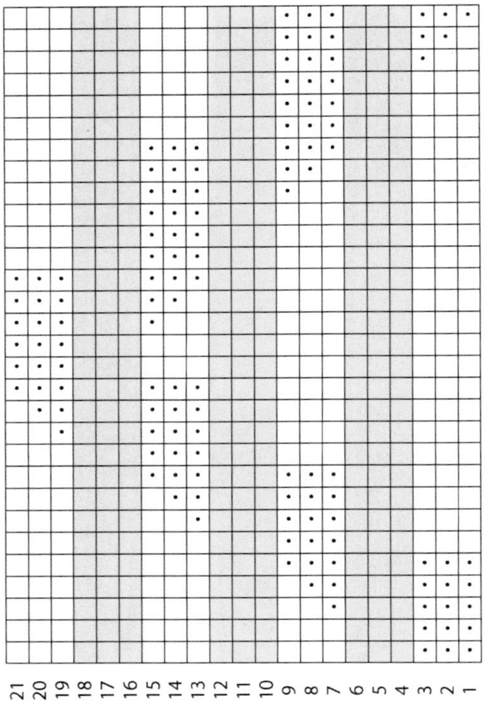

*Knit 2 rows. (Move 1 NDL at left to UWP E/R) 3 times. COL. Hold all 3 NDLS at right. Knit 1 row.** Repeat * to ** until you reach the left edge of the fabric. End the last group with 2 rows, instead of 1, and then repeat from left to right.

You can work this pattern with any (odd—numbered) size groups of NDLS in WP, but if you decide to use an even number of NDLS in each WP group, you must hold the previous group of NDLS as you move the last NDL in the next group to UWP in order to

L135

L136

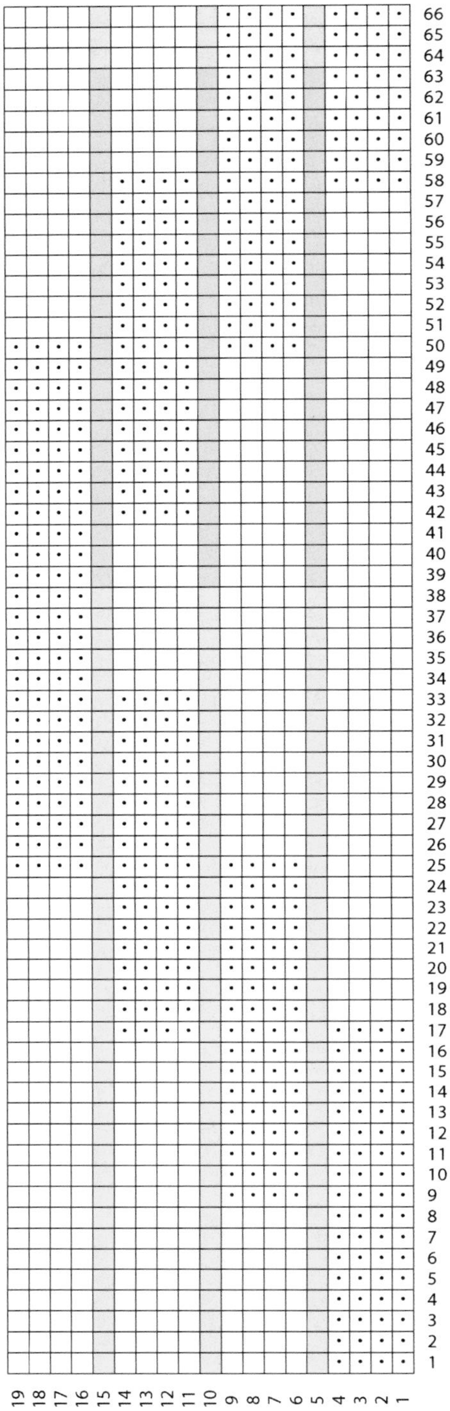

always have the carriage on the correct side to continue bridging from one group to the next.

L136 This example alternates 4 WP NDLS with 1 NWP NDL and the ladder is totally absorbed into the background fabric. The ladders do, however, contribute to the size of the open spaces and wider ladders would produce larger spaces. By the same token, eliminating the ladders altogether produces a somewhat more closed fabric. The NDLS move from WP to HP or

L136

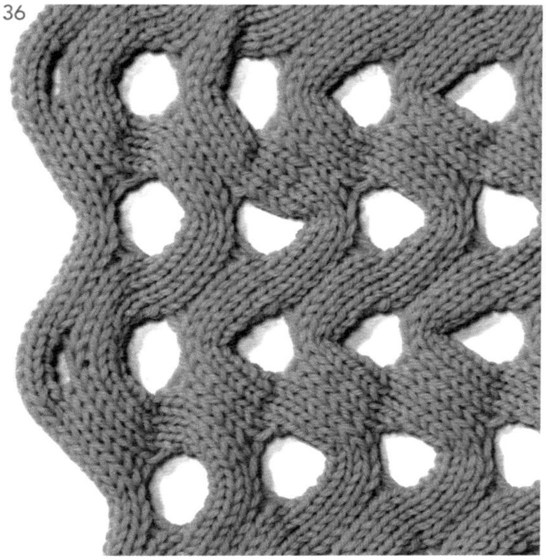

HP to UWP in groups of 4, making this a fairly quick bridged fabric to knit.

Begin COR, set to hold NDLS in HP. Hold all NDLS except the first 4 on the carriage side. Knit 8 rows, ending COR. *Bring the next group of 4 NDLS at left to UWP and then knit 8 rows across all 8 working NDLS, ending COR. Bring the next group of 4 NDLS at left to UWP and knit 1 row across all 12 WP NDLS, ending COL. Hold the first group of 4 NDLS at right Knit 8 rows.** Repeat from * to ** to the left edge of the fabric and then work in reverse back to the right edge as shown on the chart.

L137 is based on one from the Stoll archives and is similar to the previous sample except that it is knitted with an intarsia carriage and bobbins. It is important to be consistent in wrapping/crossing the yarns where the colors meet because only one of the colors should show in each ladder space and the colors alternate on each ladder. That is, the first ladder on the right will be color 1 for the first repeat, but color 2 for the second.

Here is how to maintain the correct ladder colors: When knitting from right to left across the fabric, always cross the yarns at the left edge of each ladder; when knitting towards the right, always cross the two yarns at the right of the ladders.

Just like the previous sample, the NDLS are moved in and out of position as groups of 4 NDLS, never individually. The two charts are nearly the same. There will always be two bobbins (i.e. two sections) knitting at the same time except for the one bridged row where 3 sections knit. When you knit the first row across 3 sections at once, do not cross the new bobbin. The two previous yarns will still cross, but not the new one.

You can easily play with this pattern and vary wider or narrower groups of NDLS in either WP or NWP.

L137

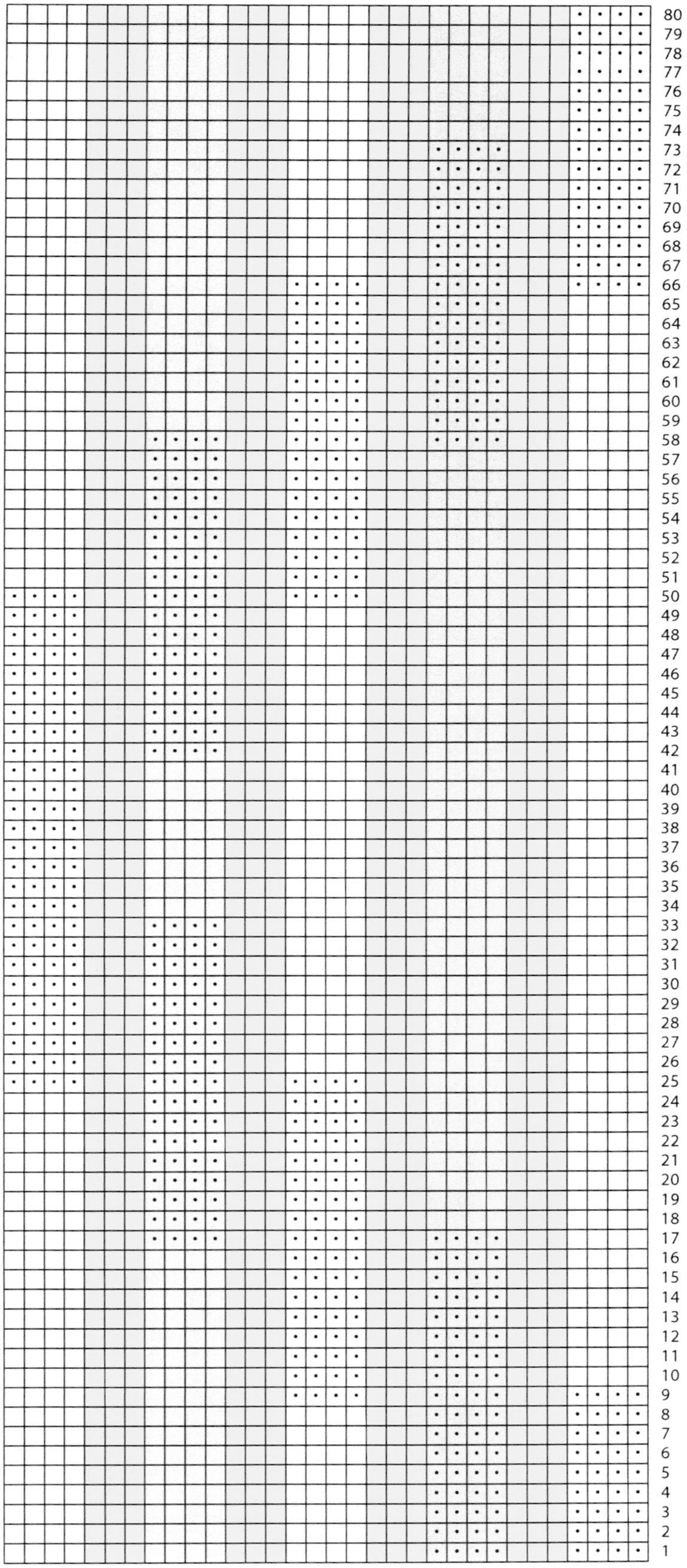

L137

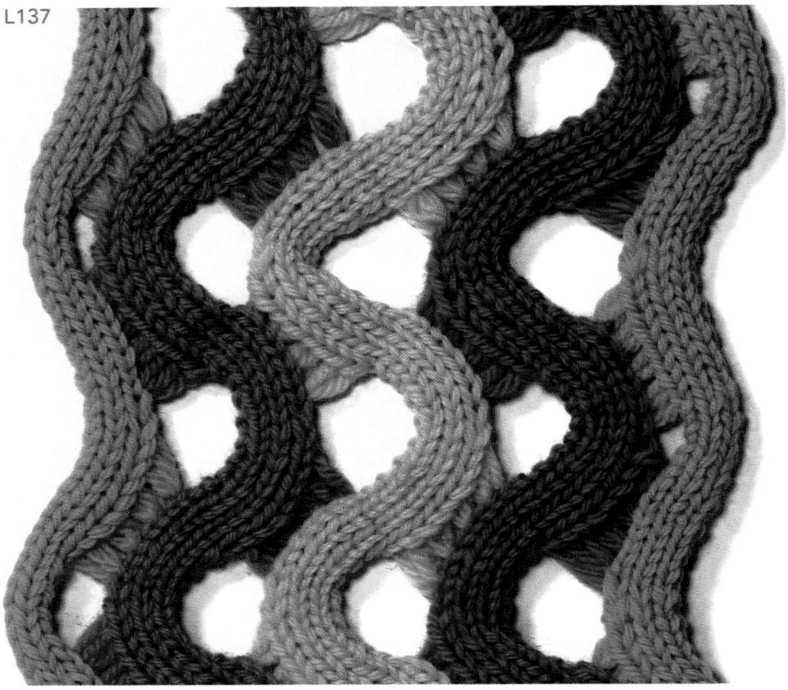

L138

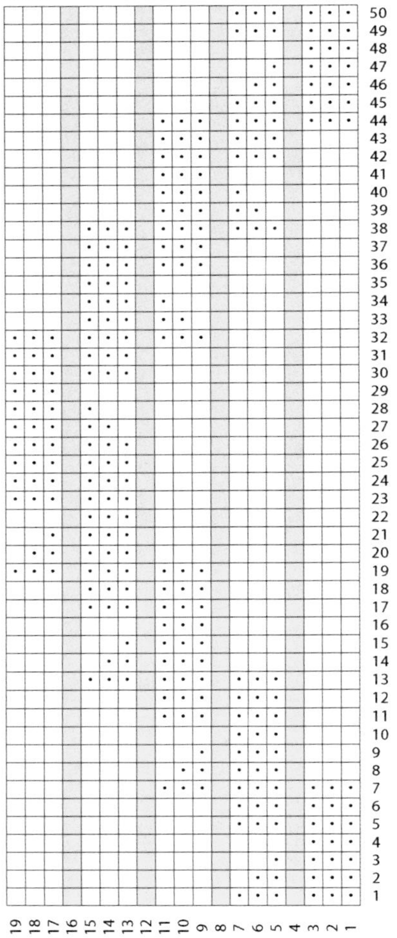

Fewer rows on each section will produce smaller holes, while more rows will enlarge them. You should also be able to apply the intarsia approach to many of the other bridged ladders in this section to produce undulating vertical stripes.

L138 Begin COR set to hold NDLS in HP. Hold all NDLS except the first 3 on the carriage side and knit 2 rows. Bring the next 3 NDLS at left to UWP and knit 1 row. *Hold 1 NDL at left E/R 3 times. COR. Bring next 3 NDLS at left (5, 6, 7) to UWP and knit 1 row. Hold the first 3 NDLS at right (1, 2, 3)**. Repeat from * to ** across the fabric.

When the work reaches the left edge of the fabric, reverse direction and work back to the right to produce the balanced fabric shown. If, instead of reversing, you knit 1 row across all NDLS and begin on the right again, the fabric will bias as shown in the photo L139. As with any biased fabric, this would probably be a problem for a traditionally knitted garment, but might open up all kinds of creative possibilities for scarves and shawls and join—as—you—knit projects.

L138

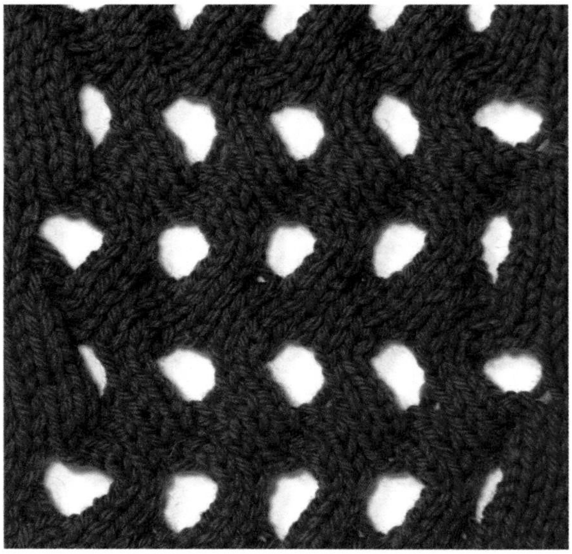

L139

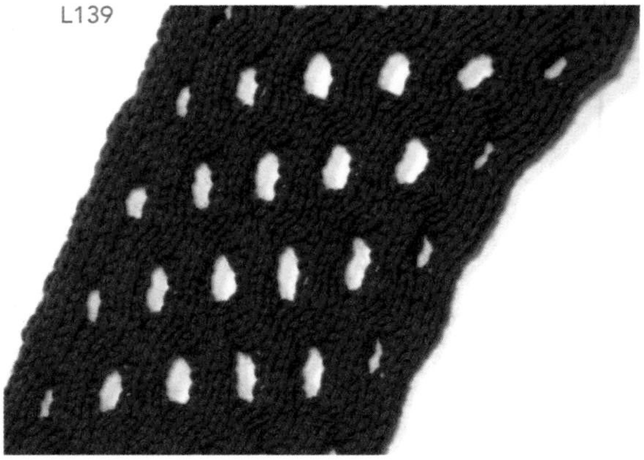

The next two examples are further variations of L138. For L140, begin COR, set to hold NDLS in HP. Hold all NDLS except the first 3 on the carriage side and *knit 2 rows. (Move the next NDL at left to UWP and knit 2 rows) 3 times. Then (hold 1 NDL at left and knit 2 rows) 3 times. Move all 3 of those NDLS (5, 6, 7) to UWP and knit 1 row. Hold the first group of NDLS at right (1, 2, 3) and knit 1 row.** Repeat from * to ** for the width of the fabric, reversing direction when you reach the left edge as shown on the chart.

L141 is similar except that instead of knitting 2 rows after each NDL is held/returned to WP, you only knit 1. It changes the whole scale of the fabric. When you compare the two examples, it is also clear that L139 creates a stronger, more raised, rectangular effect that outlines the open spaces while L140 produces a closer structure with more pronounced and rounded openings.

The next example L142 is loosely based on the previous methods with the addition of some wrapped NDLS. The chart shows a NDL set up with 3 WP NDLS alternating with 5 NWP ladder NDLS. You can vary the size of both groups, affecting either the width of the knitted sections or the ladders. In addition, you can

L140

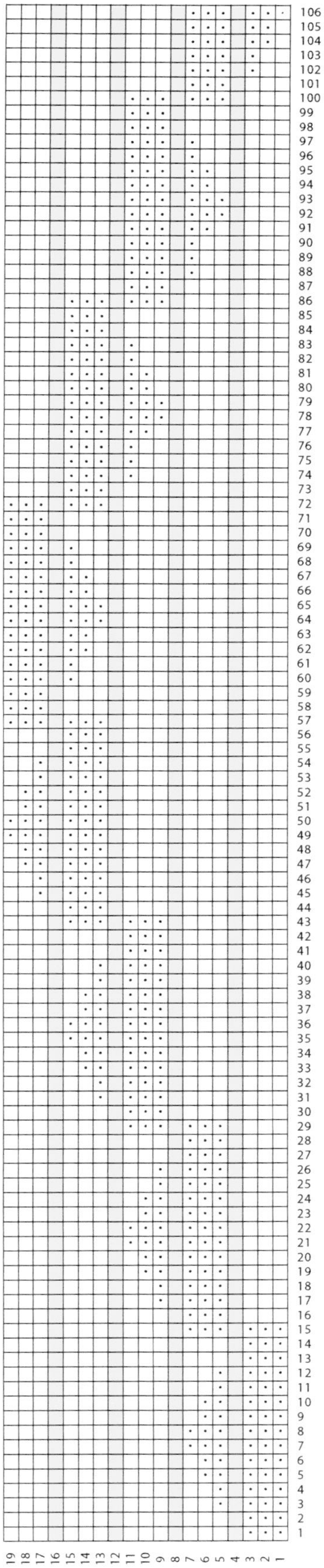

L141

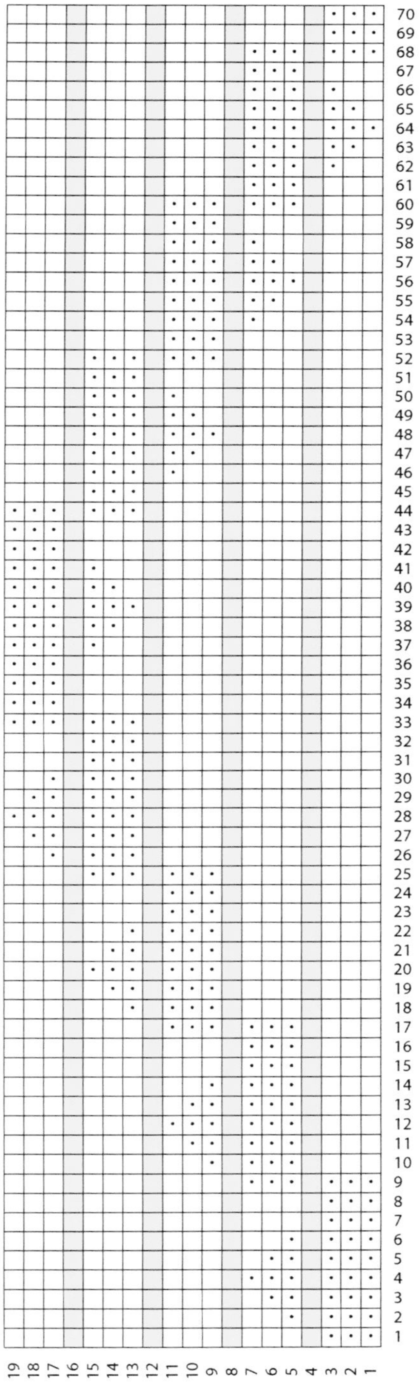

L142

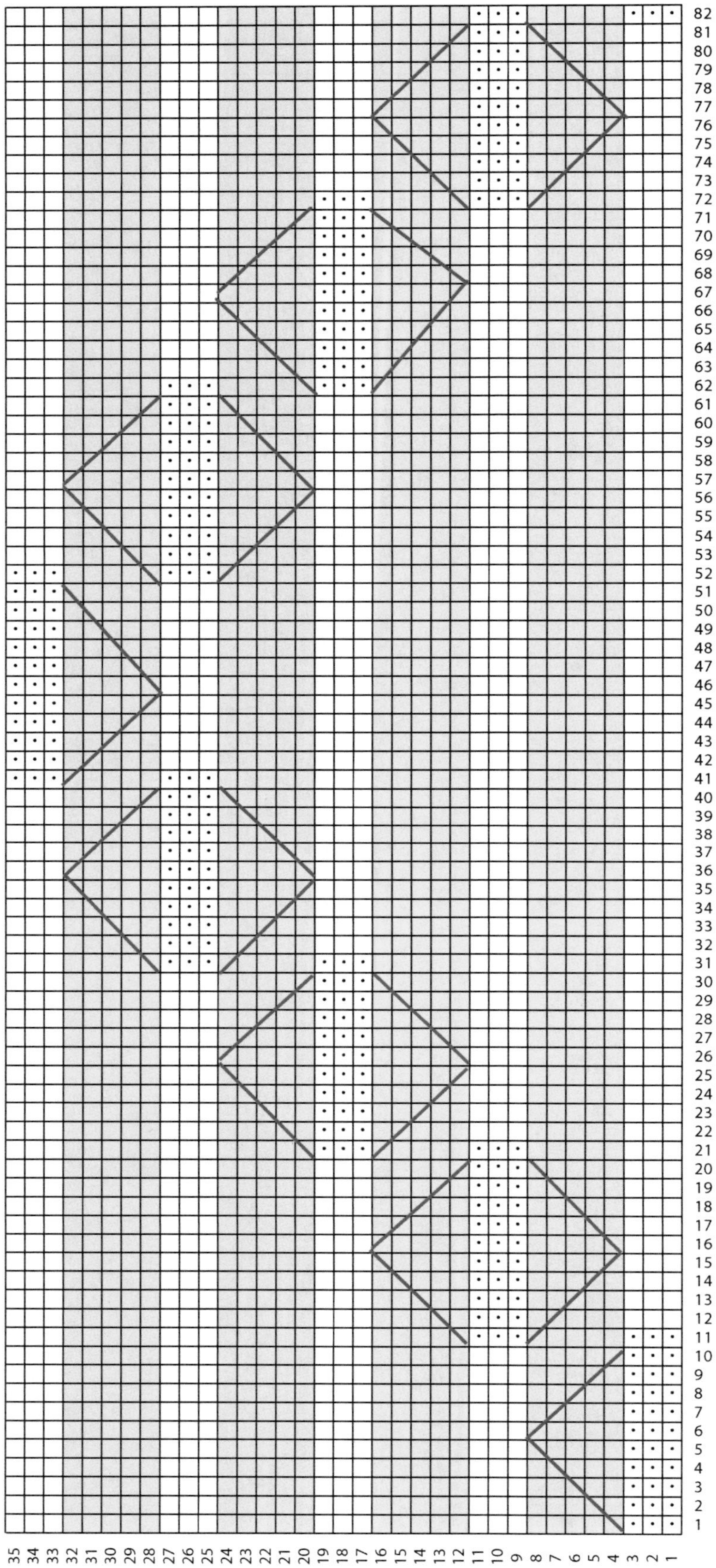

vary how many rows to knit for each section. Depending on your choice of yarn, you may want the fabric more or less open.

There are photos and several patterns and variations of this fabric floating around the internet. In trying to track down the original source, the closest I could get was a reference to Maxim Vorsin and the Russian magazine Lubo—Delo, which is out of print.

This sample is a bit different from the others in this section in that only one group of WP NDLS knits at any time except, of course, for the bridged row that moves you from one group to the next. Also, and more importantly, the yarn is wrapped under the first NDL of the next group of NDLS in HP whenever the COL (for the first half of the chart) and around the last NDL of the previous group whenever COR. The groups of NDLS at either edge always knit 1 extra row in order to reverse direction.

Begin COR with the carriage set to hold NDLS in HP. Hold all NDLS except the first group of 3 on the carriage side. Knit 10 rows, catching the yarn under NDL 9 whenever COL. Prior to knitting row 11, push NDLS 9 - 11 to UWP. Knit 1 row to the left and wrap the yarn around NDL 17.

Hold NDLS 1 - 3 and knit 1 row to the right. Wrap the yarn under NDL 3. Continue to row 20, wrapping at left and right. Prior to knitting row 21, move the next group of 3 NDLS at left to UWP. Knit 1 row and hold NDLS 9 - 11. Continue working one group at a time, wrapping at left and right as for these first few groups, reversing at the left edge of the fabric.

L143 This sample features pairs of WP NDLS alternating with 4 NWP NDLS for ladders and wrapping at the left when working towards the left edge or wrapping right when moving towards the right edge.

Begin COR set to hold NDLS in HP. Hold all NDLS except the first 2 on the carriage side. *Knit 6 rows, wrapping the yarn under NDL 7 every time the COL. Then, at RC 6, move the next pair of NDLS (7 & 8) to UWP.** Repeat from * to ** and when you reach the left edge, reverse direction.

The STS in this example zigzag back and forth and both edges of the fabric remain even and uniform because of it. L144 The next sample is similar except that the wrapping is always done on the left, regardless of which direction the bridging is traveling. As a result, all the little fan shaped ladders point in one direction.

L142

L143

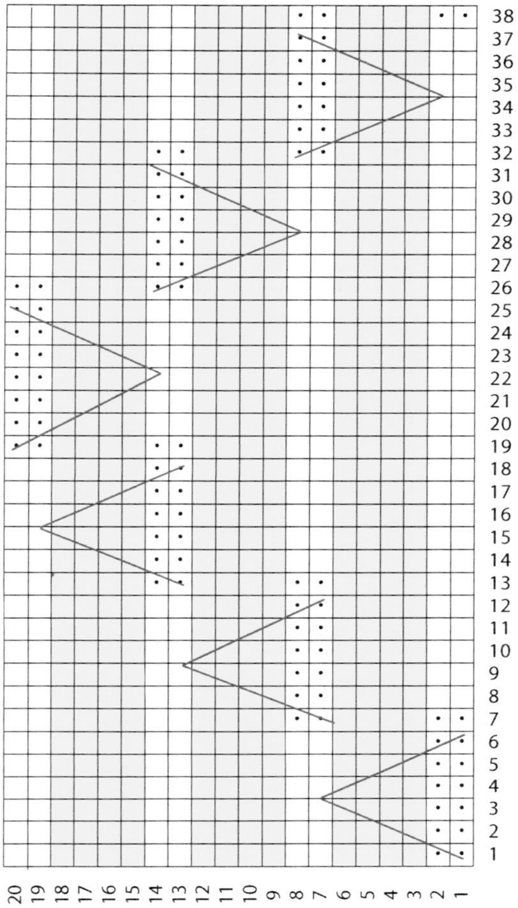

L143

L144

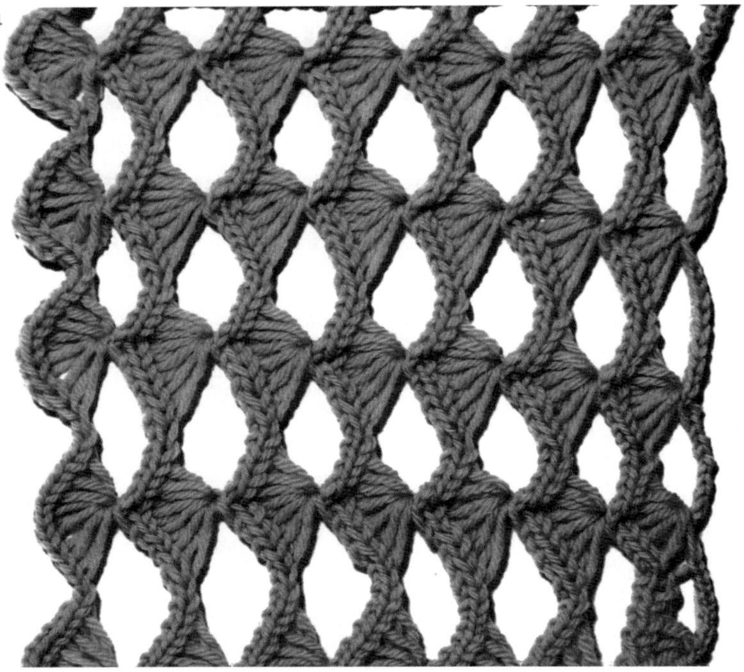

The end result is that both edges of this fabric are quite different. One edge shows the full fan shape, while the other has strips just 2 ST wide.

This second version is worked exactly like the first sample from right to left, but when you reach the left edge of the fabric, it is necessary to knit 12 rows on the last pair of STS in order to maintain the height of the edge so it matches the other side.

For the second repeat, working left to right, begin COL. *Push NDL 19 to HP and nudge the next pair of NDLS (13 & 14) to UWP. Knit 1 row. COR. Hold NDL 20 and then knit 6 rows, wrapping whenever COL.** Repeat * to ** until you reach the right edge.

Note that only the first group on the right knits and wraps 12 consecutive rows (6 at the end of the second section and then 6 at the beginning of the next). All of the others knit and wrap 6 rows in each direction, which combines to make 12 rows after 2 sections have been knitted.

Also, placing the right—most WP in HP before bridging to the next group at right helps to contain the ladder bar that forms as a result of the bridging. Without this extra step, the ladder bar will droop.

L145 This last bridged ladder example was inspired by a

L145

L144

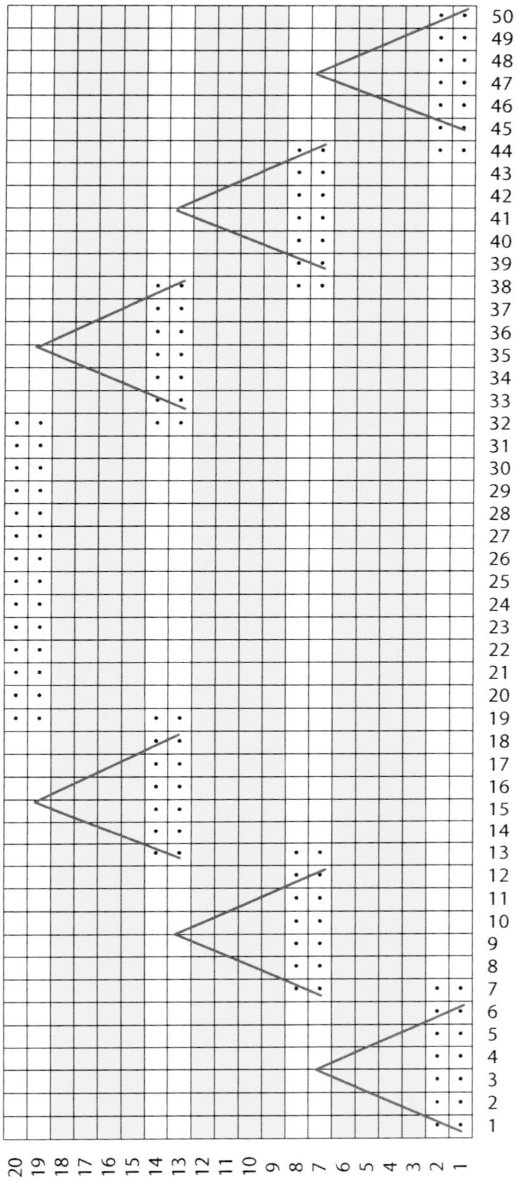

L145

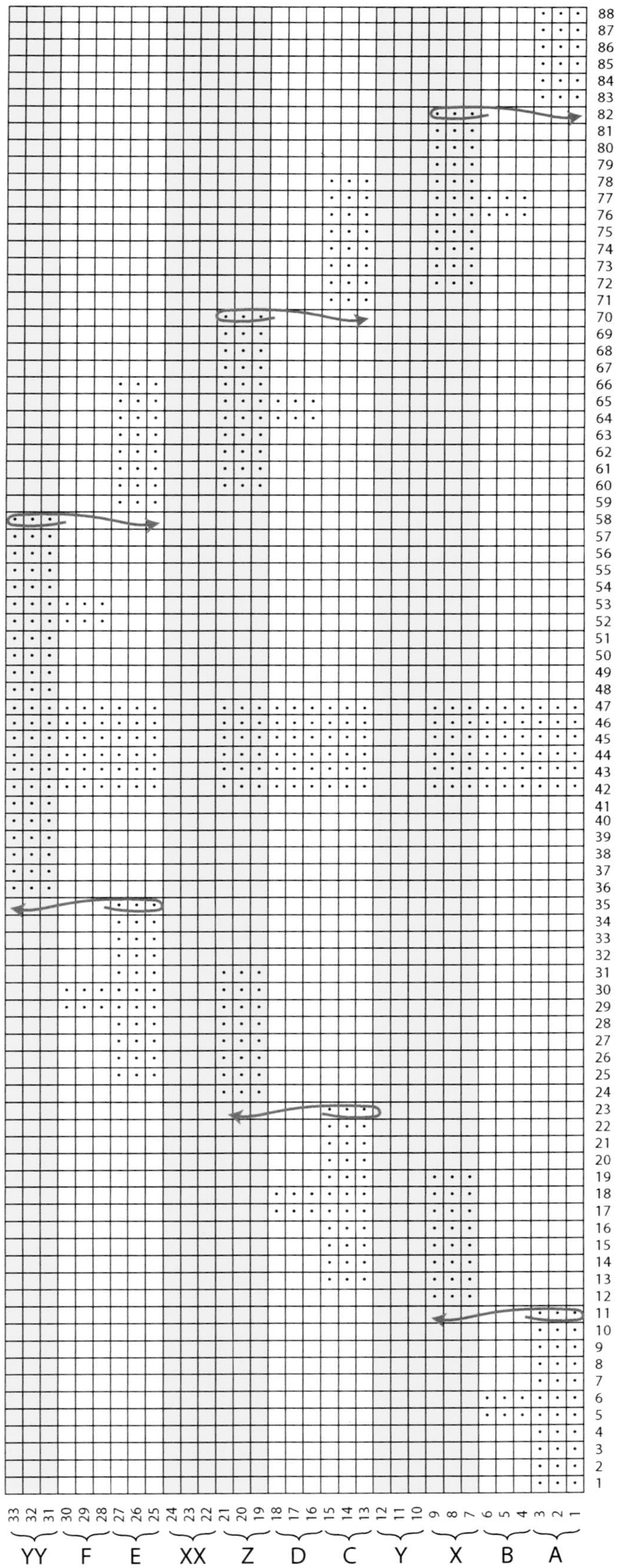

Stoll fabric that challenged me for weeks. The construction method for this fabric is very different from all the others and difficult to represent in traditional chart form.

C/O a multiple of 12 NDLS plus 6 to balance and have a group of 3 extra NDLS (shown as group YY) available at the left edge for later. To work from this chart, C/O 20 NDLS, knit 6 rows and then B/O groups of 6 for the ladders as shown. Working NDLS are labeled A, B, C in groups of 3. The NWP/ladder NDLS are labeled X, Y, Z, also in groups of 3.

Begin COR set to hold NDLS in HP. Knit 6 rows (not shown on chart) Hold all NDLS except group A. Knit 4 rows. Move group B to UWP and knit 2 rows. Hold B. Knit 5 more rows on group A, ending COL.

L146

```
|||||•••••••••••••••|||||
_________________________
••••••••••|||||••••••••••
```

Now, remove the A STS on a 3-prong transfer tool and skip past the B NDLS to replace them on the X NDLS. Put the A NDLS in NWP. Knit 1 row on the X NDLS. COR.

Move the C NDLS to UWP and knit 4 rows. Move the D NDLS to UWP and knit 2 rows. Hold D and knit 1 row. Hold X.

Knit 4 rows on C, ending COL. Remove the C STS on a 3-prong tool and move them to the empty Z NDLS. Place the empty NDLS in NWP and knit 1 row. COR.

Move E NDLS to UWP and knit 4 rows. Move F NDLS to UWP and knit 2 rows. Hold F. Knit 1 row and then hold Z.

Knit 4 rows on the E NDLS then transfer these 3 STS to the empty YY NDLS. Knit 6 rows to end the repeat. Then work 6 rows over all NDLS holding STS.

Reverse and work from left to right. Note that the beginning and ending groups of NDLS are worked differently than the other repeats. Work 6 NDLS over all NDLS holding STS after each complete sequence before reversing direction. These six rows are not shown on the end of the chart but should be knitted before returning to row 1.

You can knit fewer or more plain rows between repeats. The side edges of this fabric are particularly decorative.

L146

Double Bed Ladders

Adding a second bed of needles more than doubles your options and most of the samples I have shown you so far could be expanded to double bed versions. While some of the examples that follow are expansions of other samples, others are unique approaches to double bed knitting. Some use the second bed to facilitate drop stitch, while others incorporate stitches knitted on both beds. The most interesting samples only use the second bed of needles as a stitch holder.

L146 This fabric is just a 5 x 5 rib with the addition of 5-NDL ladders between each group of working NDLS. In this case, the ladders are formed by having no NDLS working on either bed. The 3 x 2 cables were crossed every 6/R on the MB with 3 STS crossing to the front of the fabric and 2 behind. The 3 x 2 cables crossed with less strain than 3 x 3 would have. The NDL diagram below details the half-pitch NDL arrangement for this fabric. Photo and NDL chart on next page.

The next two samples are similar and their charts nearly identical except for the number of plain rows knitted in each section and the way the repeats overlap. They are both set up with 3 WP NDLS alternating with 3 NWP ladders.

L147 Begin by C/O and transferring all STS to the MB. The beds are in full—pitch and the ribber carriage is set to hold NDLS in HP. Knit 1 plain row on MB, reset RC 000 and then transfer groups of MB STS to the RB as shown as follows: Transfer the first and then the 3rd ST from each group of three MB NDLS (STS 6 & 8) to the same RB NDL. Lastly, transfer the 2nd ST (#7) of each group to the same RB NDL. Note: For the first row only, disregard the arrows shown at NDLS 4, 10, etc as they are relevant only for repeats.

There are 3 STS on RB NDLS 7, 13, 19. Put those NDLS in HP and the corresponding empty MB NDLS in NWP. Knit 4 rows with both carriages. The HP NDLS on the RB are the only ones being used on the RB at this point and because the carriage is set to hold NDLS in HP, they tuck rather than knit.

Set the RB carriage to knit all NDLS and knit 1 row. Move the empty 1st and 3rd NDLS from each group on the MB back to WP and knit 1 row. Then transfer the single RB STS across to these NDLS. At the same time, transfer the NDLS for the next repeat to the RB as described above to triple the STS on the center RB NDL of each repeat.

It is important that you always transfer the MB STS to the RB the same way from repeat to repeat because these STS will show on the knit face of the fabric. You can transfer as I described or you might prefer transferring the center ST first and then the ones on each side of it. It won't matter as long as you are consistent

L147

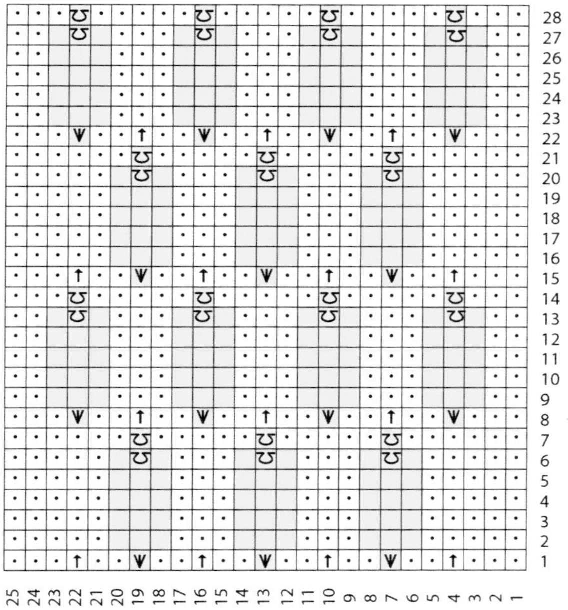

L148

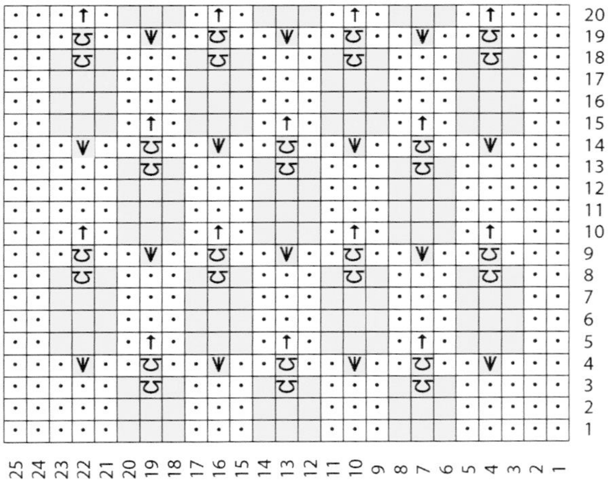

throughout the fabric.

L148 Note that these repeats overlap by only one row (rows 8, 15, 22) on the chart, while those in L147 overlap by 2 rows (rows 4 & 5, 9 & 10, 14 & 15). The spacing between the repeats remains the same, but the 2-row horizontal overlap creates a fabric with deeper, richer texture. In addition to increasing the overlap between repeats, you could also experiment further by altering the number of WP NDLS in each group or including STS on the MB that never transfer to the RB.

L147

L148

L149 The white spaces on this chart indicate RB STS. Set the beds in full pitch and, after knitting 1 row on the MB, transfer for rib as shown (4 NDLS MB, 6 NDLS RB). Knit 3 rows then cross cables as follows: Use two single—prong transfer tools to remove STS 3 and 4 from their NDLS. Cross the two STS and then

L149

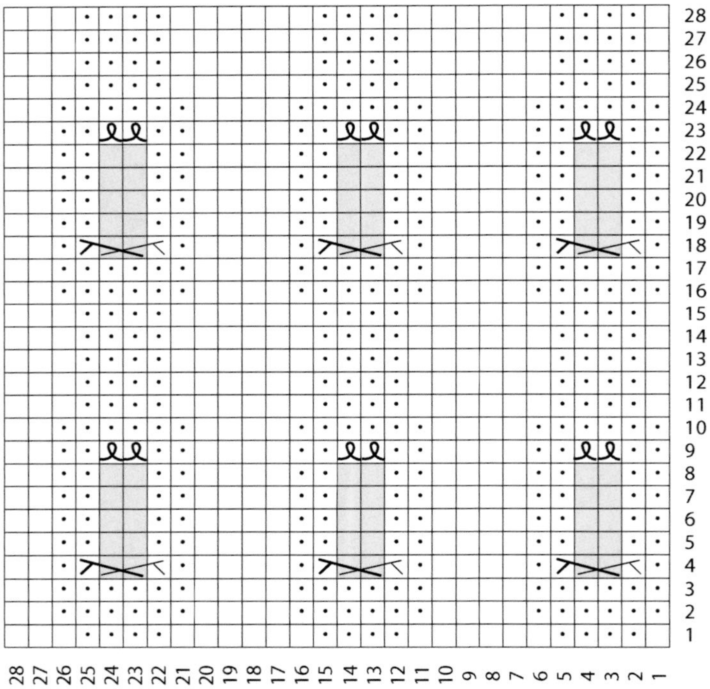

L149

return ST 3 to NDL 5 and ST 4 to NDL 2. Place the emptied NDLS in NWP and knit 4 rows.

Bring 1 empty RB NDL to WP opposite NDL 3 or 4. Knit 1 more row and then drop the ST just added and place the empty NDL in NWP. The drop ST will provide enough yarn to form two twisted increases (i.e. e—wraps) on NDLS 3 and 4. Make the first twisted increase and then keep a finger on the butt of that NDL while twisting and placing the second. Knit 2 rows.

At RC 10, transfer the outermost NDL at each side of the MB groups (i.e. NDLS 1 and 6) down to the RB and place the empties in NWP. Knit 5 rows then transfer those same STS back to the MB and work the next repeat.

L150 is worked exactly the same way except that the ladders are formed on both beds with alternate spacing.

The charts for samples L151and L152 indicate the NDL set up for these meandering, bridged, double bed ladders. Both of these samples were worked exactly like sample L136, which was a single bed version. It would

L150

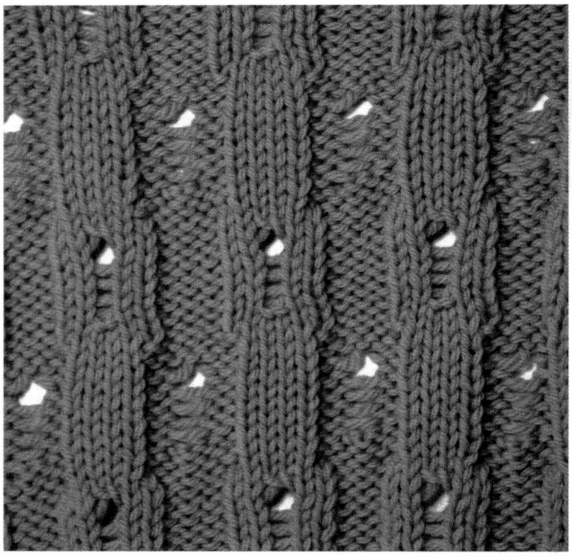

be wise to knit that sample before trying its double bed cousin. In these examples, the short rowing/bridging is worked on both beds.

I have labeled the groups A, B, C, etc as shown in the charts so the information from L136 will translate easily. All sections were worked for 6 rows, reversing the work at each edge. The difference between these two samples is the addition of some rib STS in groups A, C and E in sample L152.

The bridging becomes a bit more complex with the addition of these STS, but if you check off each sequence as you work you will find it easier to keep track of what to do when. Instead of the additional rib STS interrupting these groups, you might find it easier to keep track if you leave an extra ladder instead. Note that the edges of both fabrics are decorative and do not roll because of the rib structure.

L151

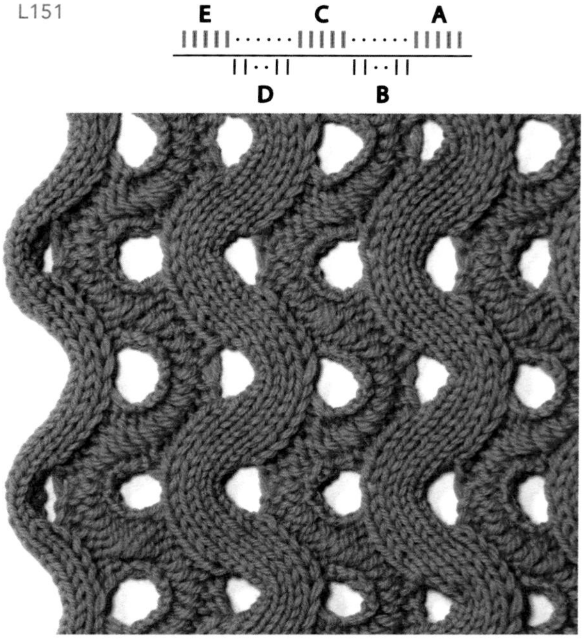

L152

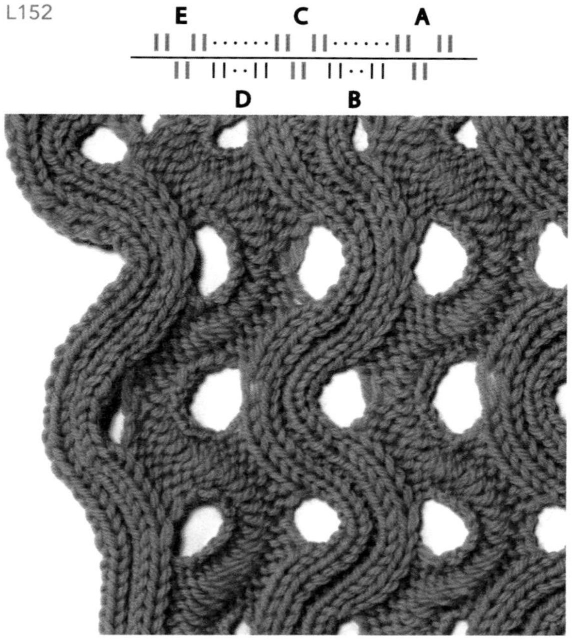

L153

L154

Racked Ladders

Every ribber manual includes a section on racking, where RB NDLS move across the surface of the MB fabric as the RB itself is shifted one position at a time. In L153 and L154 the STS also travel across the ladders.

Begin with the RB racked all the way to the left and the beds in half pitch with NDLS arranged as shown on the charts. *Knit 2 rows and rack one full HP position to the right.** (Some machines rack in half stops and alternate half and full pitch as they do so. Do not work in full pitch.) Repeat * to ** and as the RB STS begin to extend beyond the edges of the MB fabric, transfer STS from the RB to the MB NDLS; as the gap widens at the opposite end of the bed, introduce new NDLS by P/U the purl bar of the opposite MB ST.

Try to maintain the pattern as long as possible before transferring STS cross bed. When you cannot rack the bed any further, reverse direction and rack to the other side. You can also include some plain, un—racked rows or vary the number of times you rack in each direction.

L155

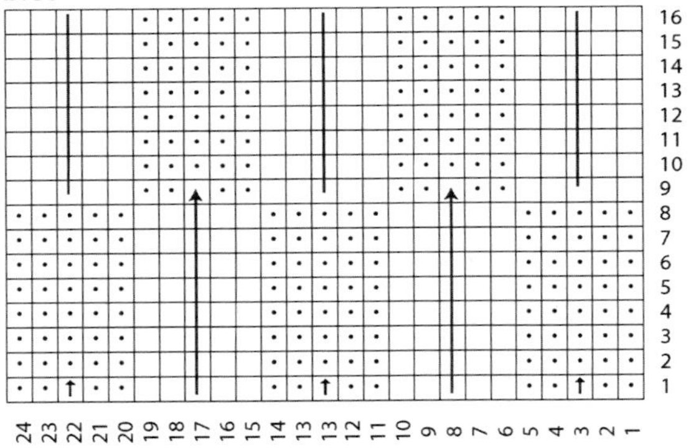

L155

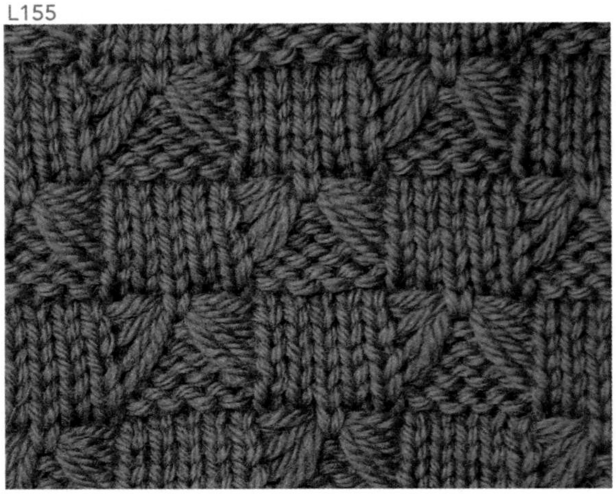

L156

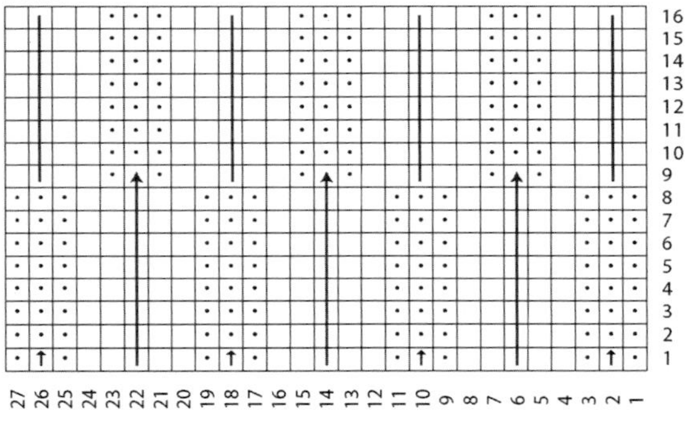

L156

L159

L158

L157

Double Bed Lifted Ladders

The next two swatches are nearly identical except for the number of plain STS between lifted sections. In L155 there are 5 STS between repeats, while in the second example L156 there are just 3. Once again, the white squares on the chart represent RB NDLS so use the first row of these charts for the NDL set up and work with the beds in full pitch.

Both examples are knitted the same way: The MB knits every row, but the RB carriage is set to knit in one direction and slip in the other (either way). Knit 8 rows. Use the ribber hook or a crochet hook to lift the four floats that formed against the RB onto the opposite center MB NDL. Then transfer the RB STS to the MB and transfer the alternate set of MB STS to the RB. For example, RB ST 8 would be transferred to the opposite MB NDL and then RB STS 6, 7, 9 and 10 would be transferred to the opposite MB NDLS. Then the alternate group of NDLS is transferred to the RB all at once for the next repeat.

L155, all 5 STS in each group are transferred back and forth across the beds in a regular checkerboard arrangement. In L156, however, only the center 3 STS in each group transfer back and forth and the outer 2 ST remain on the RB throughout. The effect is less checker—boardy and the fabric looks almost interwoven.

The next 3 examples L157, L158 and L159 (no charts) introduce color into the NDL arrangement and knitting method used for swatch L155 but could just as easily have been worked like L156.

L157 This example was worked with 2 rows/color for a total of 8 rows per repeat with the RB set to knit in one direction and slip in the other as it did in the previous examples. The lifted ladders are striped.

L158The RB was set to slip every alternate pair of rows. That is, the RB knits the green for 2 rows but slips both ways when the blue is worked. This yields single color floats against a striped background.

L159 is similar to L158 with 2-row stripes except that, instead of there being a total of 8 rows per repeat (4 stripes), there are 10 rows per repeat (yielding 5 stripes). The odd number of stripes changes the color rotation from one repeat to the next so that the solid ladders alternate color from repeat to repeat for a more interesting and complex—looking fabric.

L160

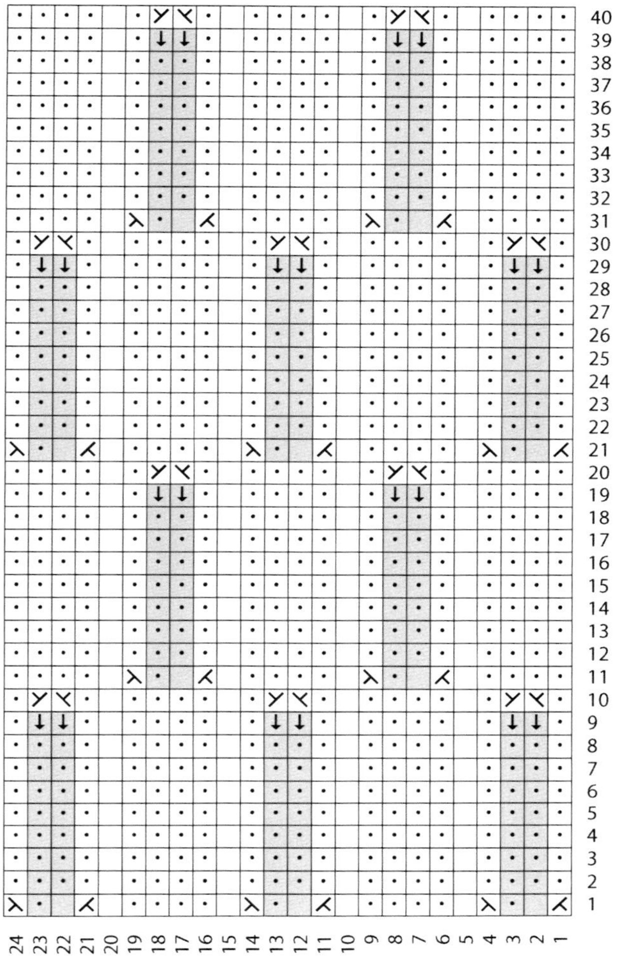

Double Bed Drop Stitch Ladders

The next 4 samples rely on drop ST for their patterning. The first sample, L160, uses drop ST for the all—over patterning as well as the open edging, which is similar to the single bed trim on L53 on page 89.

When working double bed, you can easily lose track of which group of NDLS you are supposed to manipulate and when. I find it easiest if I work an odd number of rows for each repeat so that I alternately begin on the left or right and can coordinate the groups of NDLS to that starting position. Otherwise, I keep a list of which repeats (by RC) begin on the left or right.

The white spaces on this chart represent the RB NDLS. They do not change at all throughout the fabric. Begin the first repeat by transferring STS 2 & 3 to their adj NDLS as shown on row 1 of the chart. Before knitting the row, bring one of the empty NDLS back to WP. Knit the row and then, before knitting the next row,

L160

L161

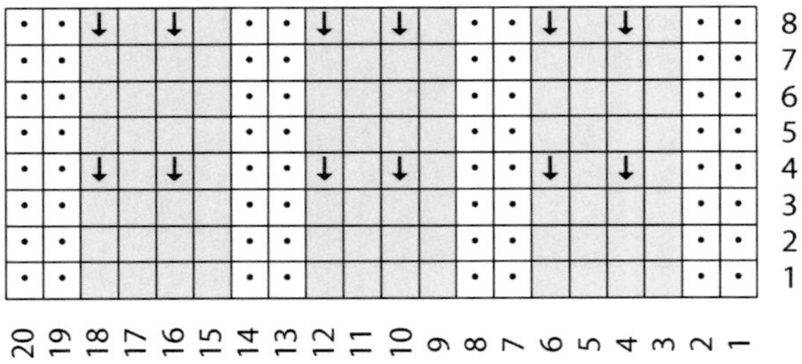

bring the other empty NDL back to WP and knit straight to RC 9. Drop the STS from NDLS 2 and 3. It is easiest to P/U the purl bar of the adj STS to make new STS on NDLS 2 and 3 before tugging on the fabric to ravel the dropped STS, Knit 1 row before transferring STS 2 and 3 to NDLS 1 and 4.

Alternate the placement for the following repeat. Both sides of this fabric are interesting and the ladders will best remain open if you work this stitch with a textured (i.e. hairy, sticky) yarn. When the effect is carried right out to the edges of the fabric it creates a decorative edge that would be great for scarves or cardigan edges.

L161 is worked on a multiple of 6 + 2 NDLS (the 2 is to balance the edge). C/O the MB only and knit some rows, then hang a comb and weights. Use bridging to B/O groups of 4 STS between pairs of WP NDLS as shown on the first row of the chart. Raise the RB with the carriage set to slip in both directions.

Knit 3 rows. Bring 2 RB NDLS to WP where indicated by the arrows on the chart and set the RB carriage to knit. Knit 1 row and then use the ribber carriage to drop the RB STS. Immediately re—set the carriage to slip in preparation for the next repeat.

First, however, twist the ladders as follows: Drop the RB out of the way. Use a latch tool to reach under the first 3 bars and catch the 4th (enlarged) bar in the hook. Pull the enlarged bar to the front, pinch with your fingers and remove it from the tool so you can add a second twist by re—inserting the tool under the twisted group to catch the same loop again. Hang the loop on the first working NDL at right of the ladder. For future repeats, alternately hang the twisted loop on the left and right to prevent possible biasing.

L161

L162

L162 (no chart) just changes the NDL arrangement so that there are 3 WP NDLS between each 4-NDL ladder. The center NDL was tucked to add some interest and texture to the columns of plain STS.

Both of these fabrics could also be knitted as single bed drop ST, but there may not be enough length to twist the last ladder bar twice without distorting the ground fabric. You would either need to settle for one twist or accept the fact that the fabric will distort without that extra ease. To work single bed drop ST, simply bring 2 empty NDLS to WP on the MB (in the ladder position) instead of the RB every 4 rows. A stretchy yarn is a must for the single bed version.

L163 This swatch is a rather extreme version of a twisted ladder and would have limited use for garments, but great potential for afghans and scarves.

C/O and knit some rows and then bridge to B/O STS so that you have 10 WP NDLS alternating with 7 empty NWP NDLS. *Bring the empty 1, 3, 5 and 7th NDLS in each group to WP and knit 1 row. Bring the remaining empty NDLS to WP and knit 7 rows.

Drop the STS from the groups of 7 NDLS and allow the ladders to ravel. Catch all 7 loops on a single—prong transfer tool and twist the tool at least 4 times** towards the edge of the fabric. Hang the twisted bars on the first NDL adjacent to the outer edge of the ladder already holding a ST.

Repeat from * to **, twisting the next and every alternate repeat towards the center of the fabric. Try to keep the ladder bars taut as you twist the tool.

L164 These twisted bundles should prevent the edges of a scarf or other straight, un—seamed project from curling under, but try a sample first as some yarns just don't respond well to blocking and may roll anyhow.

C/O enough STS for your project and knit 2 rows, ending COR. At left skip 8 NDLS and then bring 1 NDL to WP. Knit 1 row and then bring 1 more NDL to WP at left. COL. At right edge, skip 8 NDLS and bring 1 NDL to WP. Knit 1 row to right and bring 1 more NDL to WP. Knit 6 rows, ending COR.

*Drop the STS from the 2 extra NDLS at each side, leaving the inner—most NDL in WP and returning the outer NDL to NWP. Catch the loops on a single—prong transfer tool and twist the tool 8 full rotations. Place the over—twisted loops on the edge NDL of the fabric and pull it out to HP. Knit 1 row to the left and then bring the extra NWP NDL at each side back into WP, knit 6 rows and then repeat from *.

Always twist the loops at each side in the same direction. You can sharpen the edge a little more by reforming the 2nd ST from the edge.

L163

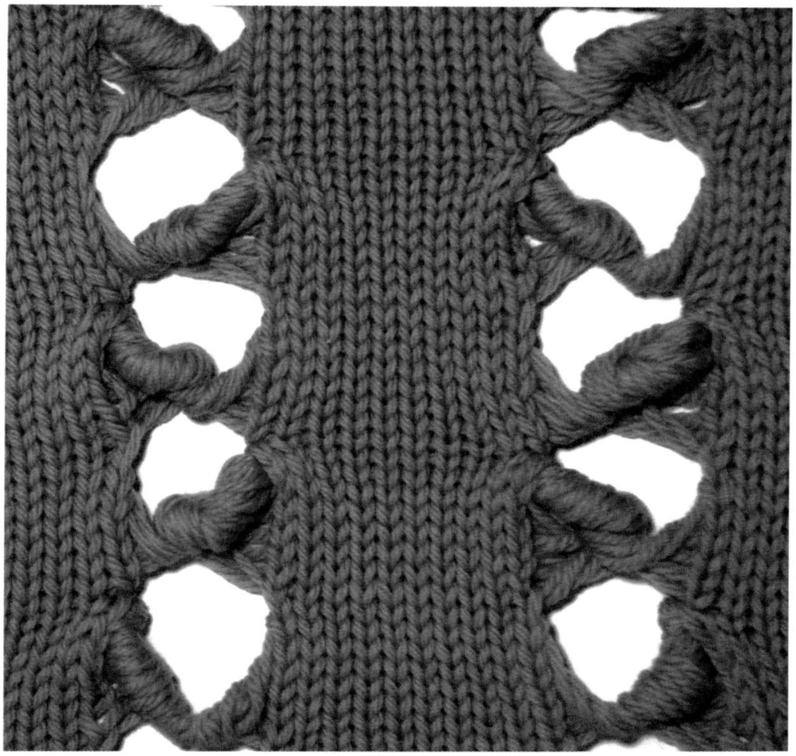

L164

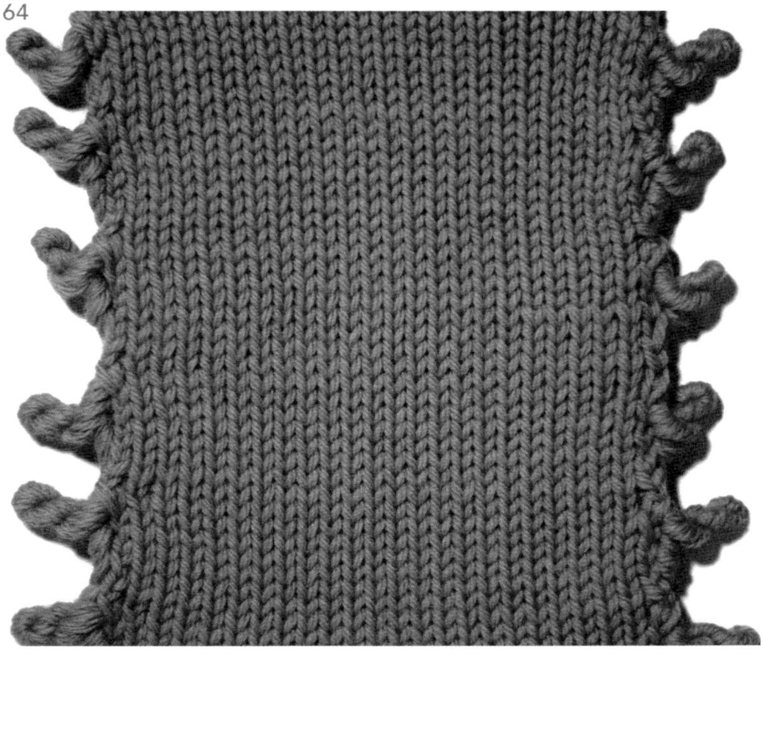

L165

L165 This sample one of the Stoll fabrics and one for which they provided directions. The MB NDLS are arranged as shown on the chart with a ladder every 5/ST. EON on the RB is in WP and the RB carriage is set to slip from left to right and to knit from right to left.

C/O with comb and weights and transfer all STS to the MB. Begin COL. Knit 1 row left to right; only the MB knits. Knit 1 row right to left; both beds knit, ending COL. Move the RB carriage across the bed to drop the STS (these passes are not shown on the chart). Tug down on the comb to help enlarge the STS.

Cross the cables, noting that the cables cross over the ladders, not on the four continuous STS between ladders. That is, STS 3 & 4 cross with 6 & 7, NOT 6 & 7 with 8 & 9. As the cables pull away from each other, it opens the spaces between them. The cables alternately cross right and left to form serpentine (open) cables.

This sample was worked with the same worsted weight yarn I have used throughout the book, but this particular fabric looks best with finer, crisper yarn like linen or cotton, which is how the Stoll fabric was worked.

Although samples L166 and L167 look fairly complicated at first glance, these are not difficult fabrics to knit. Once again, the RB is used strictly for 1 row of drop ST per repeat (i.e. rows 3 and 8 in the charts). My samples were worked with worsted weight yarn on a midgauge machine so I used ST sizes 7 on the MB and 4 on the RB.

L166

L167

L166

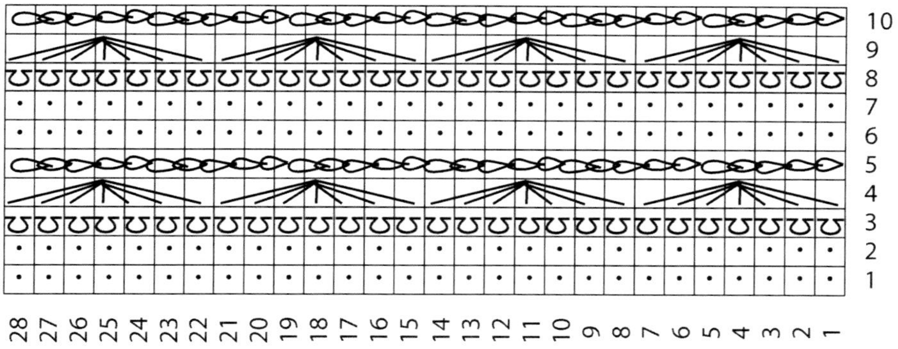

L167

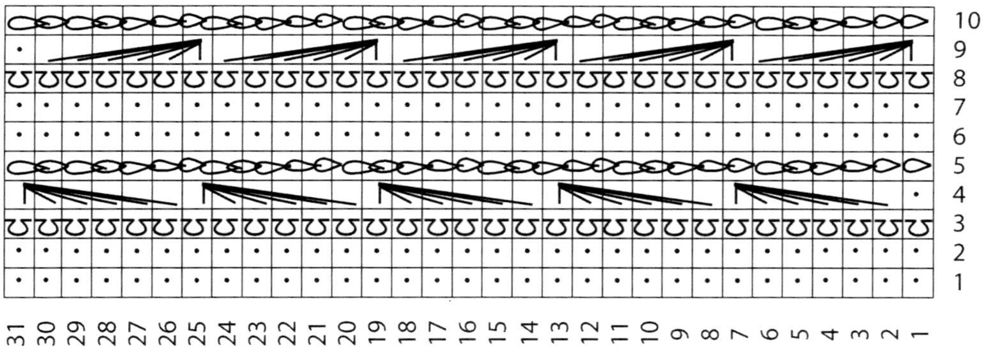

Begin with all the STS on the MB and the ribber NDLS in WP. With the ribber carriage set to slip in both directions, knit 2 rows on the MB. Set ribber carriage to knit and work 1 row full needle rib (FNR) with all the NDLS on both beds knitting this row. It will be tight so knit slowly. Separate the carriages and move the ribber carriage across the bed to drop the RB STS and then lower the RB so you have room to work.

Tug on the comb to help the MB STS absorb all the length from the dropped RB STS. Use a single prong tool to collect 3 STS from the left and 3 STS from the right onto the center NDL of each group as shown on the chart. Then work a latch tool C/O across all the NDLS and when you come to the NDLS holding 7 STS, use the ST from the latch tool to knit them back to a single ST. That is, push the NDL out to HP so that all 7 STS slide behind the latch and then transfer the ST from the latch tool into the hook of the NDL and knit it back manually. Continue chaining on and knitting the 7 STS back manually. The yarn will be on the opposite end of the bed from the carriage so free—pass the carriage to the other side and then repeat.

The row gauge for this fabric will be quite long so there won't be so many repeats to make your fabric! You can also work this fabric by alternating the placement of the repeats.

L167 is similar in construction to L166, working 1 row of drop ST and then gathering the enlarged STS to a single NDL. In this case, however, the same groups of 5 enlarged STS are gathered to the left and then to the right with alternating repeats. The 6th NDL is always the repository for the STS to its left or right and seems to undulate on the surface of the fabric.

The slightly increased pull on the STS creates a much more dimensional fabric than L166. Once again I used St sizes 7/4. Work this fabric with a multiple of 6 NDLS plus 1 to balance at the end. Continue gathering STS right out to the edges of the fabric. As the repeats alternate, so will the single ST at one side or the other. This fabric will also have an elongated row gauge, which helps minimize the number of repeats you will have to work for a large project.

Using the Ribber as a Stitch Holder

For the next 3 samples, the RB was used only as a ST holder to help position specific STS on the knit face of the fabric. The beds are in FP.

L168

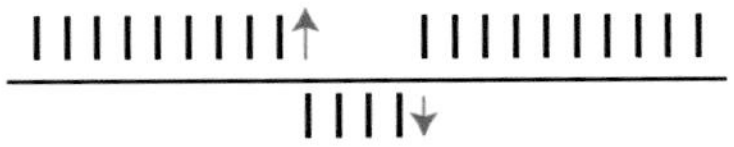

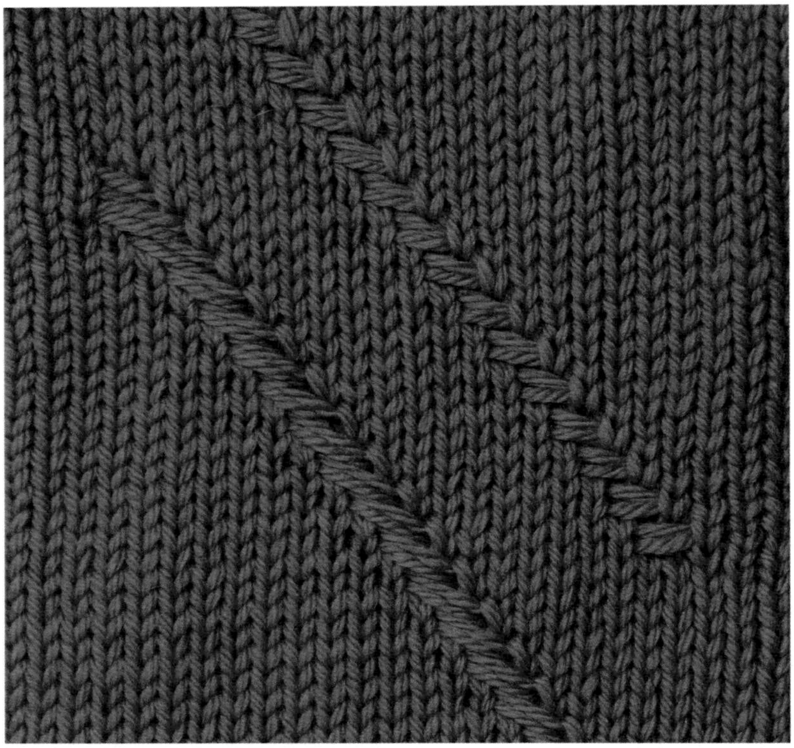

L169

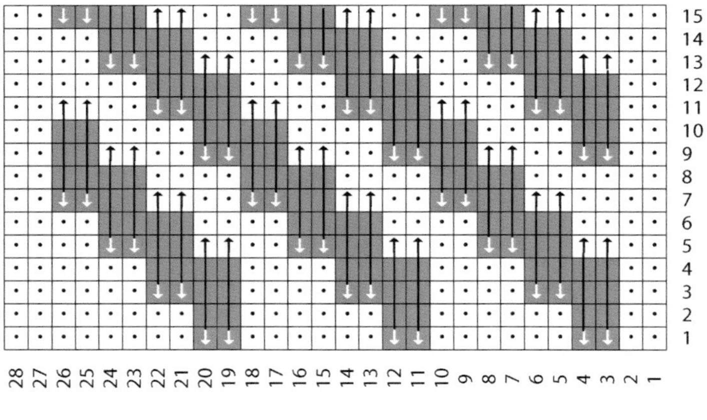

L168 was begun by C/O the MB then transferring 4 NDLS to the RB. The RB carriage was set to slip in both directions.

The diagonal at left on the swatch was worked by making transfers A/R as follows: *Return the left—most ribber ST to the MB and at the same time, transfer the next MB ST at right down to the RB.** (The red arrows indicate the transfers). Repeat * to **.

The diagonal at right on the swatch was worked with the same transfers and the added step of lifting each pair of ladder bars onto the MB NDL at left before returning the RB ST to that same NDL.

This is truly a traveling ladder, with the bars of the ladders passing in front of the knitted surface of the main fabric. It is, in fact more of a slip ST fabric than anything else, but unlike most slip fabrics, the bars are visible on the knit side, rather than the purl. The STS on the back of the ladder are vertical and decorative.

You could work this fabric on a single bed machine by using a short double pointed hand knitting needle to remove and return the MB STS as required. It won't be quite as efficient or fast as using the RB in this way, but it could be done.

L169 also uses the RB to produce slip STS on the knit face of the fabric. Set the RB carriage to slip in both directions. The slips form a twill pattern on the fabric because of the way they are transferred.

At RC 1, transfer the STS from NDLS 3 & 4, 11 & 12, 19 & 20 to the RB. Put the empty MB NDLS in NWP and knit 2 rows. At RC 3, transfer STS 5 and 6, 13 and 14, etc to the RB. Put the empty NDLS in

L169

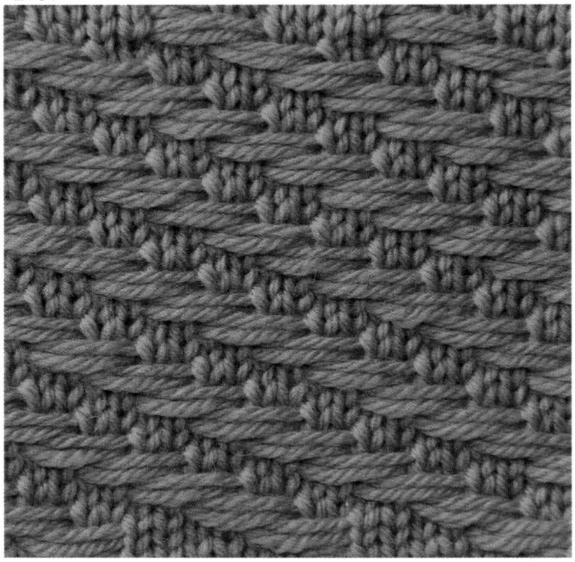

NWP and knit 2 rows. At RC 5, continue choosing 2 more NDLS to the left to transfer to the RB AND at the same time, return the first pair of STS (i.e. 3 and 4, 11 and 12, etc) to their MB NDLS.

There should never be more than 4 NDLS in each group on the RB so as you add additional pairs of STS at the left you must also return the right—most pair in each group to the MB. Leave at least 2 plain STS at each edge of the fabric (more if you want to). This fabric requires constant transferring so if you want to speed things up a bit (1) leave more than 6 STS between each repeat, (2) knit 3 or 4 rows after each transfer or (3) return all of the STS at once, rather than gradually, to create more of a checkerboard design.

L170 is worked exactly like L169 except that the pattern alternates position and changes direction, as shown on the chart. The ladder bars twist as they transfer back and forth and the stockinette areas seem to undulate and weave through the bars. Although it looks more involved, this fabric is actually easier to work than the previous sample because there are fewer transfers to make.

The transfers shown from the RB to the MB in row 1 apply only to repeats of the pattern, not to the very first row. You should begin with no STS on the RB.

L170

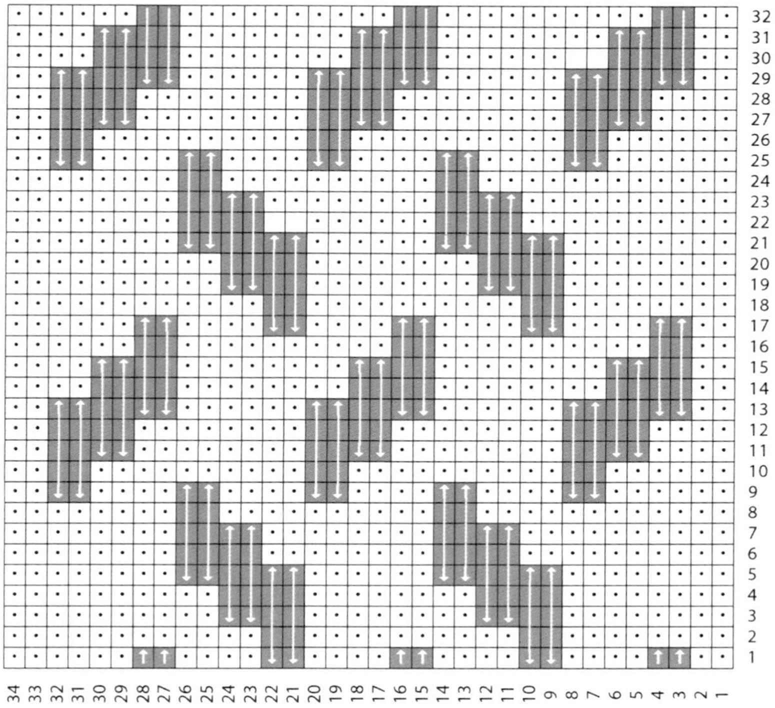

L170

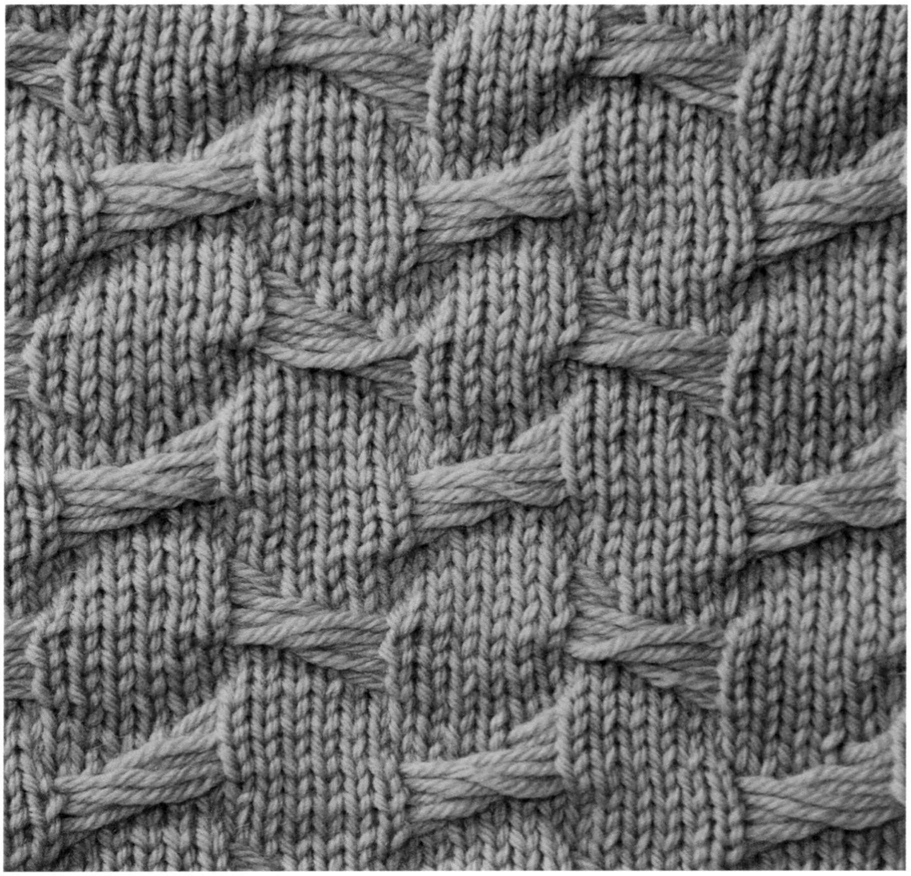

L171

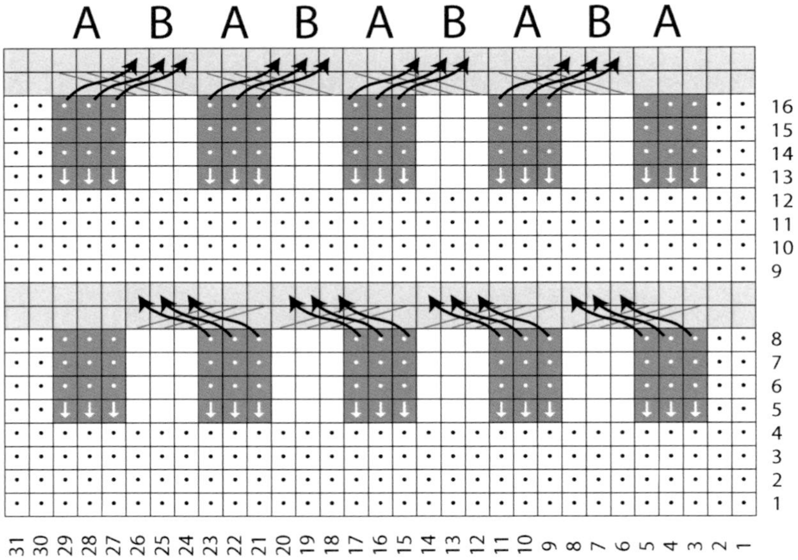
A B A B A B A B A
16
15
14
13
12
11
10
9
8
7
6
5
4
3
2
1
31 30 29 28 27 26 25 24 23 22 21 20 19 18 17 16 15 14 13 12 11 10 9 8 7 6 5 4 3 2 1

L171

Special Double Bed Ladders

L171 is one of the Stoll fabrics that kept me up at night, puzzling about its construction. After many (too many!) failed attempts, I finally worked out this method for producing basket weave cables separated by ladder bars. This isn't a difficult fabric, but follow the step by step directions carefully as I am afraid that the chart alone is of little use for this one!

The cables are not crossed in the usual way, but as groups of STS that are returned from the RB to the MB. Also, you will find that the easiest way to transfer groups of 3 STS from bed to bed is to use the 2-tool method I show on my blog. Remove the STS on one tool, insert a second tool into the same STS from above and then remove the first tool.

Note that the chart indicates A and B groups of NDLS, which are referenced in the directions as well. Maintain some plain STS at each edge of the fabric. With worsted weight yarn on my midgauge machine, I set my ST sizes 8/10 (MB/RB). For this fabric you will need larger STS on the RB, not the MB, which is not the norm.

Begin by C/O, hanging comb and weights and transferring all STS to the MB. There are two prep rows/ steps after each repeat is knitted.

Step 1: Set RB carriage to slip and MB carriage to knit. Knit 4 rows on the MB NDLS. Transfer all A groups of STS to the opposite RB NDLS. Set MB to slip and RB to knit. Knit 4 rows on the RB NDLS.

Next, transfer all B groups of STS on the MB to the empty MB NDLS to their RIGHT. This transfer is indicated by red slanted lines on the first prep row after row 8. Then return the STS on the RB to the empty MB NDLS to their LEFT as shown by the black arrows on the second prep row after row 8 on the chart. This crosses the cables and returns all STS to the MB to end this first repeat. (The last group of 3 RB STS are returned directly to the MB without crossing.)

Step 2: Knit 4 rows on the MB NDLS. Transfer all A groups of STS to the opposite RB NDLS. Set MB to slip and RB to knit. Knit 4 rows on the RB NDLS. Transfer all B groups of STS on the MB to the empty MB NDLS at their LEFT as shown by the red lines in the prep row after row 16 of the chart. Return the B groups of STS from the RB to the empty MB NDLS at their RIGHT as shown by the black arrows in the prep row. Repeat these two steps for the length of the fabric.

L172 is another one of the Stoll fabrics that I was intrigued with and after more time than I would like to admit, I still couldn't figure it out. Chui King Lai is one of the technicians at the Stoll Knit Resource Center and she worked out the charts and the method for this fabric for me. This is one of those fabrics that you can work half repeats right out to the edges of the fabric.

There are two charts included here and two fabrics to examine. The first chart and the fabric (L172a) knitted from it show a pretty basic diamond arrangement of eyelets formed by simple transfers. Keep this in the back of your mind as we take it all one step further.

172A

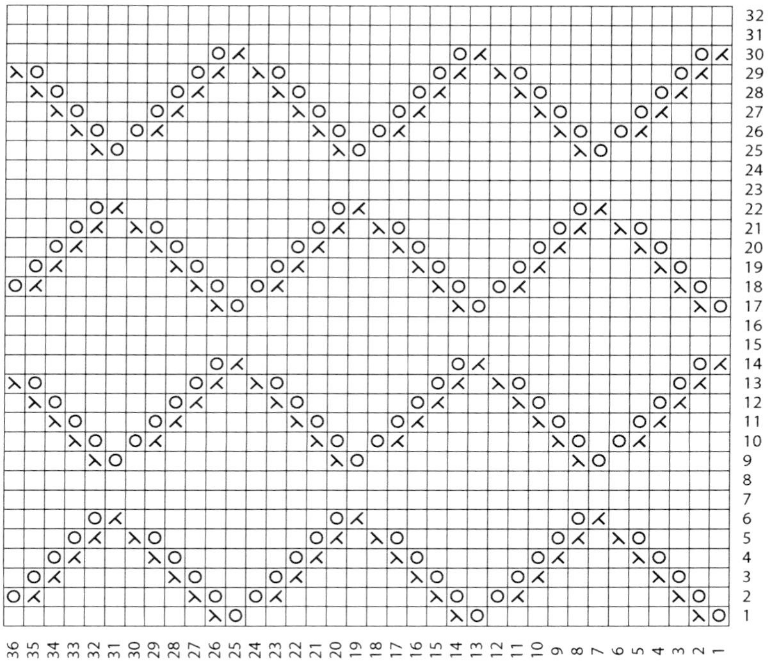

172A

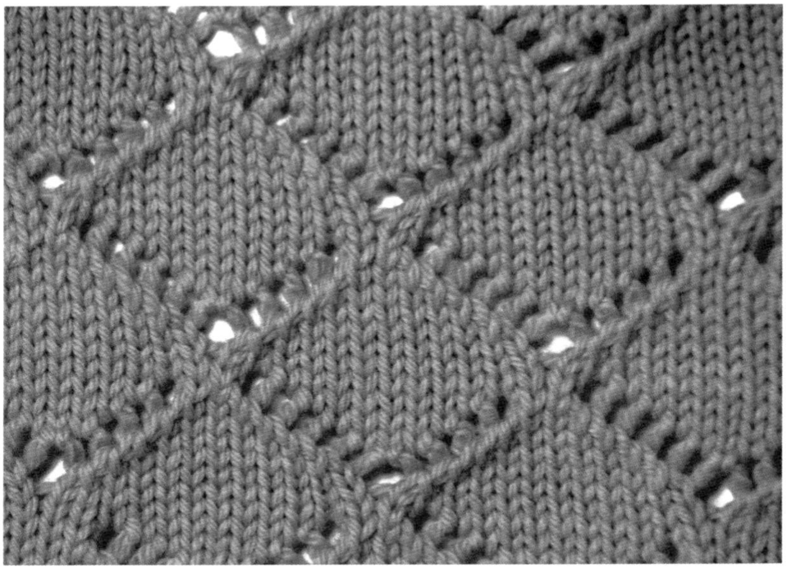

L172B

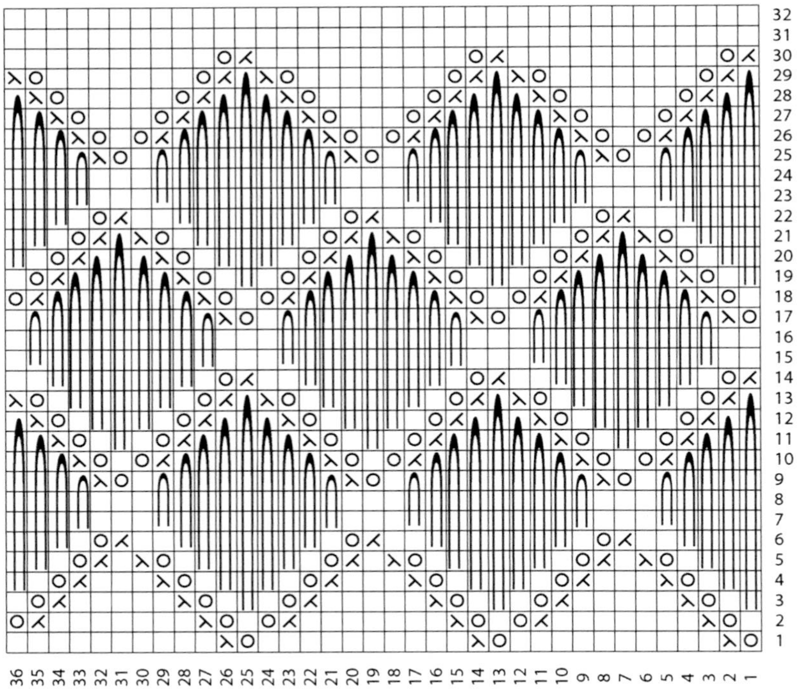

The second chart (L172b) includes some cross—bed transfers, which are reflected in the texture of the fabric knitted from that chart. This was the only fabric I examined at Stoll (not the eyelet diamonds) and without King I would never have guessed that what I saw as nearly vertical ladders between the raised sections of the fabric were the result of some fancy ST transfers!

Once again, set the ribber carriage to slip in both directions as the RB is used only as a ST holder and never knits. Begin with all the STS on the MB, with comb and weights in place.

**Work the first 2 rows of the chart, making the eyelet transfers and knitting 1 row after each set of transfers. At row 3 of the chart, make the eyelet transfers and at the same time, P/U and hang the purl bar from the center ST of each repeat (i.e. NDLS 1, 13, 25, etc.) on the opposite RB NDL and knit 1 row.

Make the next eyelet transfers and at the same time P/U and hang the purl loops from the STS on either side of the previous P/U STS onto the opposite RB NDLS. That is, P/U the purl bars from STS 2, 12 and 14, 24 and 26, etc. Knit 1 row.

Continue making the remaining eyelet transfers and at the same time P/U and hang the purl loops on the opposite RB NDLS as shown on the chart, knitting 1 row after each transfer/pick up sequence. When there are 7 loops in each repeat hung on the opposite RB NDLS , P/U the last purl loop at each side (from NDLS 5, 9 and 17, 21 and 29, etc) and then knit 2 rows. There should be groups of 9 RB NDLS holding loops with 3 NWP RB NDLS between them. This is a good time to move up your weights.

L172B FRONT

L172B BACK

L173

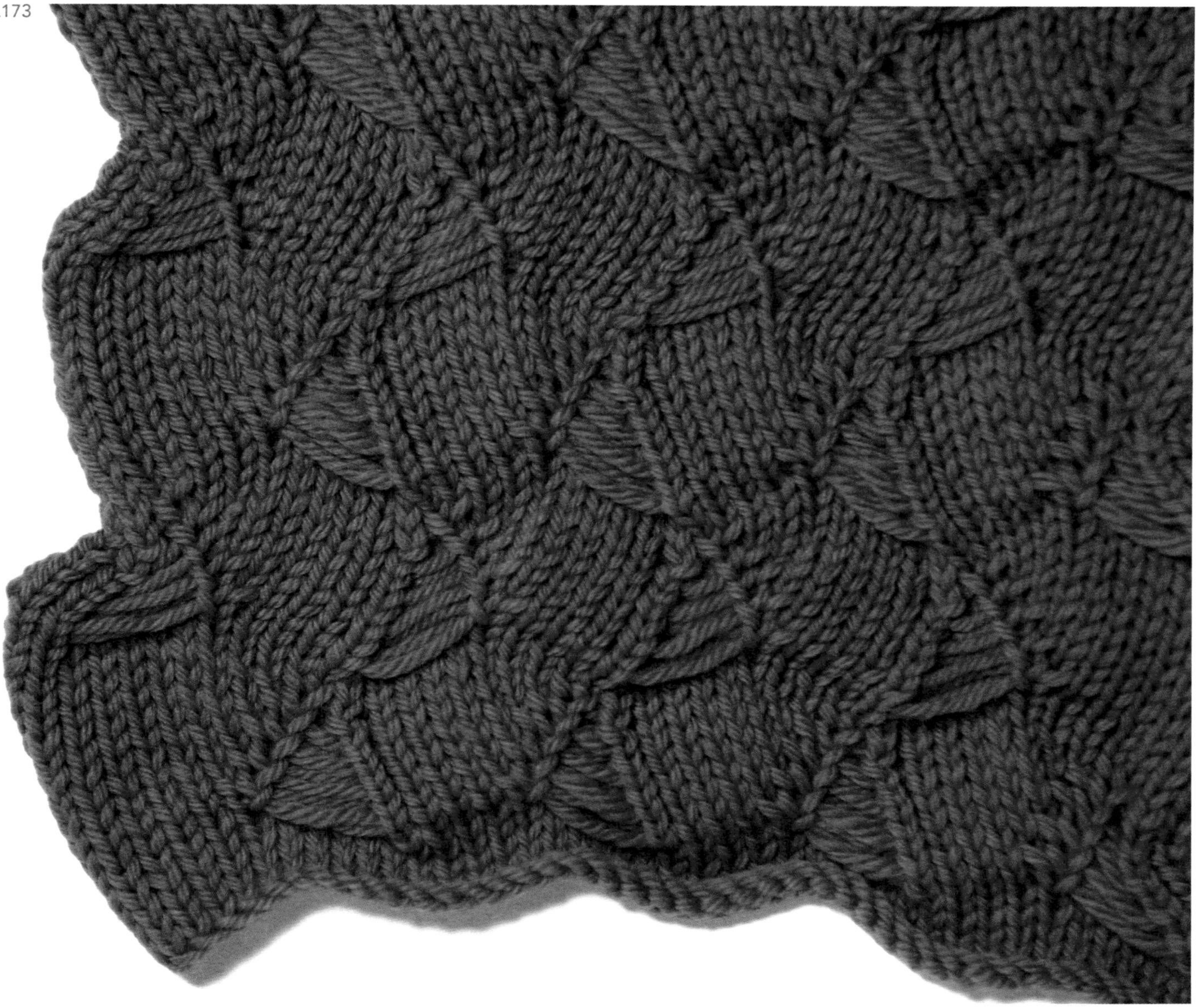

Work the next repeat from ** and note that the repeats are staggered/alternating placement. In addition to making the eyelet transfers for the next repeat, you will also need to return the loops from the first repeat from the RB to MB NDLS. So, for rows 9 and 10 you need to make eyelet transfers AND return RB loops to MB NDLS. For the next 3 rows of the chart, you will also begin transferring MB purl loops to the opposite RB NDLS for this repeat

At this point, I found it easiest to keep track of things by (1) first making the eyelet transfers, (2) P/U and hanging the MB purl loops for the current repeat on the opposite RB NDLS and (3) returning the purl loops from the previous repeat to the MB NDLS.

This is neither an easy nor a fast fabric to knit. However, I think that it opens up all kinds of new possibilities for using the RB to hold STS — in this case just purl loops — in a way that acts as a lifted ST design. Could there be a way to work something like this on a single bed machine, just lifting the appropriate loops every so many rows? Probably, but holding the purl loops on the opposite bed for so many rows helps to stretch and distort them in ways that add to the texture and depth of the finished fabric. A single bed, lifted loop would not create such a dramatic, thick fabric with vertical ladders between the lozenges.

L173 I literally lost sleep over this fabric. Another of the fabrics in the Stoll archives that I photographed and made brief notes on, but once I got home and started working on it, I was clueless! I'd like to tell you that I finally worked it out, but I didn't. The director of the Stoll Knit Resource Center contacted the German factory for the industrial charts (which wouldn't help us at all!) and then once again, King came to my rescue. She spent a couple of hours figuring it out for a domestic machine and then presented me with the chart. This is another one that I would never have figured out on my own either so am forever grateful to King for her help!

This is an unusual fabric construction and one that probably lends itself to other variations and experimentation. I've included a photo of the back of this fabric to help clarify what is happening here. I suggest leaving at least 3 plain STS at each edge of the fabric. The edge is quite decorative and could also be worked with a wider border. I especially like the way the STS seem to weave through the triangular ladders that are at slight angles to each other.

L173

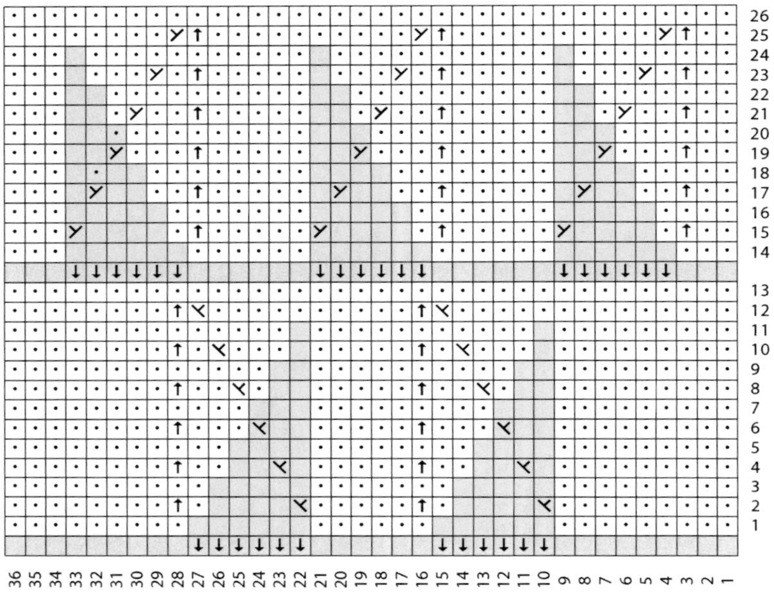

BACK L173

Begin with all the STS on the MB, with comb and weights. The RB is only used for holding STS so set it to slip in both directions.

There are 2 prep rows shown on the chart; one each before rows 1 and 14. To begin, rack the RB as far to the right as it will go, maintaining full pitch. Transfer the STS indicated by the arrows (10-15 and 22-27 on the first prep row of the chart) down to the RB. Knit 2 rows.

Rack the RB 1 position to the left and transfer the first ST at left of each RB group (originally STS 15 and 27 onto NDLS 16 and 28) so there are 2 STS on this NDL. Make a lifted increase from MB NDL 9 to 10 and NDL 20-21. Knit 2 rows.

*Rack RB 1 more position to the left and transfer the left-most RB ST to MB NDLS 16 and 28. Do a lifted increase to make a ST on the right—most empty MB NDL in each group and then knit 2 rows.**

Repeat * to ** until all of the STS held on the RB have been transferred back to the MB. The STS are always placed on the same MB NDL as they are transferred back up from the RB to the MB as shown by the upward pointing arrows on rows 2, 4, 6, 8, 10 and 12. At the same time, you need to make lifted increases on the MB to fill the one, right—most empty NDL before knitting 2 rows.

After row 13, transfer the alternate group of 6 STS from the MB to the RB to work the next repeat. Note that this second (and every alternate repeat hereafter) reverses the way the STS are returned from the RB to the MB so that they stack up on the right, rather than the left and that the lifted increases are made at the left of each group of empty MB NDLS, rather than at the right. Begin the second repeat with the bed racked as far to the left as possible and then rack it one full position to the right after every 2 rows.

This fabulous laddered sweater is by the British designer, Jo Bee. You can follow her work at http://www. instagram.com/jobeeknitwear. Photo by Alice Fisher Photography courtesy of Jo Bee.

SLITS

SIMPLY STATED, slits are breaks in a fabric. They can be vertical, diagonal or horizontal and with knits, their creation can include binding off some stitches and then casting on again. To be sure, there is often some overlap here between slits and large eyelets and ladders, but the distinctions are not always clear.

Vertical and diagonal slits are generally worked in one of two ways. You can utilize holding position to work individual needles or groups of needles. This might include bridging, carrying the yarn from one group to the next or using holding position to work with one group of needles at a time, cutting and restarting yarns as you progress from one group to the next.

In either case, weighting the working stitches is extremely important here because the needles in holding position tend to lift the fabric, instead of allowing it to drop down below the working needles which can cause dropped stitches, carriage jams and other mishaps. You need to make sure that the weights are always under just the working needles and you will need to keep moving them as you work to ensure this.

Vertical and diagonal slits can also be worked as intarsia, whether or not you change color from one section to the next. Working in intarsia mode has the advantage that the entire fabric lengthens evenly, row by row, rather than section by section as it does with the holding method. It has the disadvantage of more ends to work in later and the need to lay the yarn in by hand, rather than relying on the carriage yarn feeder. If your carriage has a built in intarsia setting, you may also be able to work back and forth between holding position and intarsia for specific effects.

I have used both methods throughout this chapter and sometimes specify which I used for each sample. In addition, when using holding position, I have employed a method of dealing with the bridge bars that in some cases (though not all) removes the need to cut and restart the yarn.

Horizontal slits, on the other hand, require binding off stitches and casting them back on in the next row. When this occurs mid—row, it usually means that you need to employ bridging to interrupt the carriage. I often find that I need to bridge the row prior to binding off to enlarge the stitches so that they are large enough to bind off without drawing in the edges of the slit.

Diagonal slits usually require short rows to build up a slanted edge prior to binding off and then again, after casting back on to level out the fabric.

In addition to these obvious, basic slits, this chapter includes some fabrics based on slits where the slits themselves take a back seat to the textures that result from lots of short rowing. Please note that when charts accompany these short—rowed swatches, the empty spaces represent needles in hold, rather than specific stitches. I have done this to keep these charts as simple and clear as possible. Many of them also include serpentine ladders and descriptive text to guide you through the charts. There are many examples of slits that are easier to understand from verbal directions than charts so there are fewer charts in this section.

As I did with the previous chapters, I have divided the examples into related groups that resulted from my "what if" queries and where one example grew from another, I have paired them as much as possible.

Vertical Slits

Vertical slits look pretty much the same whether you work with holding position or intarsia. Your choice of method may be based on personal preference for one method over another or on the availability of an intarsia carriage. It will also be influenced by the length of the slits and how often or how the slits connect to hold the fabric together because, eventually, they must connect in order to build a fabric. A slit is only a slit in the context of a complete fabric where it interrupts a continuous, connected surface. Otherwise, you simply have a strip of fabric.

If the stitch or row count or an odd/even number of stitches or rows is essential, I will indicate that in the directions There are no rules about how long slits should be or how often or how they connect. So, for example, if one of my samples indicates a slit that is connected by a single cable crossing every 12 rows, you might want to ask yourself why and, in turn, what if....

Vertical Slits – Intarsia Method

Working intarsia means that the yarn is wound on bobbins and manually laid into the open hooks of the needles. After each pass of the carriage, the needles return to upper working position with the latches open. This requires either a built in setting on your carriage or a separate intarsia carriage. Dedicated intarsia carriages do not have a yarn feeder and do not usually have any mechanism for automatically controlling needles in holding position.

You can still use holding position when working intarsia, but the needles will not knit back to working position with the flick of a lever. Instead, if needles have been in holding position, you need to nudge them back to upper working position or working position manually. You'll have to ensure that the old stitches are behind the latches and that the latches are open and ready to accept new yarn for the next row. I make a point of mentioning this because so many of us rely on holding position to more easily knit tightly crossed cables or other textured stitches. It makes it easier for the carriage to knit those needles, but, unfortunately, this is not an option with intarsia. You will, however, find that needles in upper working position also provide some relief for the carriage, but you will have to move them into that position manually.

I normally weave in as many beginning and ending yarn tails as I can when working intarsia. To do this, push 5 or 6 needles out to HP and weave the end over and under the shafts of these needles (not in the hooks) then push the weaving back against the bed. Nudge these needles back to upper working position and make sure the latches are open.

I also begin new yarns by manually knitting the first 2 or 3 needles of that color back to regular working position and then leave them there. With the next pass of the carriage they will return to upper working position. They will not drop if they are in working position. So, to sum up, I manually knit the first few needles in the first row of a new color and then, prior to the second row, I weave the yarn tail through 5-6 needles. These 2 steps secure new yarns and eliminates the need to thread a needle and work ends in later on. Once blocked and finished, you can clip the ends close to the back of the fabric.

If your carriage has a built—in intarsia setting, you may find that you can combine both the intarsia and the holding position methods for working slits in a single project. In that case, pay careful attention to your row counter and keep the weights underneath working needles at all times. Also, double check that your hand—fed intarsia gauge matches the threaded carriage gauge. You may have to make minor adjustments.

Methods of Joining Slits

S1 The simplest and most common method for joining intarsia slits is to cross the yarns where they meet between sections. It is the method that is always employed for graphic intarsia where you want a continuous surface. When working a slit fabric, depending on the gauge of the yarn, an occasional crossing may not be sturdy enough to hold a slit together so you may

S1

S2

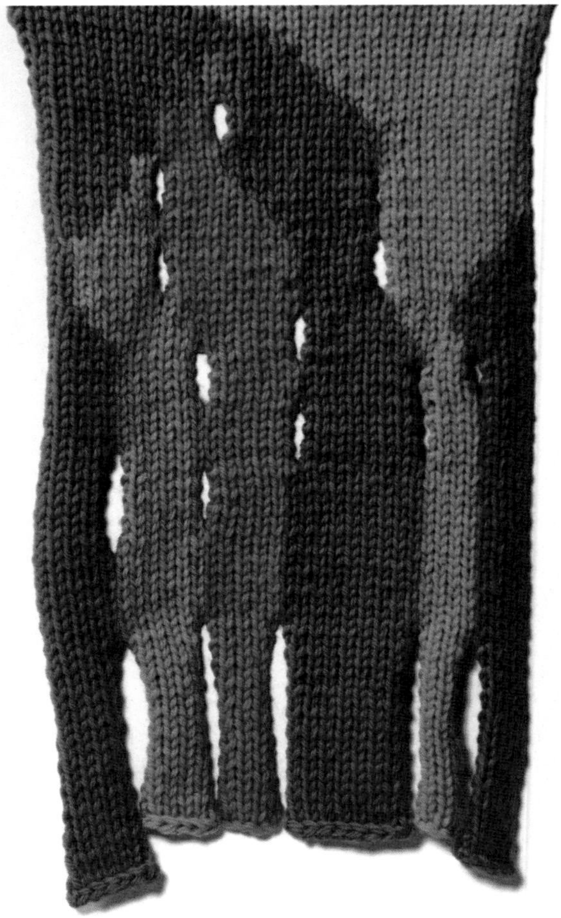

need to work several rows joining the yarn. The yarns cross twice to join the two sides of the slit and then each bobbin continues to work its own side.

S2 Based on one of the Stoll fabrics, this is a sort of "free spirit", meandering intarsia where the colors meet and cross or remain separate to form random slits. We usually tend to think of intarsia designs with all of the bobbins crossing and closing up the fabric, but there are definitely designs that benefit from the open spaces between colors.

S3 Changing the location of a slit by extending one of the yarns beyond it and creating a new slit somewhere else in the fabric will close off the slit and join the fabric. It might be as simple as a stripe pattern like the example below. The slits and the stripes are 8 rows high. The light blue yarn acts as the MC in this fabric and every 8/R knits 1 row across all of the NDLS to reposition itself on the opposite side of the work, closing the top of one slit before beginning the next. The knitting began with the MC on the left and the CC on the right. I knitted the slit for 8 rows, then cut the CC and worked 1 row across all the NDLS with the MC. The next repeat began with the MC on the right and the CC beginning anew at the left. This required cutting and restarting the CC at the end of every stripe sequence.

S4 This example employs uses alternating stripes that extend across the width of the work every 12 rows to close the slits. In this case, the full—row stripes alternate color and because they are only 4-row stripes, the second yarn can simply be held at the edge of the knitting and re—introduced after the stripe. There is no need to cut and re—start either of the yarns.

S5 This is a single color intarsia that was knitted with 3 bobbins. You could knit this fabric with HP, but I found intarsia easier and faster. The slits are 8 rows high and overlap each other by 4 rows with 4 plain STS between them. They form a nice pattern of slits just as they are, but also provide an excellent base for weaving through a cord, wider piece of fabric or a decorative scarf. Although you only need 2 bobbins for the first 4 rows, the next 4 rows require a third bobbin. I found it easiest to just maintain the 3 bobbins throughout so that the fabric at the right and left of the slits and the 4 stitches at the center have their own bobbins, crossing where they meet to join the fabric and remaining separate where the slits form.

S3

S4

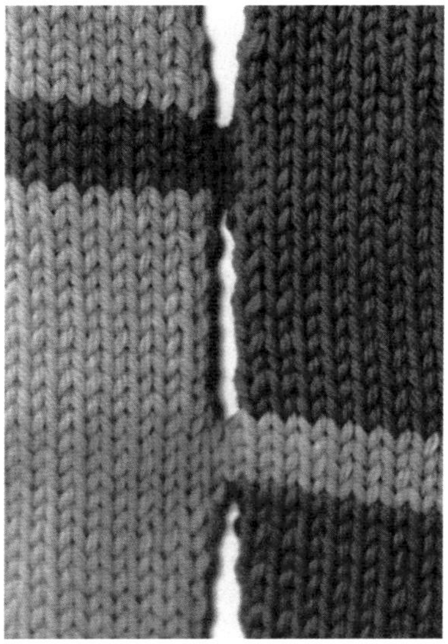

S5

S5

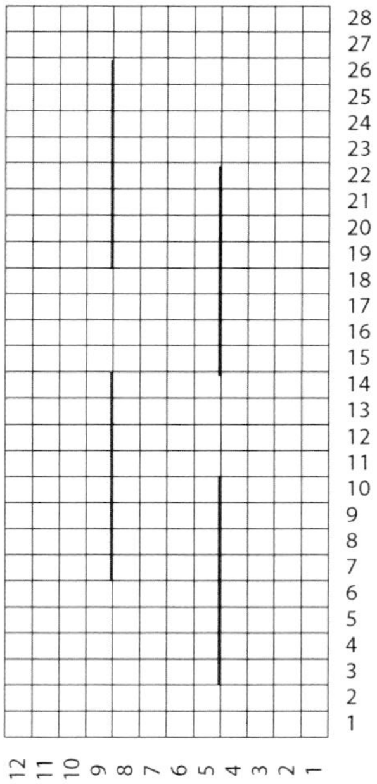

S6 front

S7 back

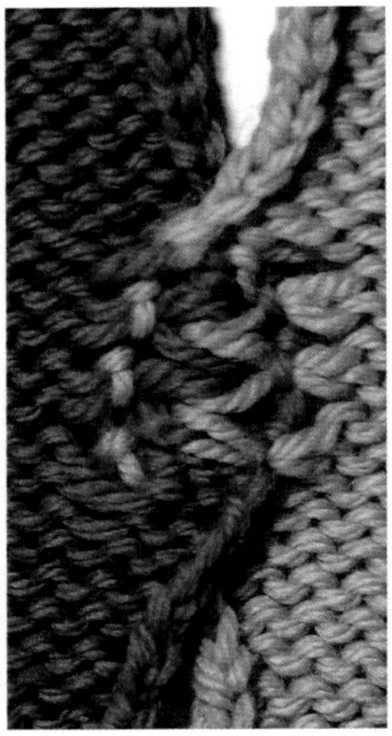

S8

S9

S6 Crossing 2-color cables to join slits may require re—positioning the yarns after the groups of stitches are crossed. This slit was knitted up to the point where the cables cross. Once crossed, the colors were interrupted. That is, a solid border of turquoise, 2 aqua STS, 2 turquoise STS and then the opposite aqua border. The color order remains like this for the next 6 rows, but once the cables cross for a second time, each color returns to its own side.

It really isn't practical or necessary to add more bobbins. Instead, I allow the two yarns to skip over the opposite color – like Fair Isle – to work the far leg of the cable. S7 The 2-stitch floats on the back of the fabric shown in S6 are shorter than most floats in Fair Isle and cause no problems. Note that the cable crosses the same direction both times to achieve this twisted look.

S8 You can also join slits by working a traditional twisted ST. Remove one ST from each edge of the slit together on a 2-prong transfer tool. Insert a second transfer tool from above, remove the first tool and then twist the tool 180° to the left or right (be consistent from one repeat to the next) before replacing the 2 STS on the NDLS. Knit 2 rows and repeat the twist a second time. This produces a delicate, linked joining that would look great alternating with modest 1" slits up the front of a simple garment.

S9 The pussy willow twists were formed as follows: With the COR (and yarns on the right of each section), use a single—prong transfer tool to remove the edge ST from the right side of the slit and hang the tool (temporarily) on the 2nd NDL from that edge. Bring the empty NDL to HP. Use a latch tool to make 5 loops abut 2" long by wrapping the left side yarn over the shaft of the empty NDL and catching it in the hook of a latch tool held below. Try to make all the loops the same length. Rotate the latch tool 5-6 times until the yarn is over—twisted and kinks up on itself.

S9

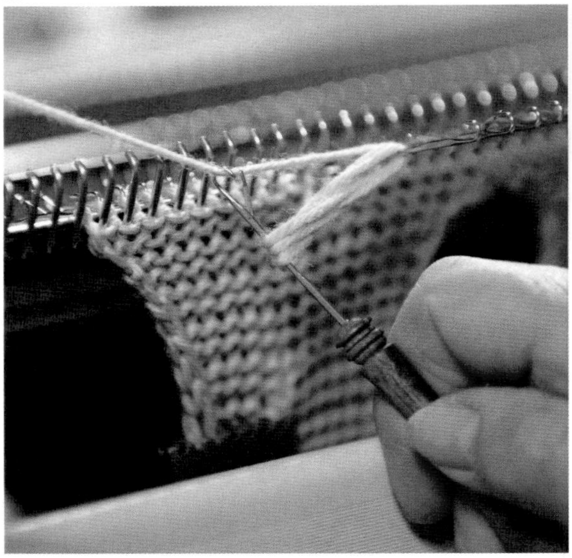

Transfer the loops from the hook of the tool to the NDL in HP. Return the original ST from the transfer tool to the same NDL, placing the NDL in UWP as you do so. Work the next 2 rows crossing the yarns between the sections to join them. Work 5 more rows, un—joined to produce a slit and then work the twisted bundles when COL with the yarn color from the alternate side. If working the fabric in a single color, the bundles can all be worked from the same side. You will probably find it more comfortable to work from one side or the other so choose accordingly.

S10 Eyelet joins are often used for afghans and large scale projects but this intarsia example is on a much smaller scale and the eyelets are used to add a lovely detail along side the join, rather than being used as part of the join. The slits were closed every 12 rows as follows:

S10

S11

S10

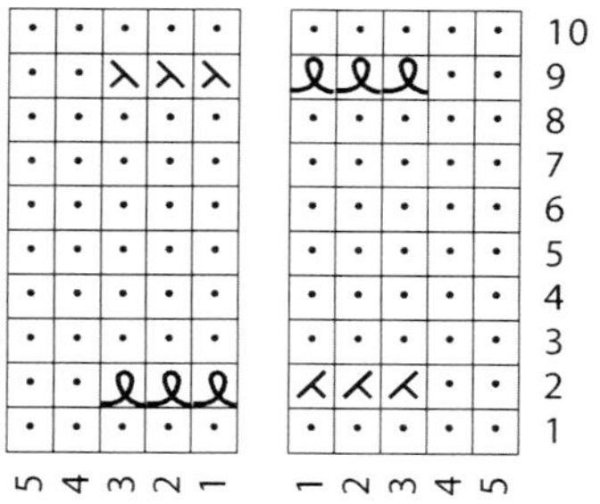

S11

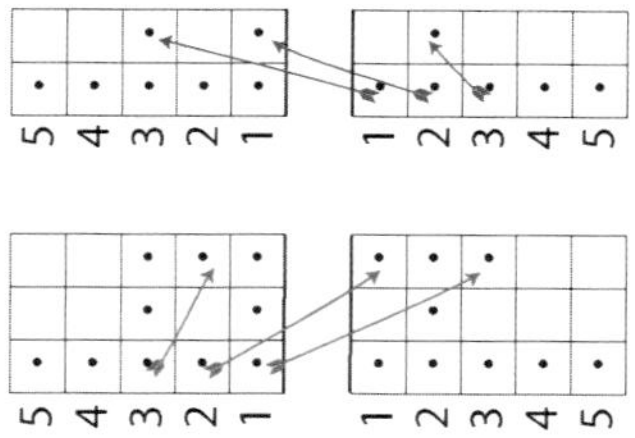

S12 front

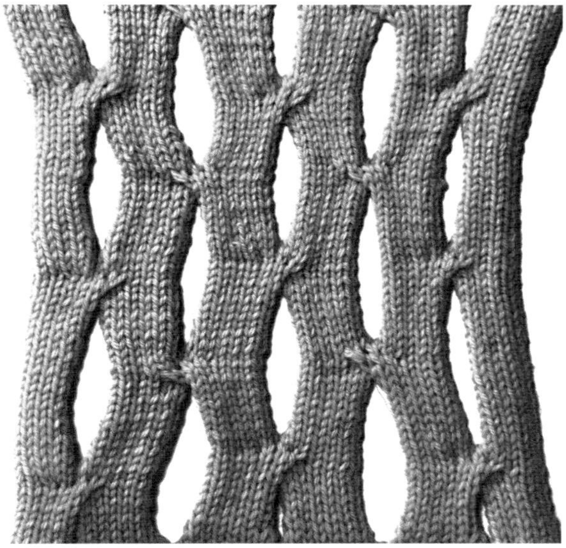

S12 back

With intarsia carriage COR and yarns on right of their sections, transfer the 3 edge STS from left side to first 3 NDLS of right side. Place the right—side yarn into the hooks of the NDLS on the right, cross it with the left yarn at the center. Then use the left—side yarn to e—wrap the 3 empty left edge NDLS, leaving the 3 NDLS in HP. Place the yarn in the left side NDLS. Knit the row. Nudge the e—wrapped NDLS to UWP with their latches open. Continue knitting without joining the two yarns so that a slit is formed for 12 rows to the next eyelet placement. Work the next repeat with COL, reversing the placement of the eyelet and the transfers.

S11 A number of the examples in the Stoll archives featured interlaced stitches like these to join the slits. Use a 3-prong tool to remove the three right—most stitches of the left strip and hold the tool out of the way or temporarily hook it on the adjacent NDLS at left (without transferring the STS) to free up both of your hands. Then use a single—prong transfer tool to individually move the three left—most stitches of the right strip to EON as shown in blue at the top of the chart.

Lastly, use a single—prong tool to individually remove each of the STS from the 3-prong tool and place them on the alternate empty NDLS as shown in red at the bottom of the chart. Make sure the free yarn/bobbins do not get trapped under any of the STS. The yarn should remain free on the purl side of the fabric.

S12 This example shows the same technique in a single color. In both of these samples I alternated the

S13

direction that I worked. In the 2-color swatch it serves to accent the color along the edges of the joining. Here, the split pairs and alternating direction of the joining adds motion and interest to the fabric.

At first glance this joining method seems similar to a cable, but it is, in fact, quite different and lies much flatter than most cables. The stitches are replaced in such a way that they alternate with each other, rather than crossing. To interlace much wider groups of stitches you would need multi—prong transfer tools or you may find it necessary to scrap off and re—hang from waste knitting.

S13 I used the same technique for this simple sweater, but regret that I wove in the ends as I worked because they show on the purl side. It turned out that I prefer the purl side of this fabric to the knit side because of the way the interlaced joining and the rolled edges of the slits add texture to an otherwise flat fabric. There is a free pattern for this sweater on my web site.

The next 3 swatches, although shown in a single color, are worked as intarsia with split pairs to form honeycomb—like fabrics. When the pairs split and the sections join, continue to use separate bobbins for each half of the group, crossing them at the center of each strip, because you will need the bobbins when the groups separate again and it makes more sense to continue with the existing yarns than to keep beginning and ending bobbins. The effect is that of traveling stitches, but these STS do not travel in the usual way.

S14 C/O and transfer STS for 6 NDLS WP/4 NWP as shown in row 1 of chart. I maintained a 2 ST border at each edge. *With separate bobbins, work 4 rows on each group of 3 NDLS. Then move each group of 3 STS over by 2 NDLS. Work the next 4 rows crossing the bobbins where the groups meet** and then repeat from * to **. This pattern alternates working groups of 3, then 6 STS, splitting pairs for each repeat.

S14

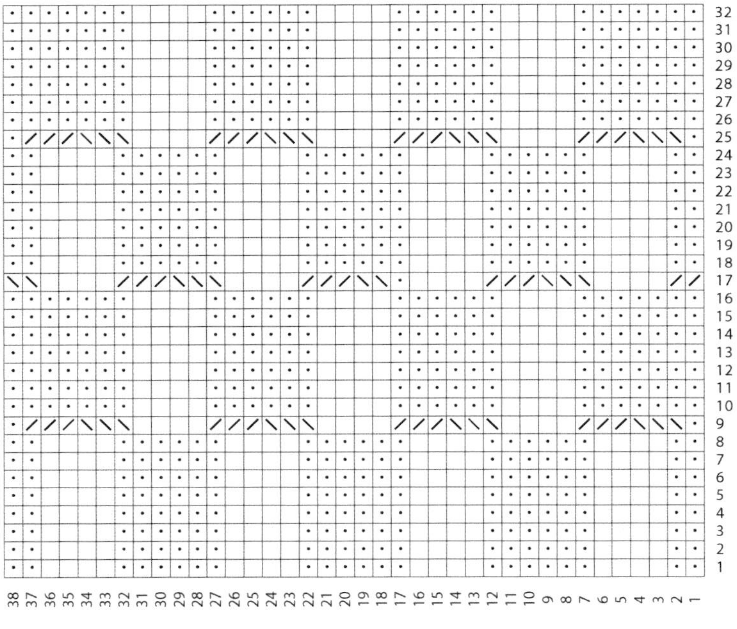

S14 FRONT

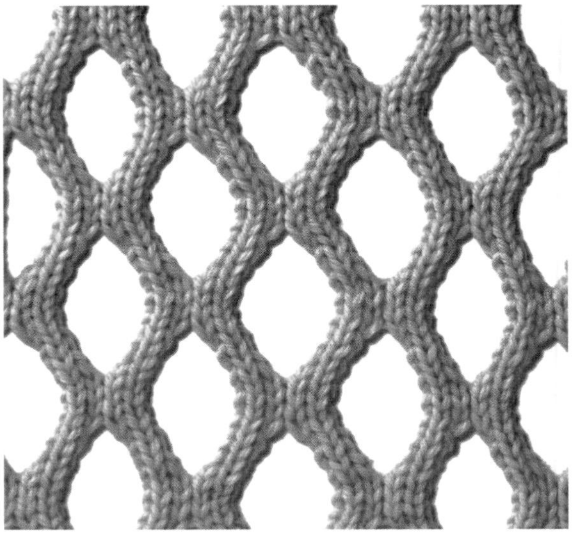

S15This swatch is worked exactly like S11 except with large r groups that knit for 6 rows instead of 4. C/O and transfer STS so there are 10 WP/4 NWP. The pairs split after every repeat to form alternating groups of 10 NDLS in WP. Once again, when the groups meet, cross the bobbins to join the two groups into a single (visual) group of 10. Work 6 rows joined and 6 not joined, moving groups of 5 STS over by 2 NDLS after the split rows.

S15 FRONT

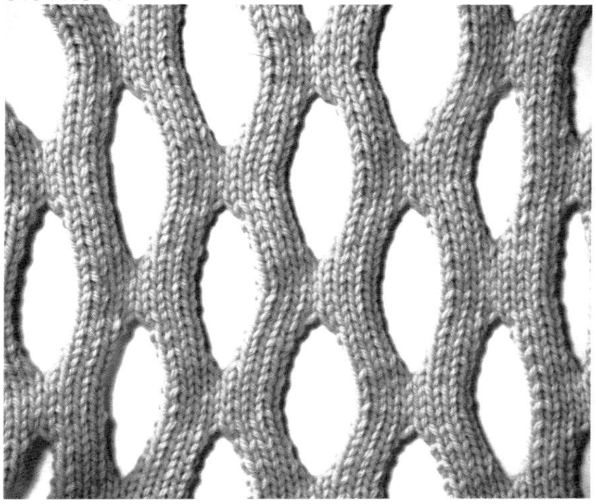

S15 BACK

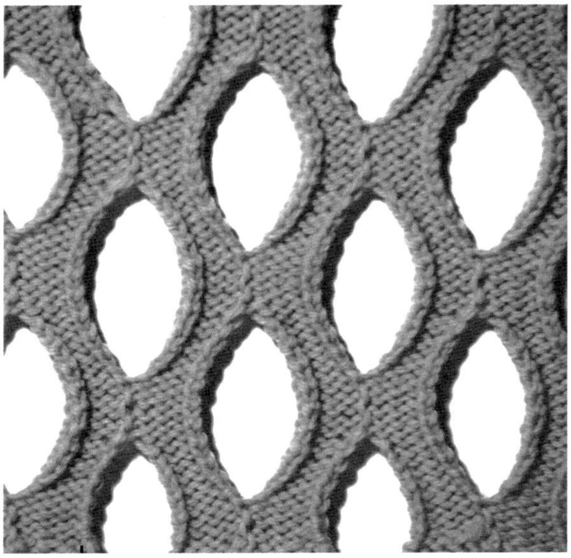

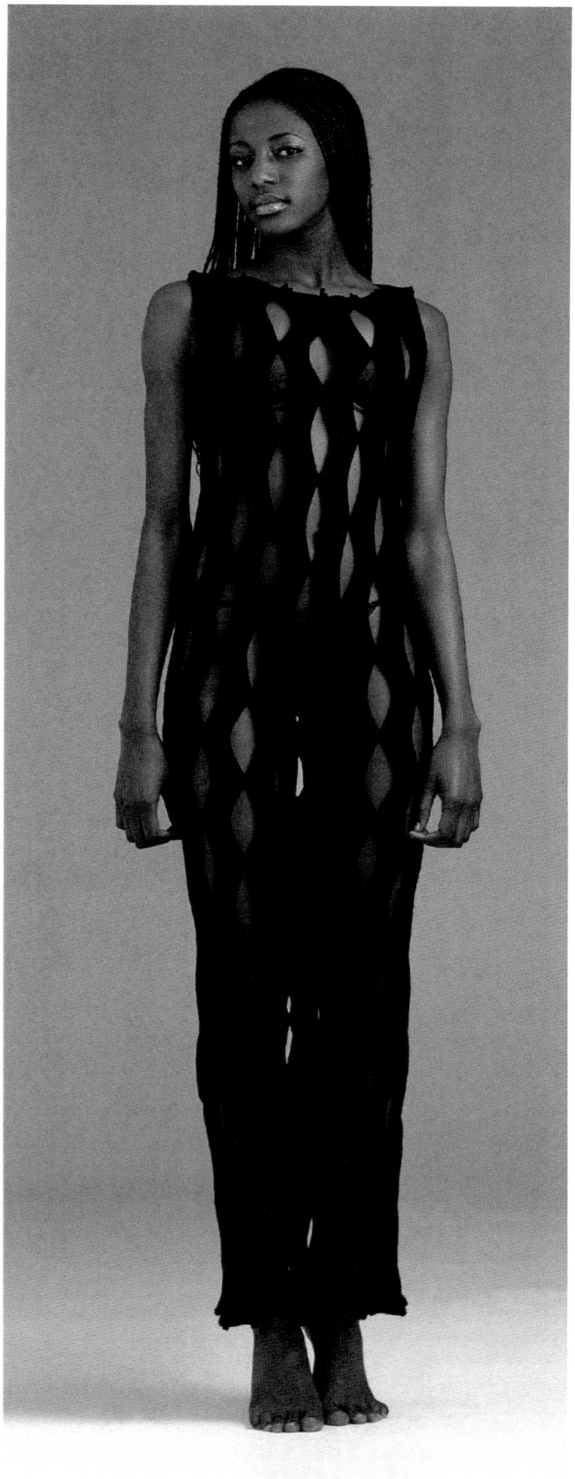

S16 Photo by Lasse Berre, courtesy of DuoDu

S16 shows a beautiful use of simple slit construction by the design team at DuoDu in Norway. Anne Grut Sørum and Rita Nylander produce very fashion forward garments on light industrial machines. You can see more of their work on page 213 and at their web site www.duodu.no.

S17 Set up NDLS as for swatch S14. Knit 4 rows joined, followed by 8 rows split. Transfer the groups of 3 stitches over by 2 NDLS and then cross the cables – spitting pairs and alternating the direction of the crossings for a woven/grid effect. Knit 4 rows joined. Start by working groups of 6 WP NDLS, alternating with 4 NWP. Keep yarns from being trapped when crossing cables. You could also use double crossings 4 rows apart for a more twisted grid effect. Note that in conjunction with the slit pairs, the cables alternately cross left or right from row to row.

S17

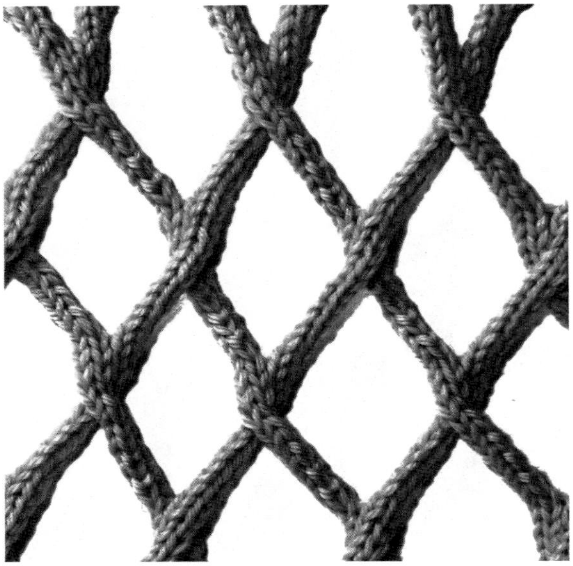

S17

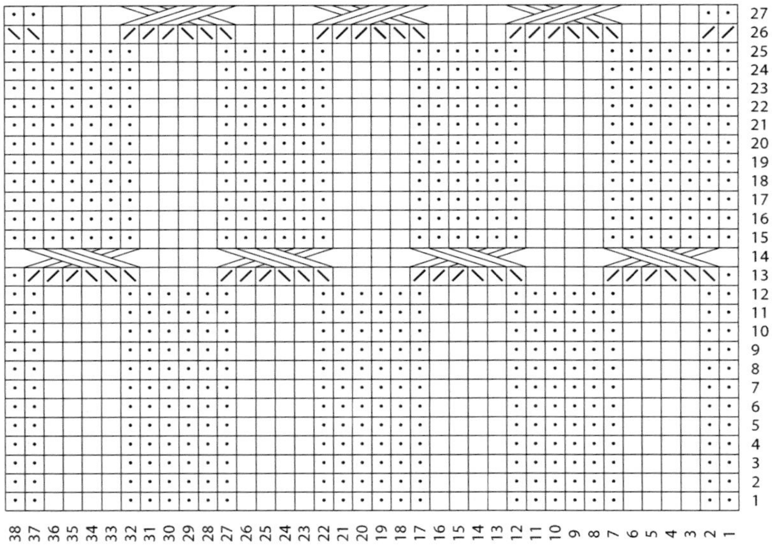

Join as you knit fabrics

The next 2 examples are join—as—you—knit fabrics that both use an alternating—stitch method of joining that is similar to the S11 and S12.

S18 This fabric is knitted in two pieces, as wide as you wish. Knit the first piece, tagging the right edge every 16 and then every 24 rows alternately for the length of the strip. You can weave a short piece of cord over and under the 8 edge needles to mark the row more exactly.

C/O and knit the second piece. Make the first joining at row 24 and then at the 16th row after that; continue P/U at the 24th and then the 16th rows. Note that this is opposite of the first strip, which is correct in order to provide the requisite ease for the fabric to undulate softly. I found it easiest to just keep re—setting the RC, but you can also make a list of row numbers beforehand and follow that.

The P/U are made as follows: Knit the 23rd (15th) row, ending COL. Hold all NDLS to the right of the 8 at left. Change to ST size 10 and knit 1 row across the 8 NDLS at left. Bring them to hold, change back to regular ST size and leave the COR.

Hold the first strip with the purl side facing you. At the first marked row, poke a latch tool through the fabric between the first and second STS and then hook the tool onto the 8th NDL from the edge of the fabric on the machine. Release the ST from its NDL, pull it through the first fabric and then replace it on the same NDL. Repeat for the remaining STS, working from the center NDL towards the edge on the piece on the machine and from the edge of the first fabric towards the center. After the last ST has been worked, bring all NDLS to HP, move COL and then place the STS to the right of the interlaced STS in UWP and knit 1 row to the right.

S18

Work the second attachment after the 15th row and continue alternating every 24/16 row for P/U the edge.

Note that 8-10 STS is the maximum you will be able to work as described above. Larger groups will definitely require S/O and rehanging. Also, when you increase the number of STS overlapping, you also need to increase the number of rows knitted for each section in order to have enough ease.

You can work this method combining knit and purl faces of the fabric. To do this, tag the first piece on the left edge instead of the right and turn the fabric so that the knit side is facing you when you overlap and interlace the STS. Alternating the number of rows from section to section on both pieces is necessary for ease. The two fabrics will match up when you are done.

S19 is very similar to S18, but worked as an edging. Knit the main fabric first, tagging the left edge every 16 rows . You'll only need to weave a short length of cord over the first 5 NDLS to mark the edge.

Next C/O 5 STS for the trim strip. Hang 5 STS from the C/O edge of the main fabric on top of the same NDLS and then knit 21 rows, ending COR. Knit 1 row ST size 10. COL. Return to regular ST size.

Pull the trim strip STS through the edge of the first fabric as described for S18 or try this method instead: Poke a crochet hook through the space between the first and 2nd STS on the marked row of the pre—knit fabric and remove 1 ST from the machine, pulling it through the fabric. Hold your finger on top of this ST and then insert the hook between the next pair of STS on the first piece of fabric to catch the next ST from the machine. Release it from the NDL and pull it through the fabric. There should be 2 separate STS on the shaft of the crochet hook. Do not allow one stitch to be pulled through the next. Continue working through the first fabric to capture the STS of the trim piece and pull them through. When all 5 trim STS are on the shaft of the crochet hook, return the STS to their NDLS. You can do this by poking the NDLS through the STS and sliding them off the hook or you might find it easier to use a single prong transfer tool to move each ST.

This method is well worth knowing because it will allow you to join wider pieces of fabric with a long crochet hook or really wide pieces using an afghan hook (a crochet hook affixed to one end of a long, flexible cable.) You can vary the look of this edging by knitting fewer/more rows between tagged rows or by knitting fewer/more rows for each section of the trim piece.

S20 This fabric was worked with 10-ST strips that were joined every 20 rows as the successive strips were knitted. To facilitate this, I used short lengths of cotton cord to weave through every 20th row of the first strip, bringing the NDLS out to HP and manually weaving the cord over and under. All strips begin with e—wrapping and are S/O at the end.

When I reached row 20 of the second strip, I held the first strip with purl side facing me and folded

S19

S20 KNIT SIDE

S20 PURL SIDE

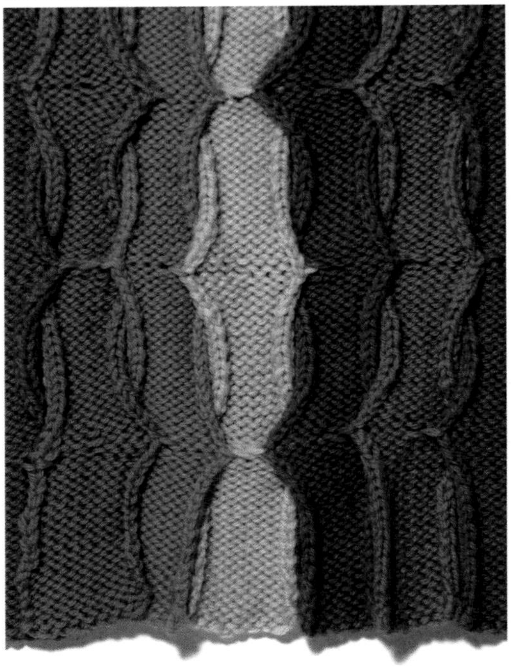

S21

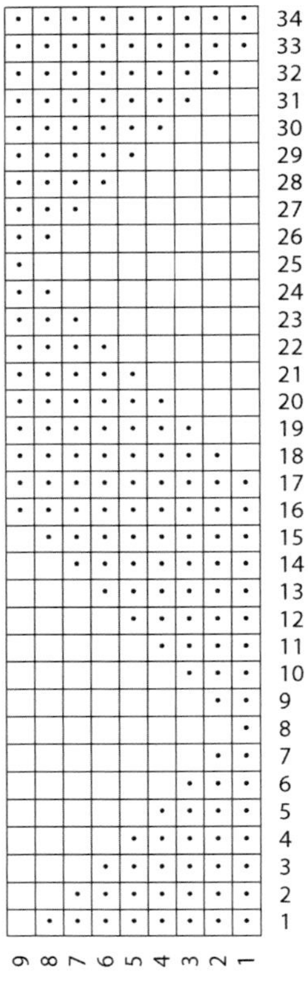

S21 Work a latch tool C/O cross the NDLS and then hang the tips of the zigzag strip on every 10th NDL. Bring all NDLS to HP to knit the first row.

it towards me at the first marker row. I P/U 5 STS from right edge on the knit side of the strip and hung them on the first 5 NDLS at left of the current strip. Then I knitted my way to the next 20 row marker and repeated the procedure. At the end of the strip I S/O the STS.

This direction joins the second strip behind (on the purl side of the first). To hang a completed strip/section on the knit side of a strip in progress, you need to work a little differently. Hold the completed strip with the purl side facing you, then fold it back to P/U 5 STS from the right edge of the purl side of the strip and hang them on empty 5 NDLS at the left of the second strip. Use a multi—prong tool (or pairs of smaller tools or several steps) to move all 10 of the second strip STS to the left, overlapping the 5 rehung STS. Knit 20 rows to the next placement. Very wide strips need to be scrapped off or you can use a GB to move them over. If repeating this hanging method on a very long strip (i.e. multiple times), begin at the right end of the bed as the work will continually shift 5 NDLS to the left each time you rehang the fabric.

When P/U STS from the knit side of a strip, it is a little trickier to stay in the same row than it is when P/U purl STS which are easier to distinguish. Once you get going with this method, you may not need any markers to guide you, but for the few extra minutes they take to insert, I think they are well worth having the first few times.

At the very end of the work, re—hang the live STS at the top of all the strips, overlapping the sets of STS or pulling one set of STS through the other to reduce bulk. B/O all together for a continuous, finished edge.

S21 —24 For years I've used these zig—zag strips to teach students how to work short rows. I've turned them sideways and used them for lower edges of various projects, sometimes working a short row fill to level off the zigs and zags and other times just leaving the open spaces, C/O over the void as shown at S21. Begin and end all strips on waste yarn so that you can work a single row across all of the strips later to join them more securely.

To knit the individual strips, C/O 9 STS with waste yarn and then change to MC and knit 2 rows, ending COR. Set the carriage to hold NDLS in HP. *Hold 1 NDL at left E/R until 1 NDL remains in WP and COR. Then, return 1 NDL to UWP E/R until all NDLS are back in WP and COR. Knit 1 row to left.**

Work the next repeat from the left side, repeating the directions * to ** and substituting right for left. Alternate the repeats, left and right, for the length of the fabric. If you lose your place, just remember that the zig—zag always points to the side where it last started. S/O completed strip.

S22

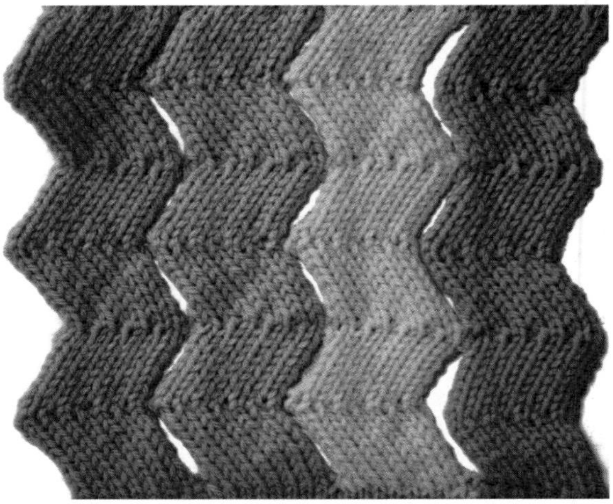

If joining as shown in S22 with each zig point nestled into a zag, start all strips after the halfway point for a right side repeat. That is, all the NDLS except the very first NDL on the right are in HP and COR. Begin moving NDLS to UWP to begin knitting the second half of a right side repeat. Then alternate the repeats, taking care to end each strip with ½ of a repeat from the left (all NDLS in HP) so the top of the strip is straight.

If, however, you want to join as in S23 with the strips joined tip to tip, begin each strip with the second half of a left side repeat, i.e. start with all NDLS in HP and begin moving them to UWP. End each strip with a full left repeat. All strips should knit the same number of rows.

To join the strips with either placement, P/U a full ST from the 1st strip and hang it on the edge NDL of the 2nd strip when there is just a single NDL remaining in WP. You can P/U STS at both the zigs and zags or just one or the other.

S25 uses the purl side as the right side to capitalize on the way the edges roll and create extra texture. Unlike most join as you knit fabrics, the STS that are P/U are the 3rd STS from the edge, rather than the edge STS.

Pre—knit the first strip, tagging wherever you want to join it to the next strip. Begin the 2nd strip and when you get to the point where the two strips should join, remove the first 3 STS on a transfer tool and hook it onto the adjacent NDLS just to get it out of the way – do not transfer the STS off the tool. Hold the first strip with the purl side facing you and roll the right edge towards you to expose the knit surface of the piece. Then, P/U just the 3rd ST from the edge of the marked row and hang it on the 3rd empty NDL. Replace the 3 STS from the transfer tool and continue knitting.

S24 A pre—knitted zigzag strip is joined to the side edge of this fabric every 18 rows. This is an excellent method for joining afghan sections.

For very wide strips, I would probably rehang pairs of STS, rather than just a single ST, for extra strength. You could also combine knit and purl sides for the various strips, but the roll will only show on the purl side.

S25

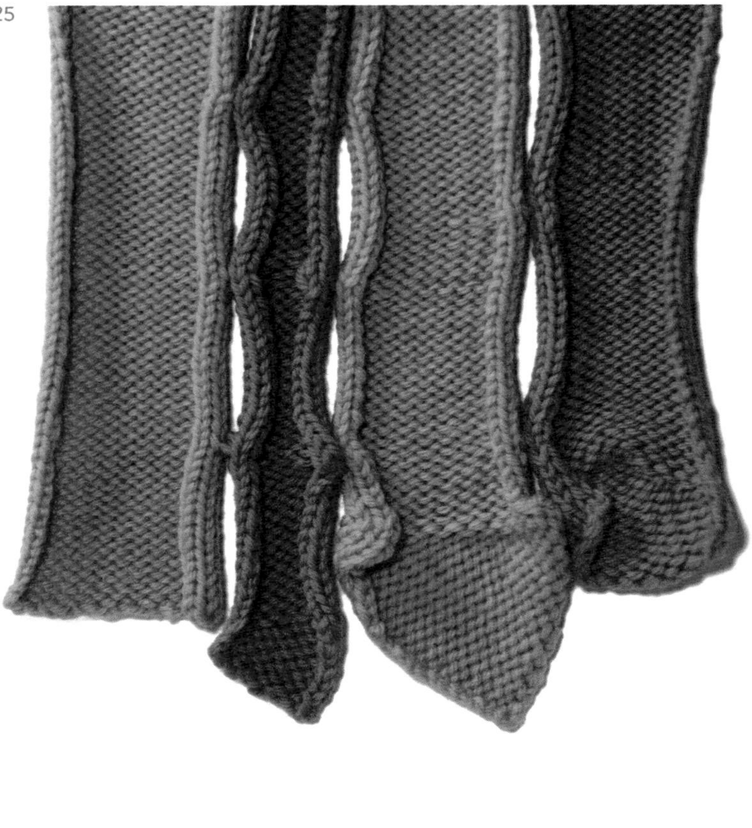

S23

S26

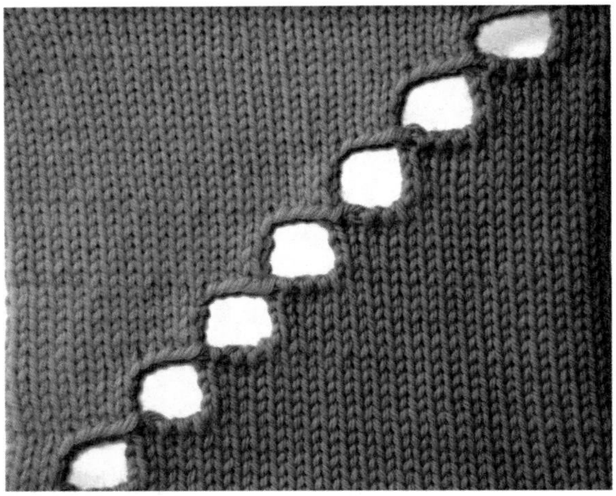

S26 These open spaces are created by working two separate pieces that are joined as the second piece is knitted. Mine were worked with a multiple of 4 STS, but you can use any number of STS for the stepped edges to create larger or smaller openings. This would be an interesting way to create a raglan seam.

Knit the first piece by C/O the full number of STS required, less 4. COR (Knit 6 rows, B/O 4 STS at the right edge) 8 times. You will produce the straightest edges by B/O around the sinker posts/gate pegs but remember to remove the loops from the posts before knitting the next 6 rows.

Begin the second piece by C/O 4 STS. COR. Knit 5 rows. COL. P/U the corner (X) (on illustration below) from the first piece and hang on the left edge NDL. (Knit 6 rows. E—wrap 4 NDLS and P/U the next corner from the first piece and hang on the leftmost NDL) Repeat for the entire fabric until both pieces are the same size, joined at the corners of the squares.

Be consistent about P/U the corner from the first piece. You can hang it on the edge NDL before or after e—wrapping the 4 empties. If you do it before e—wrapping, the #1 color will show on the front of each joining.

S27

S27 There were several of these giant, 20 x 20 ST cables in the Stoll archives, including a couple worked in pattern stitches and double bed ribs. I'll leave the more elaborate exploration up to you!

Start by making 2 identical strips, beginning and ending each one on scrap. The strips can be different colors, textures or patterns, but their length must match. C/O 20 STS and allow 50 rows per repeat/crossing, plus 10 rows to begin. Tag the strips at both edges every 10 rows to simplify matching edges and rehanging later. You can use safety pins or just hang yarn tags on the edge NDLS while you knit. Lightly steam the two finished strips to make them easier to handle. Lay one strip on top of the other, both of them with knit side facing up.

Use safety pins to match the edges as follows: Pin the lower edges together at each edge and at the 10th row markers. Cross the strips as shown in the illustration to produce the cabled effect, pinning the crossings in place at every 4th and 5th tags for the length of the strip.

C/O one side—piece and join to the main fabric A/R for the first 10 rows, consistently P/U either a full or half stitch from both thicknesses. There will be 5 joinings in those 10 rows. The next 40 rows will be joined singly — that is, only the top—most, visible layer will be joined A/R. The other strip will remain free to be joined to the second side.

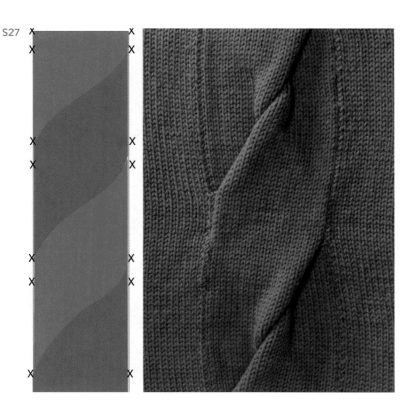

S28

Once you reach the next pin, join both layers A/R x 5 and then one layer for the next 40 rows (A/R x 20).

When the first side is complete, repeat for the second side. The width of the cable strips and the number of rows between crossings can be altered. The wider the strips, the more rows you need to allow the STS to recover so the cable does not look pinched and tight.

Rehung fabrics

S28 These interwoven strips might form the base for an interesting sweater. Begin on scrap so you can re—hang the starting STS if you want to later on – leave your options open as long as possible. S/O at the end for the same reason and once you are sure you are happy with the shape of the piece you can B/O those edges. You may also find that you want to rehang the live STS and add additional knit sections to the work, building off it in all directions.

Most of my strips are about the same width (5 STS), but they graduate in length from 30 to 80 rows. When the two pieces are woven together, the resulting piece tends to widen at the bottom, which might be good for shaping a garment piece. If all of the strips were the same length, the end result would be a square piece like S29.

Knit the first piece: C/O with scrap and knit 10 rows across all NDLS. Then work either intarsia strips or use HP and weight the pieces carefully. At the end, knit 10 (or more rows across all NDLS and then S/O.

Work the second piece like the first except do not knit 10 rows at the end. S/O each of the strips separately and weave the second piece through the first. If any of your strips are too short or too long, you can re—hang and knit more rows or rip some out. When all of them are correct, rehang on the machine to knit the 10 ending rows and then S/O.

S29

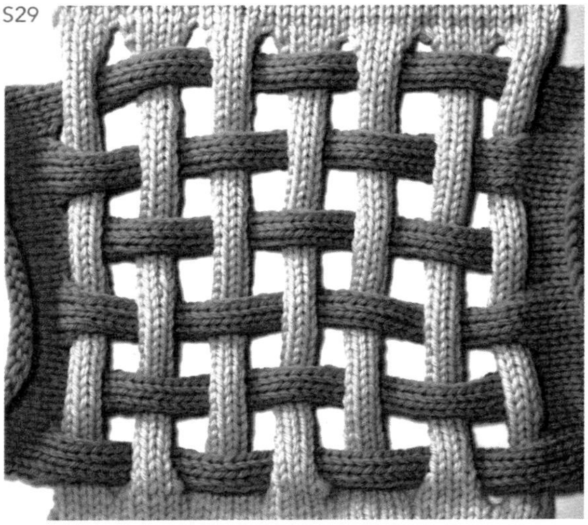

Vertical Slits Created with Holding Position

There were a number of fabrics in the Stoll archives where the bridge bars were allowed to show and actually contributed to the design of the fabric. It surprised me because I had always gone to great lengths to hide the yarns that tie one section to the next and, in fact, the horizontal cables that I developed for *More Hand-Manipulated Stitches* grew out of one approach to hiding those bars. In that case, they would have distracted from the cables, but for many fabrics, the bridge bars become a contributing design element.

S30 is a simple bridged fabric where all the NDLS except the first 4 on the carriage side are in HP. After knitting 8 rows on the first group of 4 NDLS, I returned the next group of 4 NDLS to UWP and knitted

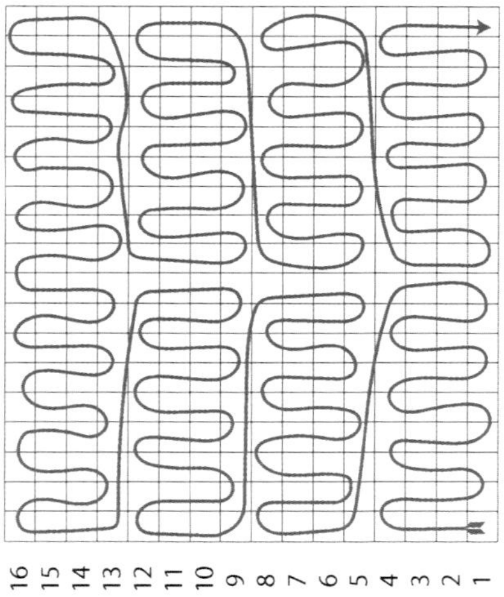

S30 Rather than individual stitches, this chart illustrates the path the carriage follows as it bridges each section of the fabric.

S30

1 row across all 8 NDLS before placing the first 4 in HP. When I reached the edge of the fabric, I knitted 15 rows on the edge group and then worked my way back across the fabric. This is pretty straightforward bridging. You can work wider groups of NDLS, fewer or more rows on each group and you could even add some cables or other detail to some/all of the groups. The BB form a zigzagging accent between the columns of STS.

S31 is a first cousin to S30 but it takes basic bridging one step further by introducing split pairs. I began working groups of 4 NDLS from the right and when the work reached the left edge, I began working back across the bed, including just 2 NDLS in the first group before resuming 4 NDL groups to split the pairs. The resulting fabric has more movement and interest than the previous swatch and the BB are smaller and more manageable. The fabric has an almost—quilted texture.

The charts for S30 and S31 show the bridging patterns for the next couple of swatches. Just pay attention to the specific stitch and row counts for each one.

S31 This chart shows the path the carriage follows to split pairs. Notice the smaller groups of needles at each end of the second tier.

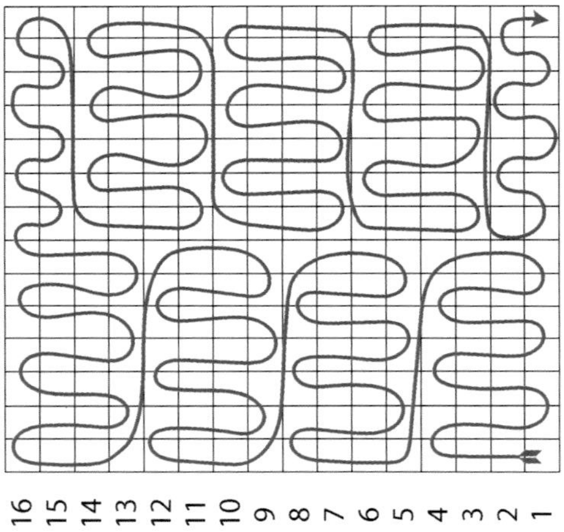

S31

S32 There were lots of cabled Stoll fabrics with exposed BB. This fabric was worked with columns of 6 STS, cabled every 6 rows. Begin COR, set to hold NDLS in HP. Hold all NDLS except the first group of 6 on the right. *Knit 3 rows, cross the cable and knit 3 more rows. Bridge across to the next 6 NDLS and hold the first group.** Repeat * to ** across the work. For the last group at either edge, knit 3 rows, cross the cable, knit 5 rows, cross the cable and knit 3 more rows before bridging to the next group. Note that ail of these cables cross the same direction.

S32

S33 For this woven cable fabric, the first tier of cables is knitted exactly like the previous swatch. End the first tier of cables by knitting 3 rows, crossing the cable, knitting 2 rows. Hold the first half of this cable (3 NDLS) and knit 4 more rows on the remaining 3 NDLS. Bridge to the next 6 NDLS and knit 3 rows, cross the cable and knit 3 more rows. All cables in this second (and every alternate tier) will cross the opposite direction of those in the first tier. The BB form a delicate, secondary pattern between the cables.

Woven cables can be difficult to knit on a machine because there is no relief between the cable crossings. Here, however, the extra rows provided by the bridging add enough extra length to each cable for them to cross easily and without straining the yarn — or your patience.

S34 The same bridging can be applied to twisted STS. I worked this fabric with 3 ST twists and maintained a 2-ST, un—twisted border. Begin COR with the carriage set to hold NDLS in HP. Hold all NDLS except the first 5 on the carriage side. Knit 1 row to the left and hold the 2 edge NDLS. Knit 2 rows. Remove the 3 STS on a 3-prong tool, insert a second 3-prong tool from above and remove the first tool. Rotate the tool 180° and replace the STS on the empty NDLS. Knit 1 row. COR. Bring the next group of 3 NDLS at left to UWP and knit 1 row across these 6 NDLS and

S33

S34

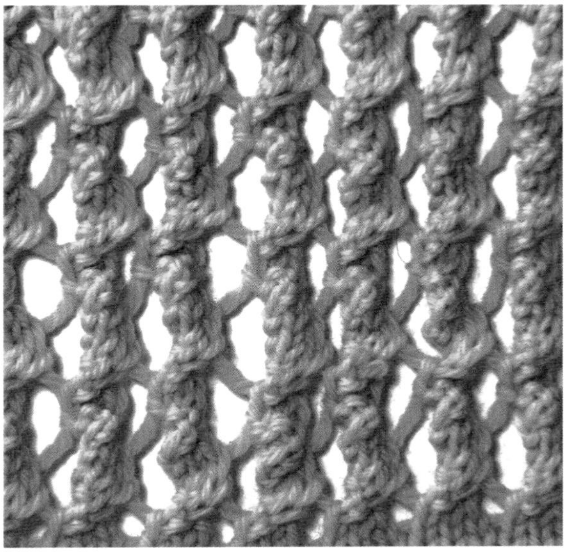

then hold the previous 3 NDLS. Repeat the twisting for each group. When you reach the left edge, retain a 2-ST border. Knitting 2 rows on the 2 edge NDLS.

COL. Knit 1 row across the first 5 NDLS and then hold the 2 edge NDLS. Knit 3 rows, twist and then bridge to the next group. The sequences are different working right to left than they are left to right so that the yarn is always on the left at the start of each twist and to maintain the bridging carriage direction. More important, it also prevents you from trapping the yarn on the knit side of the fabric.

S35 is a larger version of S34, worked over groups of 5 STS. Begin COR and work 6 rows over the first group of 5 NDLS then bridge to the next group at left. Hold the first group and work 6 rows on this and all of the following groups. When you reach the last group on the left, work 11 rows and use the 12th row to bridge to the next group on the right. Work 6 rows and bridge the 7th row across to the right side. End with 7 rows and COR. Remove each group of 5 STS on a 5-prong tool. Insert a second tool from above and remove the first tool. Twist the tool 180° and replace the STS on the NDLS, pulling them to HP. Repeat for each group, leaving the edge groups un—twisted. Bridge right to left and then left to right as before and repeat the twisting. The larger scale helps define the twists and also allows the purl STS to stand out more clearly.

S35

S36 is nearly identical to sample L133 which was worked with ladders between the working NDLS. The advantage to not having ladders in this fabric is that you can introduce a row of these open spaces mid—fabric without having to adjust the NDL arrangement. This is also a somewhat sturdier, slightly less open fabric.

S36

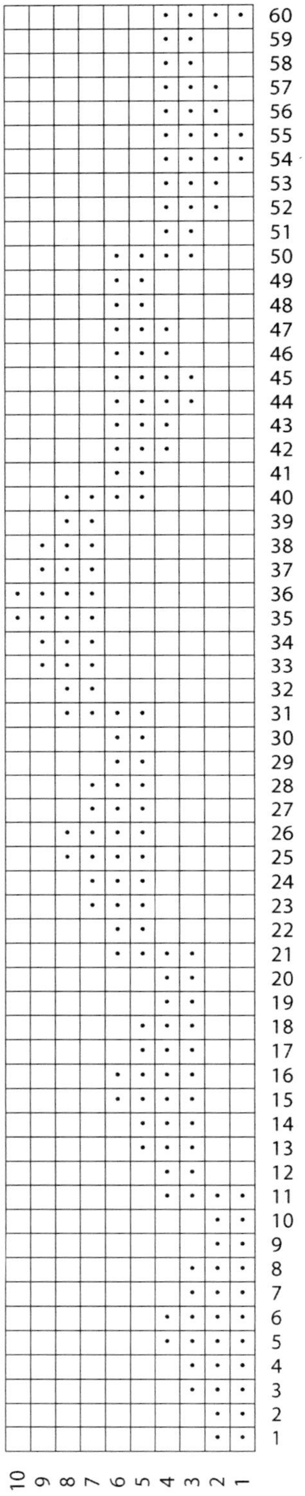

Begin COR, with only the first 2 NDLS on the carriage side in WP.* Knit 2 rows and then (return the next NDL at left to UWP and knit 2 rows) twice. COR and 4 NDLS WP. (Hold the last WP NDL at left of this group and knit 2 rows) twice. 2 NDLS WP and COR. Move next 2 NDLS to UWP, knit 1 row. COL. Hold the two right—most NDLS of the group and knit 1 row to right .** Repeat from * to **.

S36

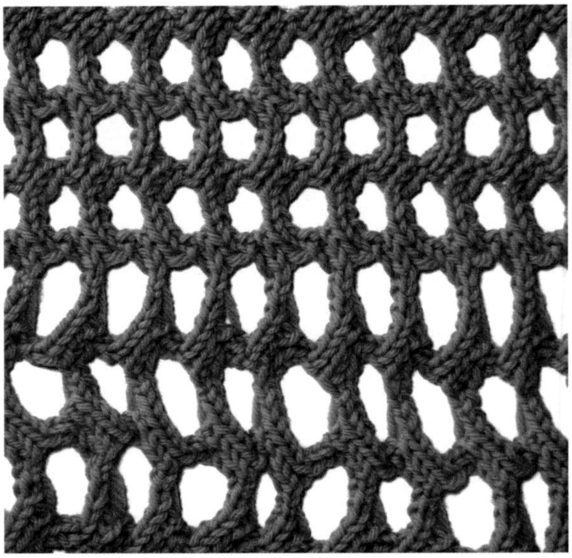

To alternate the placement, start with 3 edge STS and then work groups of 2 as described above. The smaller openings at the top of the swatch were worked by only knitting 1 row, instead of 2, after each step. If you look closely, you might see some of the BB lying along the edges of the larger openings, while they virtually disappear at the top of the swatch.

I first developed my Bridging philosophy to produce rows of popcorns. Generally, those popcorns are worked for about 5 rows and then the first row is lifted onto the needles above to force those 5 rows to pop out on the front of the fabric.

S37 is a knock—off of another one of the Stoll treasures. They showed this effect as the cuffs on a very slinky, soft garment. I bridged from one group of 3 NDLS to the next, working 14 rows over each section and then I lifted the first row of each group onto the NDLS above. I knitted 4 rows over all the NDLS before repeating. There are no plain stitches between the loops. If you would rather not be bothered lifting each group, you'll have to add a stitch or two between the loops to help lift the fabric and provide some structure.

I worked one repeat directly above the last, but you can shift the placement around and you can also work more than 3 STS per group, more than 14 rows per section and fewer or more rows between repeats.

Begin COR with carriage set to hold NDLS in HP. Hold all NDLS except the first 3 on the carriage side. Knit 14 rows, ending COR. *Move next group of 3 NDLS at left to UWP and knit 1 row. Hold the first 3 NDLS. Knit 13 more rows, ending COR. ** Repeat * to * for the row.

You'll need to tension these 14 row strips as you knit them or they will pop off the NDLS. I have worked out a way of tensioning popcorn STS that also makes re—hanging them easier and faster because you don't have to poke around to find the first row of stitches. Insert a 3-prong transfer tool through the purl bumps of the first row before you knit all the extra rows. Insert the tool from the top and then tip it towards you and use it to keep gentle tension on the STS as you work the extra rows. After you bridge to the next group at left and before you push the NDLS of the completed loop to HP, insert a second 3-prong tool through the same purl bumps from below and remove the first tool. Use the second tool to the lift purl bumps onto the NDLS above and then push the NDLS to HP. Even if you drop the purl bumps (they are not STS) off the tool, nothing is going to run and you can just poke around and rehang them the old way. There are photographs showing this method in the pattern for my Loopity Lou Hats, which is a free download from my web site. The hats are pictured on page 9.

S37

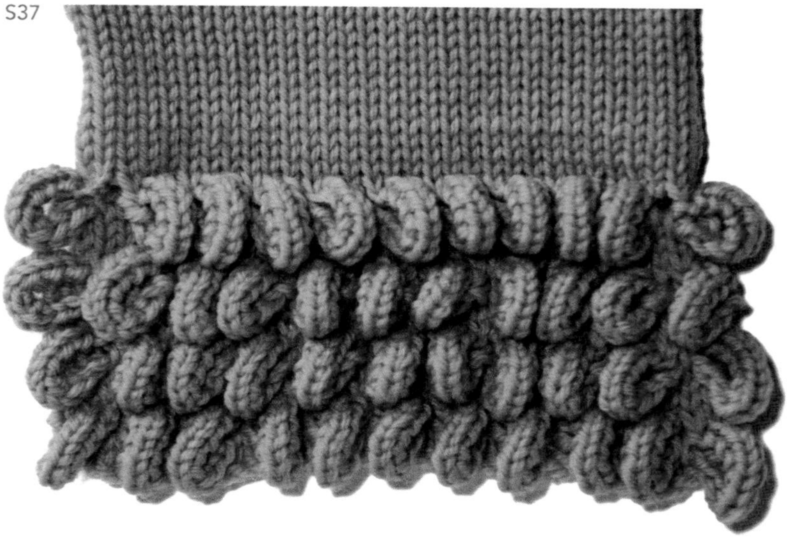

S38

S38 You can also work a whole row or column of these loops to manipulate further. These next few samples show giant loops chained across the knit surface of the fabric. Although I have worked all in one color, you could just as easily knit the loops for chaining in a contrasting color or different texture.

C/O a multiple of 3 STS and knit some rows up to the point where you want the chaining. Work an entire row of loops as described above, but do not lift the first row of each loop onto the NDLS. Work more rows of stockinette and repeat as desired. Once the fabric is off the machine, use your fingers to work a "crochet" chain across the surface of the fabric by pulling pone loop through the next, securing the last loop by tacking it to the edge of the fabric. Depending on your yarn, you may have to knit each loop with fewer/more rows.

If you choose to retain a couple of STS for a plain border at the edges, you can try chaining the loops and securing the chain by hanging a stitch or two from the last loop on one of the edge NDLS. The BB should remain on the back of the fabric.

Because these loops are not lifted onto the NDLS like the previous example, there is no reason to use the transfer tool method for tensioning the stitches, but you do need to tension them. I have some claw weights that taper to two teeth and are perfect for this purpose. Check my blog for photos and directions for recycling old claw weights. They are perfect for this kind of thing.

S39 Rather than working rows of chained loops, this example features a column of loops up each side of the fabric, 1 ST from the edge. Begin COR, set to hold NDLS in HP. Hold all NDLS except the first 4 on the carriage side. Knit 1 row to the left and then hold the edge ST. Knit 15 more rows over these 3 NDLS. Then move all NDLS at left except the single edge ST to UWP and knit 1 row to the left. Hold all NDLS except for the 3 at left and work 15 more rows over these NDLS, ending COR. Move last NDL at left to UWP and knit 1 row to left. Knit 3 (or 5) rows over all NDLS before repeating. With longer loops (i.e. more than 15 rows) you can work more rows between repeats. Just make sure that the loops do not pull and constrict the edge once chained. You can also leave more STS at the edge, but be aware that they will curl under.

S40 is worked by bridging to the center of the row to work a loop and then bridging to the end of the row. For each repeat, I simply started 3 NDLS closer to the edge so that, when chained, the loops formed a diagonal across the fabric.

S41 was worked by bridging to form individual, isolated loops 20 rows long. I P/U and hung the first row of the loop and then I knitted 3 rows over all the NDLS. Next, I removed the 3 loop STS from their NDLS on a 3-prong too and hung the tool on the 3 adj NDLS at left. I reached my fingers through to the knit side of the fabric to catch and twist the loop and then P/U 3 STS from the edge of the loop to hang on the NDLS before replacing the other 3 STS. In this case, the only open spaces formed are the edges of the loop, which allows the whole loop to be twisted and manipulated to create surface textures.

S42 and S43 Loops knitted along one edge of two separate fabrics are used to join the fabrics together. Typically, this has been used for joining afghan sections, but it could also add interesting detail for the front of a sweater, depending on the gauge of the fabric.

S42

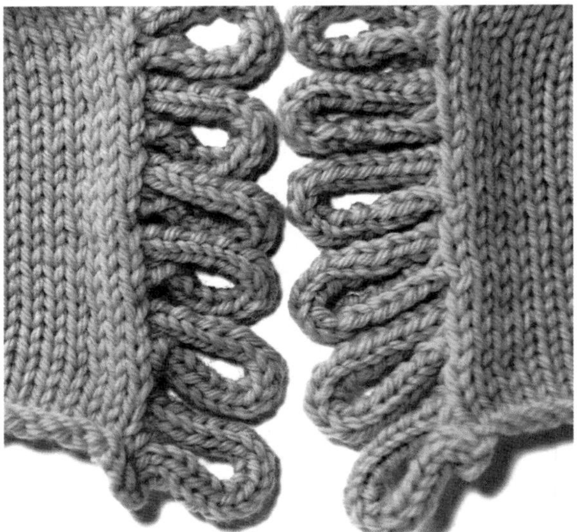

S43

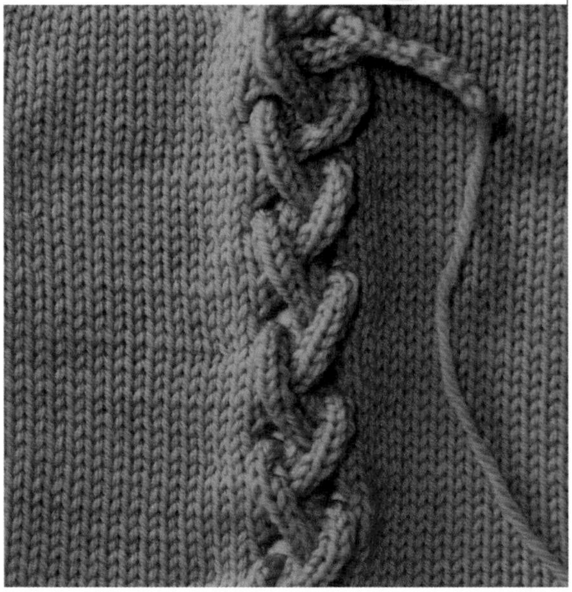

S39

S40

S41

Work the loops on the left of one piece and the right of the other or, if the direction of the stitches won't matter to you, work both pieces the same and then reverse one top to bottom to assemble. C/O the width of your piece plus 3 for the loops. Knit 4 rows, ending COR. Set carriage to hold NDLS in HP. *Hold all NDLS except the first 3 on the carriage side. Knit 20 rows on these 3 NDLS. Remove the STS on a 3-prong transfer tool and move them to the next 3 NDLS at left and place the 3 edge NDLS in NWP. Knit 4 (or more) rows over all NDLS and then e—wrap C/O the 3 NDLS you just emptied at right.** Repeat * to ** for the length of the fabric. Do not close the last loop on one of the pieces so that you can use it to secure the end when you chain one loop through the next.

You can vary the number of NDLS or rows you use to knit the loops and you can knit more rows between repeats if you want to space out the loops. It depends on the final use for the fabric and the joining. The more rows you knit for each loop, the more open the joining will be. To join the two fabrics, simply pull one loop through the next, alternating sides.

The next two examples feature inserts that can be used for color effect or to add width and ease to a garment. Although they look similar, they are, in fact, worked very differently.

S44

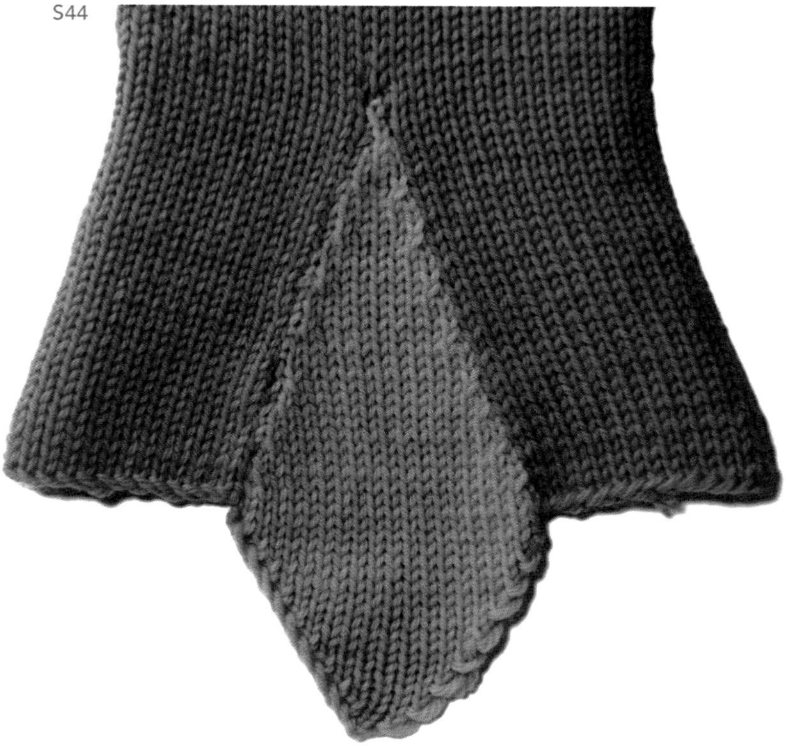

S44

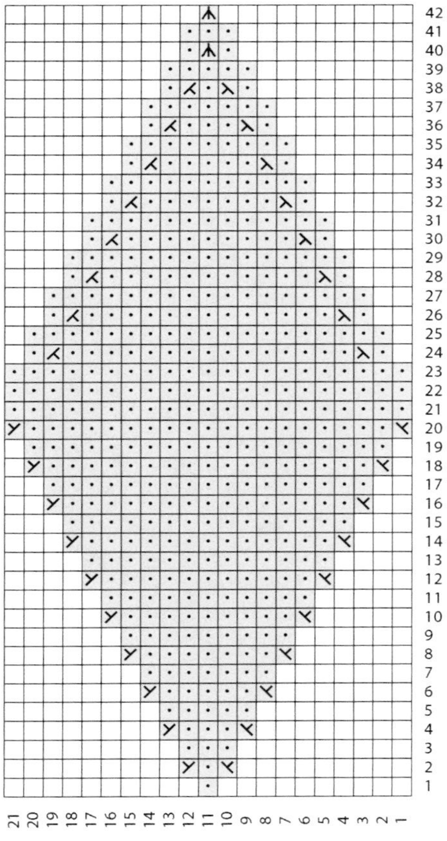

S44 was worked by holding each side of a slit for 36 rows to knit the opposite side side. There is no shaping involved. Then I knitted a separate, diamond shaped piece that I seamed into the slit later on. You could join—as—you—knit, but there really isn't any advantage to doing that and I felt like I had better control over the final appearance with hand seaming after lightly blocking both pieces.

Although the main fabric in this example was worked with a slit, this idea can just as easily be applied to the lower portion of a side seam left open for several inches or more. Worked in the same or a contrasting color, this panel is a great way to add ease to the lower edges of a garment. Also, you can work a simple triangle, rather than a diamond, if you do not want the hemline variation.

I began by C/O a single ST and increased 1 ST on the carriage side every row until I had 21 STS. (For a triangle, you would simply C/O 21 STS and begin there.) The top of the diamond needed to fit my 36 row slit so I distributed the decreases as I would for any other garment shaping by using the "magic formula". It worked out that I needed to decrease 1 ST every 4/R six times and then every 3/R four times. I worked full fashioned decreases to simplify the seaming.

S45

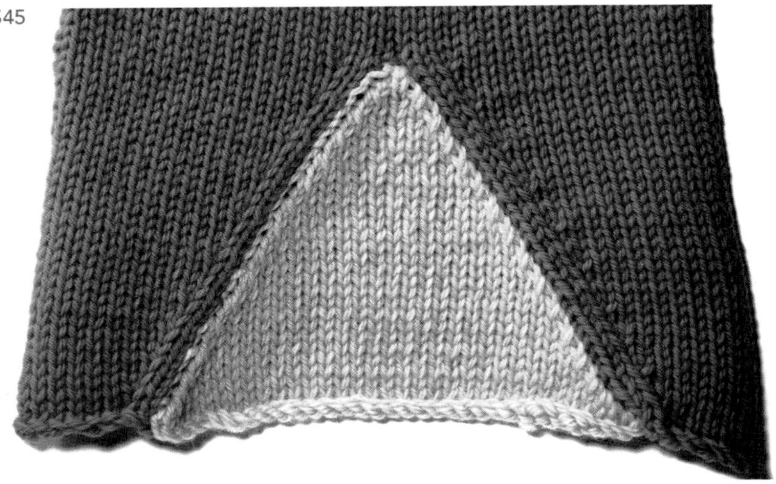

S45 adds less width to the garment as the opening in the main fabric is shaped with full—fashioned increases to begin with. I C/O15 STS, skipped the next 20 NDLS and C/O another 15 STS. First I held the left side to shape the right and then held the right to shape the left. You could also work this method with an intarsia carriage and shape both sides at the same time.

I shaped both sides of the slit by working full—fashioned increases over 36 rows as follows: increase 1 ST every 4/R six times and then every 3/R four times. I shaped the separate green triangle by C/O 36 STS and then decreasing 1 ST each side every A/R 18. Like the previous sample, the two pieces were blocked and then seamed by hand. The triangular insert was just slightly wider than the shaped opening in the main fabric so it adds just a little extra fullness to the lower edge of the fabric.

S46 Much like the shaped ladders on page 93, these shapes require bridging to B/O or C/O STS mid-row. Although you could knit this fabric with HP, I found it simpler and neater to use separate bobbins and work intarsia. The triangle and the circle both employ full—fashioned shaping, while the square is simply B/O and C/O at the beginning and end. The shapes look somewhat elongated on the chart, but remember that my working gauge was 5 ST and 7 rows to the inch and the chart accounts for the difference between the two gauges. These openings are more stable than the laddered version and the edges are cleaner. You can apply a second fabric behind the open shapes or simply leave them as they are.

S46

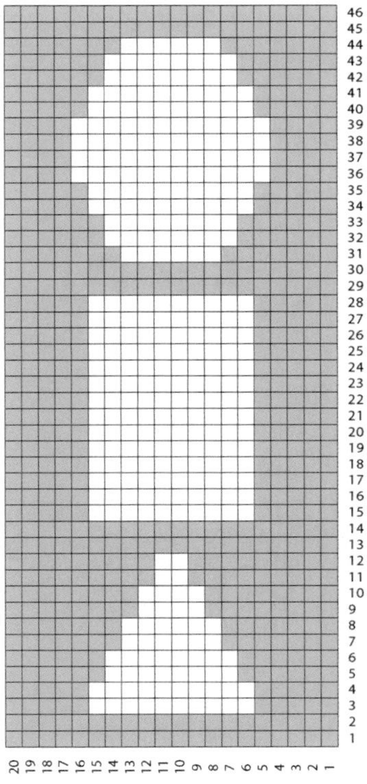

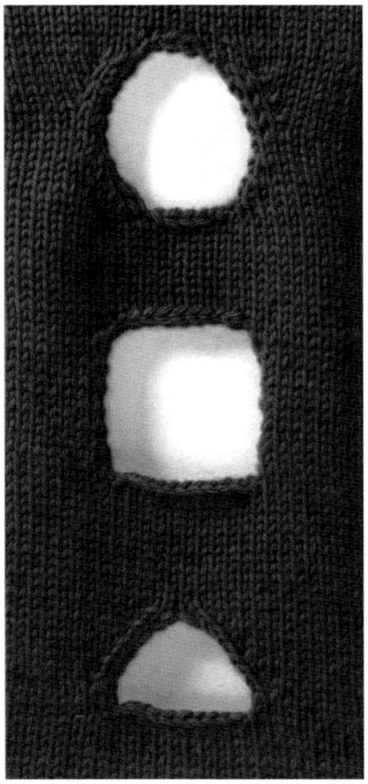

S47 I worked short rows to build up the fabric below the first half of the slit. Next, I manually knitted one large row across the top of the short rowed section and used the latch tool to chain off those STS. Then I immediately worked a latch tool C/O across the same NDLS and began working short rows to fill in the second half of the fabric above the slit.

I've included this one diagonal slit because I like the idea, but do notice on the sample that the STS at the corners seem to lie at slightly oblique angles to each other, which may or may not bother you. As many times as I approached this swatch, I was unable to totally eliminate this effect. The best solution might be to S/O the first set of STS and to use a C/O rag to begin the other. Then, when the piece is off the machine, work a single row of crochet around the entire opening to B/O all the STS at once. This might make an interesting pocket opening.

S48 I think this fabric has one of the richest, most interesting textures I developed. In addition to the pussy willow buds, the background fabric creates a secondary, undulating pattern. The slits that were produced as I formed the twisted bundles of yarn disappear into the fabric and take on a supporting role.

Begin COR set to hold NDLS in HP. Transfer 3 STS to the same NDL then place the empty NDLS in NWP. The NDL holding 4 STS is the first NDL of the next group of 3.

Hold all NDLS except the first 3 on the carriage side and knit 1 row to the left. Hold those 3 NDLS and then move COR. All NDLS are in HP. Make 5 loops by catching the FY over the last NDL knitted (3rd NDL) and a transfer tool held about 2" below. Then manually knit the loops back twice by laying yarn in the hook of the NDL. Twist the transfer tool at least 5 times, catching the FY in the first twist. As you twist the tool, the loops become over—twisted and begin to kink up on themselves, which is what we want. Place

S47

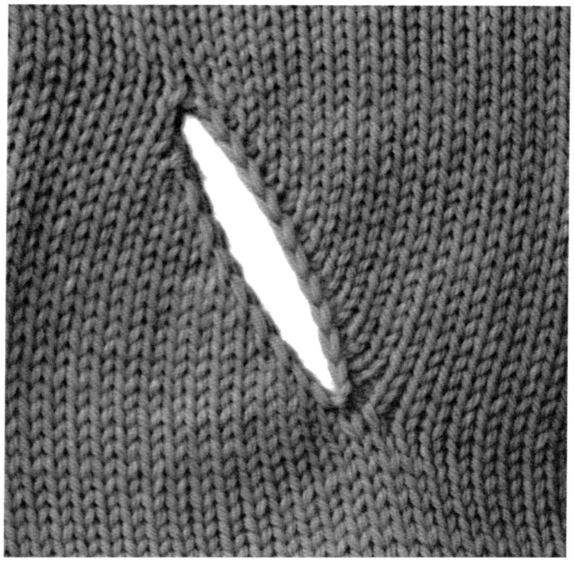

S47

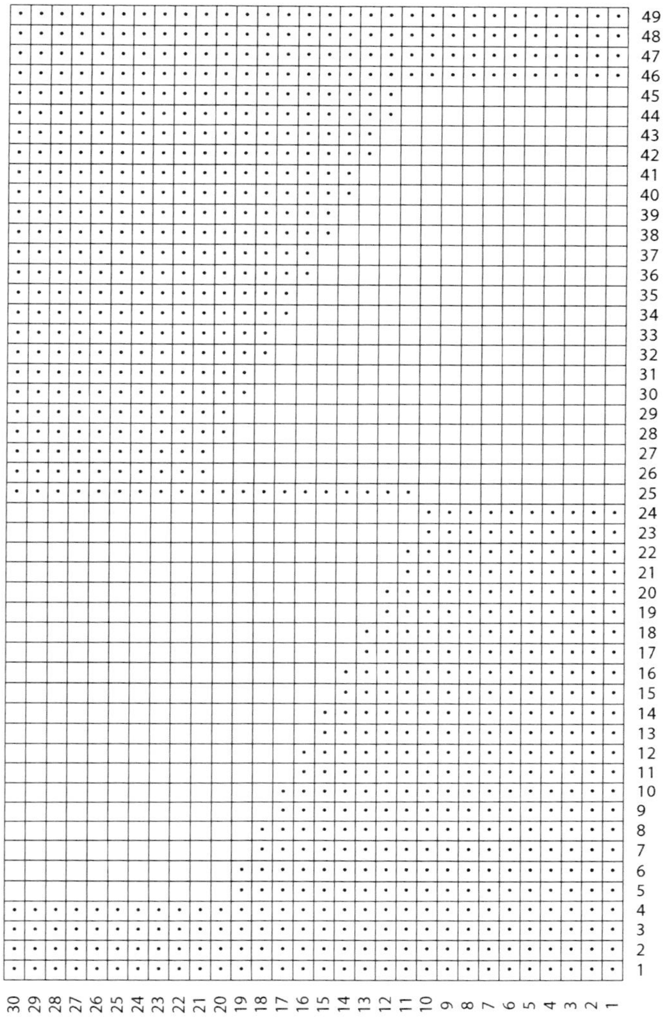

the twisted loops on the 3rd empty NDL (x) above.

Move the next group of 3 NDLS to UWP and repeat the process. At the end of the row, bridge back to the right, e—wrapping the 2 empty NDLS in each group. I knitted 3 rows between repeats and began the next repeat from the left, alternating the placement of the transferred STS and the working groups of NDLS. (See illustration S(on page 164).

S48

S48

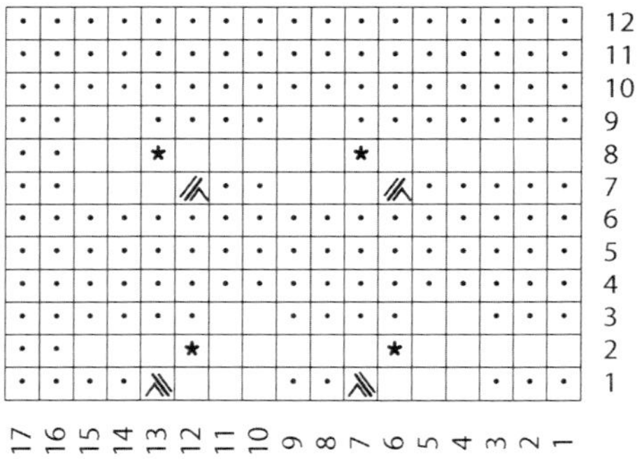

Cables

In addition to bridged cables, there are endless large—scale cable possibilities with intarsia. Normally, you can cross cables and leave the NDLS in HP to help them knit back more easily. With (most) intarsia, this is not an option. I usually push the NDLS holding the STS I want to cross to HP then remove the STS on transfer tools. After crossing the cables, I pull the NDLS back out to HP while I cross any others and then I nudge all NDLS back to UWP with their latches open. Because there are slits between the cables and each one is worked with its own bobbin, there isn't much tension on the groups of STS as you move them about. There is a little extra fussing, but it really shouldn't slow you down that much and these cables are worth it!

S49

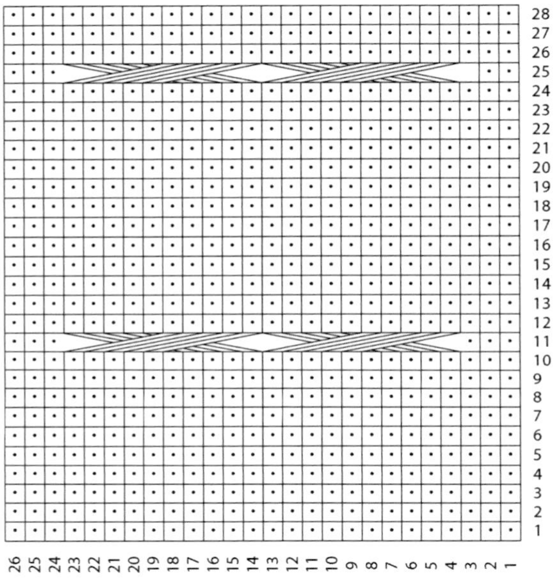

S49

S49 I hadn't really thought much about intarsia cables until I saw a sample like this one in the Stoll archives. Once it dawned on me what was happening, I realized that all of the cable variations I have used over the years could be worked this way to pump up the scale of things.

This fabric worked with 6 bobbins: one for each side border and one for each half of the parallel 5 x 5 cables. I knitted 10 rows over each section, without crossing the bobbins so that each section remained separate. Then I crossed the cables and knitted the next 4 rows (11-14 and 25-28) crossing the bobbins to join the fabric sections. Otherwise, the cables would float and turn, rather than forming a cohesive fabric. All of the cables crossed the same way in every repeat.

S50

S50 is a single 10 x 10 cable. I worked 18 rows on each cable section (only 16 on the borders) without crossing the bobbins. After crossing the cable, I worked 10 rows crossing all the bobbins to join the fabric. This would make a great scarf just as it is!

S51 is an intarsia gull or wishbone cable where two cable columns cross towards each other, rather than being parallel like those in S49. I knitted 10 rows on each group of cable NDLS, without crossing the bobbins then I crossed the cables. After the cables were crossed, I worked 4 rows with some of the bobbins crossing to join the fabric; rows 5-8 and 19-22. I did not join the two halves of each individual cable, but I did join the cables to each other at the center and to the border at each edge. Initially I found that the edges of this fabric tended to ripple a bit because, without the cable crossings to absorb some of the rows, 10 rows was about 2 rows too many so I knitted 8 rows on each of the borders strips which eliminated the ripples.

S51

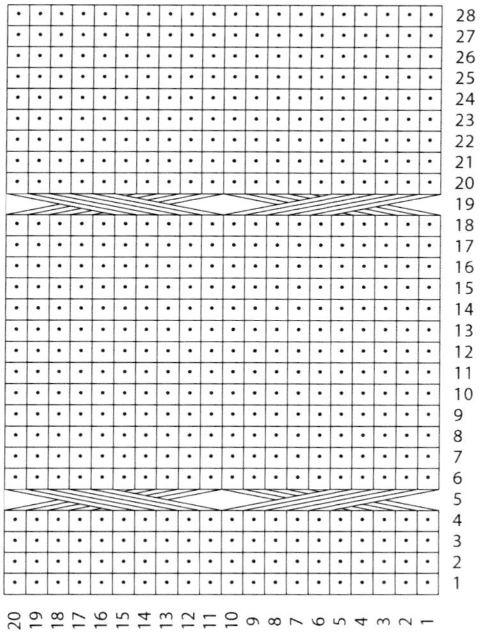

S51

S52 and S53 I worked these two intarsia samples in 2 colors to make the crossings more obvious and easier to understand. When I work with pairs of cable columns I find it easiest to think of the cables as first crossing in (towards the center) or out (towards the edges of the fabric). Remember, the STS that are returned to the NDLS first show on the knit side of the fabric.

S52 creates a 2-layered cable. The 5 x 5 cables cross every 10 rows, first crossing in (row 5), out (row 19) and in then out on each layer as the pattern continues.

I joined some of the bobbins for the next 4 rows (5-8 and 19-22) to connect the fabric. In the first cable repeat, for example, where the two light blue sections meet at the center, their bobbins cross to join them together. At the same time, the turquoise cable strips join with the background at each side, but not with the light blue strip that crossed them. I found that when I crossed all of the bobbins it tended to flatten out the effect, but you might like the way it looks and it does add a little more structure to the fabric. Because this cable is, in effect, made up of two serpentine cables traveling in opposite directions, the layers remained separate as I cross the cables. As always with intarsia cables, make sure you do not trap the free yarn on the knit side of the fabric.

S52

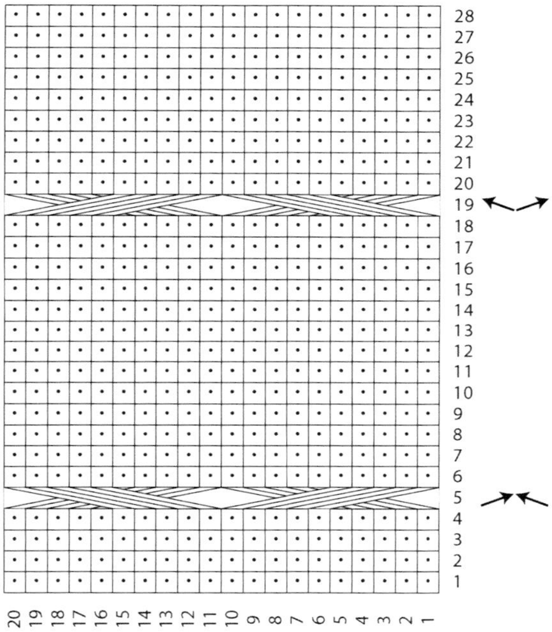

S52

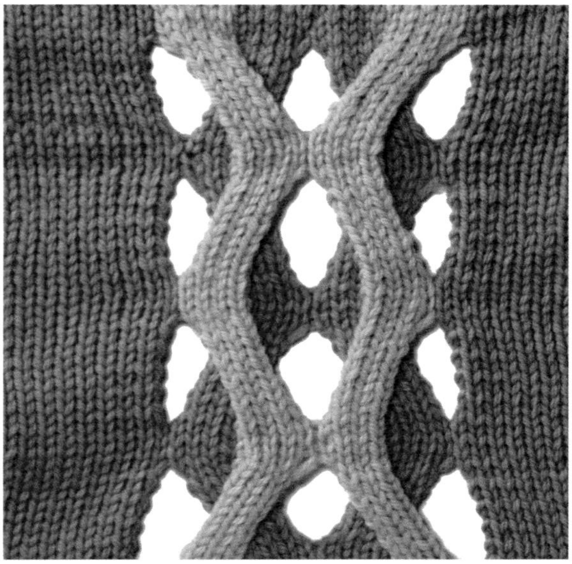

S53

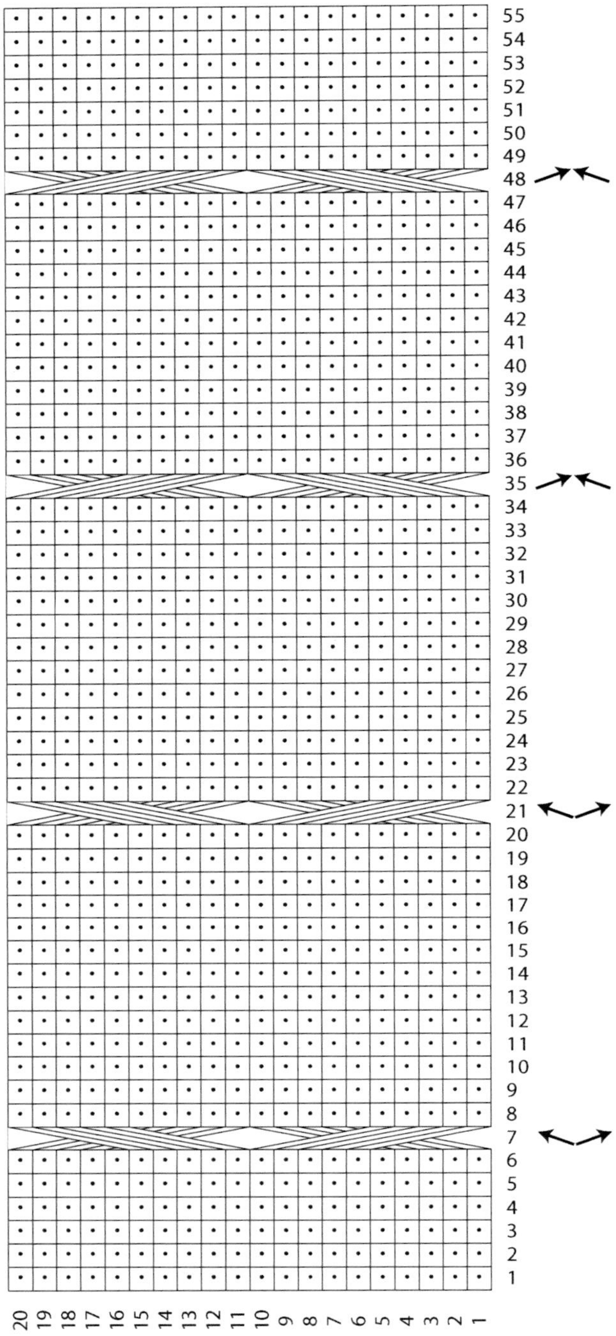

S53

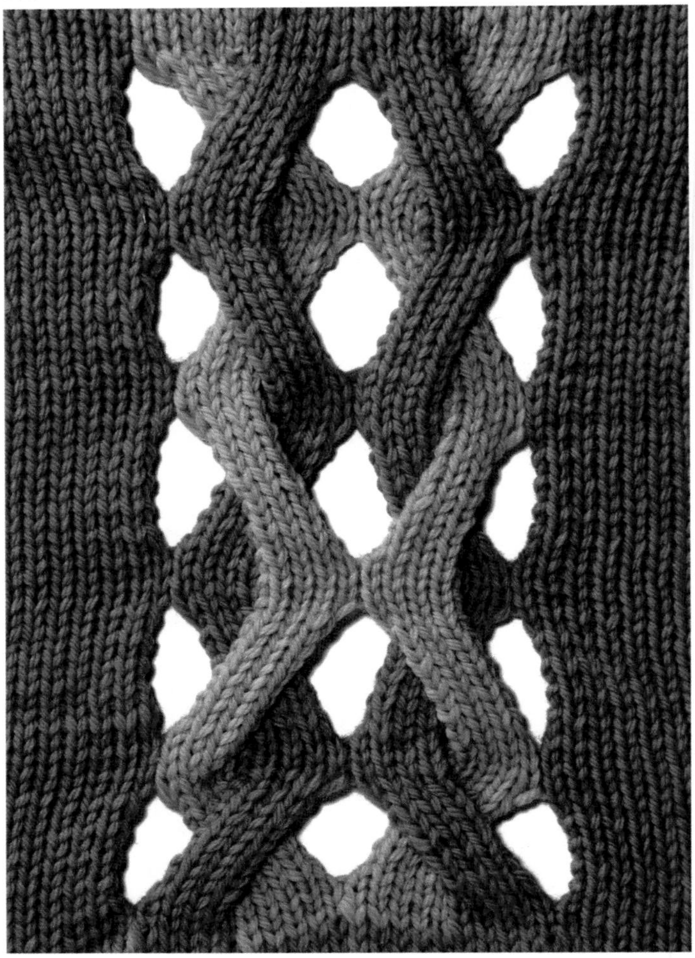

S53 is an intarsia Hugs and Kisses cable but the layers change places as the cables initially cross in (row 7), in (row 21), out (row 35), out (row 48). Once again I did not cross all of the bobbins when knitting the 4 joining rows and as I did for the other cables in this series, I knitted 2 fewer rows on the borders to account for the tension differences created by the cables.

These cables are 5 x 5 cables but you might chose to work even wider groups if you have the tools or the dexterity. In that case, you will probably need to knit more than 10 rows before crossing the cables and you might want to knit more than 4 rows to join the strips together so the fabric is more stable. When working intarsia cables, it is possible to cross really wide cables if you have the tools to do so because the separate strips usually don't pull on the NDLS or strain the stitches.

S54 is a woven cable, worked with 5 x 5 crossings and like all woven cables is constructed by splitting pairs and alternating the direction of the crossings from one horizontal repeat to the next. I knitted 10 rows on each cable strip (8 on the borders), crossed the cables and then worked 2 rows (6 & 7 and 18 & 19) crossing the bobbins to connect the fabric.

S54

S54

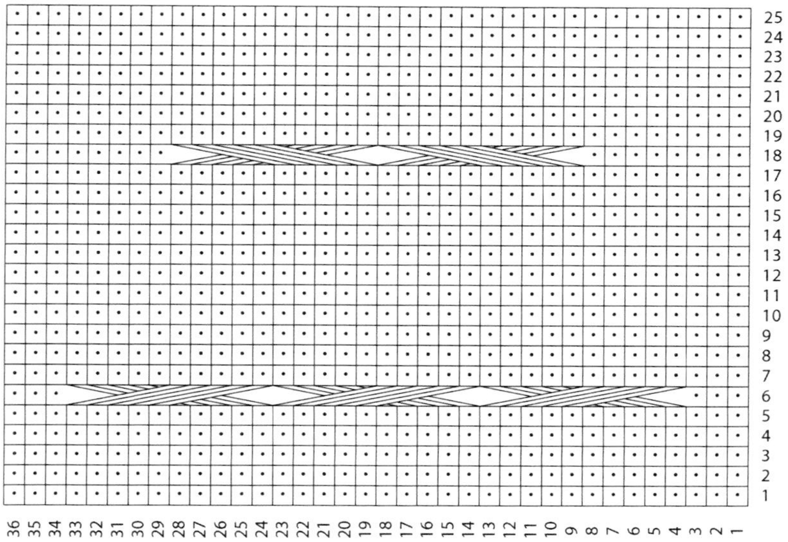

S55

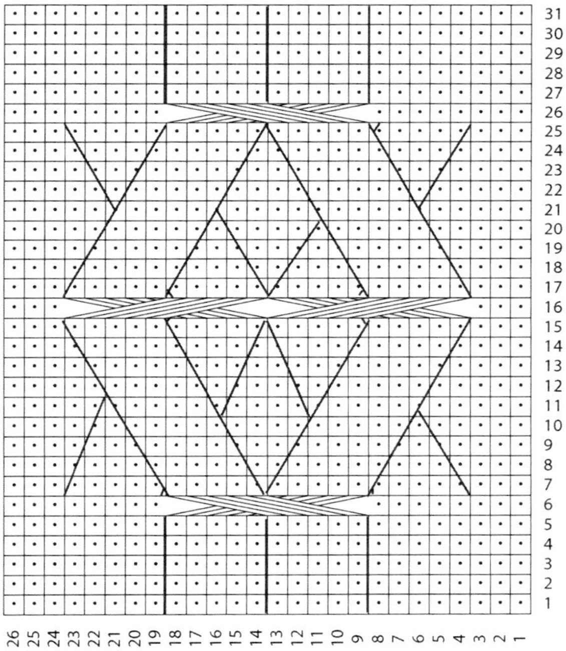

S55

S55 was inspired by another one of the Stoll fabrics where these woven medallions were scattered around the fabric. Once again these are 5 x 5 cables with split pairs and alternating direction for the crosses. What is interesting here is the way the fabric starts with two border sections and two cable strips. Then another cable strip seems to peel off the edge of each border, adding additional bobbins at row 7 and eliminating them at row 26.

Each section was knitted for 10 rows before crossing the cables and none of the bobbins cross so that the strips weave softly through each other. The slid lines on the chart are simply to give an idea where the strips cross and re—position.

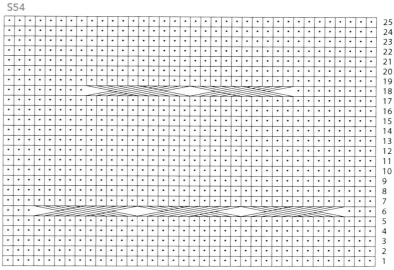

S56 I thought I had seen everything until I found Cari Morton's work on the internet and I flipped for her knotted intarsia cables. Cari is a British knitter who works with intarsia to form all kinds of interesting cables and textures, but it was this knotted fabric that captivated me. OK, so they really aren't cables in the truest sense of the word, but they seemed to fit in here. Special thanks to Cari for allowing me to share her ideas here and for supplying photos of her fabulous work for you to see a full application of this technique. You can see more of her work at www.cariandcarl.com

S56 What starts as a simple, connected intarsia stripe separates into 5 individual strips before the 2 light green strips form a square know around the center strip.

Knot Net Shawl. Photo courtesy of Cari and Carl.

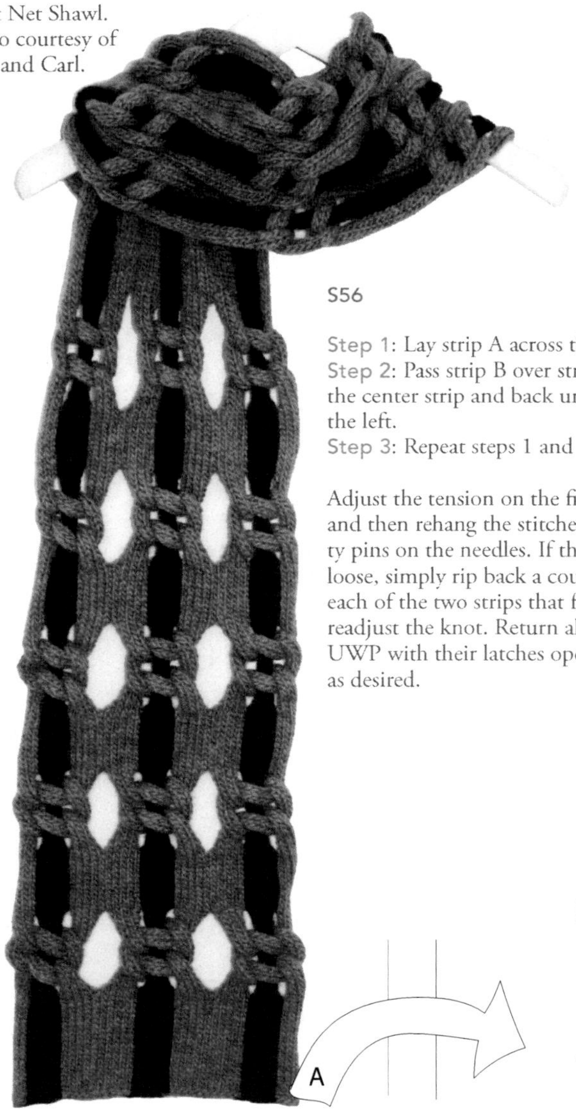

Although I usually use "Easy Bobs" for knitting intarsia and did in fact use them for the turquoise (center and border) sections because they hold more yarn, I used some narrow netting shuttles for the two mint green strips so that I could easily pass them through the loops formed in the knotting. I've had mine for years and you can find them on line at companies like jannscraft.com. They are inexpensive, come in a huge variety of sizes and hold a fair amount of yarn. Best of all in this case, they are long and narrow.

C/O 3 strips of 6 STS each at the center and wider borders at each side. *First knit 20 rows over each section, crossing the bobbins to join the fabric. Next knit 10 rows over each section *without* joining them and then hold the border NDLS and those for the center strip, all of which are turquoise in my sample. Knit 30 more rows on each of the mint green strips — the ones that will form the knot.

Thirty extra rows may be a few too many, but they will make the knotting easier and you can remove any extra rows after you adjust the completed knot. If you were a girl/boy scout, the next part will be easy for you because it is nothing more than a square knot. Use a large safety pin to remove the STS for each of the mint green strips from the machine. No need to cut the bobbin if you are using a netting shuttle. Easy Bobs will probably be too large to pass through the requisite loops in the knotting sequence so do cut those. Lift the center and border bobbins up out of the way and place them on the bed of the machine for now. Once again, you do not want to trap any of the bobbins/yarn on the knit side of the fabric. None of the center or border STS will move or interlace in any way. The strips at left and right of center will form the knot.

S56

Step 1: Lay strip A across the center strip.
Step 2: Pass strip B over strip A, behind the center strip and back under strip A at the left.
Step 3: Repeat steps 1 and 2.

Adjust the tension on the finished knot and then rehang the stitches from the safety pins on the needles. If the knot seems loose, simply rip back a couple of rows on each of the two strips that formed it and readjust the knot. Return all needles to UWP with their latches open and repeat as desired.

S57 This last cable swatch speaks more of woven—twisted stitches, but it does require split pairs and alternating directions from repeat to repeat like any woven cable. This is a fairly labor intensive fabric so probably not suitable for an entire garment, but I think it would make a great border or insertion.

C/O a multiple of 6 STS plus a border or edge at each side. Begin COR set to hold NDLS in HP. Hold all

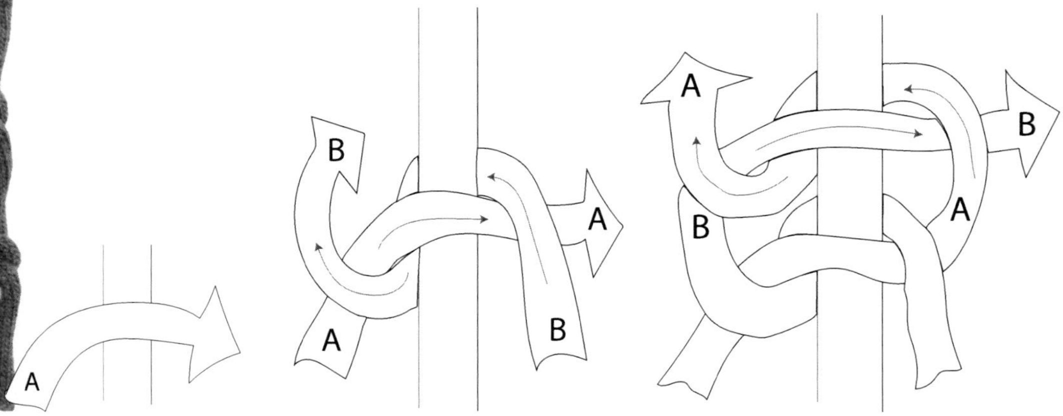

S57

NDLS except the right border/edge. Knit 1 row and then hold these border NDLS. Leave COL. Manually knit all of the NDLS back to the rail to form huge STS. Knit the left edge with the carriage if it is a wide border. Otherwise, for just a few STS knit them back manually to normal size. Push all of the NDLS with enlarged STS to HP, keeping some tension on the fabric so these STS do not pop off their NDLS.

Remove the first 6 STS on two 3-prong tools. Hook the left tool onto the adjacent 3 NDLS at left so that you have two hands free, but do not transfer the STS to those NDLS. Twist the right tool 360° to the left and place those STS on the 3 empty NDLS at left. Now twist the STS on the left tool 360° to the right and replace those STS on the 3 empty NDLS at right. Repeat across the row. Knit 1 row across all NDLS. Think of this as a cable with the groups of STS twisted prior to crossing and you will be fine.

Work the next repeat by splitting pairs (which will produce a 3-stitch wider border at each edge) and by alternating the direction of the cable, crossing left to right and then right to left. It is important that the tool always twists 360°in the direction the STS are crossing. That is, STS that will cross to the left should twist left; STS crossing to the right should be twisted right. It is a small, but important detail, because the twisted strands form the texture on the surface of the pattern.

Working with Bridge Bars

Up until now the bridge bars that connect one group of STS to the next when bridging have been dealt with in one of two ways. We've either hidden them on the back of the fabric or allowed them to show as part of the patterning. There is a third option that I had only toyed with in the past, but torn between working with NDLS in HP or resorting to intarsia I began to experiment further with a method to absorb the BB right into the fabric.

After seeing Cornelia Hamilton's gorgeous hand knits, I realized I could use the bridge bars to create a variety of openings, slits and textures that would not require me to cut and restart yarn or work intarsia. Being hand knit, Cornelia's work relies heavily on garter stitch and produces a gorgeous, dimensional fabric. Unfortunately, garter is just not a realistic option when working this method by machine.

S58

S58

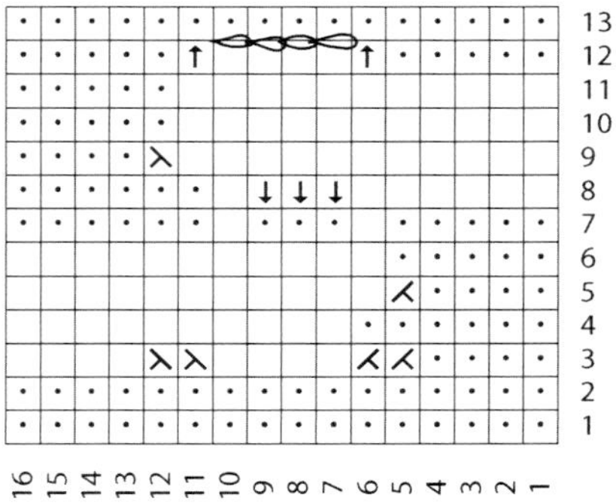

S58 This column of circles seems straightforward enough, but the increasing and decreasing that refines the shapes would have been bothersome to work in Intarsia so I started experimenting with HP and when those pesky BB presented themselves again, I finally found a way to deal with them.

C/O for the width of your project and knit a plain header to start. Knit 2 rows across all NDLS and then transfer STS as shown in the chart. Put the empty NDLS in NWP. Hold the left side and knit 2 rows. Make an additional decrease and knit 2 more rows, ending COR.

S58a There are 5 empty NDLS at the center. Bring the center 3 NDLS to WP and all NDLS at left to UWP. Knit 1 row. Hold the right side and drop the loops that formed on the center 3 NDLS and return the empty NDLS to NWP.

S58b Knit 1 row and then make the last decrease as shown on the chart. Before knitting the next row, lift the BB (lying across the center space) into the hook of the first WP NDL at the left of the open space. Knit 2 rows. Lift the BB onto the edge NDL and knit 1 row. COL.

Now, lift the BB onto the 1st and 5th empty NDLS, return the right side NDLS to UWP and knit 1 row. COR.

S59 Use a single—prong transfer tool to twist the bridge bar and the ladder bar that formed with the last pass of the carriage and as you twist, lift the resulting loops onto the empty NDLS. Knit 2 rows and repeat for the next circle. You can also use this method to produce isolated circles anywhere on a fabric. In that case, I recommend use bridging to B/O the center STS to produce a smoother bottom for each circle.

"Ursula" by Cornelia Tuttle Hamilton. Knited sideways, stitches are bound off and cast back on to form the triangular openings. The bridge bars that form are picked up and hidden in the edges of the shapes. Photo courtesy of Cornelia Tuttle Hamilton.

S58a Use drop stitch to increase the length of a BB across a wider, B/O opening. In this photo, 2 of the 4 empty NDLS have been brought to WP for the bridged row. These loops will be droppped and the empty NDLS returned to NWP.

S58b Lift the enlarged BB onto the edge NDL at left every 2 or 3/R to bind it to the edge of the slit.

This method of twisting the bridge bar and a ladder bar can also be employed to close off the tops of giant eyelets or wide ladders. Regardless of how you create the BB for this method, before beginning a large project, please work a sample first to determine just how long the BB loop needs to be for your yarn and pattern. My suggestions for length may not work in every instance.

The first time I tried working the BB into the edge of a slit, it failed miserably because the BB was too short and when pulled to the side it shortened further. This is why I have instructed you to bring the center 2 or 3 empty NDLS to WP when bridging to the left side. Even though these NDLS do not form STS — the yarn just lies across them — each of them does catch enough yarn to supply extra ease when their loops are dropped from the NDLS.

S60 is based on a much more elaborate Stoll fabric where the strip that laced through was worked in pattern. I pre—knitted a plain 8-stitch wide strip for about 100 rows and then S/O (in case I needed to re-hang and add to it). I hung the lower edge of the strip on the NDLS and then C/O over it for the main fabric and knitted to the first opening, where I transferred and shaped the opening as shown on the chart.

I returned 2 of the empty NDLS to WP when I bridged to the left side and completed the opening as I did for the previous example, P/U the BB on the edge NDL and then twisting the BB and the ladder bar together to complete the top edge. I also periodically caught STS from the strip to connect the two layers and, in some instances, in place of the twisted bar C/O to close some of the openings. In lieu of any patterning, I opted to knot the narrow strip.

S59 Alternately lift the BB and the FY onto the empty NDLS so that they twist around each other to C/O the empty NDLS. Use the same method to twist ladder bars and BB that extend across the same space.

S60

S61

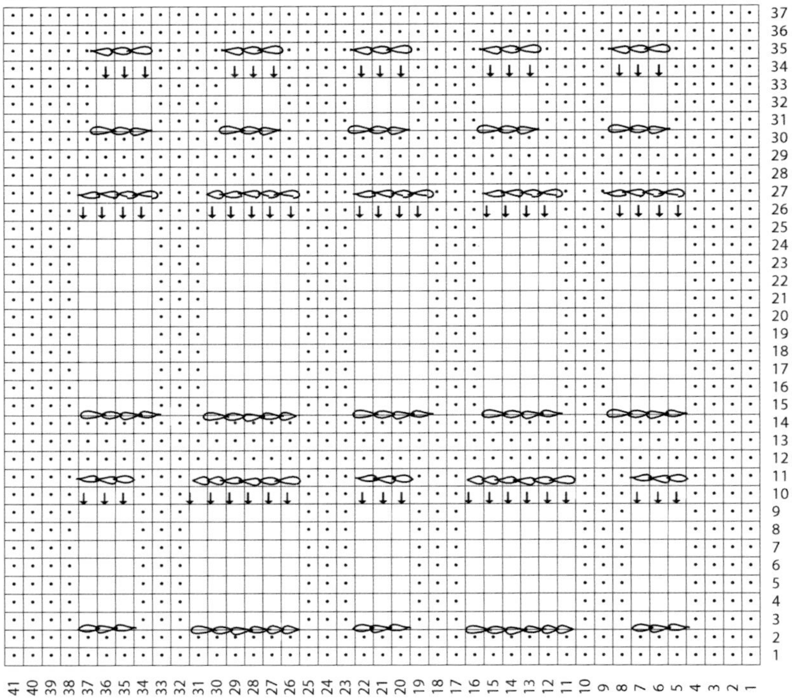

S61

"Flat Shoals" by Cornelia Tuttle Hamilton. Photo courtesy of Cornelia T. Hamilton.

S61 shows a variety of bridged rectangles and, if you compare it to the photos of Cornelia's work you will see some similarities as well as the difference between stockinette and garter stitch. Stockinette will gauge differently than garter stitch. However, you will still find Cornelia's beautiful designs and rich color sense inspiring and because the methods are so closely related you should be able to work from her patterns if you re—gauge for stockinette. You will be so inspired! Check them out at www.hamiltonyarns.com.

Begin COL set to hold NDLS in HP. Bridge the first row to B/O STS for the base for each square, increasing the ST size at the base of each so that you can chain off the STS without the square pulling in. I find it helpful to insert the latch tool through the purl bump of the adj ST to begin the chaining. It prevents a gap at the edge. I allowed 3 plain STS between each opening, but you can change that at will. End COR.

Hold all NDLS except the first group on the right. Knit 8 rows over these NDLS, ending COR. *Bring 3 of the empty NDLS (to the left of the current group) to WP and nudge the next group of NDLS back from HP to UWP. Knit 1 row to the left and then hold the previous group at the right and drop the loops from the 3 empty NDLS and return them to NWP. Knit 1 row. (P/U the BB and hang it on the edge NDL and then knit 2 rows) 4 times. Repeat from * across the work.

Once all of the squares have been formed and COL knit 1 row across the first group at the edge and then bring the adjacent empty NDLS to HP. C/O the empty NDLS by working latch tool C/O, catching the BB at the same time. Repeat across the bed until all NDLS have STS and COR.

S62

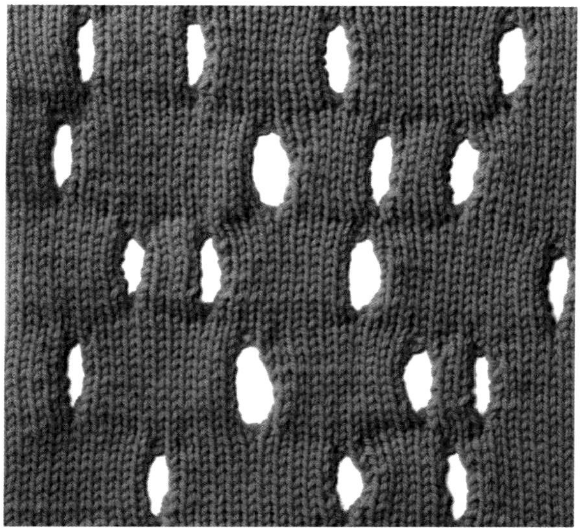

S62a For a simple slit where there are no empty NDLS to use drop ST to enlarge the BB, you can bridge to the divide and pull out a loop of the FY. Hold onto the tool while you knit the first row or two so that the loop does not close up. You could also transfer it to a short holder (even a toothpick) and catch it through the fabric to secure it temporarily.

S62 The slits in this example are worked a little differently because there are no empty NDLS to employ for lengthening the BB. Instead, you'll need to pull out extra FY between bridged sections and use that for binding to the edges of the slits. S62a Otherwise, the BB that form, working from section to section, are just too short to be P/U and manipulated. As it is, if you look closely at my sample, you can see where the STS have tightened slightly across some of the rows. In a perfect world, this wouldn't show, but with a smooth yarn like this, it is nearly impossible to hide in stockinette.

This chart is a little different from most in that I did not show any of the stitches. Instead, I've chosen to show just the serpentine arrows that show the bridging from group to group. The dark vertical lines represent the slits, above which you will see a decrease symbol.

Before starting, secure (and mark) the beginning of each slit by P/U the purl bump from the ST to the right of the slit and hanging it on the NDL to the left of the slit. This will prevent the base of the slits from gaping open.

Begin COR set to hold NDLS in HP. Hold all NDLS to the left of NDL 13. Knit 10 rows. *Hold NDL 13 and knit 1 row to the left. Transfer the ST from NDL 13 to NDL 12. Hold all NDLS and move COR. Pull down a loop of the FY between NDLS 12 & 13. I use a short hand knitting cable NDL to hold the loop and poke both ends of the needle through the fabric, in line with the beginning of the slit.

Nudge NDLS 14 to 24 to UWP and knit 3 rows. Remove cable NDL holding the loop. Use a single—prong transfer tool to catch the BB and twist like an e—wrap. (Hang the twisted loop on NDL 14 and knit 2 rows) 3 times. Make the 4th and last twist and knit 1 row. Return the transferred stitch from NDL 12 to 13, passing it under the leg of the BB. Use the remaining length of the BB to manually knit NDL 13 and then return it to HP.

S62

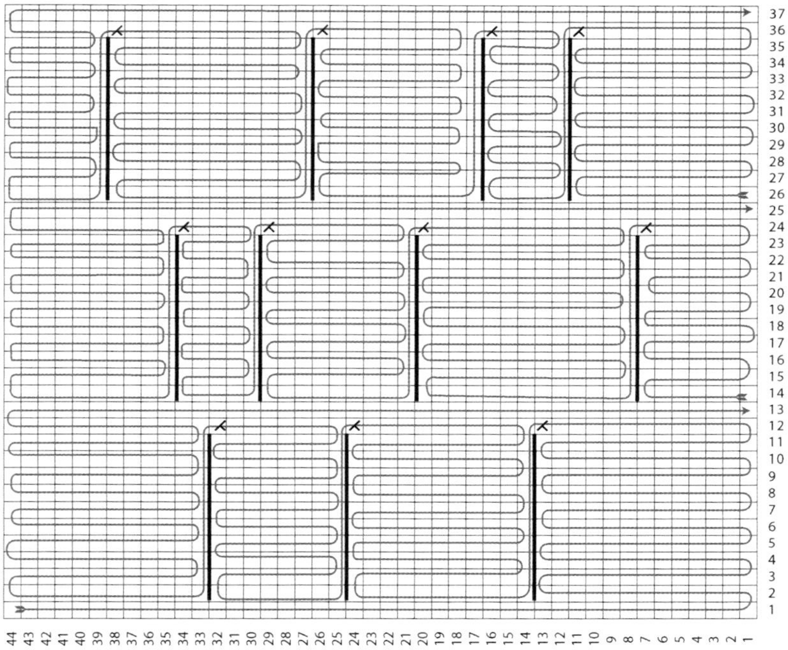

Repeat from * to knit the last row of the section NDLS 14-24 and continue bridging across the fabric. At the end of the row you can knit additional rows before producing more slits or you can follow the chart as shown. Note that I have drawn the chart so that you always begin a slit sequence COR. I have done this only to simplify the directions so that you are always working the same way, repeat after repeat. That said, if you want more rows between repeats, always work an odd number of rows so you begin COR or be prepared to reverse all of the sequences to begin COL. It can be done, but it will complicate things for you.

S63

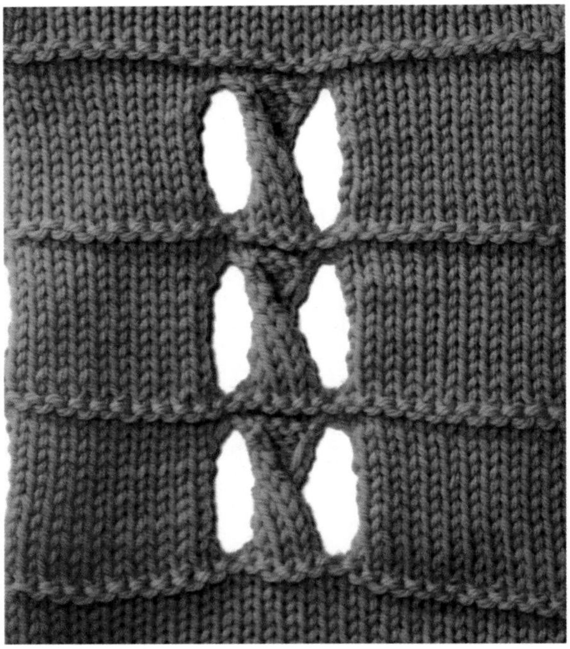

S64

S63 A garter ridge follows each twist on the center 5 STS and helps to refine the stockinette and reverse stockinette textures. Although I worked this fabric with BB, you could also work intarsia or HP, cutting the yarn from section to section.

C/O and begin *COR set to hold NDLS in HP. Hold center and left sections and knit 11 rows on right section, ending COL. Hold first section at right (all NDLS are in HP now) and use a latch tool to pull down a long (2") loop of the FY between the 1st and 2nd sections. Return COR.

Move NDLS in second section to UWP and knit 10 rows, ending COR and at the same time, P/U the BB every 3rd row and hang it on the edge NDL. At RC 10, remove the 5 center STS on a 5-prong tool (or a combination of other tools) and twist the tool 180° to the right and replace the STS on the NDLS. The yarn is on the left. Free pass COL. Use the remaining length of the BB to manually knit the 5 center NDLS and then place them in HP. Pull down a 1" loop of FY and free pass the COR.

Knit the third group, P/U the BB every 3/R for 11 rows, ending COL. Work garter ridge or plain rows and then repeat from *

Another Stoll fabric, S64 looks nearly identical to the intarsia version in swatch S49. In this instance, however, the fabric was worked utilizing HP and by pulling down 1" loops of FY to create longer BB and then P/U the BB every A/R for 12 rows as described in the previous examples. I knitted 4 rows across all NDLS after crossing the cables.

When crossing the cable, it will be necessary to pass the second tool underneath the BB to avoid trapping it on the front of the fabric. You may also need to remove the BB from the hooks of the NDLS should it get caught in the process. If the BB seems lose, you can always hook it up on a NDL on the back of the fabric, but do not allow it to be trapped on the knit side of the fabric. Bypassing the BB in this way was a major factor in creating the horizontal cable featured in *More Hand—Manipulated Stitches.*

S65 The process of working with BB became a lot more interesting once I moved away from simple slits and rectangular shapes. These triangles are worked on a multiple of 10 STS plus 2 or 3 edge STS. Begin COR. Make all of the 2-step decreases shown on row 2 of the chart, placing the empty NDLS in NWP. Hold all NDLS except the right edge STS. Knit 6 rows on those NDLS.

Bridge across the first triangle (NDLS 4-11) then hold the edge STS. Knit 1 row. COR. Make decreases for rows 4, 6, and 8, knitting 2 rows after each decrease, ending COR. *Move NDLS 14-19 to UWP and bring empty NDLS 10-12 to WP and knit 1 row to the left. Drop the loops from NDLS 10-12 and return the NDLS to NWP. Place all NDLS to the right of

S65

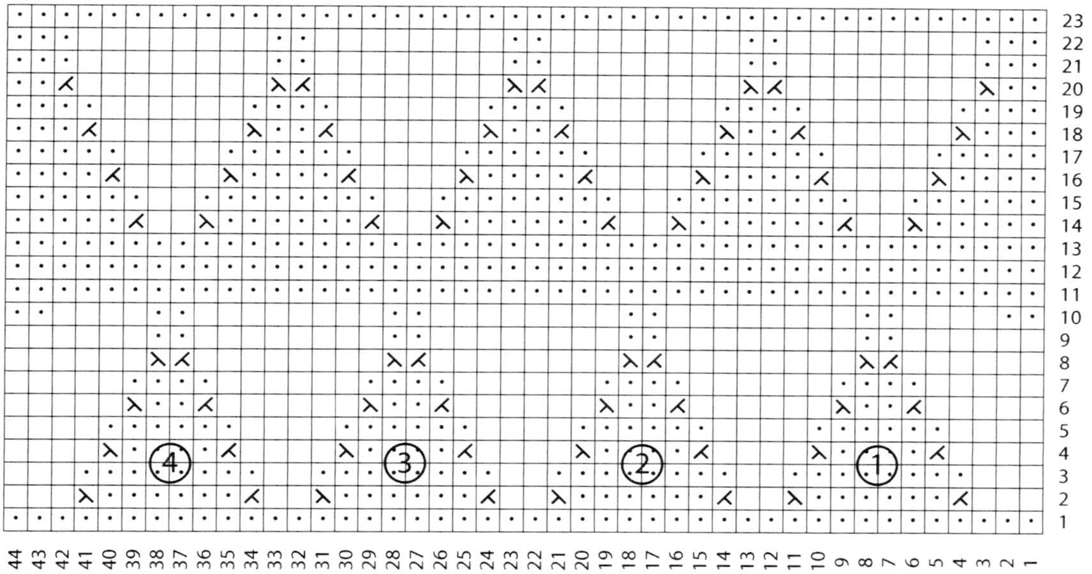

this group into HP and knit 1 row to the right. Make decreases for rows 3, 5 and 7 as before, knitting 2 rows after each decrease and at the same time P/U the BB and catch it on the edge NDL of this triangle. When working the last P/U, do so only after bridging to the next group when you bring the last 2 NDLS to HP.

Continue working each triangle from *, substituting appropriate NDL numbers and P/U the BB as you work. At the left edge, work 5 rows on the edge STS. Then work 2 rows across all NDLS, ending COL.

To C/O the empty NDLS, hold all NDLS except the left edge NDLS. Knit 1 row to the right and leave COR. Use a single—prong tool to reach under the ladder bars and the BB and catch a loop of the FY with the tip of the tool. Pull the loop down and towards you and then lift it up into the hook of the first empty NDL at left. Catch the FY by itself in the hook of the next NDL and then alternate these two motions until the first group of 8 empty NDLS has been C/O. Manually knit the next 2 NDLS to WP and repeat for the next group of empty NDLS.

When you reach the right edge, knit 4 rows over the edge NDLS and then 2 rows across all NDLS. With the next repeat, alternate the placement as shown on the chart.

S66 is a smaller version of the previous triangle fabric. Both of them were worked over an even number of STS so that I could alternate the next repeats. S67, however, was worked over groups of 5 NDLS so it really wasn't possible to alternate the placement. Instead, I moved over by 1 NDL for each repeat, which created a diagonal line in the fabric and created a less regular border in the process. Although the edges remain straight, the number of plain stockinette STS in the borders changes with each repeat.

S65

S66

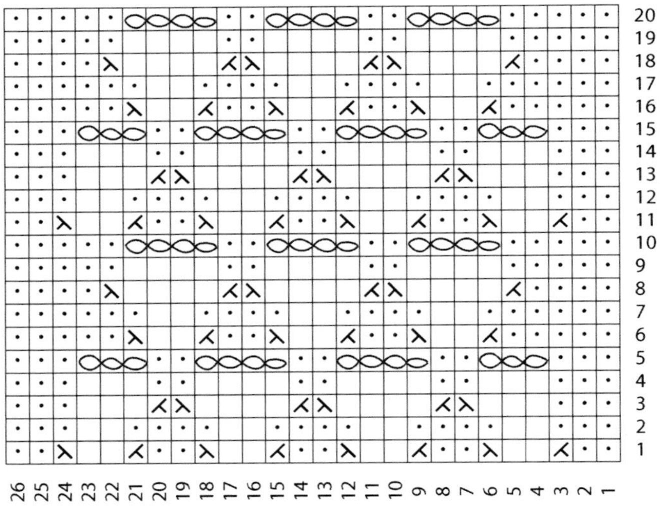

S67

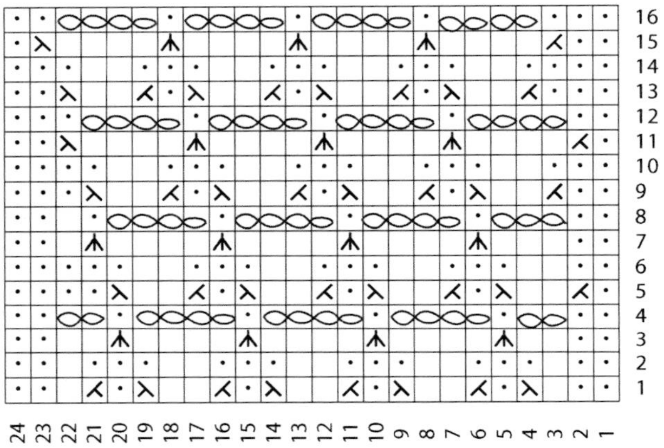

S66

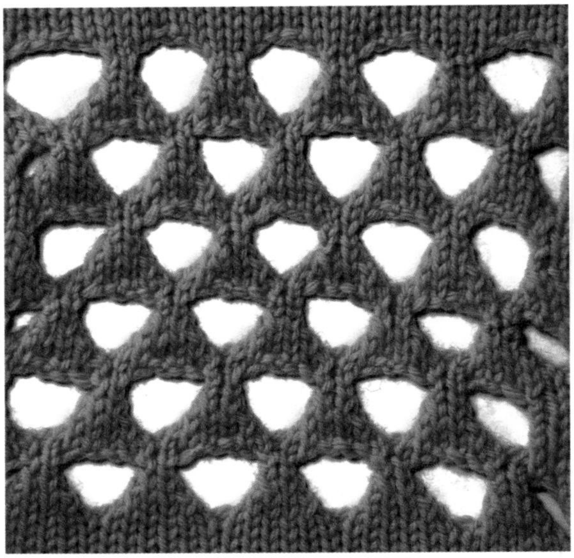

S67

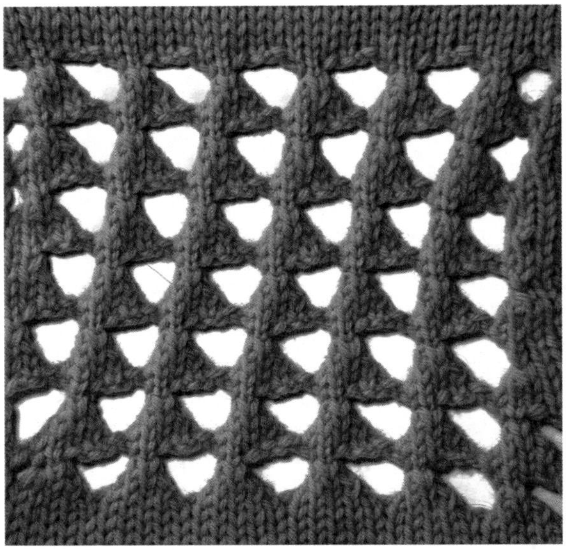

S68 is based on another Stoll fabric. Let me take a minute here to reiterate how important it is to use the correct yarn on any machine when you are trying something new and want a nearly guaranteed result. You should use a yarn that knits a balanced stockinette right in the middle of the dial. For a standard gauge machine, that means ST sizes 6-8 (depending on the brand); mid gauge with DK on size 5 or worsted on 7; bulky with worsted weight on 5. I mention it here because this technique looks terrific (if I do say so myself) in this sample, knitted with worsted on size 7 on my midgauge. When I re—proofed the directions with some leftover yarn that wasn't quite up to size, it looked stringy and sloppy because the openings were too wide and saggy. Once you know how to work any of these techniques you can experiment with different yarns, but initially I recommend taking my advice and playing it safe.

I've broken down each of the steps necessary to knit this fabric both on the chart and in the text directions. Bridging is used to knit individual sections and empty NDLS are strategically brought back to WP for drop stitch to increase the length of the BB, which are lifted onto empty NDLS to increase the lower halves of each diamond. Rely on the chart as well as the written directions as you work because there is a lot going on here. Once you get the hang of it, you will find this is not a difficult fabric to knit.

Section 1 (Rows 1-12 on chart): Begin COR set to hold NDLS in HP. Hold NDLS 17 - 35. Knit 1 row to the left, hold NDLS 1-3 and knit 1 row to the right. (Decrease 1 ST each side A/R) 5 times as shown on the chart and place empty NDLS in NWP until COR and RC12. Move NDLS 17-32 to UWP and empty NDLS 13-15 to WP and knit 1 row to left. Hold NDLS 9-11 and 17-19. Drop the loops from 14-16 and return the empty NDLS to NWP. Only NDLS 20-32 should be in WP.

S68

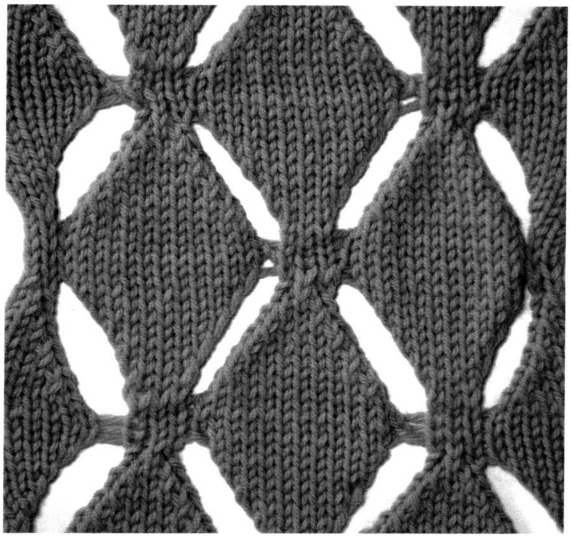

S68

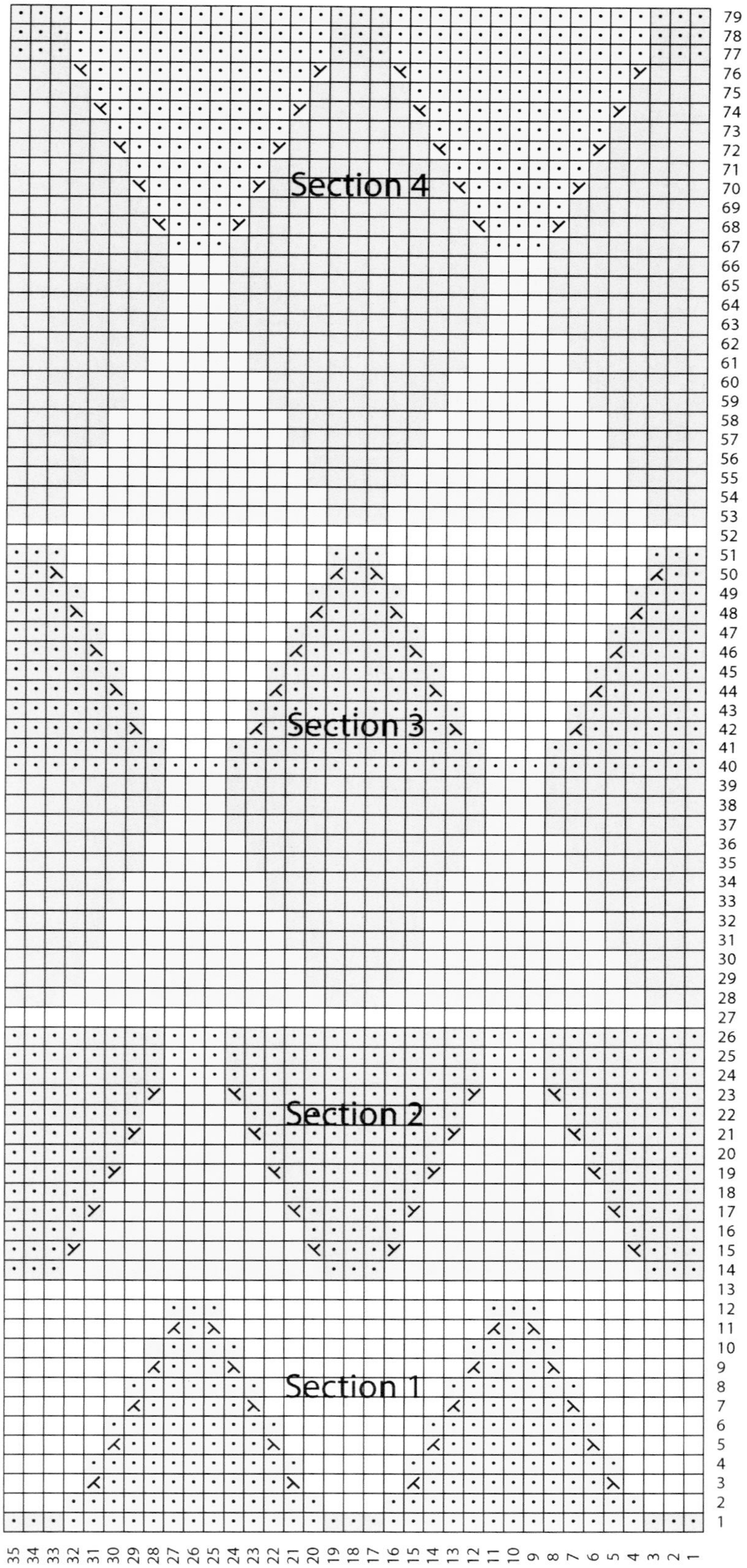

(Decrease 1 ST each side A/R) 5 times as shown on the chart ending COR. Bring NDLS 33-35 to UWP and bring empty NDLS 29-31 left to WP. Knit 1 row to left. Hold 25-27 and drop the loops from NDLS 29-31 and return the empty NDLS to NWP. This completes section 1. COL.

Section 2 (rows 14-26 on chart): COL. NDLS 33-35 in WP. Knit 1 row to the right. The BB will be used to fill the 5 empty NDLS 28-32 as follows: (Lift the BB onto the next empty NDL and then knit 2 rows) 4 times. COR. Lift the BB to fill the last NDL (28) and knit 1 row to the left. Return NDLS 25-27 and 17-19 to UWP and also bring empty NDLS 21-23 to WP. Knit 1 row . Drop the loops from NDLS 21-23 and hold NDLS 25-35. COR.

You will be working both sides of NDLS 17-19, lifting the BB as follows: E/R lift the BB on the carriage side only onto the next empty NDL at the left or right of 17-19, 9 times, ending COL. Lift the BB to fill the last empty NDL and then move NDLS 9-11 and 1-3 to UWP and empty NDLS 4-6 to WP. Knit 1 row to the right. Drop the loops from NDLS 4-6 and hold NDL 9 and all NDLS to the left of it. Knit 1 row. COL. (Lift the BB and knit 2 rows) 4 times. Lift the BB to fill the last empty NDL and knit 1 row to the right. Knit 2 rows over all NDLS, ending COR to complete section 2.

Section 3 (rows 40-51 on chart): With COR, hold NDLS 9-35. Shape first section by decreasing 1 ST on the left edge A/R, 4 times. COR. Make the 5th and last decrease and return NDLS 9-24 to UWP and bring empty NDLS 5-7 to WP and then knit 1 row to the left. Hold NDLS 1-3 and 9-11 and drop the loops from NDLS 5-7. Knit 1 row. COR.

Shape the next triangle by decreasing 1 ST each side, A/R four times. COR. Make the last decrease and return all NDLS at left to UWP and put empty NDLS 21-23 in WP. Knit 1 row to the left. Hold NDLS 17-19 and 25-27 and drop the loops from NDLS 21-23. Knit 1 row. COR.

Shape the last edge by decreasing 1 ST every A/R, 4 times. Decrease the 5th and last ST and knit 1 row, ending section 3 with COL.

Section 4 (rows 67-79 on chart): Begin COL. Return NDLS 25-27 to UWP and place empty NDLS 29-31 in WP. Knit 1 row to the right. Hold NDLS 33-35 and drop the BB from NDLS 29-31. Increase at the left and right of NDLS 25-27 by lifting the BB onto the empty NDL on the carriage aside E/R, 9 times. COL. Wrap the edge NDL, lift the last BB. Return NDLS 17-19 and 9-11 to UWP and place empty NDLS 13-15 in WP. Knit 1 row to the right.

Hold NDL 17 and all NDLS to the left of it and drop the loops from NDLS 13-15. Repeat the increases by lifting the BB as before. After making the last lift, return NDLS 1-3 to UWP and knit 1 row to the right. Knit 2 rows over all NDLS.

Continue building the fabric by repeating these four sequences. Be consistent when lifting the BB, always catching them the same way so that the edges are uniform. If there is excess BB length at the end of a sequence, lift it onto a NDL above to control and hide it.

Once you are comfortable with this method, you can always add cables or lace effects to the diamonds. You can also vary the kind of decreases you use to shape the upper edges of each diamond.

S69 This is an intarsia version of S68. Although there is neither bridging nor BB to lift, this is slow knitting because the diamonds are shaped with increases and decreases and you need to be vigilant about making sure the latches are open after every manipulation.

I used simple edge decreases, moving the receiving NDL to WP before making each decrease. Then, I pulled the NDLS out to UWP and made sure both STS were behind the open latch. For increases, I simply lifted the purl bump from an adj NDL onto the next empty NDL, making sure the ST was behind the open latch and the NDL butts aligned in UWP. The bobbins cross to join the fabric for the 2 rows where the widest part of one diamond meets the narrowest part of the next. You could work more rows here if you want to.

S69

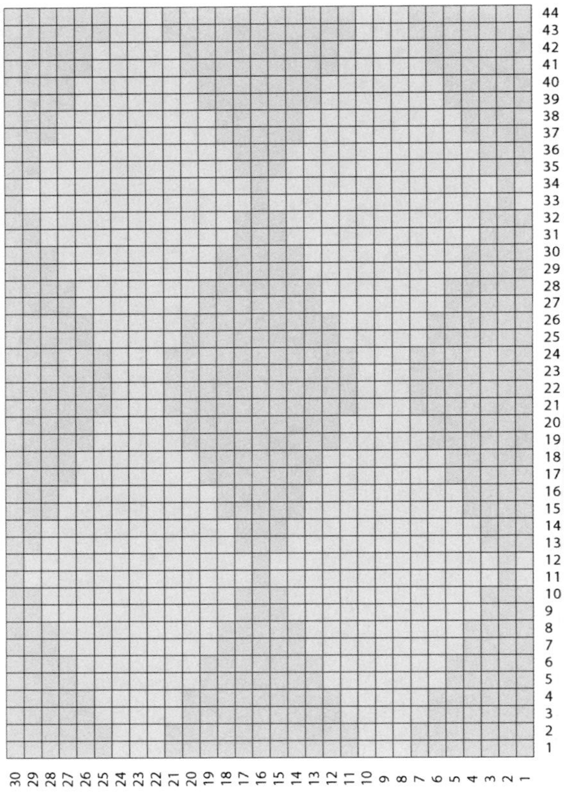

S69

S70 is an elegant cable variation and one of my favorites. Begin COR set to hold NDLS in HP. Knit 2 rows and then make both of the 2-step, full—fashioned decreases shown on row 3 of the chart. I used a 5-prong tool to create a wide outline for the openings and to allow me to re—form the 4th ST as a purl ST. Because of the transfers, you can safely drop that ST to reform it every so many rows.

Put the left half in HP to continue and knit 2 rows on the right side. Make the decreases for row 5 and knit 2 rows; then make the decrease for row 7 and knit 7 rows. Put empty NDLS in NWP after each decrease.

S70

S70

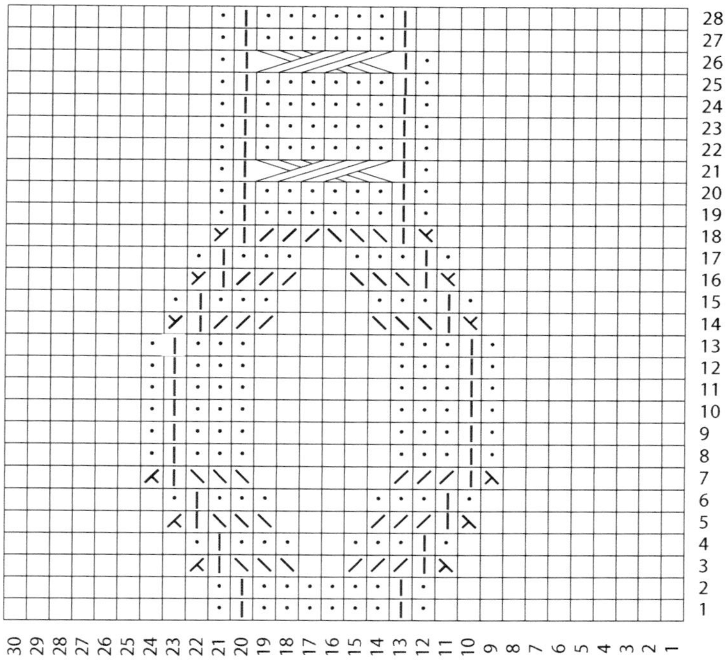

S71

At row 14, (increase and then knit 2 rows) twice. Increase 1 ST. Hold the right side, pull down a 2" loop and return COR. Push NDLS on left side to UWP and knit 2 rows. Continue shaping the left side as for the right side and at the same time P/U the BB every A/R and hang it on the edge NDL. At row 18 with COL, make the last increase and return NDLS at right to UWP to return them to work. Drop and reform the 4th ST on each side of the opening. At rows 21 and 26 cross a 3 x 3 cable, always in the same direction. Any excess BB length can be hung on the center NDL at the back of the fabric and knitted into the fabric.

S71 (no chart) is a lifted BB edging. C/O the width of your project plus 4 extra STS at the right edge. *Knit 1 row over all NDLS from right to left, set carriage to hold NDLS in HP and then place the 4 edging NDLS in HP. Knit 7 rows over just the main fabric, ending COR. Hold the main fabric NDLS (all NDLS in HP now) and then pull down a loop of the free yarn about 1.5" long between the main NDLS and the edging NDLS. Move COL and then nudge all 4 edging NDLS to UWP. Work 17 rows over the 4 edging NDLS, P/U the BB every 3/R and hanging it on the edge NDL, ending COR.

Set carriage to knit all NDLS and knit 1 row to the left. Cross the 4 edge NDLS with the first 4 NDLS of the main knitting and then knit 1 row, ending COR.**

Repeat from * to ** for the length of the project. You can work both edges at the same time for a scarf or similar project. One side will be a row behind the other. This technique can also be used as a loop—through—loop joining for an afghan or other large project and you can always knit more rows to increase the size of the loops at the edge.

S72

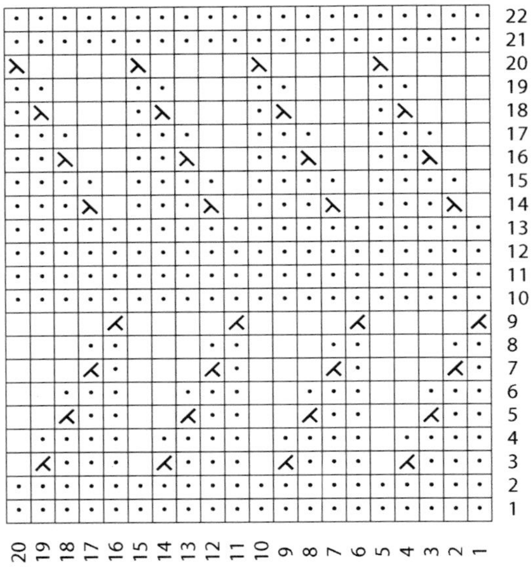

S72

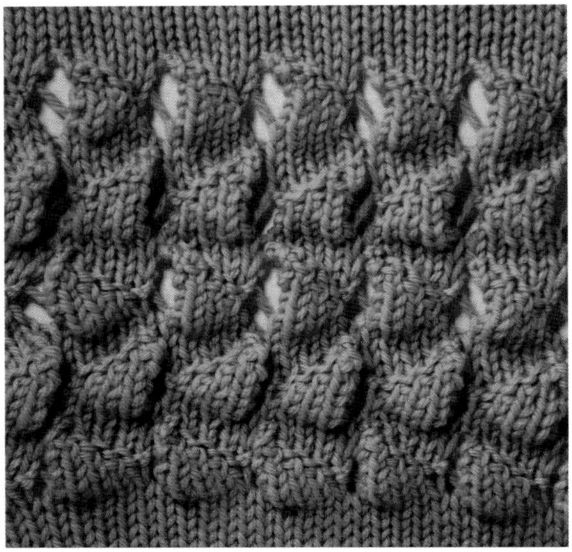

S73

S72 and S73 These fabrics are both shaped by decreasing STS, placing the NDLS in NWP and then using the FY to C/O the empty NDLS before bridging to the next group. The difference between the swatches lies in the absence/presence of BB. In S72, the BB were allowed to show in the slits between the columns of bridged STS, zigzagging left and right. In S73 I picked up the BB every 3rd or 4th row and hung them on the working edge NDL. (Note that this chart does not indicate the bridging motion of the carriage required to knit the swatch.)

C/O a multiple of 5 STS. Make the first decreases across the entire row as shown on the chart and then put the empty NDLS in NWP. With COR, hold all NDLS left of the first group on the carriage side. *Knit 2 rows. Then, (make a decrease at left and knit 2 rows) 3 more times only knitting 1 row after the last decrease so that you end COL. Just 1 NDL remains in WP on the right of the group.

To P/U the edge of the decreased triangle, use a latch tool to poke through the decreased edge of the triangle you just knitted and pull up a loop of the free yarn to hang on the first empty NDL (#2) adjacent to the WP NDL above. Beginning close to the top of the triangle and working your way down the edge, you will need to pull up 3 more individual loops to fill the remaining empty NDLS (3-5), from right to left. Try to space them evenly along the decreased edge and to be consistent in P/U either a whole or half ST.

Once you have P/U the edge, knit 1 row to the right. Nudge the next group of NDLS at left to UWP and knit 1 row to the left. Hold the first group and knit 1 row to the right.** With COR, repeat the directions from * to ** across the bed. After completing the last group, knit some rows before beginning the next repeat from the left side, reversing all directions.

I knitted 2 rows between each repeat on S72; 4 rows for S73. Both of these swatches were worked by placing each repeat directly above the previous repeat.

S74 is similar to the previous 2 examples in that the repeats stack up vertically above each other and, like S73, the BB were lifted. There are 2 rows between repeats. The texture, however is more pronounced because of the way the loops create STS on the empty NDLS. Rather than P/U and hanging all of the loops at the same time, I knitted 2 rows after P/U each loop. Also, rather then 5 NDLS/group, I enlarged the scale slightly by working 6 NDLS/group.

I P/U the BB in this sample about 4 times over the course of decreasing, P/U loops and bridging to the next group. It is not necessary or advisable to P/U more often than that unless you have enlarged the BB, which would add an extra step.

C/O a multiple of 6 and begin COR. Make the first decrease of each group, including the far left edge. Making all of the first row decreases at once streamlines the process and also helps mark each group of STS so that you won't have to count as you work.

Put all NDLS except the first group of (now) 5 NDLS at the right into HP. Place the empty NDLS in NWP and Knit 2 rows. *Decrease 1 ST at the left of the group and knit 2 rows) 3 times. Decrease 1 more ST at left and knit 1 row. COL.

[Use the latch tool to poke through the decreased edge and pull up a loop of the free yarn to hang on the right—most empty NDL above and knit 2 rows.] 4 times, ending COL. Make a fifth ST and knit 1 row to the right. Move the next group of NDLS at left to UWP. Knit 1 row to the left, hold the previous group and knit 1 row to the right to begin the next sequence.**

Repeat * to ** across the bed, ending COL. Knit 2 rows across all NDLS, ending COL to begin the next repeat from the left. Reverse all directions. Carrying the shaping right out to the edges of the fabric creates a decorative zigzagged edge that, while beautiful for a scarf, is probably not practical for a garment.

S75 alternates the placement of each repeat. My initial attempts to do this yielded fabrics with really irregular edges because splitting the pairs left me with larger groups of STS at the edges when I incorporated them into the first (or last) working group. Ultimately, I abandoned the hope of retaining the zigzag edges and knitted a plain border at each side.

C/O a multiple of 6 plus 3 additional NDLS. Follow the above directions, but begin the first repeat from the right by working 6 plain rows over the first 3 NDLS. Then bridge your way across the row, working each sequence as before. Knit 2 rows over all NDLS, ending COL. Work 6 plain rows over the first 3 NDLS at left and then continue as before. I P/U the BB as for the previous example.

By working 3 STS at the beginning of each repeat, it automatically splits the pairs so that the repeats do not stack up vertically over each other. Instead, the alternating placement creates a fabric with even deeper texture. You could also add a border to swatches 77 and 77a if you want to use either of them for a garment and require straight edges for seaming.

S76 As I worked with these swatches I found that the texture easily creased right across the fabric and realized that it would create an interesting and unique hem or pleat. I worked 4 plain rows, 1 full repeat of the technique and then 4 more rows before hanging the hem.

The next two samples differ only in small structural details, but the resulting fabrics are quite different.

S74

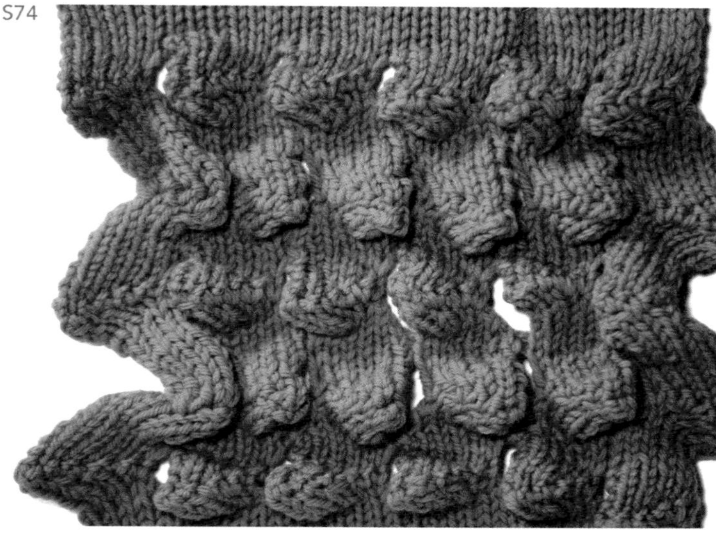

S75

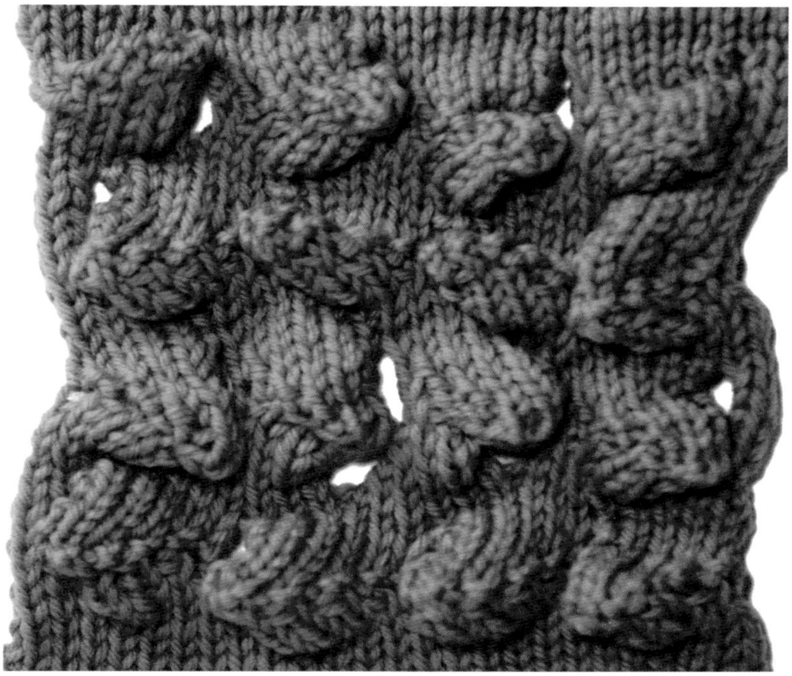

S76

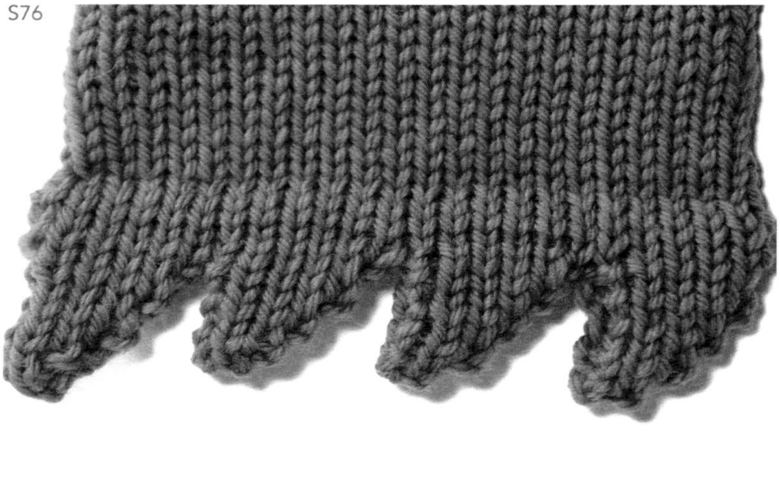

S77 C/O a multiple of 5 plus 2 (1 plain ST at each edge). Begin COR. Hold all NDLS except the first 6 on the carriage side. *Move the 2nd ST to the 3rd NDL, leave the empty NDL in WP and knit 2 rows. Move the 3rd ST to the 4th NDL, leave the empty NDL in WP and knit 2 rows. Then move the 4th ST to the 5th NDL and the 5th ST to the 6th NDL, knitting 2 rows after each transfer and leaving the empty NDLS in WP so they cast back on. End the sequence COR.** Note that the edge groups include an extra ST for the border so the first ST transferred is the 2nd from the edge.

S77

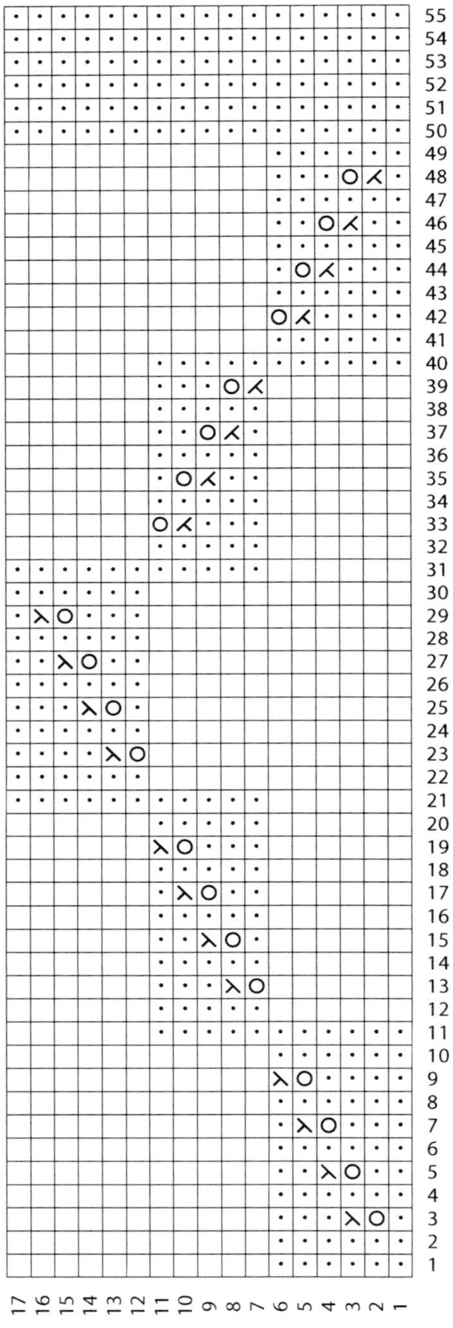

S77

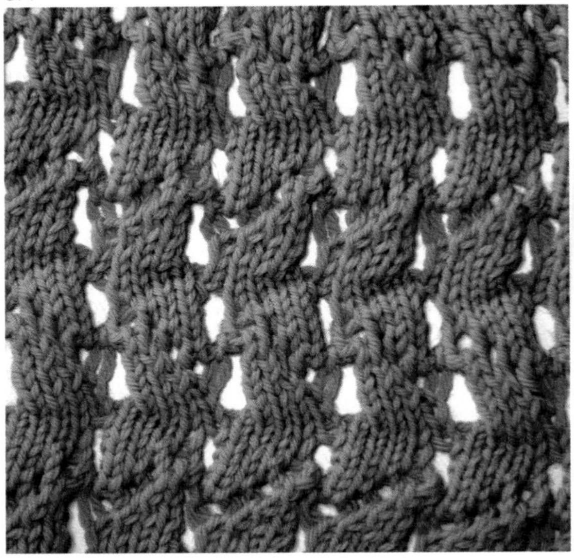

Move the next group of 5 NDLS at left to UWP and knit 1 row. Hold the previous group (including the 1 edge NDL) and knit 1 row to the right. Repeat * to ** by moving the 1st ST to the 2nd NDL, etc. This group and all the remaining groups up to the last at left will only have 5 NDLS, rather than 6, so the transfers begin with the 1st ST. At the end of the repeat, knit 2 rows over all NDLS and repeat from the left. Note that the BB show.

S78 in this version the BB have been P/U. Also, I knitted only 1 row after each transfer instead of 2. Because of that, the transfers actually formed ladders, rather than eyelets, which cause the fabric to crease for a slightly corrugated effect. Once again, I knitted 2 rows between each horizontal repeat.

You could vary either of these last 2 fabrics further by working even numbered groups of NDLS which would

S78

lend themselves to splitting pairs and alternating placements. You might also try working full—fashioned decreases, rather than the simple edge decreases I used.

Some final thoughts on managing and exploiting bridge bars: whenever a BB is simply allowed to form by bridging from one section to the next, the STS in the previous section are bound to tighten as you lift the BB. Sometimes this doesn't matter as the tightened STS are lost within the texture. If it does show and it does matter, you should review the information on methods of lengthening the BB.

These include pulling down a loop between two groups of NDLS so that, instead of bridging across the last row of one section and the first of the next, you should knit one row across the last section (heading towards the next), hold the NDLS and back up the carriage. Then, before knitting the 1st row of the next section, pull down a loop to provide you the slack needed.

You can also return multiple NDLS to WP after binding off their STS, utilize NDLS emptied by ladders, or use drop ST to create larger, more usable BB. The extra yarn is always available to increase the length of a BB, you just have to look for it.

S79 is an extreme texture that could easily be applied to a garment for accent. The shapes remind me of calla lilies and that effect could be exploited by the right color choices and duplicate stitched stems.

C/O and knit some rows, ending COR. Hold NDL 21 and all NDLS to the left of it. Knit 1 row. COL. Hold NDL 19 and all NDLS to the right of it. Knit 1 row on NDL 20. COR. Return NDL 19 to UWP and knit 1 row. Continue returning next NDL to right to UWP E/R until NDLS 14-20 are in WP and COR.

Then return 1 NDL, beginning with NDL 14, to HP and knit 1 row until only NDL 20 is working. RC 14. Repeat rows 3-14 five more times. At the end of the last repeat, when COL and there are 2 NDLS in WP, move all NDLS at the right to UWP and knit 1 row.

Remove STS 18-20 on a 3-prong transfer tool and hold aside. I usually just hang it on the next 3 NDLS without transferring the STS so I have 2 free hands. Use a transfer tool to P/U 3 STS from the edge of the slit at the beginning of the flower and hang these STS on NDLS 18-20. Knit 3 rows across all NDLS, ending COL, and repeat in reverse for the next flower (if desired) so that the slit is on the right and the flower spreads to the left. I worked the next flower from the left on NDLS 21-27, but you can work them randomly across the surface if you prefer.

Push all completed flowers through to the knit side of the fabric. The edges will curl slightly, helping to define these shapes. If you repeat the shaping more than 5 or 6 times, you can cause the shapes to ruffle, rather than lie flat.

S79

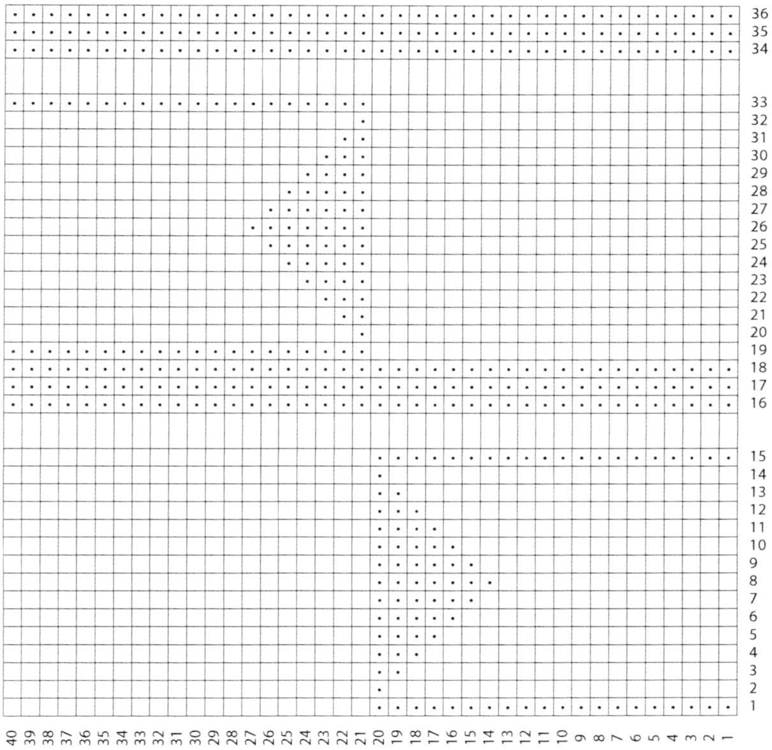

S79

S80 is a lot like some of the previous zigzag examples except that this time the effect is worked on the *surface* of the fabric. I think this texture looks a lot like leaves cascading down the surface of the fabric.

Begin COR. Hold all NDLS left of center and knit 1 row. COL. Hold all NDLS to the right of the single center NDL and knit 1 row to the right. *(Move 1 NDL at right of working NDLS to UWP and knit 1 row) 7 times until COL and 8 NDLS are in WP.

Then, hold 1 NDL at right E/R 7 times until 1 NDL remains in WP and COR.** Repeat * to * once more and then place all NDLS on left in UWP and bridge to the end of the row. Knit 4 rows over all NDLS and begin the next repeat from the left side, positioning the starting point 10 NDLS to the right of the first repeat. so that the shapes overlap.

You can also try positioning the left and right repeats closer together which will push more of the texture off the surface of the fabric.

In both this and the preceeding examples, the slits are concealed underneath the texture and take a back seat to it.

S80

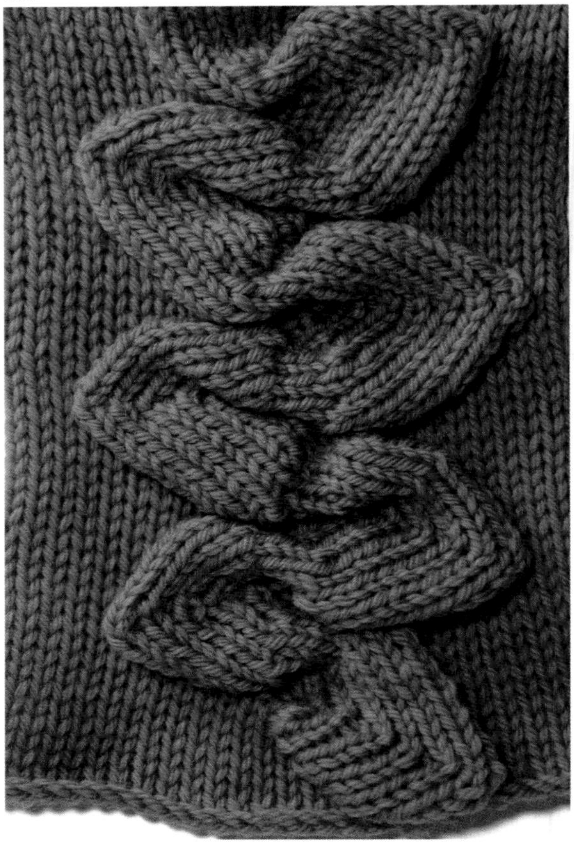

S80

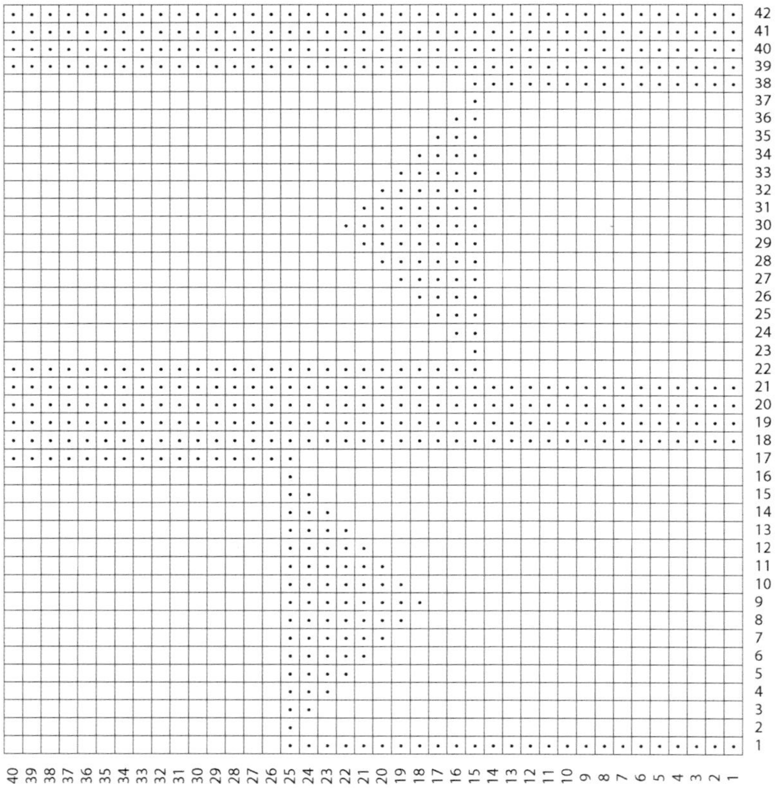

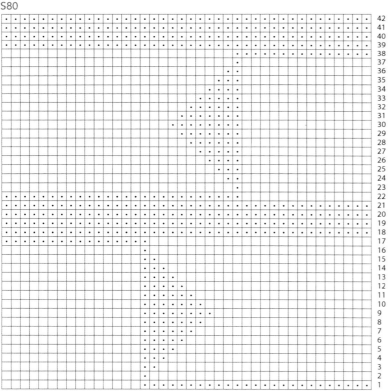

S81 is a short rowed ruffle that attaches to the background fabric for 3 rows after each repeat though you can knit more than that to space out the flounce. Each side of this ruffle was worked over 9 NDLS, but can be wider or narrower. You can also work just 2 plain STS between the halves of the ruffle if you want them closer together or many more STS between them to open up the space.

Begin COR. Hold the center 4 NDLS (15-18) and all NDLS to the left of them. Knit 1 row. COL. Hold all NDLS to the right of the 9 ruffle NDLS. Wrap the adjacent HP NDL and knit 1 row. COR. (Hold 1 NDL at left of the ruffle NDLS E/R until 1 NDL remains in WP and COR. Then return 1 NDL to UWP E/R until 9 NDLS are in WP and COR) twice, ending COR. Note that the chart, in order to save space, only shows this sequence from rows 2-18 once, rather than twice.

Move the center 4 NDLS and the 9 NDLS to the left of them to UWP and knit 1 row to the left. Hold the center 4 and all NDLS to the right of them. KWK. Repeat the short row sequence twice. At the end of the second sequence, when COR, return the 9th NDL of the group to UWP as well as all NDLS to the left and knit 1 row to the end. Knit 3 rows over all NDLS and repeat the ruffle sequences.

S82 offers a new twist on cables, if you'll pardon the pun. Using bridging, I worked 12 extra rows over the 5 STS at the right side of the cable and just 2 extras on the 4 at left before bridging my way out of the row. Then I crossed these 5 x 4 cables so that 5 STS were replaced on the NDLS first and all the extra length would show on the front of the fabric; 4 STS crossed behind.

I knitted 3 rows between repeats. The BB are hidden inside the cables so there is no need to lift them. I like the way the 12 rows curl under and look like an i—cord that laces through the fabric. Because the back half of each cable only knitted 2 rows, it helps draw the fabric in towards the cable, creating almost no gap at the edges. If you latched up the adj STS at each side, it would help the cable stand out even further.

S81

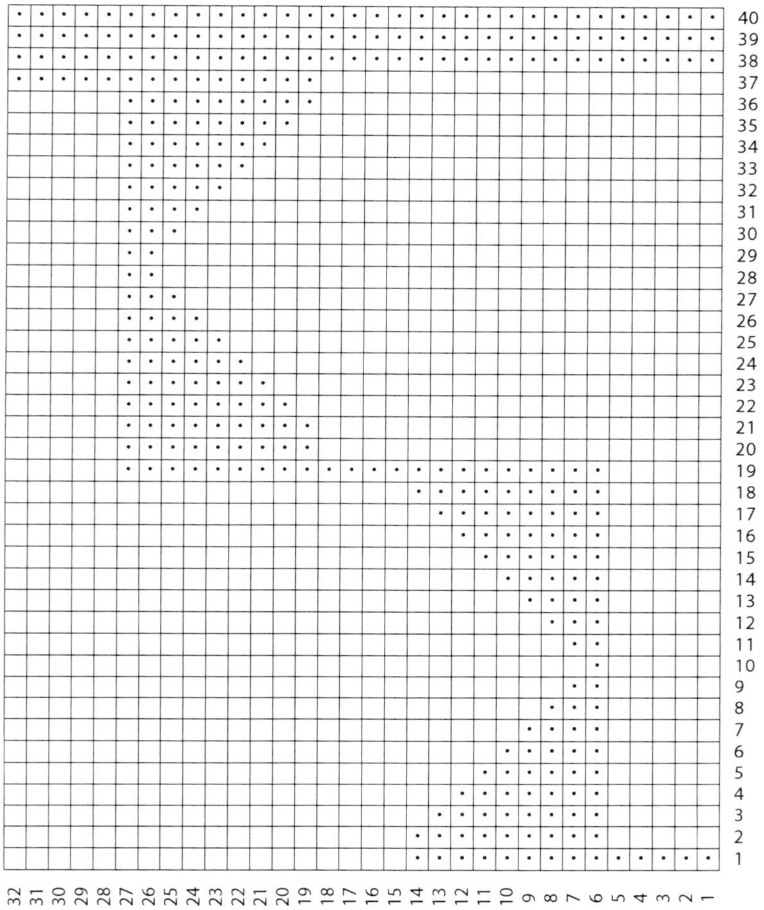

S82

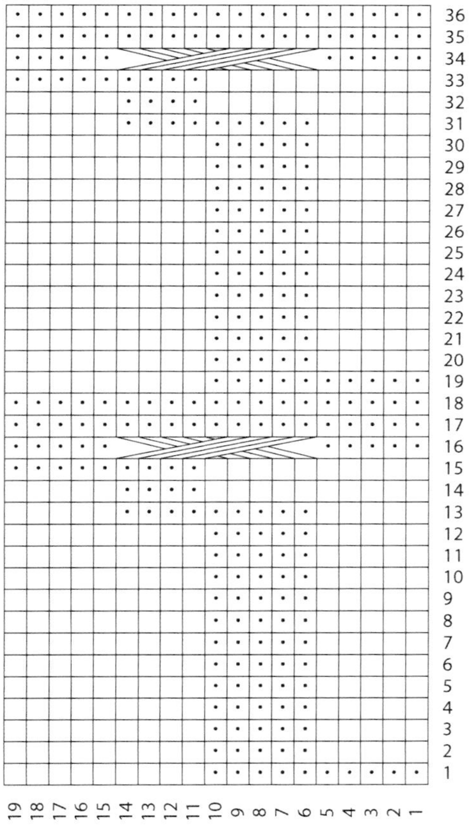

S82

S81

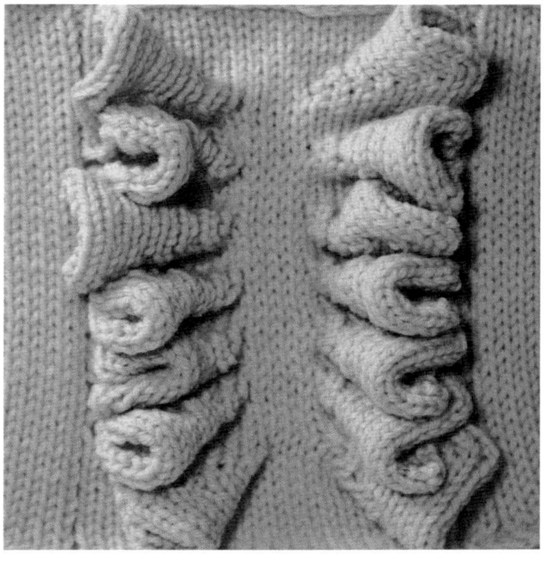

S83 shows two different, but related effects. For both of them I bridged to the NDLS where I wanted to position my texture and then I knitted 16 rows over 6 NDLS as shown on the chart. For the column of loops at the right, I lifted 3 STS from the first row of the 16 row strip and hung them on 3 NDLS above, much like a popcorn . Because I alternately P/U 3 STS on the right or left and hung them on the NDLS above at right or left, the direction the loops lie on the fabric alternate as well.

For the column at the left in the photo, I removed all 6 STS on a transfer tool (you can use a pair of tools if you don't have one large enough) and I twisted the tool 360° before replacing the STS on the same NDLS. This maneuver brings the purl side of the strips into view and adds textural interest. Because I always twisted in the same direction, all the loops lay the same way. You could alternately twist left or right and it would be reflected in the positioning of the loops. For this variation I did not lift any STS.

S83

S84 and S85 produce vertical slits at each side of the raised central texture, but the slits are minimized by further manipulation. Begin COR. Hold all NDLS to the left of the center ST of the motif. Bridge to the center then hold all NDLS to the right of it. Knit 1 row. COR. Use short rows to increase by bringing 1 NDL to UWP on the carriage side E/R until there are 9 NDLS in WP and COR. Then decrease by making a stacked decrease, moving 3 STS from each side onto the center 3 NDLS. C/O the 3 empty NDLS at right of the center by e—wrapping left to right. Push these 3 NDLS and the 3 at center to UWP and knit 1 row to the left then hold these NDLS. C/O the 3 empty NDLS at left of center by e—wrapping right to left. Hold these NDLS and then bridge to the next repeat at left or the end of the row. I worked 3 rows between repeats for S84, but I worked 5 rows for S85 and I think the effect (which reminds me of cobra heads) is much stronger with the additional spacing. It still amazes me that just 2 additional rows between repeats can so noticeably change the way the texture forms or sits on the surface of the fabric.

S83

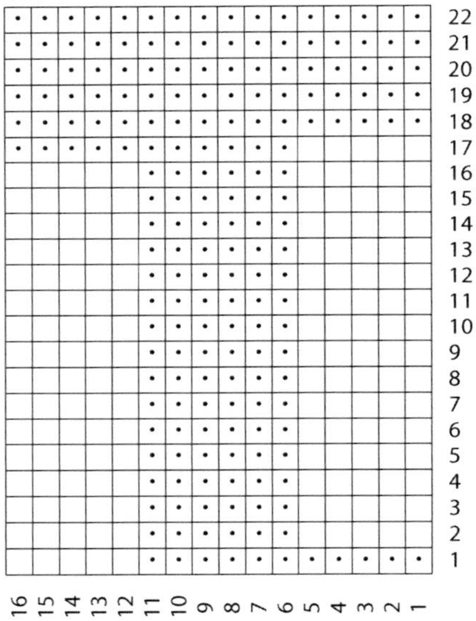

S84/85

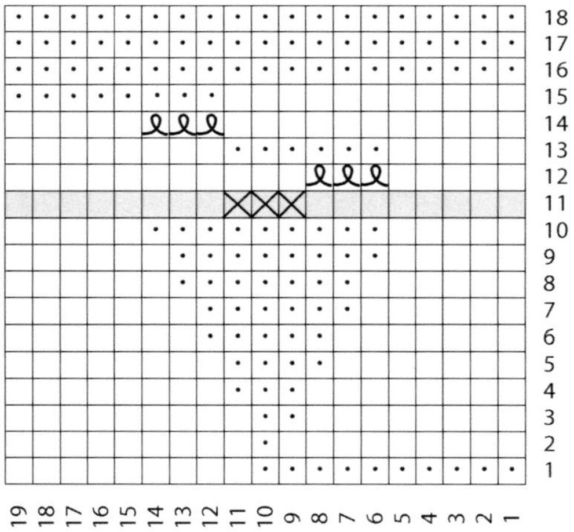

S86 is based on a double bed Stoll fabric where knit STS traveled across a purl surface before intersecting and knotting. To simplify things, I decided that traveling STS offered more than enough directionality and contrast and I opted for a single bed version instead. I began by moving groups of 4 STS towards the center

S84

S85

S86

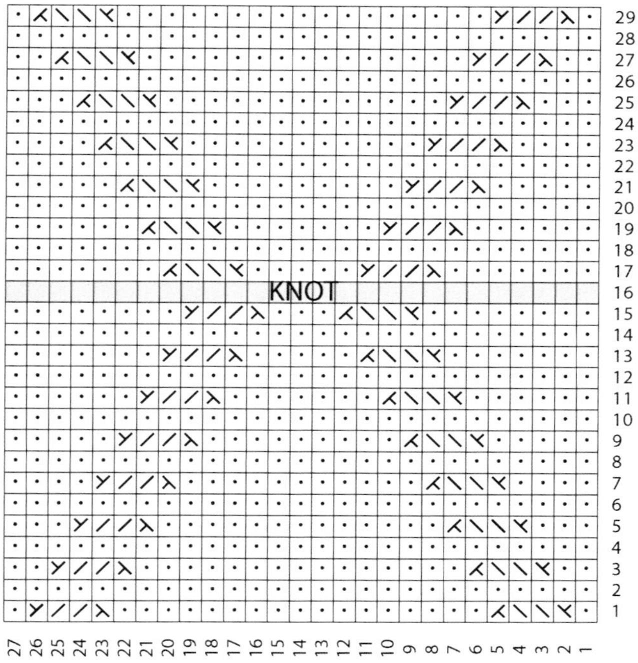

of the fabric every A/R, maintaining an odd number of NDLS between them so that, at the end, there were 3 plain, vertical STS between the two groups of travelers.

I worked all decreases as 2-step decreases in order to create a sharp division between the traveling and the stationary STS. Each decrease was paired with an increase. If you don't mind the addition of some eyelets, you could just bring the emptied NDLS back to WP and allow them to C/O and knit. It would be a little faster, but the eyelets might distract from the design.

When I reached the point where the travelers had 3 plain STS between them, I bridged up to the first group of 4 STS and worked 30 extra rows on those NDLS (9-12). I cut the yarn and removed the 4 STS on a small ST holder. Then I worked 30 rows on the other group of 4 travelers (16-19), cut the yarn and removed them on another ST holder. Next, I removed the center 3 STS on a 3-prong transfer tool, passed it in front of the left strip and hung it temporarily on the 3 adjacent NDLS at left. Then I knotted the two long strips to form a square knot by passing left over right then right over left. (See the illustrations page 186).

I replaced the left knot STS on the 4 left NDLS, moved the center 3 STS back to their own NDLS and then hung the 4 right—side knot STS. I knitted 1 row over all NDLS and then P/U and hung a couple of STS from the beginning of the knot strips to make sure I closed any gaps. I wove in the cut ends of the knot yarns and continued working, changing the direction of the traveling STS at each side so that they progressed away from the knot.

The original Stoll fabric was an all—over design and I think that this version would lend itself to an all—over

S86

repeat or perhaps a column of traveling diamonds secured by square knots. I found that split—ring hand knitting markers worked very well as tiny stitch holders. You could also use safety pins, but purchase the "loopless" pins they sell for hand knitting so the stitches don't get caught in the coil at the end of the pin.

S87 and S88 These short rowed slits are similar to S74 and S75 except they lie flatter and do not involve any lifting. Both samples were worked over groups of 4 STS with all of the repeats in S87 worked over the same NDLS while those in S88 alternate by splitting pairs. Both samples retain a plain, 4-stitch border.

S87 C/O a multiple of 4 NDLS and begin COR. Hold all but the first 4 NDLS and knit 4 rows. COR. Move the next 4 NDLS to UWP and knit 1 row to the left. Hold 1 NDL at the left of these NDLS E/R until 1 NDL remains in WP and COR. Then, move 1 NDL to UWP E/R until there are 7 NDLS in WP and COR. Move the last NDL (8th) of this group and the next 4 to UWP and knit 1 row. COL.

*Hold the first 4 NDLS at right and the last NDL at left. Knit 1 row. Hold 1 NDL at left E/R until there is 1 NDL in WP and COR. Move 1 NDL to UWP E/R until 7 NDLS are in WP and COR. Move the last NDL (8th) of this group and the next 4 NDLS at left to UWP and knit 1 row to the left. ** Repeat * to ** to the last 4 NDLS. Do not short row the last group. Instead, just work 4 rows over those NDLS and then repeat the pattern from left to right.

S87

S88

S88 I worked this second sample by splitting pairs every alt repeat in order to alternate the placement of the texture. These repeats *do* overlap each other, but you really have to examine the fabric to see the difference. The staggered placement doesn't look very different from the vertical placement and it requires adjusting the width of the border at each side. It really isn't worth the effort.

S89 based on a Stoll fabric, this fabric combines short row shaping (to build up areas), slits and ladders below the slits. I used a variety of yarns to knit this fabric and where necessary, brought the empty ladder NDLS to WP, let them C/O for one row and then drop their loops to provide enough extra length to create functional BB.

S89

S90

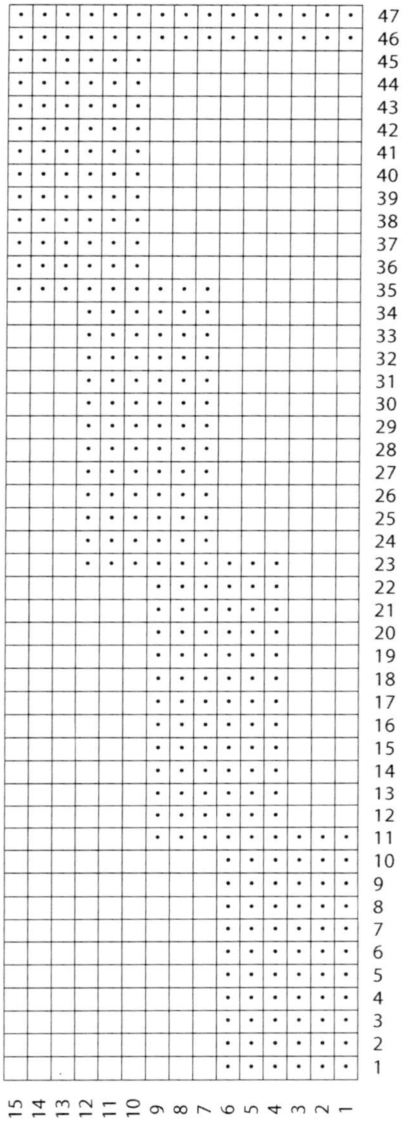

S90

A single NDL brought into work for drop stitch will provide enough extra length to bind the bridge bars for short slits, but would be inadequate for really long ones. In that case, you would need to pull out a loop as shown on page 191.

I think that one of the most interesting short rowed slit fabrics is Fern Lace (S90).The technique was first shown in a Nihon Vogue publication back in the 70's or 80's and, with their permission, I included it in my first book as a single repeat in a sideways knitted sweater. Since that time, fashion has changed and I have seen several bolder versions on the internet, including one by the British designer, Jo Bee. She added horizontal slits between repeats that gives the fabric an edgier, more contemporary look. There were also several examples in the Stoll collection where they used Fern Lace as an isolated motif.

The technique itself is not difficult and entails a short row sequence with progressively split pairs that is alternately worked from the right and left. Once you get started, you'll be able to keep the sequence in mind and work free of any written directions.

I find that fern lace has the best body when I work the short rowed portion 1-2 stitch sizes smaller than I would use for stockinette. The number of stitches you work for each section can vary. The version I first showed in HMS and these examples were worked over groups of 6 NDLS . You can work as many or as few rows between repeats as you like and I normally work those rows 2-3 stitch sizes smaller than stockinette.

For an all—over Fern Lace, C/O a multiple of 3 STS (for example) and knit some rows over all the NDLS and at least the last 2 rows with a tighter stitch size. With COR, hold all NDLS except the first 6 on the carriage side. Knit 10 rows. *Nudge the next 3 NDLS at left to UWP and knit 1 row to the left. Hold the first 3 NDLS at right and knit 11 rows, ending COR.** Repeat * to ** until all groups have been worked and you end COL.

As you work, you will always add 3 STS at left and hold 3 at the right so that you retain a group of 6 working NDLS. Note that I only worked 10 rows on the left and right edge groups to maintain a neater, less droopy edge. Be vigilant about moving up your weights.

Knit 2 (or more) rows with a tighter stitch size, ending COL. Work the pattern in reverse from left to right.

S90 I worked two repeats of the Fern Lace technique and then, between the second and third repeats, I bridged the first row to B/O 12 STS then bridged the second row to C/O the same 12 NDLS. Jo Bee's version actually had wider bands of knitting between repeats, creating a less dense, more practical fabric.

S91 was worked over groups of 4 STS so the effect is a little finer. Before beginning the Fern Lace, however, I needed to short row the fabric to create a "bed" for the leaf shape to lie in. With COR, I held the center 9 NDLS and all NDLS to the left of them. Then I shaped the right side by holding 1 ST every A/R nine times. I cut the yarn and repeated the shaping for the left side and then I worked the Fern Lace, with 2 rows between each repeat. I worked 8 rows over each of the edge sections, 10 rows over the next two and 12 rows over the center 3 sections to better fit the leaf shape into the fabric without distorting it.

When the lace was complete, I used short rows to fill in and level the work at each side, increasing by 1 NDL every A/R at each side before continuing the base fabric. Although I recommend working a regular repeat of Fern Lace across a fabric before you try dropping it into a short rowed shape, this is not especially difficult to do. You will probably have to adjust the number of rows worked over each section as I have done here.

S92 was inspired by a Stoll fabric that was worked on a much larger scale and looked more complex than it is. I began with COR and then knitted 3 rows, ending COL. (Hold all NDLS to the right of the first 8 NDLS and then knit 1 row. Hold the first 4 NDLS at left and knit 3 rows on the remaining 4 NDLS, ending COL. *Move the next group of 4 NDLS at right to UWP and knit 1 row to the right. Hold the first group of 4 NDLS. Knit 1 row. COL. Move the next 8 NDLS to UWP and knit 1 row. Hold 8 NDLS at left. Knit 3 rows on the remaining 4 NDLS and then repeat from *.

Cross all cables so that the enlarged half of each 4 x 4 cable (on the left) crosses first so that the extra rows will pop out on the knit side of the fabric. That is, cross the left STS to the right and the group to the right of them to the left. Knit 3 rows and repeat, beginning COL. Each repeat of the pattern begins by shifting the pattern 4 NDLS to the left.

Note that while I normally, purely out of habit, give directions beginning COR, in this instance, because of the way the pattern shifts to the left and the cables cross to the right, beginning each sequence COL eliminated any need to deal with the BB. Instead of having to pass one of the tools underneath the BB with every cable crossing, they simply lie, unseen, inside the cable crosses.

S91

S92

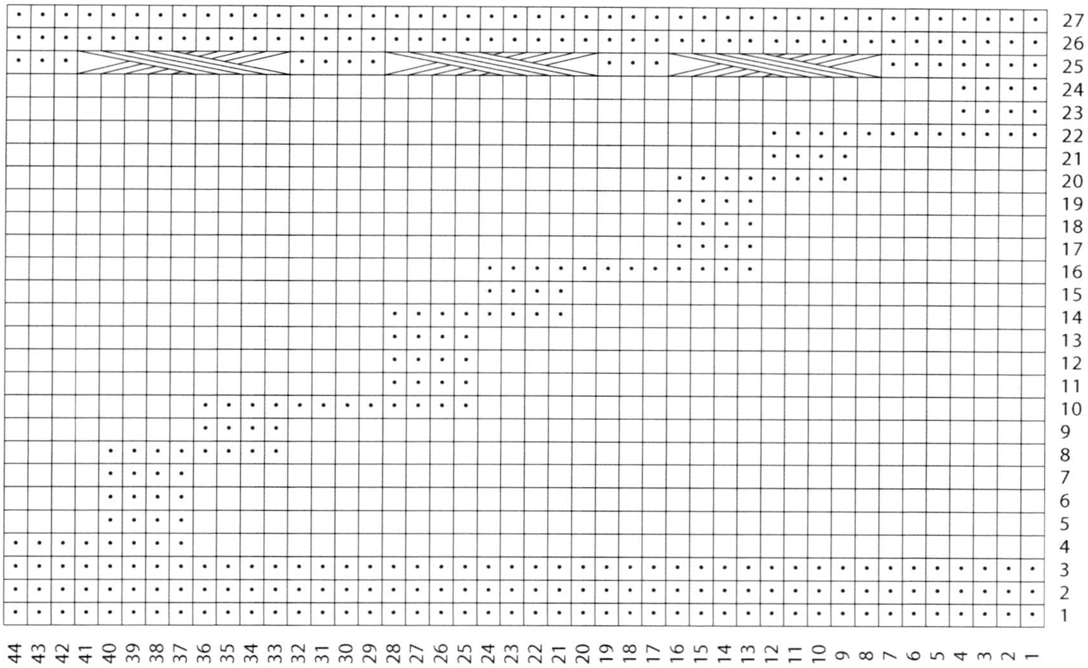

S92

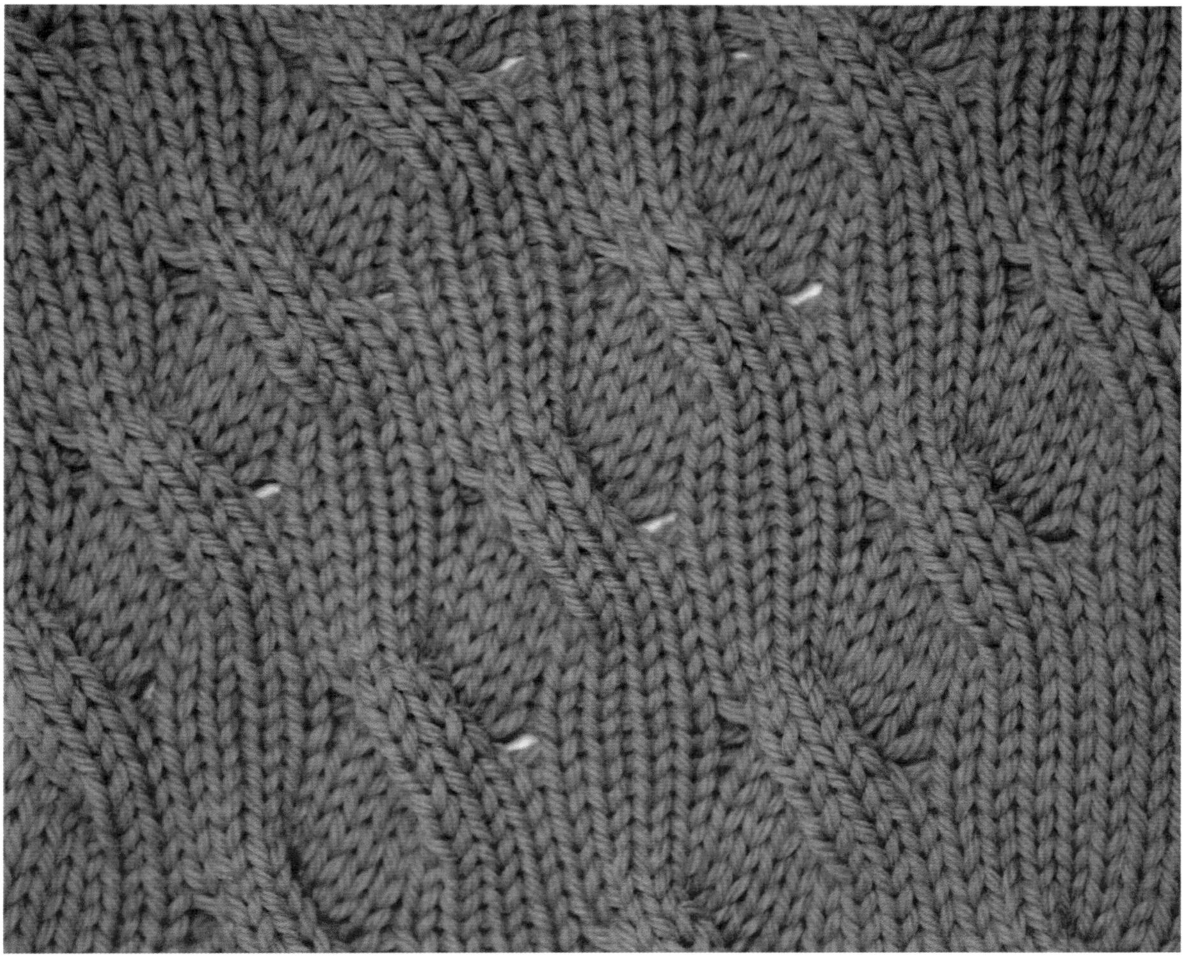

Horizontal Slits

Similar to giant eyelets, horizontal slits require binding off and casting on mid—row. You can use whichever methods you prefer for each action but it will almost always require bridging to enlarge the stitches that need to be bound off or to perform the binding off or casting on mid—row. Refer back to the information on bridging on pages 7-11 for the specifics.

S93

S93

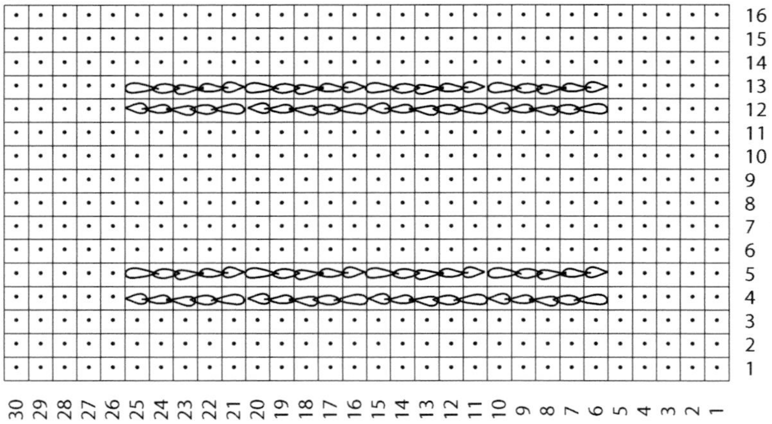

Slits within the fabric

S93 was worked by B/O and then C/O 20 STS in the middle of the fabric. I worked both by bridging to enlarge the STS prior to either B/O or C/O with the latch tool in order to produce straight, even edges that do not bind or distort the fabric. There are 6 rows between each section.

I find that the ends of the slits hold their shape better if I begin my B/O by catching the purl bar of the ST adj to the first ST B/O. It isn't invisible, but it does prevent a gap at the edge. You can also try passing the FY over the adj NDL before you begin B/O. If you work around the sinker posts as I do to B/O, make sure you remove the loops from the posts before continuing to C/O and knit. S94 While I think slits like S93 would make an interesting sleeve detail, there is a version of this fabric circulating the internet where the fabric is chained for a scarf. To do that, the slits need to be wider than the 20 ST slits I produced here and wider borders will ruffle nicely on each side of the chaining.

S95 was inspired by a garment in the Stoll collection where the entire back of a sideways knit sweater was comprised of graduated slits like these with a generous 5-6" border at each side that went into the side seams. This is an effect that definitely requires a tank top or other garment underneath, but the effect was stunning.

S94

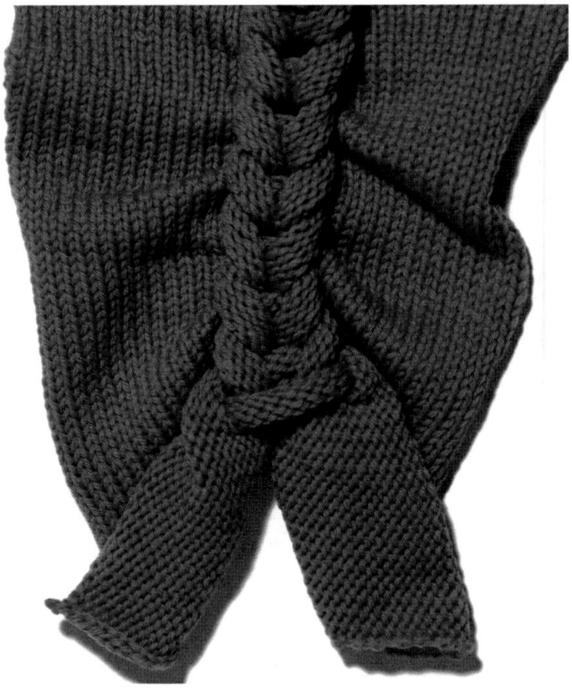

This fabric is actually worked as vertical slits, but because it is turned sideways for maximum effect, I have included it here with the horizontal slits. You could use HP or intarsia, but either way, do move your weights up regularly.

I worked each 5 ST strip 6 rows longer than the previous strip so that when the fabric turned sideways it would flare and drape well. This could be worked as an insert to be sewn into a garment or, like the Stoll design, you could work the entire back of a sideways sweater with wide borders of stockinette (or pattern knitting) on either end.

S96 Horizontal slits accent the change of colors every 10 rows. I bridged the last row of one color to B/O and then bridged the first row of the next color to C/O. I worked both the B/O and C/O with a latch tool, but you can use whatever method you prefer. Because these slits are only 5 STS wide, they are fairly stable. Wider slits would tend to droop and be more open. That openness would cause the stripes to undulate more or less, depending on the width of the slits and would look like an entirely different fabric.

S95

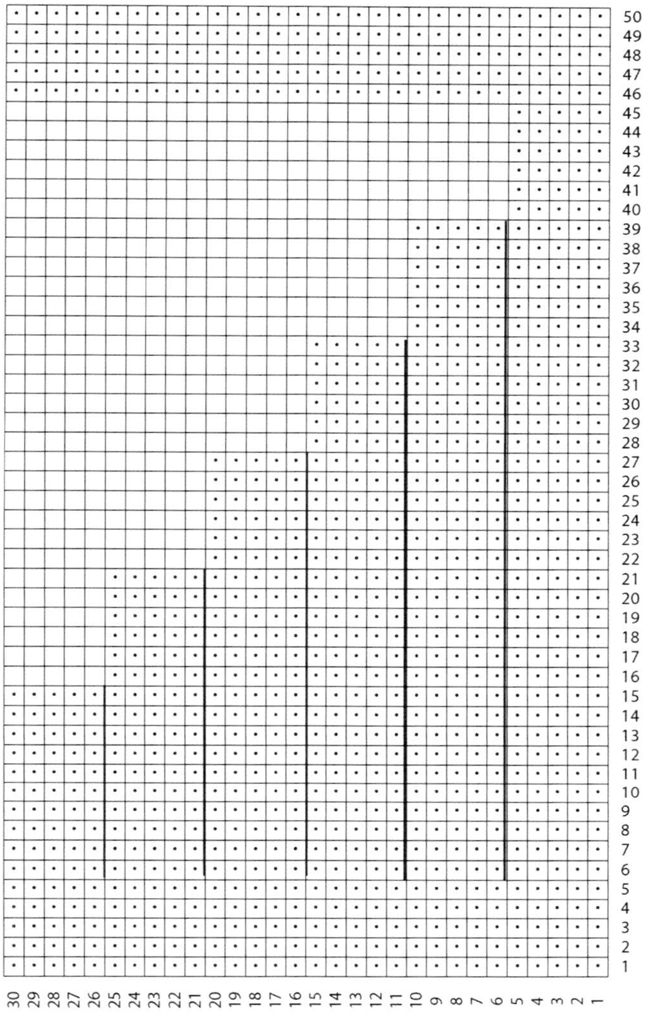

S96

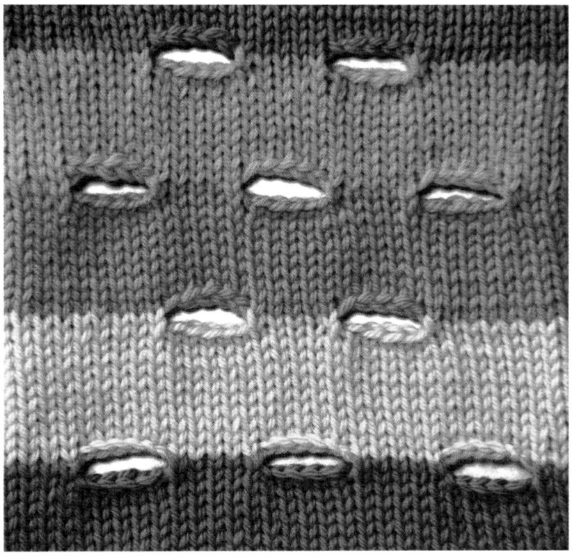

S95

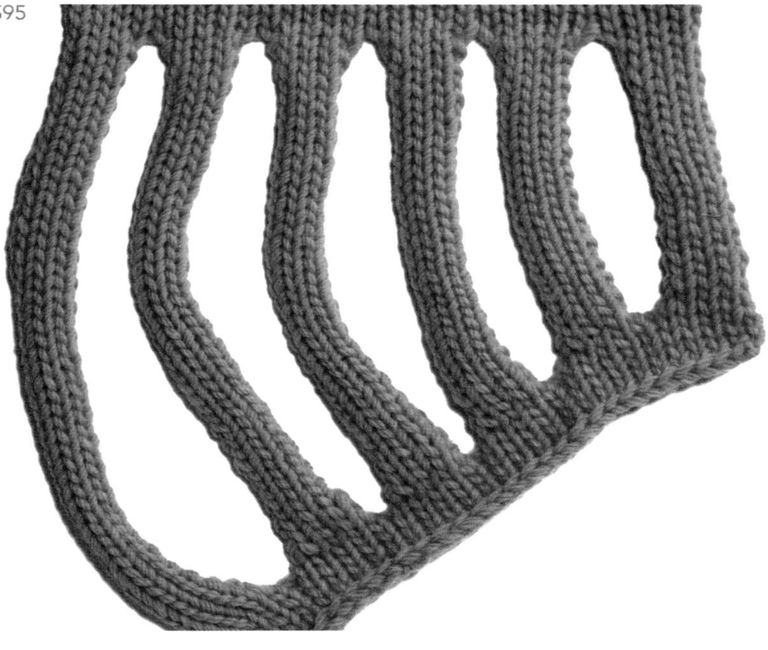

S97

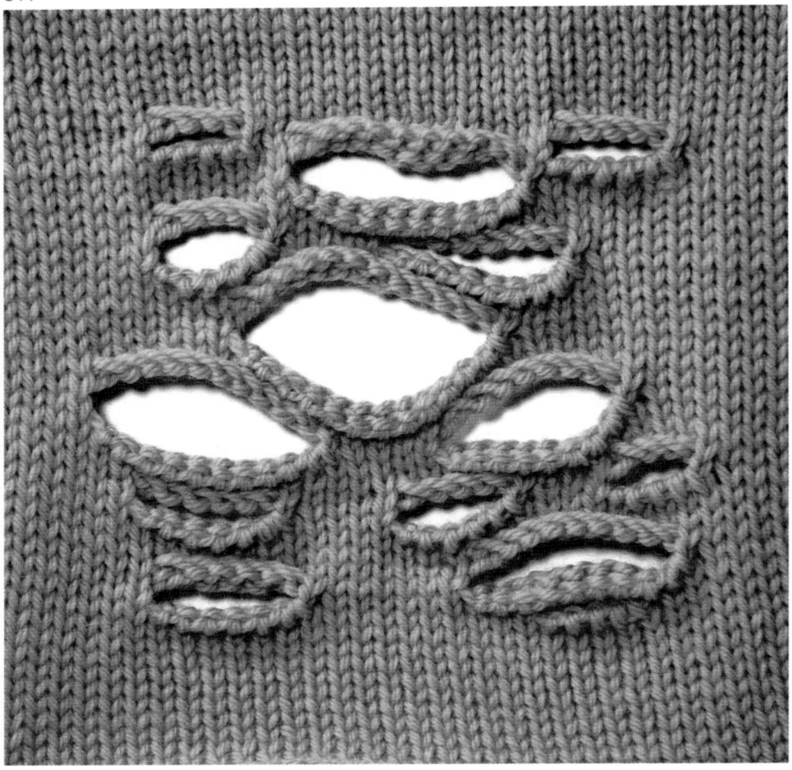

S98

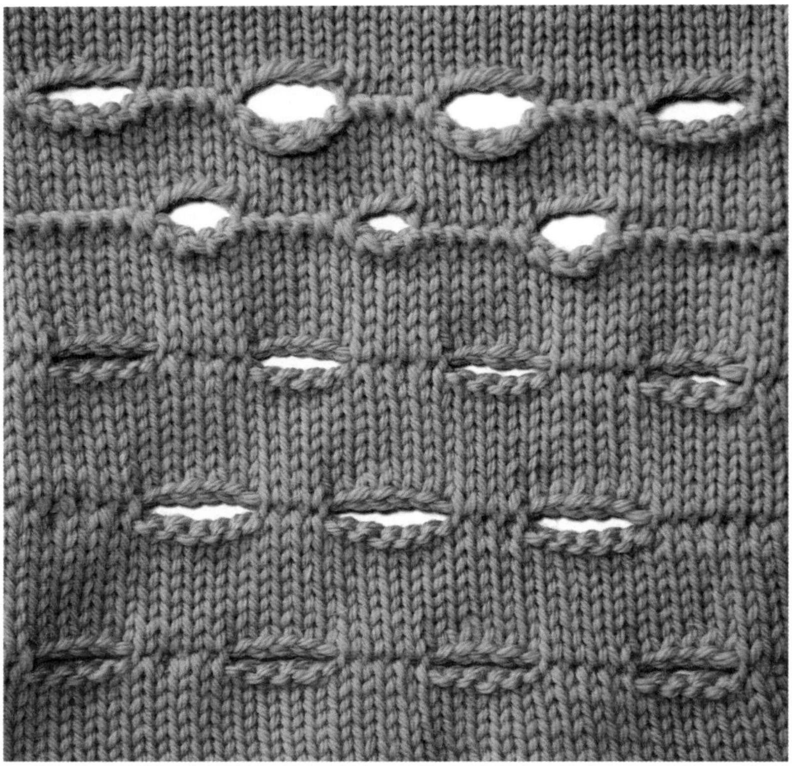

S97 Random width slits are clustered on this fabric and because I used a transfer tool B/O, the edges of each slit are considerably raised, creating an all—over texture that accents the slits. All of the slits were worked with bridging in order to more easily use the transfer tool to B/O (around the sinker posts), I bridged my way up to the STS to be B/O and used a transfer tool to return the NDLS to WP before starting to B/O.

I worked this swatch a little differently than most bridged fabrics because I B/O and then C/O the NDLS in the same row as follows: Begin COR and knit the first bridge up to the first slit position. Use the transfer tool to move the NDLS you want to B/O back to WP. Work the transfer tool B/O around the sinker posts from right to left. Knit back the last NDL of the B/O and then put that NDL in HP with the free yarn on the left of it. Remove the B/O loops from the sinker posts.

Bring the just—emptied NDLS to HP and move COR. Use the FY to e—wrap from left to right, catching the yarn under the first NDL in HP that holds a ST at the right of the slit. Nudge the newly C/O NDLS and the next bridge at left to UWP and bridge to the next slit placement or fabric edge.

There is a free video on my blog that illustrates B/O around sinker posts/gate pegs with either a transfer tool or a latch tool. You can use either method, but I used the transfer tool method for this example because I like the way it stands up from the surface of the fabric.

S98 was worked by B/O around empty NDLS as you might do on a machine that does not have sinker posts/gate pegs like the Silver Reed LK150. To do this, move the first ST to the 2nd NDL and then, before laying yarn into the hook of the NDL holding 2 STS to knit them back, bring the emptied 1st NDL to HP and catch the yarn around its shaft. There is also a free video (Latchtool B/O Around the Needles) on my blog that shows this method. This is a great B/O because, like the sinker post version, it supports the knitting all the way across the bed and prevents you from tightening up the STS as you work.

Normally, once you have bound off all the STS you would just remove the knitting from the machine, but in this case, as long as there were loops on every NDL, I decided to keep knitting. Although I'd be proud to claim credit for this variation, it was actually Sissel Berntsen, a student in my class in Rauland, Norway who produced an interesting edging when my directions for B/O by this method weren't perfectly clear. I love it when what should be an error yields a great new effect.

For the first 3 repeats at the bottom of the swatch, with COL, I worked a latch tool B/O over all the NDLS as described above, transferring the last ST from the latch tool to the last NDL at right. All NDLS are in HP and hold a loop. I dropped the loops from the NDLS

This DuoDu top is an example of wider horizontal slits creating an open, drapey fabric. If you look closely, you will see that these openings were not worked as slits. Rather, they are short, wide strips of fabric that have been joined to each other several rows from their C/O or B/O edges so that those edges roll. A garment like this needs structure so that it hangs properly and the weight of this over—sized garment is supported by close fitting sleeves. Photo by Lasse Berre, courtesy of DuoDu.

where I wanted slits and worked a row of chaining across all the NDLS from right to left, pushed the chain up against the bed and re—threaded the carriage. I knitted the first row with ST size 10 and then continued knitting with my regular ST size.

The two repeats at the top of the swatch were worked with the transfer tool B/O over all the NDLS from left to right. I dropped the loops where I wanted slits and then I bridged the next row to C/O by e—wrapping withh the FY. This method produces a raised ridge across the entire row which I find more interesting. Because I worked both of the B/O methods around the empty NDLS, the fabric does not pull in at all and retains good elasticity.

S99 illustrates a couple of interesting ways to add more texture to slit openings. For the curled flaps, I pre—knitted small 6 row pieces that were C/O with e—wraps and S/O. Then, instead of e—wrapping or chaining to C/O the top edge of the slits, I simply rehung the live STS on each piece on the empty NDLS (upper left).

Some of the slits feature a double B/O edge that was applied to the fabric after it was off the machine. To begin, P/U the STS along the B/O edge of a slit (knit side facing you) and, leaving a long tail, manually knit each of those NDLS back to WP and immediately work a (second) sinker post B/O over the same edge. Do not cut the yarn. I removed their loops from the

S99

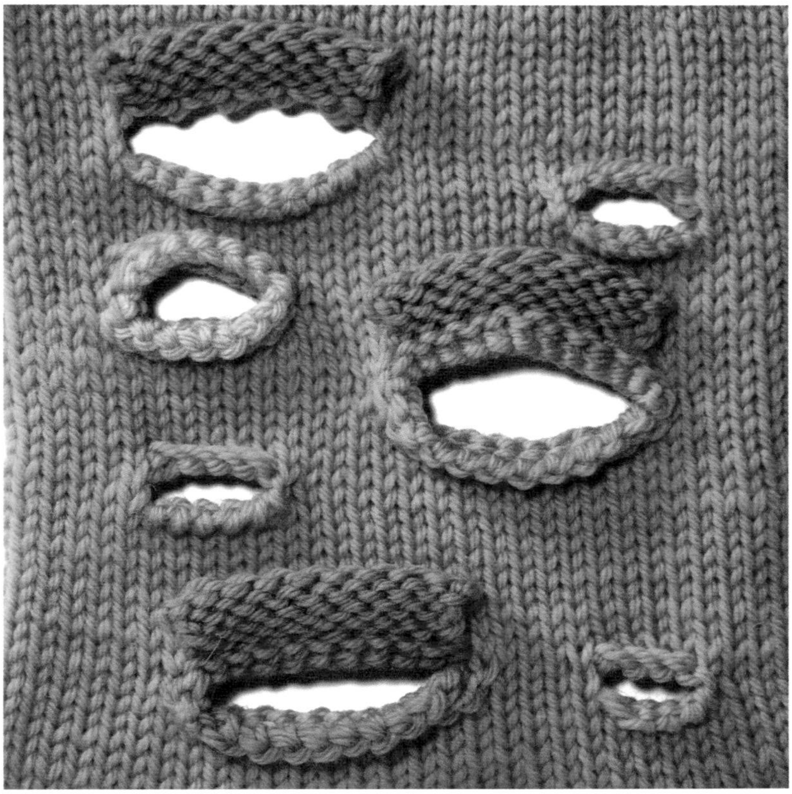

posts and then P/U the other (C/O) edge of the slit. I used the long tail to manually knit these STS back and then I continued the sinker post B/O around this edge using the same yarn I used to B/O the first side so the trim would be continuous around the opening.

The other two flaps on the swatch were joined during the process of working the double B/O edge, hanging the live STS of each flap before rehanging the C/O edge.

In addition to the double B/O or flaps, you can also employ any of the methods I described for embellishing eyelets on page 59.

S100 These 6-stitch slits are all finished with narrow strips of stockinette that roll and look like i—cording. Begin COR. Hold all NDLS at left except the first 2 STS at right of the slit location. Knit 1 row to the left. Hold the bridge, leaving only 2 NDLS in WP. Knit 1 row to the right and wrap the adjacent NDL. Move 1 more NDL at left to UWP and knit 2 rows on the 3 WP NDLS that will begin the cording.

*COR. Move the ST from the first HP NDL (at left of the 3 WP NDLS) to the adjacent WP NDL. Move the STS from all 3 NDLS 1 NDL to the left and put the empty NDL at right in NWP. Knit 2 rows.** Repeat * to ** 6 times or to complete the lower edge of the slit to the desired width, wrapping the last repeat when COL.

To streamline the transfers as you move the STS over to the left, first remove the ST from the HP NDL on the left prong of a 3-prong transfer tool. Keep that ST on the tool and then remove the 3 cord STS and move them all over to the left.

Next, close the top of the slit by one of the following methods, as illustrated from bottom to top on the swatch. Unthread the carriage and move it to the right. Bring the empty NDLS to HP and e—wrap them from left to right. After wrapping the last empty NDL at right of the slit, pass the yarn under the next NDL in HP to wrap. Rethread the carriage, nudge the e—wrapped NDLS and all NDLS to the left of them to UWP and knit 1 row to the left.

For the middle slit, work an additional 14 rows over the 3 WP NDLS, ending COR and finger tensioning or using a small weight. Use a 3-prong tool to move the STS to the right, replacing them on the 2 right—most empty NDLS and the first NDL that holds a ST. The overlap will prevent a gap at the edge. Wrap the adjacent NDL. Use a single—prong transfer tool to evenly P/U half STS along the edge of the strip and hang them on the empty NDLS. Nudge these NDLS and all NDLS to the left of them to UWP and knit 1 row to the left.

S100

To work the "eyelid" effect in the top example, wrap the left edge NDL when working the last repeat of the cord and knit 1 row. COR. Knit 1 row. *Hold left—most NDL of the 3 WP NDLS and use a transfer tool to P/U the purl bar of the right—most ST to hang on the adjacent empty NDL at right. Knit 2 rows.** Repeat * to ** until all empty NDLS are back to work. Then work once more, bringing 1 NDL from HP to UWP instead of making a ST. This will prevent a gap. Return all NDLS left of the 3 to UWP and work 1 row to the left.

S101 is a whimsical example of the way texture affects the edges of the slits and can be used to create motifs. With additional details duplicate stitched onto this face or fringed eye lashes, I think this would make a fun scarf or a pocket on a child's sweater.

I shaped the chin first by bridging to the center of the row to work a bit of short rowing. Begin COR and hold all NDLS to the left of center zero. Knit 1 row to the left and then hold all NDLS to the right of a single NDL. Return 1 NDL to UWP on the side opposite the carriage E/R until 10 NDLS are in WP and COR. Wrap every row to prevent holes.

Next I worked a transfer tool B/O around the sinker posts to B/O the same 10 NDLS, wrapping the edge NDL at each side. I removed the loops from the sinker posts and immediately e—wrapped the empty NDLS from left to right. I nudged the newly e—wrapped NDLS and all NDLS to the left of them into UWP and knitted 1 row to the left.

I knitted 4 rows and made a 2-ST popcorn for the nose. Then I knitted 4 rows and made two smaller slits for the eyes, bridging to B/O and C/O as I did for the mouth. Alternatively, you could make two (1-ST) eyelets for the nose or some giant eyelets for the eyes or work short rows to create dimensional eyelids.

S102 pairs two slits in each repeat and employs the C/O method explained for the middle example on S97. I retained 2 plain STS between the slits in the first and last repeats and 6 between the middle slits.

Begin COR. Hold all NDLS to the left of NDLS 2 and 3 left. Knit 1 row and then hold all NDLS to the right. Knit 1 row. COR. Return 1 NDL at left to UWP and knit 2 rows. Work corded B/O, moving to the left until there are 6 empty NDLS. Knit 14 rows on the 3 WP NDLS and work C/O method described for S97.

S101

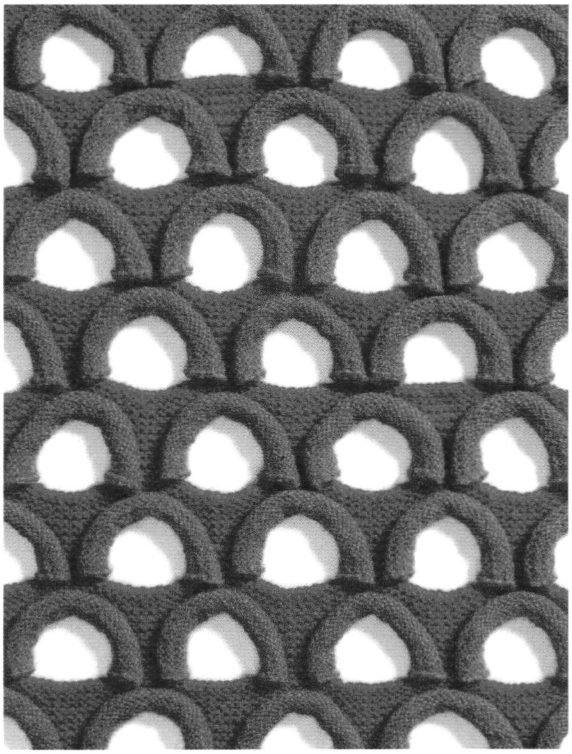

This colorful hand knit fabric by Britt—Marie Christoffersson features row after row of embellished horizontal slits and appears in her book, *POP Knitting*, published by Hemslöjdens Förlag. Photo by Thomas Harrysson.

S102

When all empty NDLS have been C/O and COL, move all NDLS from NDL 1 left to NDL 3 right to UWP and knit 1 row to the right. Hold 1 left and 1 right. Wrap the adjacent NDL, knit 1 row and wrap again. COL. Move the next NDL at right to UWP and knit 2 rows. Make transfers for corded B/O, working towards the right. When there are 6 empty NDLS, knit 14 rows over the 3 WP NDLS and continue as for the other side, P/U the edge of the strip. When all NDLS are in HP, move COR and bridge to the left. Knit 3 rows over all NDLS and then work the second pair of corded slits, beginning each at NDLS 4 & 5 left/right.

S103

S103 was worked with the corded B/O as described above and each of the slits were completed by C/O with the twisted C/O described on page XXX. Begin COR. Hold all NDLS to the left of NDLS 1 and 2 left of zero. Work the corded B/O described above until there are 5 empty NDLS at the left of zero, ending COR. Temporarily e—wrap the 5 empty NDLS and manually knit NDLS 1 and 2 right to WP. Knit 1 row to the left and work the corded B/O as follows. Return the next NDL at right from HP to UWP and knit 2 rows. 3 NDLS in WP.

*Whenever COL, release the adjacent e—wrap from its NDL and place the empty NDL in NWP and then make the transfer for corded B/O. The released e—wrap will provide enough slack to make the transfer and shift the STS to the right. Lift the bridge bar onto the left—most NDL of the 3 WP NDLS and then knit 2 rows. ** Repeat * to ** until there are 10 empty NDLS and COL.

S104

To C/O the 10 empty NDLS, begin at the right most NDL and working to the left. twist the bridge bar and the FY and beginning with the FY, alternately place one then the other into the hooks of the empty NDLS. Hold all NDLS and move the COR. Move all NDLS to the left of the twisted C/O to UWP and knit 1 row to the left. *** Knit 3 rows and repeat from * to ***.

The next 3 swatches feature a bobble—like texture. For all of these fabrics, be sure to keep moving your weights underneath the working NDLS.

S104 is an all—over, alternating placement of open bobbles. First I bridged to each placement and used the latch tool to B/O 5 STS over the sinker posts for the straightest, most even B/O. Then I lifted all the loops off the sinker posts and bridged the next row to C/O to the same NDLS with the latch tool. Beginning COR, I bridged to each of the bobble placements and shaped them as follows:

With COR, hold all NDLS to the left of the bobble placement and knit 1 row to the left. Hold the bridge at right. Wrap the adjacent HP NDL at left, knit 1 row to the right and wrap the adjacent HP NDL. Knit 2 rows with no wraps. [(Hold 1 NDL opposite carriage, knit and wrap) twice. Knit 2 rows.] Repeat [to] twice, ending COR. Bridge to the left. I worked 4 rows over all NDLS between repeats.

S105 (see chart for S104) I bridged to the bobble placement, manually knitted 5 NDLS all the way back to the rail and then removed these giant STS on a latch tool. I pushed the STS behind the latch of the tool and caught the free yarn in the hook of the tool, pulled it through the STS and placed the new, single ST on the edge NDL at left or right. Then I bridged my way to the left. I bridged the next 2 rows as well to e—wrap the empty NDLS and to shape the open bobbles as for S104.

S105

S106 is the same open bobble as the previous example, but worked from both sides so that the enlarged STS are gathered to the left (for the right—hand groups) or right (for the left—hand groups). Both groups were e—wrapped and short rowed in the same bridged rows. The texture was worked 2 STS from the edge. Because 1 ST rolled to the back, only 1 ST is visible at the edge of this (mostly) non—roll edging.

S104

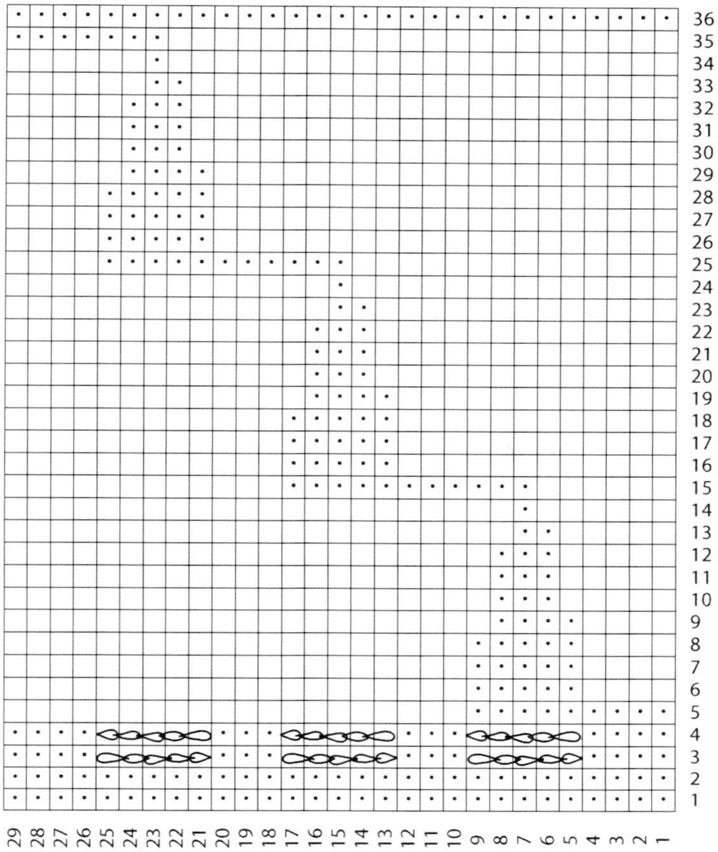

S106

S107

S108/S109

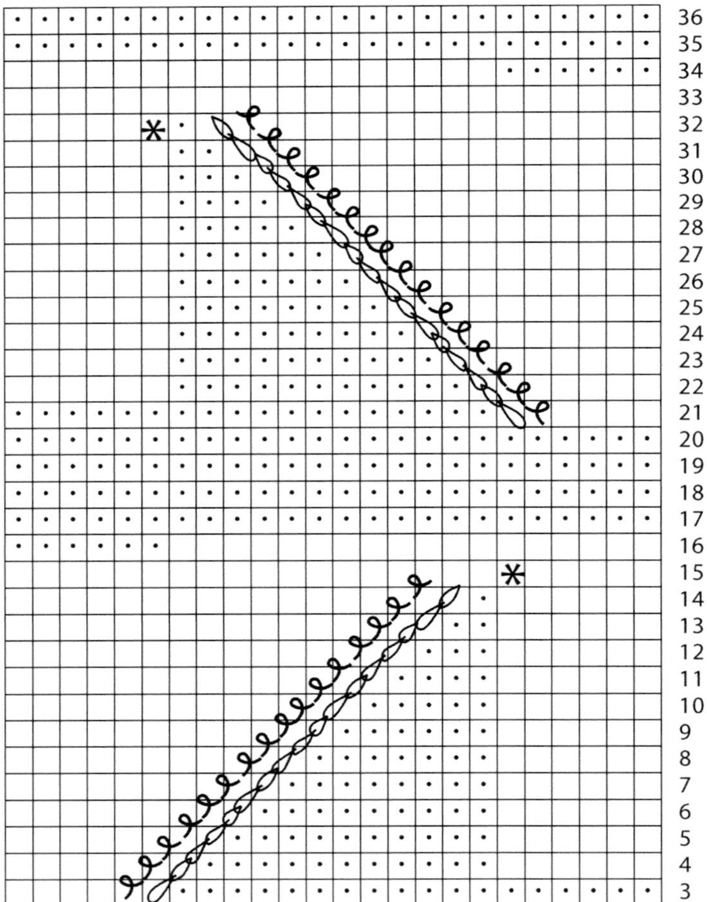

S107 (no chart) features little bands of e—wrapped C/O across the fabric, but there are no companion B/O STS to be found. In fact, the only slits in this fabric are mostly hidden on the back side of the fabric. Begin COR. Bridge to work 7 rows over each of the groups of 5 NDLS that will be worked to form the motifs, ending COL.

Use a circular hand knitting NDL to remove these same STS from the NDLS and place the empty NDLS in NWP. Make sure you choose a hand NDL that is small enough to remove and replace the STS easily, without having to poke around and stretch the STS.

Bridge to each of the groups and e—wrap C/O the empty NDLS. Then knit 4 rows over all 5 NDLS. Make decreases to reduce the group from 5 STS to 3 and then to 1 ST, knitting 2 rows after each transfer. Bridge and repeat across the bed. Finally, return the STS from the hand NDL to their original NDLS on the machine and knit 2 rows over all NDLS.

I alternated the placement of my pattern, but I also think this pattern would be interesting worked in vertical repeats. For the first repeat of the pattern, I did not do anything to close or secure the slits behind the pattern. If you are concerned about the open slits, you can do as I did in the 2nd and 3rd repeats wrapping rows 3 & 4 (of the 7 rows) or P/U and hanging the side edge of the 7-row strip.

S108

S108 and S109 offer some short rowed options for adding texture to horizontal slits. For S108, begin COR. Hold all NDLS left of the center 12 NDLS and knit 1 row to the left. Hold all NDLS to the right of the center 10 as well as the first WP NDL at left. Knit 1 row to the right. Hold 1 NDL at left E/R until 1 NDL remains in WP and COR.*

Move the center 10 NDLS to UWP and knit 1 row to the left. Use the latch tool B/O, catching the yarn around the sinker posts and around the adjacent HP NDL at the start to prevent a gap. Transfer the last ST from the latch tool to the adjacent HP NDL (*) at right. Lift the loops off the sinker posts and then e—wrap the 10 empty NDLS from right to left.

Move COR and nudge all NDLS left of center 10 to UWP and knit 1 row to left. Knit 4 rows over all NDLS and work the next repeat from the left, reversing directions as needed.

S109 is a further variation of S108 Instead of B/O towards the widest part of the S/R wedge, I worked towards the short end so that the piece remained free from the background fabric and able to curl forward. Work the same as S108 up to the * then proceed as follows: Change to ST size 10 and knit 1 row to the left. (Change back to regular ST size now so you don't forget!) Chain off the 10 STS from right to left, working a simple chain with no additional yarn fed into the STS. Then work a latch tool C/O from left to right. Transfer the last ST from the latch tool to the adjacent HP NDL. Move the center 10 NDLS and all NDLS to the left of them to UWP and knit 1 row to the left. Knit 4 rows and repeat from the left side.

S109

With either of these previous two samples, you can easily vary the number of STS over which you work each slit, work every repeat from the same side, employ a different S/R sequence for the flaps, use a different B/O or C/O method or work fewer or more rows between repeats. Working the flaps in a different color would produce some ends to work in, but it would probably be worth the extra steps.

Slit Fringes

S110 moves the slits to the edges of the fabric where they produce a sort of "fringe finger" effect. I worked this sample in two pieces with reversed shaping just as I would for a horizontally striped scarf where the bed of the machine is not long enough to work it all in one piece. I joined the two pieces at the center by rehanging the plain ends of each piece, wrong sides together. Then I knitted narrow strips of each corresponding color for about 24 rows and B/O.

To begin, work the latch tool C/O over all of the NDLS from left to right. Knit 5 (or more) rows, ending COL. Hold all NDLS right of the 15 NDLS on the carriage side. Knit 1 row with ST size 10. COR. Work a simple chain off with the latch tool from left to right and place the empty NDLS in NWP. Move COL and then knit 1 row across all NDLS to the right.

Change color and knit 1 row to the left. Return the 15 empty NDLS to WP and work chain C/O right to left. Thread carriage and knit 4 rows over all NDLS. Bridge the next row to knit ST size 10 on the 15 slit NDLS only and then chain them off. Move COL, re—thread the carriage and re—set ST size. Knit 1 row to the right.

Repeat this sequence for the desired width of the scarf. Knit the entire last row of the final repeat with ST size 10 and chain off all STS. Knit the second half of the scarf with the fringe on the right and the color order reversed so that the stripes match when the two haves are joined.

S111 is a variation on S110 in that the edge STS are B/O and C/O in the same way. It takes things a couple of steps further though because you need to work both edges of the fabric at the same time and the "fringe" sections are S/R, which causes a ruffled effect.

S110

S111

My sample is 50 STS wide, but yours can be as wide as you like. Chain C/O 50 STS then knit 2 rows ending COR. *Hold the center 20 NDLS (16-35) and all NDLS to the left of them. (Knit 1 row, hold 1 NDL at left) until COR and there are 2 right edge NDLS in WP. Chain B/O around sinker posts from right to left, remove the loops from the posts and immediately C/O from left to right on the same NDLS. Knit 1 row over all NDLS. COL. Repeat from left side. When 2 NDLS remain in WP at left, B/O from left to right. Lift the loops off the sinker posts then chain C/O the same NDLS from right to left and knit 5 rows over all NDLS, ending COR. ** Repeat from * to **.

For a very ruffled edging, you can repeat the S/R sequence a second time before B/O and C/O each side section. Also, you can knit more than 5 rows across all NDLS and change the width of each section.

S111

Chain Links

The last two samples in this chapter are join—as—you—knit fabrics that span the distance of extremes in scale.

S112 A wider version of this might make an interesting scarf. I C/O 15 STS with waste yarn, changed to the main yarn and knitted 50 rows. Then I folded back the scrap at the beginning and rehung the first row of STS on the NDLS with the end of the piece and B/O both sets of STS together. With waste yarn I C/O 15 STS for the second piece, knitted 50 rows and before C/O the two sets of STS together, passed the end of the second strip through the joined ring of the first piece. Then I bound off the second piece, securing the first. Repeat for the length of your project.

Keep in mind that if the strips get wider, you will need to increase the number of rows for each section. This would be a great way to use those odd balls of yarn that none of us seem able to throw out.

S113 For the first strip, C/O 3 STS. Every 15 rows tag the row by hanging a yarn tag or by making an eyelet on the center NDL. When the strip is as long as you want, knit 15 more rows to begin the 2nd strip and then fold the strip to P/U the edge ST 30 rows back (tagged or eyelet marked) and hang on the edge NDL. Knit 15 rows and hang the next marked row on the edge NDL of the current strip. At the end of the strip, B/O both ends of the strip together.

C/O 3 STS for the 3rd strip and knit 8 rows. P/U and hang a ST from halfway between the joins on the 2nd strip. From there on, P/U and join every 15 rows. End with 8 rows and then turn to work the 4th strip. Every time you C/O you will knit two strips, joined at one end.

For my sample, I worked with 3 ST strips, but you can work wider strips as well if you join them by their middles, rather than the edges.

S112

S113

Index

Web Sites

Susan Guagliumi
www.guagliumi.com (web site)
www.susanguagliumi.com (blog)

Cari Morton
www.cariandcarl.com

Cornelia Tuttle Hamilton
www.hamiltonyarns.com

DuoDu
www.duodu.no

Jo Bee
https://www.instagram.com/jobeeknitwear/

Netting Shuttlewww.earthguild.com/products/riff/rnetshut.htm
www.jannsnetcraft.com

Machine Knitting Monthly Magazine
https://machineknittingmonthly.net

Soft Byte (Design—A—Knit software)
https://softbyte.co.uk

Cascade Yarns
www.cascadeyarns.com/

Made in the USA
Coppell, TX
09 June 2023

17884617R00140